GW00725442

MEN, WOMEN, LOVE, SEX, GOD & DEATH

CHRISSY ILEY

MEN, WOMEN, LOVE, SEX, GOD & DEATH

The Collected *Sunday Times* Writings

CHRISSY ILEY

ANDRE DEUTSCH

First published in Great Britain in 1997
This edition published in Great Britain in 1998 by
André Deutsch Limited
76 Dean Street
London
W1V 5HA

André Deutsch is a VCI plc company

Copyright © Chrissy Iley

The right of Chrissy Iley to be identified as the author
of this work has been asserted by her in accordance with the
Copyright, Designs & Patents Act 1988.

All rights reserved. This book is sold subject to
the condition that it may not be reproduced, stored in a retrieval
system or transmitted in any form or by any means,
electronic, mechanical, photocopying, recording or otherwise
without the publisher's prior consent.

A catalogue record for this book is available
from the British Library

ISBN 0 233 99334 7

Typeset by Derek Doyle & Associates
Mold, Flintshire.
Printed by WSOY, Finland.
Front cover photographs © Rex and Photonica
Back cover photograph © Fergus Greer

To the one who loves me most

CONTENTS

LIST OF ILLUSTRATIONS

ACKNOWLEDGEMENTS

The first person that I have to thank is Julia Gaynor for her endurance to the point of dementia, for indulging me and inspiring me and showing me a loyalty that might only normally be found in a relative of Poodle. I would like to thank my parents who made me what I am and to honour Spencer Bright for dealing with it. There is no doubt that without his perseverance and patience, his Svengali like qualities and his looking after me, this collection would not exist and neither might I. For the years that I have worked at *The Sunday Times* many have supported me, many have hated me but those won't be mentioned. In the support camp: John Witherow, editor of *The Sunday Times*, without him I wouldn't be there. He is a writer and therefore understands writing and has had a go at understanding me. He delivered. Thank you. I can thank Robin Morgan for his loyalty, inspiration and support, but most of all I can thank him for standing by me at times when I know I drove him to the brink. And responsible for me being at *The Sunday Times* in the first place, the very wonderful Susan Douglas. Jeremy Langmead, Style editor, the nurturer of Never Trust . . . and Relationship Of The Week. What can I say, you placate me like no other. And 'Witness' Rachel Cooke, Style deputy editor, who takes most of the brunt of my copy. The former Style editor Alison MacDonald's unique blend of tabloid savvy and intellectual dazzlingness cannot go unremarked. On *The Sunday Times Magazine* I only work with Cathy Galvin and there's a reason for that. She is exceptional. I also thank for their steadfastness, loyalty, inspirations, observations, spiritual guidance, financial, emotional and intellectual support the following: At *The Sunday Times* – Tony Bambridge, Martin Ivens, Kathleen Herron, Vera Taggart, Wendy Holden. Chrissie Wilson – for all her hard work, Phil Symes – for making things happen, also Penny Feuer, Mark Borkowski, Carolyn Taylor, Philip Rose, Charles MacDonald; for being mentors – Corinna Honan and Paul Dacre; for everything else Sarah Miles and Sarah Green, Anna Lamm, Eric Franklin, Janie Lawrence, Marcelle D'Argy Smith, Paul Sidie, Susan Hill, Neil Shand, Sandy Williams, Henri Llewelyn-Davies, Paul Ross, Roz Poland, David Remfry, Stacey Lumbreezer, Michael Zym, Tony Rennell, Baz Bamigboye, Rebecca Hardy, Andrew Neil; the spirits of Paul Vaughan-Phillips, Jack Tinker and Dr Anthony Dean; Susan Banks, Adrienne Banks, Hilary Bright, Alex Finer, Maurice Conroy, Iain Downes, Max Clifford, Martin Clarke, Erica Jong, Joel Schumacher, Richard E. Grant, Boy George, Barry Humphries, Margaret Laurie, Kathy Lette, John Diamond, Ken Thompson, The Ivy and Le Caprice, and especially Alison Hay. And lastly, so it gets special attention, Hannah MacDonald at André Deutsch for choosing me and knowing me so easily so quickly. You can trust her even though she doesn't wear much make-up.

FOREWORD

Some people think Chrissy Iley doesn't exist. Others wish she didn't. She does of course – you couldn't invent her – but she *is* from another planet. Like Kryptonite, she strips celebrity of its power and mystique. She oozes off the pages of the *Sunday Times*, interviewing, analysing and pronouncing on the characters and personalities that reside within the Neverland of Notoriety.

It's an exclusive enclave where limos are as long as the streets and silicon and sycophants are employed to keep us believing in the Peter Pans of pop-culture. In this world people can earn a million dollars for what they call a day's work. They want publicity to multiply their earning capacity, to sell their policies or sustain their egos, they want to control what we think of them, they want us to believe the myth they create and they want us to bend the knee and thank them for the opportunity to bask in their reflected glory.

These Pharoahs of Fame will deign to give one interview to publicize a movie or cause, they will allot half an hour of their valuable time to the tiresome task. They will demand written questions in advance and strike out those they dislike, they will dictate which subject matters can be addressed or must not be raised on pain of ejection. They may even demand payment. They will produce a contract for the journalist to sign relinquishing ownership of any tapes used to record the interview, even copyright of any descriptive passage used. They will demand copy approval, picture approval and even design approval.

These are the people, *the famous*, who want to be seen through the soft-lens sham of toadyism, to pose under the flattering glow of studio lights that blind us to who they really are. These actors, politicians, rock-stars, frock stars and shock stars, these gurus of the *Zeitgeist* from the cat-walk to the boardwalk want it all. Our adulation, our patronage and our servility. Too many journalists, newspapers, magazines and television producers allow them that luxury – that's how they get to fly first-class for a guided tour of Neverland.

But Chrissy Iley would rather be an illegal immigrant and smuggle us into Neverland in her tote bag. Her *Sunday Times Magazine* and newspaper interviews take the readers on the underground railway into that self-aggrandizing millieu. Her columns, Relationship of the Week and Never Trust, are explorer's guides to the nooks and crannies of that world . . . and often ours too. Because *they* are people too, though they may regard themselves as demigods.

She writes *about* ordinary people living extra-ordinary lives, *for* ordinary people living ordinary lives, whose votes or hard-earned income are the the fuel of fame; unfortunately too many deem it a privilege extended to the reader, but Chrissy Iley disabuses them. She works on the principal that it is her readers who are extending the privilege – their time and their money – to people who regard both as a birthright. She takes her readers along with her, to read her account is to sit in on the event itself.

The acid test is that so many are angry at what she writes. They spit and snarl and scream. 'Who does she think she is? The witch, the bitch, the parasite making a living out of *our* fame?' But who gives fame? We do, readers, watchers, voters. We give it when we approve and we take it away when we don't. That's why *they* don't like it, that's why *they* seek control, they don't want us to disapprove and honest journalism may invoke disapproval. If they all loved Chrissy Iley we should be worried because celebrity is too often offended by the most insignificant truth. That she could make a comfortable living selling wax effigies of herself and the pins to stick in them, to these citizens of show, is testimony to her insight.

The pretentious and the pompous burst veins when they read what she has to say about them; the fragile egos of Neverland sleep fitfully with garlic cloves and wooden stakes by their beds for fear she'll seek admittance to their souls.

Because that's what Chrissy Iley does. She scans the horizons of celebrity with the telephoto question and zooms into the hidden recesses of personality. She shines the searchlight of perspicacity into their eyes and under their beds to diagnose and to illuminate. Some find the experience refreshing, learn something of themselves and will regard Chrissy as a confessor, a friend even, weeks, months, even years after an interview.

She'll tell them what she thinks, not what she thinks they want to hear and surrounded as they are by liggers without attitude, they recognize the value of her opinion. Some have wept in the process. Sadly, the some are too few.

How does she do it? She asks the question, WHY? One way, another way, anyway, until she gets an answer. She has no axe to grind, she has no pre-determined agenda. She begins with a blank canvas and asks. Who are you? What are you? Why are you . . .? She will fearlessly expose her own character to scrutiny in the midst of an interview, inviting comparison and debate to learn more about her subject. She will cleverly ask the impossible and take the subject by surprise. Her questions are quicksand and quicksilver. Crucially, she is shameless, brazen even in her curiosity. The reader can picture Dustin Hoffman ambushed with: *do you like my toe-nail polish?* Or James Woods: *would you bark like a dog for me?* You can almost hear them tearing up the agenda scripted by their sycophants. Their answers reveal so much.

Interviews can be war, the enemy can be silence, sullenness, procrastination, arrogance and even aggression. Chrissy Iley never charges the trenches of barricaded ego, never uses artillery where artifice will do. She wins by negotiation, woos hearts and minds, or circles round to the rear and bites them in the ass.

Of course she couldn't do it if she didn't regard herself as a star too, a black sheep in the family. She shares their insecurities, their egos and their passions and their need for devotion – that's why she understands them and meets them on a level playing field. Like them she's obsessed with her image.

She poses wide-eyed for a picture byline with an impudent innocence that asks Who me? and a seductive pout that purrs Come up and See Me Sometime. If a photograph could wink, hers would. She's like the love-child of Groucho Marx and Mae West, or Violet Elizabeth and William, vampish, spoilt and invariably getting into scrapes. In another age, she'd benefit from a good spanking but would probably enjoy it because Chrissy Iley makes mischief, demands attention and glories in it.

From head to toe in black, hair, clothes and even beloved poodle at heel, she's a gothic cherub firing arrows dipped in wit, erudition and reproach into the rump of fame. In her interviews and columns the reader can picture her sliding the darts between moistened lips, and tucking her tongue into the corner of her mouth as she closes one eye and takes aim. Chrissy Iley knows her target. She has an uncanny, almost genetic understanding of fame, its attendant emotions and insecurities, its necessary mechanics and dynamics.

She isn't fooled by it and, in consequence, neither is the reader.

Robin Morgan – Editor, *Sunday Times Magazine*
July 1997

INTRODUCTION

Why I do what I do and how . . .

I do what I do because I can. I mean, I'm good at it and the *Sunday Times* provides me with the perfect arena. Don't think it came naturally. There's nothing natural about what I do: seep into someone's psyche and strip it – snatch the bits out that I want and then display them so they glisten. I didn't start off as a writer. I wanted to act, but I was not good at it and this depressed me. Then I sold vintage clothes and jewelry. I was good at this, but it bored me. What I do now is a sort of combination of the two. I become a person who is going to be the kind of person that the person I meet will want to open up to, and then I rummage. In the same way that my heart used to skip a beat when I found a piece of Schiaparelli that crouched unnoticed and unknown among junk, and I'd have to keep a straight face so that the dealer wouldn't know how good my treasure was, when the famous person casually tells you something you nod, unconcerned, but inside you're punching the air, thinking 'Yes, yes, yes!'

My first proper job was with the *Daily Mail*. My husband, Spencer Bright, had typed my features for me and John Diamond had written the intros, yet Sir David English said, 'You're obviously a natural.' But of course, he knows too, there's nothing natural about our profession. It's an unnatural world where a truth is not a truth. It's either a good quote or an impressive PR job. The only thing that remains constant, the natural force, if you like, is a voice. On one of my first days at the *Daily Mail*, Jack Tinker told me just that: 'You have to have a voice.' It was that simple and it was that complicated. You have to have a voice. That voice has to be you. Your voice has to have a rhythm and you have to know how to speak to your reader the same way as you speak to your friends because how you write is who you are. And that's how you make the connection with other people, and that's what this is all about: connection. Once you have your voice, it can be measured or sweeping. You can use it to amuse or betray or redefine who someone is, who you are. People say that journalists are either good at writing columns or good at writing interviews and they're rarely good at both. That's very limiting and often the muscles you develop for one are the very opposite you develop for the other, but that shouldn't be the case – not if you have a voice. Sometimes when you write about something you have a less cluttered vision, a less emotional one. You have to keep that. All the best interviews should feel authored. You display facts, then you interpret. So, in a sense, an interview with a person is not approached entirely differently from say, a Relationship of the Week. A Relationship of the Week, though, is more of a vivisection and they don't get to answer back.

Relationship of the Week was created by Jeffrey Archer when I was examining why he is so much of who he is because of Mary. Then it hit me how interesting the symbiosis always is: who's doing what to whom and why and how is it flawed. That's what we spend most of our time thinking about. I took the idea to John Witherow at a drinks meeting. He'd just been made editor of *The Sunday Times*. Relationship of the Week was born thus, proving his impeccable taste and faith in me. I loved him for it. It was kind of plugging into the universe and making it specific. Although the Relationship of the Week was usually about two people or one person's relationship with a place or body part, it was also about me. It was also about you. In the way that I've had the same relationship over and over again, but with different people, everyone has had that same relationship, or a version of it, a detail from that place. And everyone has had a different relationship with the same person. I think the variations are not as wide as you might expect. That's why we like looking at celebrity relationships. We like to feel pain with them, we like to feel anger through them, pull them down to our level or restore our own belief that true love is possible through someone else's shiny eyes. They are the conduits to the place we don't dare go.

Relationship of the Week is a vicarious thrill. Its love-child is Never Trust. The love-child is less angry, less disappointed; knowing, but funny. Never Trust is not as tortured, but it's still identifiable with. And more people write to me asking me for love advice – well, as Boy George once told me, 'We all teach what we most want to learn.' Not that I really know what to say to the women who write to me saying, 'How can I make him not want to go Dutch?' other than say, 'Don't go out, or dump him,' but it's important for us all to know we've been there, the place where all the best pop song lyrics take us.

The best thing about Never Trust is that I'm allowed to be funny. When one starts out as a journalist, the subs take out all of the jokes, and with your wit goes your ego, buried under facts and quotes. Thank God I've paid my dues.

Columns are one-way conversations though. And while I love having the final word, more than that, I love the combat. I love the war zone of the very important person and me in the interview scenario. Is there such a thing as celebrity truth when they're so good at presenting and perfecting the illusion? My job is to decimate the industry that creates the veneer. The point of the interview is the *frisson*, the tension between what they want to say, what they want you to hear and how you interpret that: how the public image is at odds with the private mess. Never interview a happy person. No point.

The interview is about breaking barriers, crossing borders and enjoying the landmines, and the setting is relentlessly artificial. The classic is hotel room suite. Four Seasons in

Beverly Hills, Dorchester in London. It could be the same place. Sometimes it's nice to snoop around their homes, but I love the anonymity. It makes us almost equal. Anything can happen. They could tell you anything. They are much less secure in a hotel room. So transient. Sometimes I think they're defined too much if they're sitting in their own furniture. Somehow I don't think James Woods would have barked like a dog for me in his own home.

Martin Amis thinks the interview is a dying art form and the way of the future will be fly-on-the-wall pieces. You get to be with them for two days, but only the public persona; no intimacy, no interaction, no one let in, no *frisson* from the duality of the two faces. I think it's dying because, in the PR industry, protection is kind of like a non-intellectual mafia. It used to be the PR's job to set up the interview. Now it's the PR's job to prevent the interview from happening.

They are the body-snatchers. I have met so many PR's who want to suck the life out of their client. They are psyche vampires who pretend to treat their clients like gods and they'll punish you for blasphemy. What are they afraid that their client is going to do? Be too boring or too racy?

Bad behaviour is easy. It's instant good copy. You don't have to do anything. So if you know somebody is an old soak, a misogynist, an exhibitionist, a control freak, you don't have to do anything. But it's not very challenging, and why would you want to spend time in the same room with someone who is spiritually ugly unless you are on a tireless campaign for the exposition of the truth, which I suppose you always should be. What is much more interesting is the murky grey area of someone who is adored, but you need to know if they're real. Or someone who is brilliant and you need to know what made them so. Brilliant people are always neurotic and neurosis is interesting because we're all neurotic and we all want to enjoy other people's neuroses. So, you have to get them to share.

Why share? Partly because it's the nature of what a very important person does. The strange artificial world of a performer or a politician. They think in terms of masses, an audience to which they are forever playing. They see me as the conduit through which they can communicate. They share because it's their job, it's their business to spill their guts, smear their souls and it's my job to pick at it. Sometimes they share because they're paid to. It's called a buy-in and it means that the newspaper has bought them, mind, body and soul – or at least it thinks it has. This is boring and tawdry, and I've done it, in my tabloid days. You spend, say, two days with this supervictim, feigning sympathy when actually you're disinterested because your conniving talent seems superfluous, and instead you have the voice of your editor screaming in your head: 'We've paid £60,000 for this and I want to know every spit and comma, I want to know what position, how often, and what she looked like when she came.' So you say something like, 'Was she very noisy?'

Much more fun to get them to share because they want to. They also share because they want to share with me because wherever they've been, whatever festering hole or euphoric vault, I've been there or as near as makes it still interesting. I mean, everybody's been there, and that's my point. You make yourself the same as them. You show them empathy. You give them the idea of possibility. You're their lover, their healer, their soulmate, their shadow. You give them respect but you never treat them like they're some other special breed from you. All the best interviewers: Oprah Winfrey, Jean Rook, they have empathy. Empathy hurts. Once, I went on prozac for a month, and nothing hurt. I lost my ability to under-stand. Could have ended my career. Curiously, it also prevented me from having an orgasm. The interview process is most definitely a love-act, an intellectual seduction, but you don't know who is seducing who for what. I just read Iris Murdoch's *Existentialists and Mystics*. She defines love as one being having total knowledge and total awareness of the feel-ings and mechanics of another. So therefore, the interview process is a love-act. It is the flush of first love and true connection and the sadness of the valedictory fuck, all in an intense, short time-phase. It's very draining. Afterwards I often have to lie down because it's like some whole being's energy has consumed me, and that's when you know you've done it right. Then, in order to make your experience meaningful, to make this one-off meeting into something that will last forever, you have to write it with the same heart and soul. And you do it knowing that you're never going to see the person again. That's the only way.

What happens when you like the person, when you want to be their friend? Then it's very hard to write the piece. The reader is your friend. You are there on their behalf. You are the everywoman. That's why you've been given the gift of empathy. Not that empathy is a natural. You create it. But more of that later.

You ask what everyone wants to know. The reader is your friend and you are obligated to share with them everything. And if that means insulting, humiliating, or perhaps just slightly embarrassing your new friend, the interviewee, then that's the deal. It's the sacrifice you have to make. Otherwise, you would have crossed over on to the other side. It's very tempting to cross over to the other side, the other side being the parallel universe where celebritude is real, where confidences shared between you and the person remain secrets. But if you cosy-coo with them, you betray your best friend the reader and then you'll lose that best friend and you won't be who you are or do what you do anymore. This is how unnatural you have to be.

When I worked in one office, a colleague of mine was determined to ensnare a famous person – not for an interview, but for marriage. She did. Her first technique was called mirroring. He wore big suits; so did she. He scraped back his hair; so did she. He hated smoking; she stopped. She feigned an interest in curry. I was very impressed with this. What worked romantically works professionally. I look at what sort of clothes they wear and try to capture it, or if it's a man, the broad perimeters of their style. It's all fairly logical. Why interview a rock star in a suit? I put my breasts away for Howard Stern because, really, he talks about them so much it's obvious that he fears them. Sometimes, I might wear a pouty little bra if I was meeting a gay man and I wanted to look like a drag queen. If I think the character is bright and colourful of ego, I dress like that. If I thought they were sombre, I wouldn't want to be at odds with their psyche, so I would be black suit, grey suit. You might only have an hour. You have to bond with them quickly so you encourage sameness as opposed to alienation. You want to precipitate the bond. For Donna Karan, I thought it would look too ridiculous to wear all Donna Karan, so I did just a shirt. But for Barbra Streisand, a friend of Donna Karan, I did the whole Donna Karan suit. Manipulative, eh?

Not really, because you too are being willingly manipulated. Because you are giving them the celebrity plug or the politician's soundbite. Best to get this over with in the first ten minutes. Otherwise, they're nervous, fidgety. You give them that and they give you as much of themselves as they/you want in the time given. Time is very important. And once you become practised in your science, you'll know that 20 minutes in, there's the first high. That's how long it takes for you to really get something. Sometimes, it's confusing if you spend too long with a very important person. You become less, not more, aware of where the importance and the person merge. And that's another unnatural thing. In the real world, you'd expect that the longer you spent with a person, the more you knew them. On the rare occasions where I've been allowed all access in all areas for a couple of days, the piece becomes almost impossible to write. Your perceptions are confused because either they've irritated you too much or you've become their friend. One and a half hours is the perfect time. If you've done your job right, both of you are too tired to go on after this and you will have gone through them like an espresso. You don't need any longer than that once you've been honed. You're a missile. You might implode if you go off course. I was honed by Corinna Honan who was then the Showbusiness editor at the *Daily Mail*.

It's very different being an interviewer for a tabloid than a broadsheet. The tabloids aren't really interested in the journey. They're interested in arrival. The arrival of the quote. They don't want nuance. They want confessional hell. You may as well not exist. The tabloids simultaneously deify the celebrity because all we want to hear from is them, and then condemn them, because they are always reduced to 'My battle' with this or that, 'My drug hell', 'How he beat me, left me, loved me'. Loss is always more interesting than gain. I'm not knocking this process. In fact, it helped form me and I truly appreciate how wonderful it is that the *Sunday Times Magazine* lets me write 7,000 words uncut, if that's how much I have to say about a person. I am eternally grateful to Robin Morgan, my editor, mentor, guru and shiny knight, for showing me that I could demand and command that space. But even in the weighty, all-encompassing, definitive interview you have to have a line and the *Daily Mail* taught me that there always is a line. You know, a new twist on a person that tells you the whole story, or as whole as you can manage.

The *Daily Mail* teaches you competitive savagery. You got the cut up, you read everything forensically. You knew you were going for the definitive. You have to go where no other interviewer has gone: further, faster, deeper. You knew that time would be limited – an hour, perhaps. The PR might sit in. You'd learn to build your psychic wall so that they won't interfere with you. They don't exist. You'd get the killer questions lined up. You only need two of them. It's a panic, so you think fast and sharp. You know when to listen. You know when to speak because you have to go to some dark place that no other interviewer has ever been before. So the person is telling you how his mother left him to be eaten by the pet alsatian and you nod nonchalantly and you bring it back like a bone. Actually, it's more like that *Daily Mail* series Quick Cuisine; something that looks extravagantly gourmet, but is delivered up really fast but with total detail. The excavated soul served with fast-food relish. I'm very grateful for the fastidiousness of Corinna Honan. She used to drive me mad at the time. She taught me to be that terrier for detail.

You miss nothing. Everything you have learned in your life about betrayal, love, hate, sex, joy, pain, you recognize. Every time you see it hidden or disguised, and just as you know it among your friends, you know it among your enemies, you know it in the parallel universe of the celebrity. You know the nuance, how to recognize its mark where it's been and how it has affected the person that you must know so totally in such a short time.

Who are the best interviews? Invariably Jewish people make the best interviewees because they are sensates. They like to eat and, on the whole, they don't like to exercise. This means their intellectual muscles are very formed and flexed. They'll do debate. They'll do confession, because they need more to be liked. Happy people who are self-assured people are boring plunder. Dustin Hoffman is the perfect interview because he makes it easy for you to know him. He gives you nuance. He gives you detail. He gives you edge, misery. Meg Ryan is the perfect nightmare. She doesn't play the game. She doesn't give you anything, so you have to take from her. When the interview with Dustin Hoffman was over, I wanted to know more of him. I could easily be his friend. With Meg Ryan, a one-night stand was enough. But that doesn't necessarily mean it's not interesting to write about. Sometimes, the reverse is true. The metaphor, I suppose, would be messy sex. Bad sex is sometimes more haunting than good sex. You just don't want to do it again. The interview process is like taking a polaroid. You get one shot. If the polaroid doesn't come out, you've got a blurry thing. But you haven't got nothing. It's your job to make sense of the blurs. There's always something that comes out.

There's a couple of key questions that I always ask and they'll always deliver, no matter who or what. I'm afraid I can't reveal what they are because it took me a long time to reach them. Everyone has a repertoire of things that they are interested to talk about. Mine is Men, Women, Love, Sex, God and Death.

It's a much more exacting process interviewing someone

you admire than someone who makes you angry. For a start, you don't want to play the tape back and hear yourself fawning. The point is, whether you like them or not, you have to pull them away from their constructed reality. James Taylor said that sex and death were the same thing because they both did just that, pull off the constructed reality that you depend on to live. It is the same with the interview process. That is why it is often seen as a seduction and it's assumed that females are best at it. They probably are. It's like why are all the famous hairdressers men? There's an analogy in that somewhere. If I let you think I was this temptress, seductress, implacable, that would simply be an image I was trying to create. Or maybe one that's been created for me. I've been blacklisted by many PR's. They don't tell me to my face, but oftentimes, the *Sunday Times Magazine* has set up an interview. They have been eager beavers about it until they heard it was me and they asked for someone else, and Robin Morgan, to his credit, always tells them where to get off.

Sometimes I go to an interview extremely vulnerable. Something dreadful has happened in my life and it's difficult to separate from it. Sometimes it's imperative that you do. Sometimes it's interesting if you don't. Allowing the very important person to know that you are raw and stripped may heighten the mood. You plug into each other quicker. It's unnerving and interesting for, say, a buttoned-up politician suddenly to have someone vulnerable in front of them. All their synapses are trained in the covert of combat. I am not one of these interviewers who think it's a good idea to be like a Jungian therapist; you sit, they talk, pretending you're not judging them. I think people need points of reference. They need to know some of who you are. The problem is when they want to know too much of who you are. Sometimes they do this as a charming avoidance technique – they spend an hour asking you questions – so that you won't have found out much about them, although you can learn much about a person by the sort of questions they ask, almost as much as by the questions they answer. Or, ridiculously, they think they're there for a nice little chat. And although you have to make it seem as though they are, absolutely they are not. So I like to reassure them with a little bit of who I am – but not too much. I like interviewing politicians because it's an opposite process to the celebrity. Politicians have developed a knack of being ambiguous, which is irritating if you are after policy structures, which I never was, but fabulous if you're after emotional range. Invariably, they will present both extremes that they are trying to avoid. At the beginning, it is always important to listen.

I remember reading Joan Didion, whom I always admired for being so fast and seeping completely into your own body rhythm. She said that she was always nervous when she turned up, didn't know what to ask them, so said nothing and they just spilled. As long as you remember to keep interjecting with the word 'why', then that can work. 'Why' is such an important word.

Who are the worst interviews? People who are less intelligent than you, but not entirely stupid. The middle ground. Always the worst. The reformed psychotic is also bad. They give you therapy-speak which is a blandification of pain. We like to explore weakness but we don't like going down that preacher road. You also don't want to be going down the conveyor belt. You know, person in hotel room affords you twenty-five minutes, one after another. The idea is to make you feel small and unimportant and they are huge and very important. Well, you don't fall for that. There is no great divide between you and them. What you have to find is someone who will talk well and excitedly, with new perceptions and acuteness, of stuff that has happened to them, the stuff we all want to know about. That's Men, Women, Love, Sex, God and Death.

DOGS

All Men are Dogs
15 August 1993

I love to go out with my big silver poodle. He's always on his hind legs doing tricks. Flouncy, quirky, clever, literary tricks. He likes to be the centre of attention. He likes to show off, use the odd French word.

The silver poodle is a really good friend, almost as good as my black miniature poodle who is a real dog. All men are dogs. It's just a question of identifying breed, sifting out the spaniel souls, the bright and manipulative poodles and the stupid rottweilers.

Men call women dogs as a term of abuse and that's because men know themselves. Men fear themselves.

I keep my real dog because I like the thrill of unquestioning loyalty, unconditional love and affectionate licking when I am in the mood. He's clever, he's funny, he's entertaining. Pretty much the same stuff that any woman would want from any man, except you're more likely to get it from a real dog.

The confusion is, dogs and men are of a similar psyche. They wander round permanently oversexed, slaves to the power of their biological urges, their tongues hanging out. They don't know a lot about emotions other than being little puppies dependent on their mothers. The emotions that are sated with this maternal bond easily transmute to their dependence on a mistress when they become full-grown dogs.

I've always felt particularly thrilled with poodles. They are so deceptively multifaceted. You never know who's poodling who.

Some poodle men: columnist Matthew Parris, theatre critic Jack Tinker, a toy poodle because he does such marvellous tricks, Jeremy Paxman and Mick Jagger. They like an audience.

You can't really enter into a serious relationship without knowing the breed. Its temperament and how you'll get on with it. I once made a terrible mistake. I had this feral dog, a fascist with a thick neck, a brute of a dog, an indeterminate breed, always raking around. The kind of dog that ends up a misfit in Battersea Dog's Home because this breed doesn't want to belong. Now I hear he's running around on television, calling into the homes of strangers every morning. There are some dogs whose nature it is to bite any hand that strokes them and some women get off on the idea of taming beasts.

If you want something a little neurotic, but not too much of a brute, you couldn't find anything more excitable or reliable than a collie. Collies want to learn and love to please, have kind, intelligent eyes, a mixture of stability and deep passion. However, they can sometimes be embarrassing when they go gangly-legged and bark with enthusiasm. They can be irritatingly animated. Richard Branson is a bouncing collie. Donald Sutherland is a collie. So is Peter O'Toole. So is Bruce Springsteen. They're quite good at leadership and dominating. They order your food for you in restaurants. The down side is that they get a little bossy, sometimes go crazy in cars and sometimes try to round you up. Neil Kinnock was a collie. Typical boss dog that went wrong. I once knew a border collie and found that too much love damaged him. He was keener on the pursuit of power and the key was sex, aggression. He suffered from too much testosterone.

Dr Roger Mugford, the dog psychologist, feels certain species of dog, such as weimaraners should be routinely castrated and that future generations should come from a sperm bank. Personally, I can't recommend castration. I've always found that when I've emasculated my dogs, they have become bad-tempered and fat and have taken an unsettling interest in other things such as face creams, gardening, golfing or drinking calvados.

Some of my girlfriends have gone for what they have assumed were easier breeds. I have never for example been attracted to a cocker spaniel. But Janie has sadly become an expert on recognizing their peccadillos. 'They suffocate you,' she told me, 'they drown you with their saliva.' You're an hour late and he's still waiting. He says it's his fault. Spaniels roll over and you stomp on them. They are only suitable for women who see themselves as corgis.

Prince is a perfect shitzu. Axl Rose is a yorkie because he's always yapping and he's so fond of tartan collars. Tiny terriers have phenomenally large egos and are control freaks. Dachshunds are so dwarfed and miserable about it that they have testosterone overload and have been known to sever the arteries of their owners near the jugular. Bill Wyman and Dudley Moore are waddlers with nodding heads, but you never quite know when they're going to bark.

Most women like a touch of terrier. They are spirited, tenacious, emotionally cool and then suddenly roused to a passion. You find a lot of terriers in politics. Dennis Skinner is a Jack Russell. Fox terriers are brainy and biscuit-coloured like Clive Anderson. It's such fun to see him snapping at ankles.

Again, you have to be careful with some terriers. They steal, they like to possess a person and stake out no-go zones. Terriers can be calmed with rejection. I am told a nice kick in the face will do. But I've never been a terrier sort of girl because I've always lived by proxy. There was Janie's affair with a terrier who turned into a rottweiler. She recalled, 'There is a difference between snapping at my ankles, which I like, and ripping out my pancreas.' Some men misjudge this because they think all women are masochists.

Spaniels can be surprisingly diverse. They are a dimorphic breed; the multicoloured, sloppy-jowled and bad-breathed sort with a bad haircut that invites you to kick them and the solid red or solid black spaniels who are stricken with an unfortunate schizophrenic gene. One minute they're affable, fuzzy, friendly, your closest friend, and the next they have an avalanche of rage as the canine syndrome is known, and they turn to snarling, unthinking monstrous beasts.

Bruce Fogle, the vet and columnist, a golden retriever of a man, is informed about their eccentric behaviour. 'They are

Jekyll and Hyde dogs, one minute a dog on a chocolate box and the next depraved. It's an incurable syndrome.' Golden cocker spaniels with raging syndrome are Gazza, Prince Charles and Roy Hattersley. Michael Heseltine may look like an afghan, but actually he is an alsatian. He's bitten too many people in all the wrong places and he's strayed from the pack.

Beware of having too close a dealing with pack hounds, slim-hipped beagles and stag hounds. They are bred to chase, they protect each other. Team spirits who are not pushy are labradors and retrievers. Sensible and true, they pant to please. Political labradors? There, there Paddy. Good boy.

Aristotle said that the only difference between men and dogs was that dogs didn't know reason. Mmm. They scratch us, they leave us, they go out of our control, they slobber, they twitch, become irrepressibly enthusiastic for all the wrong reasons, they travel in packs, they can't think straight when they think about sex, it curdles their vision. There seems little difference to me.

I was very wrong about the silver poodle. He turned out to be a sly, rabid wolf dog with a perm. He barked bad things about me, loudly. In my head I have had to put him to sleep.

James Woods
Sunday Times Magazine
24 January 1993

Mike Tyson used to prepare for his fights by screening three days of James Woods movies to get his blood up. A few hours in a hotel room with Woods and it's easy to see why. He's like an incendiary device turned in on itself. An amalgam of complications: sensitive, psychotic, creepy.

He has been called America's most hostile actor. One is used to seeing him in searing portrayals of weirdo sleazebags like the cop killer in *The Onion Field*, the slinky gangster in *Once Upon a Time in America*, the amphetamine-enhanced neurotic in *The Boost*; in his latest offering, *Midnight Sting*, he plays a shifty but sexy ex-con hustler. His performances are so lingering, it's hard to disentangle him from them, but that's only part of why Woods is unsettling. The big-screen intensity, when delivered in small hotel rooms, is maniacal.

His face is cheekless and mouldy with pockmarks. An eel with slitty eyes, he slithers across two chairs. And he talks in torrents of foreboding, like an Old Testament prophet, spitting pitchforks about revenge and using the word 'whore' a lot.

It seems like James Woods has a problem with women. He'd say he has a problem with just one woman, but it's not human nature to make the same mistake only once. Unprompted – we were chatting about his mother, a school-teacher who read him Flaubert in his pram, about his near genius-level IQ, and about illiteracy. Mere warm-up stuff. Unwittingly, I'd pressed a button.

'This sociopath I was involved with, she didn't burden herself with the finer things of mind and spirit. She had more money socked away in her safe deposit box than most people who really work hard for a living ever have in their lifetime.' One woman, a cataclysmic effect. He always refers to her as 'the sociopath.'

'This person has caused an evolution in my life,' he says. 'Now I have definite standards of a person's worth. The only two things that I ever demand of anybody is that they never hit me and they never lie to me. That's all they have to do and they can be my friend for life. The first time they do one of those things there is no second chance. No court of appeal. The relationship is over the second it happens, in the blink of an eye. If you hit me or lie to me, you are dead. No reprieve, no purgatory, no probation, you don't exist anymore. It's real simple, real easy.'

He's twitching his foot. Big, beige, thick washed socks waggle up and down, up and down.

Does he not think that everyone deserves to have a second chance? 'No. The sociopath was a liar, and I've never been with liars again. This is a non-negotiable conversation.'

I'm afraid of any man who could hate one woman so much, and I've already lied to him. He wanted to know why the maids hadn't been in to clean my room. I told him I didn't know and he was on the phone hollering, 'This is James Woods. Why is room 713 such a mess?' The affronted Hispanic voice on the other end of the phone said I'd shooed them away.

How big does the lie have to be? 'Any liar will detract from your life, never enhance it.'

I suggest that people can both enhance and detract at the same time. And he retorts, machine gun rat-tat-tat: 'Never. It's a constant undercurrent, and you start to smell a detractor in everything that they do.

'There are those people who are socially responsible and there are those who are not. You watch how people treat other people, because I promise you, if they are going to fuck someone else over, they are going to fuck you over. Not a question of if, but a question of when. Simple, works like a charm. Weed them out. Why do you need greedy exploitative people?

'Don't you know people who forgive too much? Accepting an apology is giving permission for them to do the same thing over again. Most people forgive and tolerate

7

because of fear of loneliness. They haven't got enough confidence to believe they deserve better, and I spent twenty years of my life compromising, saying, "They lied to me, but I know they really like me." Fact is, they were scumbags.

'For all of this steam that I'm letting off, I am the most gentle, loyal, forgiving friend that anybody could ever have. I was so sweet to the sociopath because I thought she was good. But she was evil. She didn't care how she hurt me.' He speaks not sorely or plaintively, but with hard words from an ancient canker.

'She would say "Maybe I could really provoke him, and then he could do something and then I could do a lawsuit and make some money. I'll threaten his brother's kid's lives, and maybe they'll get so shaken up they'll . . ." He swallows the rant, blinks and manages to look wounded and predatory.

'This is an evil person and that kind of person should die of cancer. She would lie about the colour of the moon. She has caused a lot of damage in my life. But now I have learned something.

'It was hubris for me to think I could deal with her. I thought I could change this wounded bird. She presented the "I am just a poor little girl . . ." Well, let me tell you honey. It was arrogance. I thought I could fix her. Men can be abused by women, even though it is political flavour of the month to look at it the other way round. I was a fat, rich movie star. She came in for the kill. I was just a big fat sheep standing in the meadow and she and her coyote friends came in to rip out my underbelly, hamstring and the arches of my feet.'

It's always 'this person' or 'this sociopath'. He'd gag if he had to speak her name. 'I think we know who we are talking about, but I am not saying the name. For me this person does not exist, although she continues to harass me legally. I just get the pest control people to take care of the pests.'

Sarah Owens was his wife for a short time. She looks like your regular Californian babe, boufantty blonde, pure essence de bimbo. She used to train racehorses with an outdoorsy smile and high-octane lipgloss and as soon as the relationship soured, she kissed and told. She talked to *People* magazine about what a bad time Woods gave her.

She talked about verbal lashings that turned physical. She talked about how his sexual habits troubled her. How he was supposed to have pressured her into having an abortion. How she threw him out of the house, but how he returned, lurking with a shotgun. She claimed he ordered her to strip at gunpoint, lie on the floor and repeat parrot fashion, 'I am a whore. I am a baby killer.'

Apparently blinded by love and pain, they forgave each other, married in 1988, and divorced four months later. Intense legal battles and recriminations have followed. Woods seems to be obsessed with being taken for granted.

'I do honestly think there is some self-preservation instinct on my part that I never had children with her – I say to myself every day, "I know there's a God because he didn't let her spawn."

'Other people would have looked at this as an embittering experience, but I don't.' He's po-faced when he says this. For someone with an IQ of 180, he seems markedly lacking in self-awareness. 'I thought of it as a personal evolution. I was never going to make the same mistake again.

'People do make the same mistakes, until they learn from them. If I hadn't learned, I might as well have killed myself, because I couldn't have gone through anything like that again. I now know never to go for these damaged birds. I was always a fixer, and that was my inclination.

'My dad died, God rest his soul, when I was 12. My mother worked very hard to put my brother and me through school, so I felt that I had to look after her. Here was this woman, incredibly bright, who grew up in the Depression, and had nothing. It was my inclination to take care of people. My first wife came from an abusive and battered background, and I really helped her. We talk twice a week now. She's married to somebody else. She's a good mother to three children and she says, "You saved my life. Now I'm living a sober life."'

His first wife was a model, Kathryn Greco. They married in 1980 and divorced three years later. She described him as a very loveable control freak. 'He loved the way I looked, but never really trusted me. Jim thinks his way is the only way,' proffered the formerly wounded bird.

'The sociopath only pretended to be wounded,' says Woods. 'This woman's got chromium steel for tendons and mercury for blood. She said, "I'll suck him into my lair, rip his throat out, drink his blood, eat his brains." After her, no more damaged people.

'If you look for dysfunction in families and you find someone comes from an abusive, alcoholic divorced family of car thieves, chances are, they're not going to be much fun. Crappy people come from crappy families. As the divorce rate soars in America, I realize they had it right a century ago with arranged marriages. Common values, common background, common religion, heritage and aspirations are a bond stronger than true love.'

He has happily put into practice his vetting process. What a wholesome thing his new girlfriend, Heather Graham, is. Heather is beautiful, Heather is wonderful. Her hair is the colour of wheat. 'She comes from a totally loving family. Her father was head of counterterrorism in the FBI. My father worked in army intelligence. She is an Irish Catholic and I am an Irish and English Catholic. Her family are still together, the parents love each other. There is no alcoholism, no abuse and surprise surprise, she happens to be one of the most loving, caring, independent, thoughtful people I've ever met. She comes from a healthy, functional family that has great values and self-respect.

'A friend of mine once said, "If I could meet a woman who hadn't been raped by her uncle, been a drug addict since she was 14, was a feminist and had four abortions and gonorrhea, I might just meet one woman who is decent."'

Heather is so decent. She's cherry pie. Tom Robbins wrote an ode to the American waitress for *Playboy* and the picture they used was of Heather. She's now starring in the film of his novel, *Even Cowgirls Get the Blues*. She played a waitress in *Twin Peaks*. Agent Cooper fell in love with her. David Lynch then had her warm and breathy in his Calvin Klein ad for Obsession. She and Woods met on set, the way all great arranged marriages begin, when she was providing the love interest for *Midnight Sting*.

He talks euphorically about their shared interests. 'We both love nothing more than to walk. We love to stay in and read. We are redoing a house together that was once owned by the musician Jascha Heifetz. She is so unbelievably beautiful in the film, it's astounding. She's in her twenties, but she can look 14.'

She looks nubile, she looks gorgeous, and Woods explains that since knowing her, he's given up smoking, his only addiction. He says she has produced a chain reaction of positivity. He goes on and on about it, in that patronizing way that reformed addicts do and, at the same time, his foot is waggling up and down like a maniac's. I wanted desperately to give him a cigarette to calm him down. But he would only tell me how relaxed he is, how wonderful golf is, how straightforward and straight-talking he is, how happy his life is. How he's not at all like the nefarious, sick and blighted souls he likes to portray, although he has given us a relief from them in *Midnight Sting*, which is an unpretentious, fast boxing film.

He plays Gabriel Caine, an ex-conman, who arrives in mythical Digstown and fixes a fight to beat the town's slithery crime boss (Bruce Dern) at his own cold and crooked game. It is a cute macho movie, a much needed counterbalance to those grizzly performances that leave blood on the screen.

He was nominated for an Oscar for his role in Oliver Stone's 1985 hit, *Salvador*. He played Richard Boyle, a manipulative American photo-journalist who finds personal redemption in the midst of moral and political squalor. Stone thinks that Woods is not the easiest of actors to deal with. 'He's a lunatic. He always knows better, which is very irritating. In the end, it was like a fifteen-round fight. We were both beaten, but we respected each other ... If he's right for the role and you want to make the best possible film, you've got to go with him.'

He recently played Roy Cohn, in the film *Citizen Cohn*, the repulsively hypocritical gay Jewish lawyer who was a right-hand man to Senator McCarthy. He prosecuted Jews for communism and homosexuals for perversion. Critics used that 'seminal' word to describe his performance. He was exhaustingly frightening. Woods likes nothing better than to frighten people in this way.

'I find my self-worth is enhanced by what I contribute to others. I have people coming up and saying, "You saved my life" because of the film *Bill W* which I did about a recovering alcoholic. I have raised political awareness about *Salvador*. I have touched people and in some way they touch me back, and I feel part of the community. I feel comfortable being part of what I have achieved and it is what, in an existential sense, makes us function as a civilized global community.'

His hatred for 'the sociopath' is so virulent, his face grey with bile, yet he is coming out with all of this 'I'm just a homespun boy' stuff from such a loving, normal background. Something, somewhere, must have gone terribly wrong. He insists he's not like the characters he plays onscreen. 'I'm so mild-mannered, which is a little unsettling for most people.' What is unsettling is to have glimpsed the persona from which the madness and the maniacs are culled.

We are to meet again the next day. I suggest dinner, I suggest drinks, I suggest the golf course. But he wants my hotel room again. The next day, he is another person. A pair of horn-rimmed spectacles make him seem kinder, more open.

'I am the most direct, least duplicitous person you'll ever meet. I never pull punches. I never play subterfuge,' he claims. But for a person who doesn't like subterfuge, there were certainly many variations on the 'truth' in a court case that involved voodoo dolls and the actress Sean Young.

12

A mutilated doll was mysteriously placed on Woods' doorstep. Its neck had been cut, iodine was spilled on its chest and its face was smeared with white panstick to make it look like a rancid corpse. It was wrapped in a newspaper from Vancouver, where Young happened to have been filming. They had briefly enjoyed some kind of soured romantic dalliance on the set of *The Boost*. She is known to be feisty, volatile, an easy target.

He had her questioned by the police and finally decided on a $2 million lawsuit for the harassment. He alleged she turned his hair grey and gave him constant tinnitus. He claimed that she had put his and his wife's names on the mailing list of anti-abortion organizations and he was flooded with pro-life literature. Court battles began. Young's lawyer had Woods' police record checked and unfortunate shenanigans concerning Sarah Owens and her shotgun claims were uncovered.

Nobody seemed to win. Who paid what in costs and damages is not clear. Young vehemently denied the dolls. She said that she decided revenge was best left to God. She dismissed Woods as a sad character. 'He suspects the world. He barricades himself accordingly. Jimmy appears to behave as though nobody suffers as he does, and at the rate he's going, it may one day be the truth.' She wrote this in her diary when they first met. It was the beginning of a bad cycle for her because everyone had her branded as a vengeful dipsomaniac. So, did she send you the voodoo dolls? 'No, she didn't.'

Rather a shame for her, then, that she had to be dragged through the courts. 'It was just . . . I had this incredibly jealous girlfriend who was upset by the fact that I was working with a very beautiful and talented actress, and all hell broke loose. Once I got rid of that girlfriend and never thought about her or talked about her, my life was fine.

'They were not voodoo dolls. It was a doll that was made to look like a dead infant, because this person, the jealous one, thought of it as a clever, self-serving little drama. It was an incredibly evil thing to do, not quite as evil as making it seem like Sean Young did it, who, in my heart, I don't believe did it. It was this disturbed and awful and evil human being. But I guarantee that this person is not in my life anymore. She does not exist.'

The feet are starting to wag again. So what does he think of Sean Young? 'I think she's terrific. But I was really furious with her when I thought that she'd done those ugly things. My brother's children's lives were threatened. They were kept in the house for eight months during this period. And pictures of dead babies in garbage cans were sent to my house.

'I wasn't used to dealing with this kind of person. I've always dealt with decent people. There were attempts to smear me, but those attempts were incredibly transparent and everybody in my business saw through this little charade. I think you know what was going on, so I don't have to lay it out for you, do I?' He sighs, cathartic, sweet, sad.

He tells me about other deeply sad things. About 'this person, who destroyed, or took most of the stuff that was important to me, including letters from my family, my dad. All destroyed. This was one of the greatest losses of my life. I have nothing of my dad's left.'

Gail Woods died suddenly, during routine surgery. 'He was a big, strong country guy, but his hands were very soft. He would make my mother breakfast in bed every Sunday. He'd sit me on his lap and quote Shakespeare to me.

'I didn't much like being a child; I always wanted to be an adult. I said my first words when I was 7 months and could carry on full conversations before I was a year old. I was a phenomenon. A forceps delivery and five days after I was born, when I was safely home, a tornado hit the hospital and it burned to the ground. It was like I'm a catalyst to disaster ... I'm only teasing.'

Today he really wants to be a puppy dog. 'I'm just a big old mutt running through the mud with a big, wet, cold, black nose. Running around the wood, rolling in dog-poo. A big, old, stupid dog.'

We enter dog mode, which is as sweet as yesterday's rant

was bitter. He talks about all the dogs he grew up with; there was Biscuit who rang the doorbell, Tinkerbell Tiger Lily, who was a sheltie showdog, and Fluff, who looked like a little koala bear. 'She was retarded and sort of blind, but the cutest dog you ever saw. She was sweet, and so undaring, except she'd always come running over to you.'

I am perched on my hotel bed and he's on all fours with his tongue out. 'She'd start licking your leg and look up at you.' He cocks his head, sad. 'I'll tell you this story that will tell you more about me and my mother than anything. We were so poor it was ridiculous. My mother hadn't had an education, she had to work, but she was determined to make something of herself. She opened a pre-school in Rhode Island which became tremendously prestigious, famous and successful. The kids put on a play in French when they were 5. All the top senators and psychiatrists and lawyers wanted to send their kids there. Yet my mother always took 20 per cent of the kids for free because she knew about the stigma of poverty.

'The school did well and she wanted to have one little symbol of wealth, because she'd never had any wealth in her life before. So she went out and bought herself a mink coat. She came home on the first day that she had her mink coat. She picks it up and swirls it about and sweeps it over the floor. And Fluff comes walking over, sniffs the coat, thinks great, crawls up on it and falls asleep. My mum doesn't want to disturb Fluff, so she picks the whole bundle up and puts it in the closet where Fluff likes to sleep. She never wore that coat again because Fluff liked it, and it became Fluff's bed. Fluff had a mink bed.

'Years later, when Fluff's distemper caught up with her and it was clear she was in pain, we had to have her put down. My mum felt so bad, and wanted to make sure that she wasn't afraid. She picked up the coat with Fluff asleep on it and put it on her lap. The dog slept all the way to the vet in the mink coat. He gave her the injection and then my mother had Fluff buried in the mink coat. She never wore it once. It was Fluff's bed and then Fluff's burial shroud. If you live in a home like that, you have a clear understanding of the priorities of life.

'Now I'm going to do my greatest imitation for you,' he says. He's on all fours, looking extremely stupid, poking his little tongue in and out and doing little breathy noises near my ear, trying to conjure everything that is loyal and sweet and good, even if it is a creature from another species.

'My main affirmation, my belief in God, is because he invented dogs in all their stupid, fabulous glory. He had such a great idea. Here's people, they have to live their life, their toil will be arduous, rewards will be few. But just in case they think all will be lost, we're going to give them sex and we're going to give them dogs. And the dogs come free.'

Since this was written, Woods has become a lot more famous, but is still a serial fiancé, and I wonder if he still barks like a dog.

Relationship of the Week
Oprah Winfrey and Solomon
August 27, 1995

There is a higher form of love between living things. It's self-less, endless, and unconditional. And it's canine. Earth can deliver no greater bond than that which binds woman and dog. Oprah thinks so. And Oprah knows. Oprah's known all pain, all angst, all love, all fat, all thin things that it is possible to cram into one life. She's every woman. That's her theme song. What cares she for a non-marrying fiancé? Or the warm feeling that cheeseburger and fries used to bring. That was conditional love. It made you fat and it made you cross. It made you shrink a little inside yourself. But the love that Oprah Winfrey has for her dog Solomon is a much, much tastier, much furrier, and a much more devouring delight.

Last week it was reported that she spent £75,000 to save the chestnut-coloured cocker spaniel's life. £50,000 on vet's costs and the rest on travel costs, transporting him and her to the genius vet in Denver Colorado, 200 miles from Telluride where she was vacationing with Stedman Graham. Solomon was a Christmas present, but thus was much more than a simple love gift. Solomon is a love-child. She calls him surrogate baby. She rang the clinic where he'd been taken to be treated for parvo, a killer intestinal virus. 'Please save him. I love him as if he were my baby. I spend more time with him than I do with anyone else.' Not a dignified confession, but then love isn't about dignity.

She flew Solomon several times back and forth to Denver where he has been responding encouragingly to her treatment and love. Spending £75,000 on saving the dog's life is no big deal because A) she is so rich – she earns a reported £25 million a year and B) she is so generous. It's not like we can put her into a 'this woman is so loopy and dejected, she loves animals more than people' box either.

Last year she surprised Stedman with a $130 million stake in her company, donated millions to the United Negro College Fund, handed over one million to the run-down school Providence in her home city Chicago, paid for her sister's kid to go to the élite Wellesley College in Boston, she tipped the crew of her Caribbean cruise boat holiday $1,000 each and gave her best friend Gayle King a $1,000,000 check so that she too could be a millionaire.

She grew up dirt-poor, deprived even. She packs a lot in and chucks a lot out. It's a frenzied, generous existence. Her gift to her dog should be seen as relative and therefore it is totally in proportion.

Much is made of strong women who have small dogs, no children and busy lives. It's not that the dog's love is less complex or less demanding than a child's and it should never be assumed so. It is that Oprah's relationship with herself is complex. When she was 14, she was raped by a relative, made pregnant and had a miscarriage. This is bound to have distorted the loss and the desire for that baby. Until she met Graham, she had a history of abusive relationships with men.

When she needed their approval so badly, she turned to suppressing her feelings in mounds of food. 'It was a way of cushioning myself against the world's disapproval. I needed everyone to like me because I didn't like myself much, so I'd wind up getting involved with these cruel, self-absorbed guys.'

Children can be cruel and are self-absorbed. Spaniels are sweet and giving. They approve of everything. Oprah's desire for children has been as elastic as her size. One minute hungry and desperate, another, she wouldn't want to make the sacrifice, wouldn't want to take the risk. A child involves another parent and the emotional risks that go with him. The love for the nine-month-old dog comes after a difficult year. Her publicist, who's been with her for eight years, quit in a huff and filed a lawsuit against her former boss for back-pay and severance. Her personal assistant of six years, Beverly Coleman, also backed out of her life saying she couldn't cope with the exacting demands on her life. She offered her a million-dollar salary to stay, but the woman wouldn't be bought. People who give often do so because the giver is always in command. Takers are the needy, the vulnerable. Givers are the empowered, Oprah's favourite word. How irksome when something can't be bought, even with your great big generous heart. Solomon's life, in terms of getting him to the top specialist, is certainly something that can be bought. Although, it is wrong to assume a dog's love is easy and comes as a token exchanged for a choc-drop. Oprah has had other dogs like she has had other boyfriends, and just as one can have many loves in a lifetime, only with one is there that piercing connection in the heart chakra. It's the same with dogs. Sometimes you find one with whom there is a perfect and limitless connection.

For instance, I have known dogs before, but I have never known a dog like my dog Poodle. We are as one. We intuit each other's thoughts. We are boundless. The dog psychiatrist said that I had given Poodle a superiority complex by his name implying that he wasn't a Poodle, but *the* Poodle, King of Poodles. And that is exactly what Oprah has done by giving her spaniel the name Solomon after King Solomon, an exemplary chap. Very wise, very strong. Solomon is a black icon, even though in dog form he's chestnutty silky brown. But then again, so is Oprah. And he wrote songs.

He wrote drooling, fecund, sexy songs. 'Let me kiss thee with the kisses of my mouth for thy love is better than wine.' King Solomon in the Bible was an instinctive genius, an almost telepathic know-all, and the Bible says, 'King Solomon loved many strange women.' There now, that must have made Oprah feel at home. Because she knows she'd had a strange life and is adored for being the kind of peculiar that women identify with. She needed, of course, a male to acknowledge this. And then came Solomon, a gift, all chocolaty, with those big aching eyes. A perfect combination. A male she has created to revere her who also follows her from room to room wagging his whole body. She can transfer all the feelings she doesn't want to show on to him; he can cry at doors and at partings, however short. He can beg, like strong women learned not to do. Solomon will not flee from her cuddles and he will no doubt creep up on her bed where he can make those sad eyes, all loving and loyal and scared of life without her. She can nurture his dependency and he can host all her own fears of failure to please and abandonment. She can hold his paw and release her own insecurities.

Woman to dog is not a simple love, but the dog's love is more enduring and less flexible than of any man. Dogs don't lie. They demand attention, not restriction in your life. And dog spelled backwards is God.

This piece was inspired by and in honour of Poodle.

Marquesa de Varela
Sunday Times Magazine
18 August 1996

She'll tell you herself that she's fun to be with, and her predilection for rescuing things that don't need rescuing is charming.

She's sitting in the very front row of club class, poised, always ready. She waves languidly at me. I am the last on the plane. Slowly, she smiles. 'Ah, the star. Only the star arrives last. They held the plane up for you.'

It's corny and you don't want to believe her, but you do. You're in her web and it feels good. The Marquesa de Varela has fixed you with her eyes, her incredible, unbelievable eyes, not quite green, not quite grey and not quite brown. You know she has something. You don't know what, exactly, it is. Charm would be too soft a word. A well-flexed manipulation technique would be too hard. The world is her friend and she gets her friends to do what she wants. There's my friend the Duchess of this, the Princess of that. She'll beckon you into the Taras and the Camillas to make you feel you know them too, and with equal ease she'll glide you to the brash, the *arrivistes*, the Gazzas, the Mandys, and asks them all when they last cried. She has opened the doors, the porticos, the haciendas. New mothers scarcely recovered from the anaesthetic blearily reveal their new arrivals. Specials on Fergie becoming a model. Fergie changing nappies and seen as intimately uncoordinated and gauche as a Royal was never seen before. Mia Farrow, after the case with Woody Allen, all that nasty business, all washed up first in *Hello!* magazine.

She's the international fixer, though she does not edit the magazine. Her exact title is international editor and she is the reason that the rather mundane Spanish *Hola!* was transformed into the soon to be global *Hello!*. Without the

Marquesa, there could be no curse of *Hello!*. There could be no hard-core fawn, no stroking of the *nouveaux*, the nearly-had-it-alls and the now-I've-got-everythings. As everyone knows, doing the interview is the easy part. It's the fixing that takes the time.

Here we are on a plane, headed for Sotogrande, where I've been invited to the christening of her daughter Valeria's third child, the first of her current union. Very intimate for people who don't know each other. But of course, we do know each other. She is fierce in her vulnerability, her desire to expose regret, foible, pain. She not only opens her wounds, but she lets you sit in them like armchairs. And then, with a beguiling nosiness, she'll wonder, have you too been to that place? You trust her, you'll tell her anything.

She tells me she has always made terrible choices. Then, rather skittishly, 'I'm a gypsy.' This is because she is never settled, never comfortable anywhere for long. She has homes in Madrid, London, Montevideo and Punta del Este in Uruguay, and has just bought a villa for her daughter in Southern Spain. She comes from a good family, but her three brothers got most of the family wealth. Eduardo Sanchez Junco, the publisher of *Hello!*, pays her well, but not that well. It doesn't sound to me as if the choices have been so terrible. But yes, she says, they have, because she's riven. She's two people, two entirely different people.

Actually, she's more like fifty-six people. She says all she wanted was to be happy, a family woman, a woman in love, but she wanted to be stimulated and is easily bored. She never wanted to work, but she needed money. There is that need to be protected, a wistful woman, but it can quickly translate into the predator, the business-minded woman who needs to control – 'a silken enabler,' as she was once described. 'Silken enabler': we both think that is a tremendous phrase for her.

Even if this is false intimacy, it feels real. She makes flattery seamless. This is by no means a ten-a-penny talent. Those who know how to apply it are exotic creatures indeed. I notice men looking at her. She is sexy, very sexy. She is about

50, but a lady doesn't tell her real age. There's something about the way she sits, her legs slightly apart, the way her mouth goes from small and pursed to laughing and pillowy.

I have read that she keeps a full wardrobe in each of her houses and so only ever needs to carry her Louis Vuitton hand luggage, containing little more than a nice fat cheque for the person she has fixed to interview. She travels the world, I have read, in her leggings and her knickers. But no, this is all wrong. She meant sneakers, not knickers. And she hates labels. She'd never have Louis Vuitton.

We're at the luggage carousel. Five suitcases are off already and there's a disastrously heavy, suspiciously Vuitton-like trunk filled with mirrors and paintings she is taking to furnish the house she has just bought for her daughter. She is looking to see if any men are looking to help her. There are none, and we drive the lot on various trolleys to the hire car. We try to fit it all in the little Peugeot. She drops the heavy chest. Her knee is slashed, gushing blood. She's holding her leg and still trying to lift the trunk and looking askance, helpless.

The man from the hire-car company has already left his office. She cries something in Spanish to the car lot attendant, who explains that we have to have a code to start the car. He brings her a bottle of antiseptic lotion and looks longingly at her leg. He gets another man to start the car. The Marquesa is so stressed, she has to get yet another man to fetch a cigarette. She had given up smoking. Funny, she had never asked me for a cigarette.

The next day, she takes me on a little tour. Not of the nice pink and sandy villas, although she shows me where Prince Andrew stays to play golf, but to the run-down little town where the hippies and drug dealers hang out. We drive past a chained husky guarding a second-hand car lot. She explains to me that this is where she saved two other dogs, who were also chained in 'little houses' that were too small, without water. In her home country, Uruguay, she has rescued fifty dogs and she walks for miles and miles with them. Animal love is unconditional, not like human love. Rescuing the dogs was

woman wants unconditional love

the best she'd felt in years because it was dangerous. She hired a car and two gypsies. She waited in the car under the bridge for the getaway while the gypsies clambered over the wire mesh with spikes on top and brought the dogs back. She likes the contradiction of her elegance, her manicured life, and saving the starving dogs with the dirty gypsies who are her friends, along with Princess this and Princess that.

She was her father's favourite, brought up very strictly, the kind of girl who is shown her place. 'At lunch and dinner, the only talk was business, so I absorbed it and was never expected to speak. My mother is red-haired, thin, and very elegant. I am like my father, who is very sexy. In fact, I am my father. Although I loved Uruguay, when I was 17, I was already in New York bringing things back to South America and selling, because I wanted to be independent economically. I wanted freedom. That is the basis of my life – not to depend on anyone else. That is why I took nothing from my husbands.

'My first husband doesn't want to come to the christening because if I am there, he is suffering. But for me, when something is finished, I become completely cold. I always think I am like mafia to people. I can adore you and you can be protected by me forever. I can honestly give my life. But if you betray me, I will never forget that, even thirty years later.' There's an arctic chill and her eyes narrow.

Her first husband was Julio Cesar de Montenegro. He told her he was a prince, but he wasn't. 'He said he had a palace in Florence and all he had was debts. He was a gambler. He said on my wedding night, "Tomorrow morning some people are going to come and we're going to have to pay them." We were in Madrid and I remember walking in the streets crying. I was 23. I was an idiot. My father had left an amount of money in cash – the value of a flat in the best area of Madrid. I had to give it to him. And I could have had anybody. I had been engaged three times before, to wonderful men, elegant. But I wanted my freedom. I was not dreaming to get married at all, although I always wanted to be loved.

'My parents were very good together, but there was a big difference in age, so I never really saw a big love-affair. I wanted this, and I wanted an international life, travelling. Now I regret that life.' She shrugs, makes big eyes of remorse. You don't regret it, really? 'Well sometimes I think it would have been better to have married a farmer and live with animals and the children all together. We are all living seperately.

'When I was a child, 5 or 10 years old, the game they played was, my brothers were Indians and I was a prisoner, so they would put me in a barrel and I was there, all afternoon. Imagine the respect they had for me.' It is not surprising that young Neneta (which is what her friends call her) wanted to get away.

Getting away meant going to Europe, going to New York on studying expeditions. When she was 14, she had her first fiancé. 'But he had a terrible accident and became a cripple. This was very difficult. The wedding was postponed because he had a depression. He was in the hospital for nine months, and when he came out he was different. He became very jealous, so my father sent me to Europe. Anyway, I could have had any man. If you think I'm beautiful now, imagine then.'

Although the Marquesa is at the helm of *Hello!* magazine, she does not always like its imposed self-censorship. She's fun and she's funny. She's indiscreet in an endearing way. She would have been much funnier had she been allowed to say what she really felt about some of those she has interviewed. Sometimes she despises those with no money and no taste or no brain. Sometimes she argues with Eduardo, but she concedes that he is usually right. He was perhaps the first man to respect her talents, to realize that her connections could be useful.

After splitting from her second husband in 1985, she worked as a researcher for a Spanish television station. But when the Socialists came to power, they despised anyone with her background. Eduardo knew he could use it. Her first job for him was to persuade the daughter of the King of Morocco to allow pictures to be taken at her wedding. She posed with her sister as they had never been seen before, with diamonds all over their faces and their shoes encrusted with emeralds and rubies. The Marquesa had been a guest and this combination of tenacity and exceptional society contacts convinced Eduardo to hire her full-time. It made sense to move her to England to use her talents to set up the big international stories. She says she knows that people love to be with someone who is fun, but when she has to be tough, to push, she will do it. That is why most of the specials that have made *Hello!* famous, the scoops that have made its covers, the marriages that have been cursed after welcoming *Hello!* into their lovely homes, have been generated by the Marquesa. But *Hello!* only wants beautiful things and beautiful people, only the good news. She recalls telling Princess Anne that she had come to do a nice positive, happy story and Anne replying, 'Well, you've come to the wrong place.'

The Marquesa tells me how she has a wistful longing for Uruguay, for its elegance. How she never wanted to be famous. How all she wanted and still wants is not a man who is glamorous, but a man who will protect her. And yes, she does feel she needs protecting because she has many enemies. 'They are all jealous of me. Always, since I was a child, I have created jealousy. I have never asked for it. I cannot be nicer with people. But even my mother – and my mother is a cold woman, not someone who will flatter – even my mother has seen something that she has never seen in anybody.' At school, that something made all the girls want to tell her what eyes she had, and would she be their friend? That something made women fear she would eat their husbands. That something makes her catnip to men.

She discovered her own charisma. She could channel it into getting any man she wanted, and to begin with, that's where her sights were set. 'Except I always got the wrong man. Had I found the right man, who knows, I might have stayed married and created a different family. I have had an interesting life, but I have sacrificed a lot.'

After her two daughters, Natalia and Valeria, were born, she made a plea to the Vatican for an annulment of the first marriage.

'I am stupid, stupid.' She shakes her head. 'I have made terrible choices. I always choose the wrong man, the bad man, the naughty.' She says this with a conspiratorial glint and waits for me to say, 'Naughty is the most interesting.'

The second husband had a father who was General Franco's right-hand man. The title Marques de Varela San Fernando was given to him by Franco. Her mother-in-law was the richest woman in the Basque country. She was already dating Henri Roussel, the father-in-law of Christina Onassis, but Enrique, the Marques, had asked around those jet set 1970s friends who was the most beautiful woman on the circuit. Everyone agreed it was Neneta Marin.

'The Military was so sexy. Those boots, that uniform. He was the sexiest man I've ever had. He knew how to command a woman. You forgive everything. He would just take me by the waist, very tight, just to let you know that this is a man who knows how to sleep with a woman when he holds you like this.' She puts her arms out with military precision. 'He would say I had the most beautiful eyes in the world, the most beautiful body, the most beautiful everything. It was love at first sight, from the very first date. I didn't mean to go out with him. My boyfriend had gone on a cruise and was coming back twenty days later, and this one rang and wanted me to go to dinner. Everything said go, you're stupid if you don't, he's so much fun. I wore this dress, sexy, sexy but elegant and it was red. And I put on platforms to be taller. And he had a velvet jacket, blue eyes, so elegant.

'I like cashmere, I like lovely sheets. I like things that you touch. I couldn't go out with a man who had bad taste and I like men to be macho, to organize everything, to choose the right colour, the right car, the right suit, the right restaurant. I want them to give the orders and hold me like in a tango. That's what I want, a tango man. I miss that now, that passion.'

Enrique was a hard act to follow. He would say to her, 'Just obey. Don't think.'

'He was a spoilt, domineering boy, but I was a slave,' she says, her eyes getting bigger and greener and swirling about the place. Did you find yourself addicted to that? 'Yes,' she says shyly. You didn't really like it, but you were hooked. 'Absolutely. I couldn't let go, and – you know what? – I never met a man who could give me orders like that again. That person I would have died for. I lived with him for four or five years in a little town on the Costa Brava. I never rang anybody and nobody rang me and I couldn't care less. The only thing for me was getting up in the morning, making sex, going to do the shopping, coming back, making lunch. Then we would sleep together again.

'I cannot understand how it is that I could have lived without my daughters. That's the big drama I have now. How could I do it? I left them in South America. They will never know how much I love them. I would give them everything I have. I feel terribly guilty. I stole from them their childhood. From when they were 2 or 3 till when they were 11 or 12 I never saw them. It was unbelievably bad, but it was a passion, all-consuming. It was something like a sickness.'

She bows her head in shame. 'I used to think I wanted love, and then with my second husband I realized sexual love was for me more important than romantic love. Without sex, for me, there is no love.'

Valeria is now 24, Natalia 25. As toddlers, they were sent to Uruguay to be raised by Neneta's mother, returning to Madrid all those years later. In those missing years, she saw them twice, once when she went to Uruguay as her father was dying. She stayed until the funeral. Then they came for the wedding with the Marques, with whom she had been living for several years. She hoped they would all live together. 'But he never liked children and he insisted that they were sent to boarding-school in England. Valeria was very unhappy and went back to South America. Natalia was more adaptable, but suffered more and stayed. My husband made no effort to love them. He even wanted to eat alone with me and sent them to eat with the maids. Valeria once wrote me a note which said, 'You are never there when I need you', and that is the only time she has referred to it.

'He would cheat on me sometimes, and then I would try to kill him. On the day I said I was leaving, he would go on his knees and cry and make a big scene. He was a very spoilt man, born with all you could dream of, power, floods of money, deeply intelligent. He knows about everything and he knows how to make you feel a slave. I never have found another man to treat me like this.'

The final straw in her marriage was that there was another girl. 'The problem is that he is a womanizer. He never remarried – that's why I can still use the title.' According to Spanish law, if you're divorced you shouldn't use the title. She uses it when it suits her. Sometimes it suits her more to say she is the mother of Valeria, who is famous in Spain as a top model, the Bennetton girl.

'Meanwhile, since the birth of my son, Bruno Mauricio, I had changed. From the moment Bruno was conceived, I knew everything about what Bruno was going to be, exactly his face, exactly his behaviour, when he was here inside of me. He was the angel I had waited to have.' Do you think the great sex made a great baby? 'Yes. It had to be a result of that great sex. But my husband got jealous. I was asleep and put the baby like this.' She clasps her arms to her breasts. 'Bruno was all my conversation, Bruno this and that. I was becoming a mother, not a wife, and this was distancing me from him, and the more he womanized, the more I was completely in love with Bruno.' Bruno is now 17, just finishing school in South America.

Her love life after Enrique? Well, there was a boy who followed her while she was walking the dogs. The dogs liked him and that was a big plus. But because of her love for her son, she would be embarassed to go out with a younger man: it might offend Bruno.

There was another man she liked, in Europe. But she went

28

for her sojourn to South America – she is two months here, one week there, which she thinks makes it very difficult for a relationship – and when she came back there was a message on her answering machine telling her how much he loved her and telling her everything he had to say to her because he had very little time left. Terminal cancer. He was already dead when she played the message.

She asks me, beseechingly, why do I think people are so jealous of her? After all, she hasn't always been Marquesa World-Class Concorde Club. She used to travel economy. In fact, when she first started out working for Eduardo, she was free-lance, and had to pay her own fares. Recently her Gazza scoop saw *Hello!*'s circulation top the million mark for the first time. But in the beginning, things were different.

This is a woman who frequently begins sentences, 'My friend the president', 'My friend the king,' but this is also a woman who is unspeakably lonely. Sure, everyone wants to be her friend, but real friends, friends who would die for her, she says there are only a few. 'I would die for.' 'I would suffer for.' She says that a lot. Her daughter, Valeria, the model: sure she would die for her, but they have a ferocious non-understanding. The Marquesa thinks Valeria has let herself go. Three children, no make-up. On the first afternoon of our trip, the Marquesa takes me to the new villa she has had built for Valeria. One of the builders asks Valeria if the handsome woman is her sister.

On our way to visit Valeria's new pink house, with the Marquesa driving like a maniac as usual, we see a perky little black kitten, trotting very fast, following a couple who turn out to be German lesbians. 'The cat is starving,' she says. 'It is lost. Shall we save it?' She had already planned for us to save the husky we had seen earlier. She would go and get the gypsies and they would climb the fence, clip it free, and we would be waiting in the getaway car. That would have been exciting and a nice story, but I imagined we'd never get round to it, what with the christening and the Marquesa itching to decorate Valeria's bare house with the lovely exotic antique rugs, the tapestry throws and the paintings she had lugged over. Then there was the photo shoot. It would be quite a story, showing the Marquesa's rescuing nature, to just rescue this kitten. I blame myself: I encouraged her.

We ask the German women if it is their cat. No, they can't stop it from following them. 'Ah, he has been abandoned,' says the Marquesa with a face of horror. 'Let's get some milk for him.' Well, if he has indeed been abandoned, he has not been treated cruelly. I say that milk isn't good for little kittens. It makes them sick. 'Nonsense, he needs it for nourishment,' she says. She drops me at Valeria's new, unlived-in house and goes to look for a shop.

She returns with a banana milk shake for the cat and a huge tin of cat food. Valeria is not pleased to see the stray kitten: she doesn't share her mother's love of stray animals. It is quite ravenous and eats the cat food in the back yard. 'He will be all right here while we look for places for the photo shoot,' says the Marquesa, whose grandchildren look at her sullenly because she has not given them much attention. As we wave goodbye, one of them is sucking the milk shake through a straw.

The Marquesa was anxious about the Valeria situation. I could see that. We'd had lunch, Valeria, her man, the Marquesa and me. There'd been an explosion. Hard words in Spanish. The Marquesa let the row happen knowing that I could understand Spanish. Afterwards she asked me, 'Did you know what that was about?' And I said basically she likes the life here where he can play polo and play with his dogs and not have to work very hard and you were saying, why doesn't he want a better life? Why can't he work? 'Yes, you understood perfectly well enough.'

I understood what was being said, sure. But I am not sure why the Marquesa is supporting her daughter, giving her a villa and discount towels from Conways when the very rich boyfriend won't work and she was a substantial earner as Spain's top model. I think perhaps it is guilt. 'Yes. I cannot forget their childhood alone, so I have to spoil them now.

And even though Valeria and I, we have a good relationship, after a while, there's a silence that will never be filled, never. Never did I say the reasons why I left her. Never does she ask and the hole will be there forever. Such anguish.

'That dog is lost,' she says, pointing to a Yorkshire terrier with a bright yellow collar sitting by a pink-skinned couple. No, he's not lost. There is a tendency in the Marquesa to rescue things that don't need rescuing.

The previous night, we had gone to a charity dinner in Marbella. There was a little man there, a former bullfighter with a sprig of rosemary in his lapel, who now has an animal sanctuary on his farm in Marbella. He has fifty stray dogs and more cats. He is a millionaire. He loves animals. He offered us his farm for a photo shoot. So we ended up going to the bullfighters for the photos. It was all very contradictory stuff: a front room with huge heads of dead bulls, his trophies on the wall and a couple of arthritic live ones that he had kept for thirty years in the back yard. It seemed ludicrous that he was offering us rides on Julio the bull. Julio's fur was very greasy and I didn't like the look of him at all, but the Marquesa is game for anything. I also noticed that his cats were teeny-weeny, thin things, as if they had been ironed. We should have brought that other cat here, I said to the Marquesa. She looked horrified. In our busy day, we had forgotten to collect it from Valeria's. We went for it afterwards, but, of course, it was gone. If it wasn't lost before, it was certainly lost now.

Our last day together, the christening. The Marquesa was in a diaphanous silk chiffon. Only beautiful fabrics touch her skin. She was to be the godmother, but we arrived five minutes before the ceremony ended because we had been taking more pictures. Valeria's face was thunder. The Marquesa was concerned that my face was also thunder. I was upset about the cat we 'rescued.' She knew we shouldn't have left it with Valeria, who doesn't like animals. She said she was furious with Valeria for not looking after it, but she was really furious with herself for forgetting it. She said she had not slept for worry of it and I believe her. I told her that she reminded me of men I'd known. Lovers who promised me things, wonderful things, and then I never heard from them again. It's a very masculine thing.

'Oh, my God, I'm not like that at all,' she said. She was supposed to be at the christening brunch but it seemed that they were already so cross with her that she stayed to talk some more. In the grounds of this tiny, stern, stone church, she started talking about Eduardo, who is very Catholic. She told me he never spends a penny on advertising, only on stories. She talked, suddenly eager for the future, for *Hello!*'s launch in America, another apartment in New York or Miami. And then there's *Hello!* the television show – beautiful homes, beautiful stories.

It seemed rather odd that on a day that was supposed to be spent in the embrace of her family, she should start talking about Hector Barrante's cancer, and how she had cried during his final moments and taped it all for an exclusive. She talked about that quality of empathy she has, to feel others' suffering, others' sadness, anything instead of feeling Valeria's crossness.

When we were back in London, she was still worried about the cat. She said how she'd had a big fight about it with Valeria and that Natalia had turned up at the hotel we had been staying in, carrying a black kitten and saying, 'Look, mummy. I've found him.' But it wasn't the same one; she had just brought another kitten. They took this new kitten to the bullfighter's house to join the ironed-thin cats draped around his pool. She said this one was in even more need of being rescued.

She sent me clippings about people who save cats. She says it still keeps her awake at night. So why did we make the big gesture and fail? What is it with this rescuing? 'I am frightened of death because I am frightened of being a nothing. That's why I always think and dream to be a swan, a dog or elephant, but something. I read this book about a letter from a baby who is about to be aborted. The pregnant woman says to the baby: you will find traitors, unhappiness, illness, wars, lost loves. IS that fair? Is it better to have nothing? To me, nothing is the most terrifying thing. That's why I don't like anaesthetics. I would rather suffer physically. At least you know you're alive.'

Then she muses about being a swan, how they are so beautiful when they die, how they are monogamous, how she saw in the paper a swan that had lost its mate and was going to die, but then it found another one who had lost its mate and they were pictured nestling into each other's necks, together forever.

Perhaps she represents the paradox of the malcontent who has everything she says she doesn't want.

'Supposing I had got the right farmer, supposing you had got what you dream – that is the worst thing that can happen to you. It would be awful. You would have nothing to dream of, no expectations and I would be nothing. In order to live, you have to struggle.'

GOD'S CHOSEN

Dustin Hoffman
Sunday Times Magazine
27 October 1996

*Dustin Hoffman is God's most perfect interview. He answers
every question with a personally honed nuance. Every revelation is fresh and deep. He'll show you his wounds, then you
bathe them. Perfect.*

I hadn't seen him come into the room. I turned round and he
was there. He must have been there already for a few seconds.
It's not so much that Dustin Hoffman fills the room, but he
fills you. Intense ears and eyes locking the world in. Pained
mouth. Sensuous combination. But it's not that. We're
nervous of each other, assessing each other. His voice a
chewy, gravelly lull. It lolls in a rhythm, it moves you, it
moves into you.

Somebody told me that it takes four seconds to fall in love,
to subconsciously read the life maps presented behind the
eyes. Well, it wasn't quite falling in love, but it was a very
intense reading of each other that in ten years of doing interviews has only happened once before, and that's another story.

The interview situation, particularly the interview junket
situation, is a very false one. Fawning, flattery, cajoling,
pretending to be interested journalist, and actor gets to talk
about self and sell movie. This is a junket for the movie
American Buffalo, the film of the David Mamet play where
Hoffman plays a hopelessly conniving, lost loser. It's not a
big-budget movie. It's a movie of minutiae and nuance. It
seems incongruous that this junket day, a day of soundbites
and superficiality, has been organized to promote it.

He gives me some of his beer and tells me he knows how I
am feeling terrible about this junket situation where journalists and TV crews from all over the world are wheeled in
and out of this Beverly Hills hotel. Some of them at intervals

of fifteen minutes running over a forty-eight hour period.

He is supplicant. He decides he would like to do a movie called *Junket*. It would be about a celebrity and the various agendas of different hacks. What does he want to give, what do they want to get, how is he under the microscope, the intellectual seduction, maybe an actual seduction, and this one, nasty, short-haired, hard-bitten woman perhaps, who really is out to destroy. Wouldn't it be interesting to see how she did it and how he avoided her? Wouldn't it be intense? Well, we could practically write the script just from the day.

He invites me minutes into knowing me to break through the junket-barrier. He wants me to be with him all day. And the role he wants to do today is 'experienced icon has fun'. He is a conspirator, but you don't know exactly who he is conspiring with, you or himself.

Everyone's read how fanatically private he is, how he likes to reveal nothing. He manages to do this by being utterly vulnerable. You read about him being this incredible perfectionist, doing Method world-class. You know, actually not sleeping for a weekend for *Marathon Man*, studying autism so hard for *Rain Man*, uncovering uncoverable research. You read about heightened discourse on set, tantrums, forever-fall-outs because of his all-consuming need for detail.

He was born fifty-nine years ago in the same year as Warren Beatty and Jack Nicholson. He once said, in relation to their respective labels, 'I'm the perfectionist and Warren is the womanizer, and so on, but all of us know how simplistic those tags are. I mean, if anybody thinks that Jack Nicholson and me got laid less than Warren Beatty when we were single, they're wrong, but that's the way we all got tagged.'

I also read that he has an ex-wife, Anne Byrne, with whom he had Jenna and Karina; and a current wife Lisa, who has borne him Jake, Rebecca, Max and Ali. He says that he wishes that I hadn't read anything about him, that I hadn't prepped for the interview. He says that he's not a perfectionist. 'That's a media distortion. Everybody is incredibly hard-working. To say that no one else is a perfectionist demeans them.

Anyway, being a perfectionist is a contradiction in terms if you make movies. You shoot a number of pages every day. You're spending $150,000 a day on a mainstream studio picture, so you can't get behind, they don't allow that. The suits arrive on the set. This is not a place for a perfectionist. In a low-budget movie like *American Buffalo* it's probably worse, but it affords you liberation because you know you're not going to be successful. It removes the pressure of having to be in the first three or four of the box-office when it opens; you know you're not going to be.'

He says he's not commercially motivated. But constantly there's this duality, a man that's totally comfortable with himself and a man who is mocking himself. So comfortable he's mocking? Or so mocking he's comfortable? He says you can't be famous and not sell out, that fame is too seductive, that there is no doubt he would have done better work if he had not been famous, it's just no one would have seen it.

He's done some pretty good work that's been famous. The autistic Rainman, the vulnerable seducer of Mrs Robinson, and the sad Ratso Rizzo in *Midnight Cowboy*. The insecure, the failed outlaw, the neurotic, the credible cheat. They're all puns, all shadows, they have a slinky seduction, but not enough to comfort him. He's quizzical, watchful, clever. Says that he made the Mamet because it was like doing the film of *Death of a Salesman*, it was giving the play a life, putting it on the shelf. Arthur Miller said that he wrote it for the guys in the bar in Brooklyn who were never going to pay $50 a ticket, and it was the same with this. Is Mamet going to like it? 'I think he did.'

American Buffalo is about honour or non-honour among almost-thieves. It's low-life, it's men not trusting men, it's men after the main chance, it's chasing the deal. The deal's not interesting, it's the way they chase and deceive each other. It's set in a junkie place called Federal Hill in Providence, Rhode Island. It's a film that haunts. You think about it afterwards because of that rhythm that David Mamet writes in. The rhythm stays with you.

'Yes, that's him. He's a jazz musician in his soul. I've been told that when Mamet was rewriting stuff and the actors were on stage he'd be walking back and forth with the rhythm. Do-do-do, do-do-do, do-do-do-do-do. He'd get that right, then he'd fill in the words. Shakespeare writes in a kind of jazz, the iambic pentameter is a kind of Elizabethan rap. Did I ever want to play jazz? I grew up wanting to be a piano player but it never happened.

'I wasn't gifted in two areas, I didn't have an ability to play by ear, I read music very slowly, and it didn't come easy to me. I didn't have that kind of brain. You know, where you hear it and you play it. But Mamet can do it with language and I can do it with people.'

How do you mean? 'You feel a rhythm, actors feel a rhythm, an essence of a person, and you can get that. You can replicate it. Like you, I have a sense of you, even though I don't know you.'

And what is this sense, I'm wondering? Just how intent have those ears been? 'You appear, like most interesting people, to be one thing on the surface, and underneath there's something that totally contradicts it. On the surface you are very yin, very serene, very cool, and it's a total contradiction. Inside there's not only turmoil, but heat.'

It could have been flattery, it could have been a wild gener- alization, but I had felt him the whole time trying to get the rhythm of me, just as I had been trying to get the rhythm of him.

He tells me now that he usually gets killed in interviews. 'You know, there needs to be something provocative to say about you.' He tells me about a female journalist and how she set him up.

'For three hours she was asking me the same question and I guess I was closing my eyes, and she said, "Is something wrong with your eyes?" I must tell you that sometimes when you are asked the same question fifty times in a row and try to find a fresh way to answer it it makes you close your eyes. She pointed to me and said, "Look at the way he smiles, his eyes are one way and his smile is another. His eyes are nice and his smile is mean." '

How very existential to have an interview about another interviewer, which is essentially saying, I know you're not like that. The risk is the trust and suddenly it's me who is vulnerable and saying the reason I seemed double-edged was that I didn't want to ask him boring old questions about the movie, but I didn't want to look not interested in him, so I was quiet in my confusion.

He says, 'See, I wouldn't have guessed this in a million years. I thought she hates this set-up, she doesn't look happy about being rushed in.'

No, I tell him, sometimes you can get to know people too well if you spend too long with them, like them too much. I prefer the restriction. 'Ha, are we talking S&M, handcuffs?'

Well, I like handcuffs too, I just bought some the other day, actually, but only so I could get a carrier bag from the shop that said Religious Sex.

Dustin Hoffman perks up. Small, beady eyes become large, beady eyes. His voice is saying that his son gave him hand-cuffs, Dick Tracy handcuffs as a Chanukah present and put them in the drawer in the bedroom, and every time the house-keeper comes up she sees the handcuffs. He can't throw them away because they were a present. But handcuffs aren't really his thing. Religious sex on the other hand . . .

'What a powerful thing those religious people did realizing that there is something very powerful with sex. Give you something wonderful and make you feel guilty about it.' How very Jewish of him to be guilty about sex. 'Not in the least. George Burns said, when they asked him what his worst sexual experience was like, he said it was pretty good.' What was your worst sexual experience like? 'Very good. No, but that's not true. Of course it's not true.'

And we're coming to the nub of him. It seems to me that he is defined by two things, things he knows very well. Doesn't necessarily like them but he knows them and he's lived with them a long time. His comfortableness with his

Jewishness, and his discomfort with sexuality.

He says he's had bad sex and he defines it as when two people realize they don't even like each other. I tell him that it's possible to have great sex with people you don't even care about. He looks horrified. 'Do you think men and women are different,' he says. Yes, how do you think they're different?

For a long time he doesn't say anything. He sits very still, prim in his fresh blue jeans and blue and white striped shirt. As if there's a real hot agenda going on underneath.

He answers. 'There are three (sic) types of men. There is the Milan Kundera category, they really love women in a sensual way, they bow at the shrine. And other men who feel indifferent. And then other men who really don't like women. There are some men who not only like women and need them, but prefer them as company.'

We agree that Milan Kundera man is the biggest bastard because he loves all women, there's no selection process. 'And it stops intimacy.' Intimacy, we decide, is what men and women are really different about.

'Women I think find the orgasm a bridge to the next moment, and men find it the end. And that is the tragedy. It takes men, some men, a lot of years to wake up one morning and not be chained to that maniac.'

Which particular maniac is that? 'His cock, which is something where there is a constant battle. To use your word 'selective', I have often thought I would have been more selective with the women I've been sexually intimate with if I'd had a vagina instead of a cock because letting someone inside you is different to putting it somewhere. It makes you detached, compartmentalized. And when it's over the woman, by instinct does . . .' We stand up, the both of us, cocking our heads to one side, doing *faux femme*, needy and bondy after orgasm, with arms outstretched. And he continues, like we're *Playschool* presenters, 'And the man does . . .' And we both stretch our arms out and push away. What a moment. I faked an orgasm with Dustin Hoffman.

'For a man, it's a great feeling when you reach a point

where that feeling doesn't exist anymore.' What, when you can have sex for hours without having an orgasm? 'I wish it were so. No. We have something in our country called blue balls, which is very painful. I used to get them in high school. If you don't have an orgasm you build up incredible pressure in the groin, your scrotum was in great pain. You never heard that expression? I mean you can't walk and it's too painful to masturbate. A lot of times, it happened in the car when the girl wouldn't let you go all the way, one of the tricks was to go round the car and lift the car by the fender. The myth was the lifting would make the blood leave your scrotum. I tried it and it didn't work.'

Do you think that Teach (the character he plays in *Buffalo*) ever had sex, I muse. 'You get the feeling that no one has sex in that play. Teach's room is so grotty and horrible no woman would go there unless they were paid. I've never paid in my life. It's hard for me to envision any man being able to get an erection with a prostitute. But with Teach I have a feeling there's no sexual drive at all, although I guess he masturbates.'

The whole play is full of that inverted masculine energy. The language is full of expletives. 'There's an inability to communicate and be articulate. Teach has lost his soul and he didn't know how lonely he was.' It's the way he chews on the words 'know' and 'lonely' that reveals he knows lonely.

He knows things with almost an extra sensory perception. He might say it's his job, but I've never met another actor that could see into souls and reassemble them. Before he was an actor, before his big break in *The Graduate* aged 30 – after which he was never again to play sexy leading man – he was a psychiatric assistant, a seller of toys, and an assembler of Hawaiian leis. I agreed that I wouldn't take much notice of the stories that I've read. And if I reported anything that happened that didn't happen between us at that moment I would say someone else had said it.

So, someone else said, if Dustin Hoffman is not the greatest actor in the business it's a photo finish. Someone else said that he once threw a director into a lake. Someone else said that when they went to interview him and they said they'd liked his movie, which happened to be *Outbreak*, he had an assistant bring in a piece of paper which said 3:28 minutes, which was the length of the helicopter scene which the writer had already written that he hated.

It was said that the thought occurred to him that wouldn't it be nice if children could be at their own parents' wedding. So that's what he arranged and in a Polynesian ceremony he and his wife retook their marriage vows with their children in attendance.

It has also been written that his mother gave him the inspiration for the woman Dorothy that he played in *Tootsie*. Actually, I think it was closer to him than that. 'It was the first time I really authored something. I was at a fiftieth birthday party and this guy said, "There's a Shirley inside of you." And somehow the question came up that I'd never pondered, what if I'd been born a woman, would I be essentially the same person as I am as a man, how would I be different.

'And the first thing I thought was, it depends what I look like. So much of what I am as a man comes from what I look like, acned and short, and thought to be unattractive by the hierarchy and the girls.

'In those junior-high-school years I was watching it all happen, the walking surfboards and the football players, and I wasn't in any of the clubs. We started working on *Tootsie* and I said, "Let me start working on make-up tests before we even have a script because I don't want to do this if I'm going to look like I'm in drag. Let's see if Hollywood and all its magic can transform me."

'We did everything. Prosthetics, rubber lips, Anne-Margaret wigs. I learnt that you're flat right there,' he presses his hand on my forehead, 'and men have a bump. We tried to feminize me as much as possible. My fantasy was they would be able to do anything. They said to me, "What do you want to look like?" and I said, "I want to be beautiful," because that's what I would like to be as a man so why wouldn't I want to be beautiful as a woman. I kept saying, "No, this is not enough, make me more attractive." And finally one day the projectionist was rolling the test and it was silent and I heard him saying, who's that actress? And I thought, "I'm home." And I looked at myself and said, "Well you're not very good-looking," and I couldn't stop thinking about it. I had these discussions with my friend and he asked, "Why does it bother you so much?" And I said, "I think I'm interesting as a man, and interesting as a woman, but I know if I went to a party and saw her I wouldn't go over and talk to her because she wouldn't meet the criteria, the physical prerequisites", and I started to cry. And it was a kind of important moment in my life where I felt closer to that character than anything I'll ever do. It's the kind of information you get in ten years, not one day, and it all rushed on to me.

'How many interesting women I'd never gotten to know because I'd never allowed myself to get past whatever it is, that trophy, what a loss. I would never have asked myself out and all we want to do is meet someone who knows us and we know them. In other words where two makes one. I'd passed up people who might have given me that feeling, and also I knew, that however painful life was for me as a man, it didn't hold a candle to how painful it would have been if I had been born a woman and looked like that.'

It's an intense moment again and we're nearly crying. He doesn't think that women are less trophyistic, not in junior high school anyway. But in a way men don't get past adolescence, while women do.

He's just had his fifty-ninth birthday and his card from the same male friend said that he'd wanted him to know that 59 had been his best year sexually. All his life he's waited to feel sexy, he doesn't really think that at 59 he'll do it, but he tortures himself with the hope.

'No, I never felt I was sexy. Not in the thirty years I've been doing this did *People* magazine put me on the cover of their fifty most sexy people. Sean Connery is always on that list.

'It stunned me when I started acting that these attractive women in class wouldn't look at me twice, but after they'd seen me do a scene they'd come up to me. Girls who were models taking an acting class wanted dates with the good actors.'

A woman is attracted to a man because of how good they are at something, therefore they become sexy. Also, in England the perception of Dustin Hoffman is sexier than in America. In England he's fanciable because he's funny and he's clever and he's fast. In America there's no concept of fancying, there's only sexy or not sexy.

'But these models, when you look back on your life, these are not the most exciting women. In the old days when they used to say, which actress do you want to work with, I could never think of one.'

Which is more important for you, to be loved, respected or understood? 'Well, unconditional love you get from animals, never from human beings, it's always conditional, even from your parents. It's very conditional, it's all to do with that first dump you don't do correctly. So I suppose understood. Generally I'd rather be understood, particularly by a journalist.'

We go back to yesterday and the one with short hair from the *New York Times* who accused him of calling people honey. Yes, he did call someone honey, he was looking at her toe-nails. He says that my toe nails are a metaphor of me. Iridescent paint, doesn't look what it seems, to see it you've got to look closely or you're not interested.

Don't I get to see your toe-nails, and he says, 'If they're painted red will you not print it?' He stands up and takes his socks off and the PR comes in looking askance. Junket-land is awaiting and I have his toes in my hands. Very clean, very white toe-nails, with the second toe bigger than the big toe which allegedly means he's a genius.

The PR tries to hustle me out, but Hoffman says, 'No, she's staying.' He says, 'I want you to watch how these people work.' What's more interesting is how he works them. There must have been fifteen interviewers from all around the world, asking the same questions, and he never gave the same answer twice. He delivered.

He wound them all up. They had fifteen minutes each, he didn't necessarily answer their questions, but his answers were perfect soundbites. Sometimes he pretended I was his girlfriend, sometimes his assistant.

The man from British Cable TV comes in. The film rolls. Instead of answering the questions about the movie, Hoffman's banging on, 'Tell me about the girls from Newcastle.'

'They're hard and tarty . . .' And he lets the guy ramble.

'She's from Newcastle.' The guy is embarrassed, bemused. Another time he's searching for a word. 'Hypocryphal story?' he asks me. 'Is that the word?'

'No, you mean apocryphal,' I say.

'Apocryphal,' he says to camera.

'Beautiful word,' the TV man says fawningly.

'Beautiful girl,' Hoffman says slyly, further embarrassing him.

For the main part of these interviews he tells jokes, and he is a great teller of jokes because of his sense of rhythm. And, despite the tears over *Tootsie*, he is categorically nicer to women. He flirts with all of the women, but flirts particularly with the attractive women. He might be being ironic. A creamy Latino woman he can hardly speak to because she's so gorgeous. He asks her why couldn't she be an actress, why does she have to be a journalist, didn't I think she was sexy?

Part of the reason he's still uncomfortable with women is that he doesn't give them a chance to respond. This girl, totally overawed, is embarrassed by his attentions. By the end of her fifteen minutes she is saying yes to everything. But he's already dismissed her as too beautiful for him.

'We're all acting all the time,' he's saying to Spain in answer to a question that the guy didn't ask. 'We get up, we make certain choices. You look in your mirror and open your closet, you put on a costume and that costume alters you. If it's a business thing it's a suit, it's all fake, it's meant to be fake. I know a woman who has breast surgery twice a year. Larger

46

breasts for summer for bathing suits, smaller for winter so the clothing hangs better.'

Why did he do *American Buffalo*? He needed the workout. Is Teach going to go to Heaven or hell? He doesn't know because he wasn't taught about Heaven and hell when he grew up. Teach is lonely and alone. Did he think he was evil? Did I think that evil existed, he asks me. The TV man from Spain looks at me like evil exists, what am I doing in his interview?

Everybody likes the movie, or at least they say they do. His eyes glint at me every time a journalist comes out with a particular fawn, and they're fawning all over the shop, and it forces him to be even more self-deprecating. 'I still don't expect this movie to be successful. We tried to stop the audience from fidgeting, but we are doing a film that is language-driven, character-driven, it is not a roller-coaster ride like big movies. The blockbuster movies that exist today are blow jobs basically,' he's saying to the Japanese interviewer.

'I know that Japan knows something about blow jobs because they're taken very seriously as an art form, but when you go to these movies, you know, you're expecting you're going to get head. This is the other end of the movie spectrum. This movie is a first date where you're not going to have sex, this movie you're going to spend an evening getting to know someone and there might not even be a kiss goodnight. A blow job doesn't stay with you for a long time but that will stay with you, it's that addiction that you need to repeat. The big studios are increasingly going for this thing where you pay your money, get your popcorn, sit down and unzip your pants.'

The TV man says, have you any idea where this film is playing? And Hoffman says to the TV man how handsome he is, how he bets he never had a problem in high school, he got all the girls. Then he segues into Freud who said unfortunately what we think of ourselves is based on how others perceive us. In other words if people think we're nice we're nice. So we go through life not based on self-worth but on what others perceive us to be.

47

He is both terrified and beyond caring what others perceive him to be. Recently they showed a rerun of a Parkinson interview on TV. It was done in 1975 and he said how carbon copies of *The Graduate* kept coming his way but he didn't want that, he didn't connect to that. Instead his next big part was Ratso Rizzo in *Midnight Cowboy*, a character that people keep comparing to Teach.

But this one wasn't a cold soul, he was a lost soul. He told Parkinson that that character was part of him, that scabrous, greasy nobody, that was his connection.

'It was a feeling that I've had about myself for years, that I look like that in an inner way, through school. Unattractive and anonymous and a great anger to be neither. But we are all Ratso, we are all JFK. When we look at the Bowery bums and imagine them as infants, they were all beautiful then. And you have to think what makes a person sit here and what makes that person be on the street. I could have been Ratso and I am Ratso, we all are.'

Asked then what his ambition was, he said that he'd like to do a love story about elderly people. Even then it seemed he had the hope that appearance meant nothing. Decrepitness on the outside should be disregarded. He said that we are all five years old but it's just that we see ageing in the mirror and have to act old. He said then that he wanted to do, 'a really sexy movie about two elderly people who make love like no one else.' And I'm sure he still wants to make that movie.

Some people might think it's easier to feel sexy when you spend a lifetime coming to terms with the fact that attraction and compulsion is beyond physicality, and some people might think you can simply look around at other 59-year-olds – paunchy, balding, whatever, and feel comparatively pleasing. But I don't think that's why he would want to make that movie. I think it's because he still needs validation, he still needs someone to tell him, 'Dustin Hoffman, you're pretty damn sexy.'

Barbra Streisand
Sunday Times Magazine
2 February 1997

She's a small frail thing wrapped in black cashmere, security-tag designer-label Donna Karan, curling into herself on the stiff Dorchester sofa. At odds with herself, always. Complexion, translucent; reputation, control-freak-fever diva; demeanour *t'mished*. Candid as an open wound and then paranoid, covert, fiercely guarding her privacy.

Terrified of not getting what she wants and all the time wanting more. Complicated, introverted, and yet she reaches and she touches. The voice, the visceral connection, pure yet searing, with the intelligence that could cut through everything, including herself.

Her famous fingernails, which used to provoke her mother to tell her, 'Cut 'em off, become a typist,' are neat, short, French-manicured jobs. When a man I know saw them on Oprah he said, 'Ha, she's happy in love at last. No one could have had sweet sex with those fingernails.'

Women I know love her. In some curious way they have been her or she's been them. The put-upon victim and the relentless survivor, a woman turned inside-out by rejection, disappointment, not being wanted enough. When she sings it, and sometimes even when she acts it, it touches you.

But women I know also hate her. She's everything they don't want to be, or they think she is. She's always had a huge range of who she is. The Cleopatra-eyed siren, the passionate liberal, the emotional neurotic, demanding that men protect her and letting them destroy her, naïve and knowing. She claims not to know why people react to her so vehemently.

The new movie, *The Mirror Has Two Faces*, interweaves old but not tired premises: that you can't be loved unless you're beautiful and beautiful means conventionally pretty and thin, that men can't cope with having sex and true love all in the same package,that men and women can never really be friends, that true beauty might be beyond the physical but how can you reach it, and that the cruel mother defines what we think of ourselves.

She produced, directed and starred in this latest emotional roller-coaster. When I went to see this movie at a Los Angeles matinée screening, the audience loved it. The critics, particularly in Britain, have hated it, finding it egocentric and indulgent. ('*The Mirror Has Two Faces* and all of them Barbra.') There is no doubt Barbra-bashing is easy, she's an easy target with a difficult reputation.

Much is made of her tantrum-throwing. She wants to control her picture and how the picture turns out. But why wouldn't anybody want that? I think people hate her because she makes demands that they are afraid to make. And her press constantly surprises her. It's not that she believes that women journalists have given her a tougher time than men, but she often feels bemused by having a female bonding session with an interviewer and then finding herself spliced in the piece. This she says has happened time and time again.

She quotes a particularly vitriolic review of *Yentl*, a movie she made fourteen years ago, that concentrated on criticizing her for providing designer yarmulkas when the yarmulkas were real – everything had been researched minutely. And how a reviewer from the *New York Times* had wanted to write an amazing piece about *Yentl* but the editor chucked it out because it was 'too nice.'

'Why don't they like me?' she says. It is not a rhetorical question. It is one she has asked in song, ('Will He Like Me?'). And which has been wrapped one way or another into every theme of every movie she's ever been in, including the award-winning *Prince of Tides*, the big-box-office *Yentl* and those weepy nuggets *Funny Girl* and *The Way We Were*.

Can she be who she is, not conventionally beautiful, demanding, questioning, passionate, and also transcendent, so that the lesser-evolved and extremely handsome man will be smitten forever? Or just will they like her, will they think she's clever, will they understand her? Of course not, that's why she has to keep trying, pushing. As I said, this is by no means a rhetorical question. It's a theme that we are going to be coming back to throughout our meeting. Do I have an answer? Well, I'd better find one because she wants to know.

For a while I feel like her therapist. It's easy to slip into therapy speak in interviews. Particularly easy with her because you want to protect her, or destroy. I suppose she is the place where extremes meet.

'People either love me or they hate me. Is it a kind of love that is hate? People have made up stories about me from day one. Really terrible negative stories that were not true. In my earliest days coming back from *Yentl* I was so proud of being only 11 per cent over budget and I came back to America to read I was 100 per cent over budget. A lie. To diminish me, to diminish my accomplishment?

'My first time ever I was in a movie, *Funny Girl*, there was a terrible story about me fighting with the cinematographer. An absolute lie. We adored each other. We went on to do four movies together until he died. We had a great communication. They talked about fighting. It was like how dare this girl have an opinion about lighting. That's why I had to direct, because as a director you're allowed to have opinions.'

Well, sometimes you are. She says she hasn't read the reviews for *Mirror* because she doesn't want to be in pain. But she is anyway because even if what they say isn't true she thinks they hurt business. So of course she's paincentric. In this movie and indeed the others in which she has directed and starred, she has been accused of self-indulgence. She thinks this is a sexist thing. That's the easiest way of dealing with it.

'A woman is called demanding, a man is called commanding.' She points out that Mel Gibson was never criticized for how many close-ups he gave himself in *Braveheart*. 'Women are control freaks, men are perfectionists.'

Then she wonders, still on the theme of why don't people like me, whether it's simply the power of women that is

51

abhorrent. 'In the Jewish Bible,' a book she reads a lot, 'it talks about women being closer to God because of the creative process, able to bring life into the world. I think ever since cavemen it's been that way. Cavemen watched a woman stretch her legs out and out came human life. Men come from women, they gave life to them, they could take life away. It's a primal biological fear, the man separating from the mother. He has enormous dependence on her for nurturing and then he has to leave her, so he gets angry.'

Angry at being dependent? 'Yes. In love relationships you get angry at the person you love the most because you need them so much.' And she says it like she knows, like she invented bad behaviour for lovers.

She's off on the woman thing. 'The mother is a representation of the woman they first love, and you don't have sex with your mother.' A reference, perhaps, to *Mirror*, in which a befuddled mathematics professor is so distracted by sexual relationships that he wants to have a platonic friendship with a plain woman (Streisand) so that he won't be driven crazy, can get on with writing his books and can have a peaceful life, because men have a problem being intellectually and sexually stimulated at the same time.

But it's like she's done with talking about the movie. The movie was already a conversation she had with herself, as all her movies have been similar conversations that have begged, some day will my prince come? In the movies she's always been too much for the men. They've left her on a learning curve, but disappointed. In life, too, all the love-affairs had endings where the man was not a prince.

She married young to Elliot Gould in 1963 when he was a bigger star than she was. They had a son, Jason, now 30. Gould was a perplexed introvert from a similar Jewish background who probably came along far too early in her life. She could have handsome, she could have sexy. Warren Beatty, Ryan O'Neal. Don Johnson. She wanted glittering, gorgeous prizes to reflect her perhaps, to be one of those mirror's faces. Her long-time lover was John Peters, a millionaire hairdresser who came from a slummy background, was a streetfighter and ended up one of Hollywood's most successful producers. They are friends still.

From 1994, after André Agassi, she was alone for a long time. 'To have someone that you are intellectually stimulated by and also one to fuck is hard to get. But nothing below that is worth much. But it is hard to get, that's why I feel very grateful to have that in my life now.'

She says that when she made movies with sad endings life imitated art. She gave this movie a happy ending. It seems that in real life James Brolin, the actor-director, is the prince who came. Handsome of flesh and soul. She calls him the masculine to her feminine and the feminine to her masculine. 'He's unafraid of his feminine side. Totally accessible emotionally and also like a father, proud, supportive.'

Why does she think she's fallen in love? 'There is a cabbalistic concept of soul connection. The idea that only when you've learnt certain lessons in life do you meet your soul mate.'

She's big on Cabbala, the mystical branch of Judaism encompassing numerology, astrology, the symbolism of names and reincarnation. She recommends this book, *Wheel of the Soul* by Phillip S. Berg.

'The book is based on paying karmic debts and when you've learnt lessons you're open to your soul mate. You know who they are. It's mystical. You know how alcoholics are attracted to other alcoholics? Well, something is set off in you and transmitted that you'll be compatible on that level. Or incompatible.'

Don't you find that you have the same relationship over and over again but with the same person?

'Yes, you repeat it. You try to repair the damage. You pick the same person who will give you the same person so you can make it different. So you have to get to another level of consciousness where you can pick another person that won't give you the same pattern, that is the different person. But it's interesting because you can say "I thought you were totally different", but then there are patterns that are the same.

'If you love each other enough you can try to change the pattern.' What was the man in your pattern and how is James different? 'I would go back and forth. I would choose an abusive man.' Her stepfather was the one who said, 'Why couldn't she be quiet like her friends', and that she wasn't attractive enough to be an actress, and that forged the pattern of self-hatred. 'And what I really wanted was a man like my father, which is Jim, supportive and loving, kind. Within that nothing is perfect. There are moments that things go funny, but the nice thing about getting older is that you have moments of strength at this age.'

Her father Immanuel, a teacher, went to Columbia where the movie is set, was a sweet man, stoical. Died at 35 when she was 15 months old. Ever since he had a car crash on his honeymoon he got killer headaches. One of these was blighting him and the hospital gave him too high a dose of morphine. It killed him and deprived Barbra of the love and support she craved.

Her mother, sad and embittered, took it out on her. Diana Streisand, also a singer, whose name was formerly Ida Rosen, told her that her voice was weak and that she needed to put eggs in her milk to make her voice stronger. She said she didn't want her to get a swelled head. She once asked her mother, 'Was I pretty as a baby?' The mother said, 'All babies are pretty.' And she said, 'No, I mean, was I pretty?'

'What's pretty anyway, look what good it did your sister.'

In the film the dialogue is transported from life to art. 'If you don't feel loved as a child you spend the rest of your life trying to get love. This movie is about the mother's influence, about what a person thinks of herself, the roles that are assigned to children by their parents' vision of them.'

Visions are so often distorted. Does she think she's pretty now? 'Like all women, sometimes I think I look good, sometimes not.' She professes that the theme of the movie is that beauty is not in the eye of the beholder, but in the head of the beholder. A theme that perhaps turns in on itself. Yes, we see

Barbra Streisand as the plain professor, lumpy, badly-coordinated clothes, low self-esteem displaying itself as a baggy face and disgusting jumper.But can we really believe that Barbra Streisand is ugly? She can certainly believe it of herself.

It is her distorted vision of herself, though, that made this movie, that made her. Bette Midler recently quipped, 'So her mother wasn't nice to her. Couldn't she get over it?' The fact is, if she had got over it she wouldn't have become a legend. 'Because if my mother had said, "Oh my God, you're fabulous" I might have just given up. I might have said I'm going to get married, have some kids and lead a happy life. I'm grateful. I'm not complaining about anything in my past because I think it's a gift. The wound is a gift.'

Maybe that's why you attract so many wounds, because you think they're gifts. 'Yes, that's true.' She's always going on about the vulnerable side of herself in a cherishing way. Everyone has commented to her that the most powerful scene was when she was the most vulnerable. The one where her hormones are giving her hell, she decides she loves him, she wants him and he tells her he doesn't find her attractive. It's a brutal moment. Has a man in real life ever said that?

'No, not in real life,' she says, almost sadly. She made it real enough in the movie though. Gaining weight, puffing out, and focusing on all her worst features. It must have been hard because in real life she doesn't let a picture go out unauthorized. Much is made of this, and all I have to say here is, I don't let unauthorized pictures of myself go out.

This is all to do with the fact that in real life her mother made her feel ugly. Has her mother seen the movie? 'Yes, but she didn't recognize any of it.'

Are there any women that you strongly admire and identify with? 'I admire Virginia Kelly Clinton. She was a loving person with a confident attitude, supremely giving and joyful.' (She sang at her funeral and now wants to do an album of inspirational songs). 'She told her son that he could do anything he wanted, he could become president of the United States, which he did.'

Do you tell your son that? 'I just try to make him feel smart and thoughtful, talented and gifted, special and handsome. He is. Did you know that his film just got accepted at Sundance. Thirty-two films out of 1,200, and he's one of them. He wrote it and directed it. It's called *Inside Out*. It's about his personal journey and about paparazzi making up stories about him and following him. It's painful out there.

'I guess if you don't give them other stories they have to make them up, is that why they do it?' she asks, flecked with paranoia. She's still curled up slightly, touching into herself. 'I wish people believed in the power of the truth,' she says, without a hint of irony. The paparazzi guy that followed Jason was interested in outing him. There's been constant debate about how she feels about having a gay son. She has said that if her son wanted to marry a chimpanzee she'd support him.

She is extremely committed to Aids causes but was forced recently to abandon the filming of the Larry Kramer play about Aids, *The Normal Heart*. She couldn't raise the money. She is a constant fundraiser though, money from her concerts going to various liberal-minded charities and her association with Clinton is a far-reaching and heartfelt one. She recently did a speech at Harvard staking the claim of artists who wanted to be associated with liberal causes.

Because she is a Jewish liberal and a vociferous one, she thinks this is another reason that people don't like her.

She is glad, though, that she has spent the past few years without the conflict of a relationship. 'You have to appreciate your aloneness before you can be with someone.' She thinks that that was what Brolin was doing too. He was also at some spiritual crisis. He divorced his second wife and the reason he gave to *Hello!* magazine at the time was because they 'weren't really the key to each other.' And he was going to dig deep to figure out what he wanted.

'I think we both found each other because we spent time alone and surrendered to the fact we were OK.'

Is part of her pattern surrendering to strong men to feel more womanly, and have the men she sought sometimes been authoritative to the point of abusive? 'I don't think abuse and cruelty is ever a strength, but I think I also want excitement and passion and kind, sweet men.' You don't often get excitement and sweet men. 'No, I like the complexity, I like the dance. I want excitement, I also want serenity, peace and comfort and security. If you find the right person you're dealing with the conglomeration of things. You basically have to want the same kind of goals in a relationship.' Is that true of her and Brolin? She does a slow, steady smile. The eyes glitter a bit. She wants to talk about him. If she can't talk *to* him she wants to talk *about* him. As if that in some way makes him there, with us.

'A friend of mine met him and said "I think you'll like him." I was editing my film. I used to work till midnight. She said, "I'll set up a dinner party and I'll leave you to sit next to him." I thought, oh God, I have to leave my work to go to a dinner party. We always used to eat at the editing table, we never broke for dinner. I told my editors I'd be back in a couple of hours.

'When I first saw him I thought, oh, what happened to his beard. I couldn't sit down so I went and played with the children for an hour, I was too shy because I knew we had both been set up. It was terrifying. Once I sat down I saw that he'd cut off all his hair and I thought he'd cut it too short on the sides and I remember saying, "Whoops, what happened to your hair, somebody cut it too short." I thought, oh I shouldn't have been so critical. I never talk about my son's hair, he hates it when I talk about his hair. And I told him all of my thoughts and he said he fell in love with me instantly because I was right, it was too short on the sides, and also I was not afraid to touch him.'

Are you often afraid to touch people? 'Yes, but with him it seemed normal and natural. We just talked about architecture and lumber and building and gardens and psychotherapy and seminars and learning and books. He's a worldly guy, he's been around. He's interested in the things that I'm interested in. We talked for hours and he asked if he could take me home. I had to call my editors and say, "OK, go home, I won't be working." And we haven't stopped talking since. He more or less moved straight in.

'We saw each other for two weeks then he had to go to Manila to make a movie where we had amazing conversations on the phone. One day we talked literally three and a half hours in the morning, half an hour in the middle of the day and three and a half in the evening. When he was in Ireland and I was in L.A. I would literally fall asleep on the floor talking to him as if we were together. Can you imagine talking to someone seven and a half hours out of fifteen hours, it's spectacular.'

She says this in a stretchy, surrendery, fluttery sort of way. But not so much quirky, vulnerable, gauche, although that's all in there. There is a kind of serenity, a kind of poise, but not too much, that might diminish who she is.

In the movie when she is transformed she gets pencilled into a sexy little dress and has a kind of hard glamour. In reality it's all the reverse. She's very soft and exudes, she doesn't contain. And she has that glow that they say women in love have.

Are you going to marry him? 'I'm not sure, maybe. I just don't want marriage to hurt our relationship. If it helps make it stronger and deeper then we will.' Do you think every time you fall in love you've never been quite in love this much before? 'I never felt quite like this before. I never thought it is as much to love as well as be loved. This is new for me. In Ireland I would get up at 5.00 or 6.00 every morning and make him breakfast. I couldn't sleep while he was dressing and having to go to work. I wanted to make him breakfast. You get love back by loving more. I want to protect and take care of him and help him through this movie-making process.

'He also said to me, "I want to empower you more." And that's a spectacular thing. A man who wasn't frightened of my power. He sees the child in me. He loves the child in me.

'He's never even seen *Funny Girl*. He did remember seeing me in *The Way We Were* and he also remembers he went to buy an apartment in Central Park West and I had just been there and didn't buy it because it needed air-conditioning. He said "I'll take it" and he sweltered that summer because it was devastatingly hot. So I had always been somewhere in his consciousness.

'We wish we'd met then. We almost met then at that apartment. But maybe we wouldn't have been ready for each other.' She feels they are now though, ready for each other. And I hope she's right.

'Of course I've had a soul connection without a sexual one and a connection that's purely physical. But when you have heart and soul and sexual connection, then I just think that's what life's all about. It's a taste of heaven on earth and I think this is the closest I've come.' A happy ending at last.

It's no fun being an icon. I mean, what if you aren't going to like her? What if you are? The reader becomes an eavesdropper on how much you want to be Barbra? I thought I should hide my love, but I so didn't. It was unlike any other interview because I wanted to be her friend, I wanted to confide in her. It's usually only the sad interviewer's role to be therapist. Here, I extended mine and found myself saying, 'What should I do about . . . ?' I listened to her, as I had been doing all those years, by the record-player, at the cinema, at the concert-hall. 'Was it all so simple then, or has time rewritten every line? And if we had to do it all again, would we, could we?'

Howard Stern
Sunday Times Magazine
11 May 1997

When you hear his voice coming out of the radio, it's a rat- a-tat missile voice of vengeance and combat. Sometimes it's low and drooling. The voice goes down, down, down into the microphone so you can hear breath over spittle. It is the voice that has shocked America for over a decade, a voice that has alienated and endeared all at the same time. Howard Stern is the original shock jock. He talks about douching and masturbation. He likes inviting on lesbians who will share with him the intricacies of their sex life. Sometimes he'll spank a stripper and then swoon to the sniff of her panties. He'll heighten his prejudices into unruly campaigns. He once ran for the governorship of New York because he wanted to introduce the death penalty. Later he changed his mind about this. He wants to scare you with his prejudice and then lure you into scaring yourself that you might think like him, then scare you because you don't. He is now tuned into regularly by 18 million listeners. His book, *Private Parts*, was the fastest-selling autobiography in the history of Simon and Schuster (over two million copies) and the signings ground Manhattan to a standstill for twenty blocks.

Some people find *Butt Bongo*, *Lesbian Dial-a-Date* and *Who's the Jew* offensive. He likes to demean the handicapped, the occasional ethnic minority. He likes big-breasted women to appear on his radio shows regularly. How do we know they're big-breasted? Because his radio show is televised on E! Television which reaches 40 million households, while his 1993 pay-per-view TV special was the highest grossing event of its kind since the invention of television – grossing upwards of $40 million.

He has contempt for journalists usually – not because he doesn't want to reveal. Rather, he takes such extreme and wincing pleasure in the revelation of personal circumstance. That his penis is the size of a raisin is now a given, just like Niagara Falls is wet and the Empire State is tall. The average radio listener tunes in for eighteen minutes. The average Stern-lover listens for one hour, fourteen minutes because they want to know what he's going to say next. The average Stern-*hater* listens for two hours eighteen minutes – because they want to know what he's going to say next.

I'm quite interested in what he's going to say next. He rarely grants interviews. When I saw him for the first time a person, not just a voice, it was in itself a shock. A cartoon of a man – long feet, long hair, lots of it and lots of nose. Eyes blacked out by little round sun-glasses. It's early in the morning but it feels late at night. The studio is aquarium-quiet with his side-kicks, Jackie the Joke Man and the sound man, Fred Norris, gurgling placidly in one corner. His voice mesmerizing and harsh down the line. In real life, it's clownish, giggling and playing to the gallery. Every time he says something cruel, he looks up with his naughty-boy eyes to check that I'm laughing. There's never quite a commercial break because mostly he does the commercials himself after realizing the value of protecting the advertisers. Some of them he's shocked so much, they would take away their business. But usually it works in reverse. The product wants Stern to endorse it. People want to be a piece of Howard. He is loathed and he is worshipped.

Friends fretted for me, told me not to do this radio show because he makes women take their tops off. It's easy to make him into a savage, but it seems like a lot of women want to be savaged. They want to take their tops off. The cameras are filming Sheryl Crow who is still wanting to know if it makes you happy, why the hell are you so sad? Stern thinks he's constantly sad, born to be miserable and his misery has made him happy, made him millions. Today though, there's no stream of filth, bile, hate, humiliation flowing from out of his mouth. He's too nervy about his upcoming première for the film *Private Parts*, which is based on his autobiography.

A woman rings up in tears saying that she's bought airplane tickets from California to come to New York because she heard that there were still some première tickets left, but actually they went days ago to the people who stood out all night for them.

'You bought tickets? You bought airline tickets before you had première tickets? What? Are you stupid? You're a nurse? What do you look after?'

The woman says, 'My boyfriend. He's my reason for living' but she's bawling her eyes out because Howard has given her a reason not to, and all the time he's checking me with his eyes. 'She's stupid, right?' they're saying. 'We'll humiliate her, yeah?' It's all so conspiratorial.

His sidekick, the dreadlocked and juicy news-reader Robin Quivers is nodding and shaking her head in empathy. She says he's one of the most sensitive, loyal and trustworthy people she's ever met. Of course, none of these things fit together. Angry, vile and reviled and the sensitive, loyal family man, the libertine who is monogamous and constantly grateful to his wife of nineteen years whom he met at Boston University. Some people think he must have sat down one day and made a list of all the taboos, all the don't-dare-say-this-on-air subjects and words, everything that humanity thinks is unspeakable and fears most, and constructed a radio show around it. This is the Stern that my friends were horrified that I could be in the same room as.

He is driven not so much to outrage, in fact, as to bond us all in his outrageousness, which is not outrageous at all. He claims that he simply says what most people think. He is motivated by the American challenge of freedom of speech. He is motivated by his prejudices, which might be cruel, but they are also other people's.

He grew up in Roosevelt, New York, a strange outsider; the only white boy in a black community. This feeling genuinely disarranged him in his own skin and made him want to commune all the more. He says that this film, which tested higher than *Forrest Gump* and *Indiana Jones* before its release, and did $40 million in its first weekend, is about following your dream. Hardly a rebellion. In fact I can't think of anything more apple-pie American than having a yellow brick road to follow. He says that when you grew up having your father tell you you were a moron every day, you had to constantly prove yourself. His father was a radio engineer. He thinks that he is one of the most articulate, intelligent men he has ever met. Stern is deeply hung up about that. The way in which he felt forced to prove himself was by being uncontrollable. He proved that WNBC could not tame him. (WNBC is the radio station which first brought him to New York and number-one New York ratings after having been number one in Washington.)

The traffic stopped again for twenty blocks at the Madison Square Garden première. Five thousand Sternettes had queued for tickets, sleeping three days in the street. No wonder he despised the woman who thought she could just hop on a plane from California. 'Without Howard Stern, white trash would have no role model'. Buildings flashed with this slogan. Howard Stern is a role model. He may look like some heavy-metal-brain-dead shock rocker, but students see themselves, blue collars want to be him. The man who works for computers at AT&T Connecticut and sat next to me at a talk show had stolen the day off work to be there and wanted to know me just because he had seen me walk in with him.

There is a chapter in his book called If You're Not Like Me, I Hate You. A lot of people think they're like him, or at least there's some secret gridlocked gremlin in their head that threatens to become him and maybe comes out when they're having a row or having sex or some such explosion. People who are not like him hate him. He likes enemies. Enemies keep him going. Hatred drives up his ratings. The new shock barrier that the movie breaks is that he'll tell you that *Private Parts* is not about genitals, it's about exposure – exposing those vulnerable squidgy bits. It's about his insecurities. It's a love story. It's about his wife, Alison, played in the movie by

Mary McCormack. When he talks about Alison, he always calls her 'my wife Alison', territorial – checking wife and Alison are one and the same, the same way as they have been for the past nineteen years. How can you be married to that man, that man who, when you had a miscarriage, said that they should send polaroids of the blood blob to their parents, telling them they're pictures of their first grandchild, that ranted that 'those of us in formaldehyde have rights too.' That same Howard whose naked body was oiled by *Knots Landing* actress Stacey Galina, and when Alison phoned him to complain he put the call on the air. Stern likes to obliterate. His audience like to watch him obliterating celebrities, taboos, his own soul.

The next day was the day that I went to see him do the Maury Povich show and he appeared to want to obliterate Maury Povich. It could have been a nice easy ride. 'Let's plug your latest movie, Howard'. But no. He was right in there. He accused Povich of having sexual problems because he has adopted children and is married to a well-known sex-symbol news anchor, Connie Chung. Povich, wearing a devil's costume, remained with a face of purple velvet while Stern was relentless.

He is extremely polite to me and extremely graceful even though everything in his head jangles and jars with itself. He is lean and rangy, long bony fingers, sliver rings and a pin-striped suit. Controlled and anarchic. He has this heavy metal mane of hair so that you might expect some relentless guitar-chord outburst. What you get is sophisticated, articulate and, at the same time, ridiculously eager to please. He's worried. 'Will they get my movie in England?' because he doesn't have a radio show there. He'd really like to be in England. There have been talks with Channel Five, but no more than talks, to run some back copies of the edited version of his show that appears on Entertainment Television, an American cable network.

'You know,' he says, 'There are guys in England doing sort of their version of Howard Stern. It makes me angry that I don't have a presence there. There are some markets where I'm just not heard.' He is incredulous, plaintive. 'So people have this perception that I'm just some guy who goes on the air and says penis a lot.'

Has he heard of the recently dysfunctional Chris Evans? No he hasn't, but he has heard that guys have had a nervous breakdown trying to be him, because, after all, it's hard to be him.

Despite his onslaught into movies, he still finds the radio the most piercing and effective media. His ego is bemused and entranced with the idea of being an actor, just like it might have been with being a governor. But he's not going to leave because, 'there's so much more I want to do and I want to get on in all those cities and prove that I'm the guy that started all this.'

The movie, which went through twenty-two rewrites and seven years in the making, was produced by Ivan Reitman (*Ghostbusters*, *Twins*) who took the project to Paramount and turned it into something else so that it was not just the studio chief that tried to thwart him and stop him using the seven dirty words but 'something that made you feel like you were eavesdropping in my life. Nothing over the top. I wanted to play each scene for real.' He says that with an endearing 'Like me' look, as if he no longer wants to be that dark pudding of prejudice and perversity; suddenly he wants to taste sweet.

But just which Howard Stern is real? He says that it's the radio character, the one who says anything, who doesn't care about anything, the one that keeps pushing because he wants to be funny, wants to be successful, the one who never assesses what he's talking about because he's already gone too far. 'I know that's the real me.'

And this other one, the polite one, the one sitting with his bony fingers clasped neatly on his knees? This one is the pretend. 'It's the guy who my father taught me to be, who bowed to authority, who played by the rules, and the guy in my head said something else. My father was very respectful of authority.'

Maybe the radio guy is the guy your father always wanted to be.

'Probably. I think he's the guy everyone wants to be, the guy on the radio, and I always had that guy trapped in my head. The guy on the radio is so much healthier than the guy I am in real life. In fact, I get upset when my real-life guy interferes with my radio guy.'

Does he ever try to impose reasonableness?

'Yes, and I have to fight that every day.'

That would be the day that he'd get a bad show and every day is only as good as his last show.

He gets up every morning at 4.30. His driver collects him and, on the hour-long journey from Long Island to KROCK in midtown, he does transcendental meditation for twenty minutes. He says it's a technique he's learned like brushing his teeth. It's spiritual and it's disciplined and he's felt a profound change in himself since doing it, has more energy. After the meditation he then reads the papers, absorbs the day's news. He's on the air at 6.00 and he is joined in the studio by Fred Norris, a dead-pan sound man who plays himself in the movie, as does Jackie the Joke Man and his long-time female radio consort, the juicy Robin, who reads the news, keeps him in line and occasionally crosses it. He introduced her today on the Maury Povich show as the most important woman in his life, and then he said that that was because Alison probably wasn't watching. There is enough realness in this statement for it to be just one of the things that make Alison irritated, angry. 'When I talk about my wife's miscarriage in the film, there's a second where I look down just before I do it.' He demonstrates the forlorn, guilty, 'oh she's going to hit me' look. 'There are a lot of times that I'm thinking I know that when I walk through the door at home I'm going to get yelled at. I always walk in "Hi!" Like I'm not going to get yelled at, but I know I am.'

Maybe you hope you're going to get yelled at.

'No. It's never pleasant.'

Maybe not. But it's what you're addicted to. His father,

every day of his life, used to tell him to shut up, moron. His father's favourite sport was yelling. He got his frustrations out. His mother would prepare him a Rob Roy cocktail every day for his return from work, and sometimes didn't get it as right as she had done the day before. She liked it when he yelled at Howard because it took the heat off her. Yes.

'I was the designated yellee,' he says. 'Now I'm afraid not to do what I do because I think my show would be boring and bland. I'd hate to give that up professionally.'

So you'd rather be yelled at?

'Yes. It's weird being me. But you can't go on the air and be totally honest and safe and say I masturbated last night, then go home and . . .'

Masturbation. Of all the things that he loves talking about, bring back the death penalty, then recounting it; his hatred of Roseanne, then recounting it, there is one thing on which he is a constant – masturbation. He says, 'I probably wouldn't masturbate so much if I didn't have to go to sleep every night at 8 o'clock.'

That's not why I think he does it. I think, despite all of this sex talk, he's really asexual. You know, like the amoeba. They're kind of sexually self-fulfilling, self-sufficient anyway. His preoccupation with lesbians allows him to receive sexual stimulation without any commitment to anything else except his own gratification. He never has to have any sexual guilt and it's the very essence of the contradiction that makes up Howard Stern. All this loose talk and hot lesbian action on the radio show, and a marriage nineteen years long where he has never been unfaithful. It is positively puritanical and he thinks that most people can relate to his masturbation fixation. They can feel sorry for him and self-aggrandised by the fact that he's always talking about his little penis. He says that he wouldn't dare be sexually unfaithful and I believe him. What I don't know is if he's being truthful about the rest of his bravado.

'My point is that I will go on the air and say that I masturbate. I go home and my wife will say to me, "Is that true what you say on the air?" and I'll go, "no" because I know it really upsets her. She'll go, "Are you lying?" And I'll go no. Then my wife will read the interview with you and you will bring this up and she will say, "Wait a minute, I've just read in his interview that you were lying to me" and I'll go, "No. I was lying to her." But the real truth is the guy on the radio. He's the truth,' he says with an earnest, almost pained smile and lollops back on the sofa.

Why do you masturbate when you can have sex with your wife?

'Because it's going to take too long and I have to get to sleep. You know, the foreplay. I have to do that. Plus, I've been married twenty years, you know? I like your jewellery. I like silver. I don't like gold.' Suddenly, truth man, who's afraid of nothing, is deflecting sex questions and I don't want to allow that.

He sighs and says, 'What I'd love to be able to do right now is to drill a hole in your head and hear everything and see everything that you're thinking. You might be thinking that I look hideous.'

Interesting, I think, that he turns it around to about what he looks like. But then all the bravest brains and sharpest intellects are sad in that way. Do you think you look hideous? 'Yes I do. I hate the way I look. Hideous. If I had any balls at all, I'd get a nose-job, fix my face. But I'm afraid because I talk so much for a living, I don't want to mess with that whole area.'

He says he is insecure all the time. 'If I wasn't, I wouldn't be human and I think that my humanity is what people respond to. You see some people who get so carried away with themselves, so impressed with their own success they stop functioning in a normal way. It's the insecure individuals who keep creating and trying to prove themselves. When I'm going to a book-signing, people flocking all over and I'm signing 25,000 books, you must think that I would feel great inside. I swear to you I don't. I don't know what that is. Some guys must feel fulfilled and then they stop doing anything, like Quentin Tarantino. He made a great film, *Pulp Fiction*, and now you don't hear of him anymore. I think in his mind it's like, "I've created a great film" and now he's going to parties for the rest of his life. Even though people are reacting to this film the way they are – phenomenally – I feel that I have so much more to prove. It's that insecurity, wanting to impress my father and my friends, that keeps me going.'

He loves his father enormously. 'When someone tells you that you are a moron every day of your life, you feel stupid. At the same point, I always felt that my father loved me and he did it out of love. I have him to thank for my whole life. My whole success was me trying to prove myself to my father. He did me a favour.'

He presents his childhood as something wacky but intense, something that he is almost disjointed from. He is all reverential, positively coochy-coey when he talks about his mother, yet he alleges she had such a cleanliness patrol that she ran her household with the intensity of a Hitler. She complained to his father that her hand was hurting from smacking. She would generously offer all the local children lifts to school. Yet she made him walk. Was she insane?

'No. It was her theory that I should get some exercise.' In choosing the scenes for the movie, he feels that the one that reveals who his mother is is where she turned on a lot of kids who were complaining about their neighbourhood being overrun by black people and said, 'I am half negro.' He says this portrays his mother's courage and that there is not one bone of hypocrisy in her body.

'I lived in a black neighbourhood and every white person left and they all preached about how we should live with our black brothers and there was a mass exodus. It was only she who preached it and lived it.'

He thinks that he is like both of his parents. 'Although I'm like my father I'm a different kind of father. I am much more distant to my kids.' (There are three girls. Emily 13, Debra 10, and Ashley, 4.) 'I find myself sounding like him on air and I don't mean saying shut up moron. I mean my father is a wit, the brightest guy I know on the planet. He could razzle-dazzle me with his grasp of world events, his analysis and his humour. I have a lot of things that are fucked-up about me that probably come from them. My parents have a weird line they drew. Like I was allowed to have porno-graphy in the house all the time, but growing my hair long was a major issue. There was this weird liberalism and conservatism going on in my house.'

Just like now, there's a weird combo going on in his head. The libertine pioneer that is totally faithful to his wife, a man who plays Fartman, and yet protects his children from seeing *Batman* because it's too violent. Certainly, they're not allowed to listen to the show. 'I wouldn't have trouble with any other 13 year old listening to the show or seeing this film, but I think it would be very hard to sit there and hear about Daddy masturbating the night before. It would be a bit like watching your parents have sex.'

He says that his mother gave him the great inner morality and sense of crusade. She says that they would never have left Roosevelt had it not been that he couldn't take it anymore. 'Growing up in an all-black neighbourhood was very confusing. I was fucked in the head about it. It made me introverted, very much upset with the world and very much betrayed. It took me forever to come out of it.'

The coming out of it, the road from alienation to 'in your face', the path from sensory exile to the bathing in fleshy graphics, is what comes out of his mouth into the air and onto the airways. Even now, before his show, he gets nervous. He used to be so nervous that his voice would go high and he'd get the shakes. Now, he just has a horrible nausea at the start of every show. Yet his radio show is his life. It's about everything that comes into him having to go out of him. It's feast and purge. He never takes time off, gets extremely antsy if he's ever forced into a vacation. And while he's happy to pioneer the Marilyn Mansons and Porno for Pyros on the show, if you ask him what music he likes to slink back and relax to, he doesn't know. He doesn't relax. He prepares. 'I always feel like it's Sunday night the night before school. I get up at 4.00 a.m., never rested, and I always feel that I'm going to go on and not be as good as my last show. My books get critical praise, but not the radio show and I feel it's the thing I do best. And I have always felt that no matter how these guys, these bosses, were real terrors, no matter how much my father tried to knock me down, I had this notion that I could do it . . .'

Then he waxes lyrical again about having the courage to follow your dream. God, he's so American. The real guy and the radio guy are both maniacally insecure because they are sensitive. Those who feel pain sharply need to wound, to get it out of them. The thinner the skin, the heavier the missile action.

Yet he says, 'there's nothing that you could say that would offend me. What could embarrass me? It's just words. Perhaps that's the Howard off the air. But the Howard on the air can't be embarrassed by anything. For instance, I even talked about the fact that I was obsessive-compulsive for years. I had a real disorder, would never admit it. Finally I admitted it and I got rid of a back pain that I'd had for years. I was embarrassed by it. It showed weakness. But I could only admit to it once it was gone, once it left me.' I wonder, is there no length to which he will not go to reveal, admit, to take you to some dark, pathetic place.

'I never feel like I have to apologize when I come home. You can't say what is on your mind and then have to apologize for it.'

But all the time he's talking to me, he's looking for my sanction, looking at me with his sun-glasses off, a very rare thing. His eyes are a very pale, splashy, teal blue, a baby blue, angelic blue, crystal-bottled-mineral water blue. Do you think that you can be sexually faithless and still be loyal?

'Woah. That's good.' He looks very shocked. 'In my warped mind, being sexually faithful is the one thing you can't break. Yet I never expected women would be attracted to me. I think it's exciting. Whatever I've become is more attractive to women than what I was. Of course I don't think of myself as attractive, but famous is attractive, so today when this beautiful girl comes on, Jenna Jameson and says she wants to sleep with me' (she gave him her underwear to sniff on air) 'I'm like, oh my God. I would like to experience that. Who wouldn't? She is a beautiful woman and it would probably be fantastic. At the same point, what do you do? Give up your marriage and the loyalty? How would you find that again?' his voice rising with panic as if he genuinely believes he wouldn't. 'I know couples that aren't uptight, the woman understanding when a guy goes out and has affairs, but we don't have that kind of relationship. Alison would freak. I am tempted every day. All the time. Every fucking day. I'm pretty sure it would be a lot more exciting to be in bed with someone new, but I can't do that and it's a torture.'

It shows his ineptitude with women. His cackhanded, brutal, stupid way of handling them. Of course he could never be friends with a woman. He says that if he had learned how to be the smart guy, how to be friends with women, he could be doing them all simultaneously. But he didn't. After a few girlfriends but no real relationships, he met Alison and knew instantly that he wanted to marry her. He still feels grateful that she stuck with him. He says their sex life is not at all kinky and he's conventionally like Elvis, can't stand the female form pregnant.

I tell him that I've met many men in my life who are sort of all mouth and no trousers. You know, they talk about their penis being huge. 'They're assholes,' he snaps. Yes, but you talk about your penis all of the time.

'I'm very upfront. I don't have a big penis.' And I tell him that I don't believe him. That all men, with the exception of one, who have talked in great detail and excess about the size of their penis are putting on a front, a diversion, a lie, and any man who talks about it a lot does it because he wants women to get curious about what it's really like. And I tell him that I think that he does it because the man from AT&T Connecticut and all the other AT&T guys who think

Howard is absolutely fabulous and worry that they have a small penis think, 'I have a small penis so I am Howard. Howard could be me.'

'I like how you're looking down as you say that.' I say, 'I wasn't looking down. We're not on the radio.' Horribly, Howard has gone into his radio persona, the kind of person who goes on automatic flirt, a kind of mocking flirt that is not real, that is the amoeba, the asexual, the flirt without guilt because it is not real.

'I'd like to be happier. I really would. I'm not a particularly happy person. Are you a happy person?'

He always wants to bond, to drag me back down to some basic insecurity or empathy. I tell him no, and he says, 'OK then. So we're alike. Maybe that's what people respond to in me. Also though, I'd hate to read an article where someone appears to have so much and says they're unhappy. You know, you think you've got a career, a wife, money in the bank. But some people are just born miseries and I'm one of them.'

We're back on to 'it's hard not be Howard' because relaxing doesn't appear to make him happy and working obsessively doesn't appear to make him happy. The pursuit of any interest not pertaining to his show would be disorientating. 'In fact I hardly like to leave the house if ever I'm not working. I like to watch television and sit like an eggplant. I've heard celebrities go "being famous really sucks because you can't go to the supermarket." Who ever wanted to go to the supermarket in the first place? Fame is a great excuse for staying in your house but I would stay in my house even if I was a garbage man. I'd rather stay home, eat dinner, watch a movie. It's so romantic, even if I'm by myself. I love doing that, don't you?'

He doesn't even comfort-eat. Much has been made of the fact that he has a food obsession that might almost be a disorder. He talks like a supermodel about being ten pounds overweight. There's only a total of five things he likes to eat: tuna fish, baked potatoes, fruit, Paul Newman's salad dressing and oat bran. He's obsessed with his own digestive system, always talking about vomit and the other stuff. He's kind of an intellectual bulimic, if not an actual. 'Yes,' he says. 'I have a need to spew and it's not healthy, not good for a relationship because my wife doesn't understand. She says, "Can't some things be private?" This is a constant discussion.'

There is of course one thing he's desperate to keep private. He will never admit how much money he earns. He pulled out of the governor's race in New York because you have to reveal what you earn. An unauthorized book written about him recently alleged that in 1996 he earned $17 million. The figure is usually estimated to be in excess of $12 million per year and that was before the movie. Is the man who is happy to reveal the size of his penis, the intricacies of his sex life and to humiliate celebrity guests, is he embarrassed to reveal his income?

'I think there's such a class struggle in this country. It's weird when you start talking about how much you make and you're trying to live among people, and your kids have friends and it's very difficult to get a plumber to come in if he thinks you're making millions of dollars. Then there's also that it becomes an issue, a value judgement. People might go, "Is that all he makes? He can't be very good." If I start asking you how much you make I start to evaluate you as a writer. How come she makes that much? She must be terrific. And that would not be a judge of your writing. And my father would never admit to what he earned. I used to say that when I worked at WROR, my first radio station, and the guy upped me to $250 a week, I thought that was more money than I'd ever need in my entire life. And my life hasn't changed that much. Money is only important in my radio career so I can't get fucked with as much, because it's like "Hey, I'll leave." That's why it's called fuck-you money.'

At the première party, the man who is content to earn $250 a week surrounds himself with white-trash heros: The Buttafucos, several relatives of Ron Goldman and Donald Trump. There are breasts everywhere. Porn stars shimmering and lesbians with breasts, who are showing them to each other and to the crowd who are waggling their fists below. Despite all those guys who want to be him, there are women everywhere who love him – including his mother, who didn't seem to notice the section of the film where he accused her of making him wear her underwear and take his temperature every day rectally until his teenage years. In fact she announced, in line for the bathroom just ahead of me, 'I didn't see it before today because I wanted to see it with all of you. You guys, you who make him. Besides it was special, more of an event. And you know? It was just like giving birth to him.'

Far from being offended by him, I have concluded that most women go on the radio show because they want to expose their breasts to him, the idea of the bile-at-heart but loyal to the core, monogamous American who wants to touch, but not do, is a challenge. And, of course, they find him intelligent. He's flirtatiously lewd with women to their face and he bonds with men in a different way, with the crudeness of a vendetta against Richard Gere or sharing the graphic detail of what it must have been like to have been John Wayne Bobbit's private part. He has always been anti-P.C., and America has always embraced and loathed that kind of redneck, never more so than now, when Stern seems to be at the helm of the liberal-fascist split personality of America, both opposing it and embodying it.

Stern tells me how privileged he has been to meet me and I tell him that I have been privileged too. It's nice to spend time with a phenomenon. It's interesting to reaffirm that what makes a person extra-ordinary is the depths to which they will plummet to find their ordinariness. He's quite carried away with the acting malarkey and says next he'd like to play a retarded person or a romantic comedy lead. I doubt he will. He's far too busy playing at playing himself.

Howard Stern is used to people being scared of him and that's just the sort of man I love. American girlfriends had warned me of his routines but of course he was too reverential to even look at my breasts. He wanted to shock me so I didn't have to bother trying to scrape out his fingernails for clues to his make up. He's a great combination of brazen and vulnerable and he's the essence of neurotic manhood. Men listen to him because he knows the secret. He lets them all think they have a bigger penis than him.

Erica Jong
Sunday Times Magazine
19 December 1993

Erica Jong has talked sex voraciously, thighs dripping with it, stomach liquid with it, her fingers tweaking it, her brain creaming it into an unstoppable voice, a voice of her generation that seems sweetly nostalgic now, probably impossible even then.

Her book, *Fear of Flying*, changed lives. Fifteen million copies were sold and it was translated into twenty-two languages, languages like Serb-Croat, indicating that it probably reached people who had literally never read a book before.

If you read it now, you would see that there's very little hydraulic action, very little sex. It is the story of a woman finding sexuality, fantasy, and growing up. It is the story of the confusion of a woman's proactive, unashamed and predatory desire. In the 1970s, predatory desire was allowed. A decade and a half later, 'predatory' got made into movies like *Fatal Attraction*. *Fear of Flying* was a funny, deeply ironic book, in which the quest for the most wondrous sexual encounter ended up in limp impotence.

Jong wrote it when she had just turned 30 in 1973 and since then, of course, sexuality, repression, puritanism and backlash have all turned themselves inside out. But what is still startling and absorbing is the voice. It is a warm, embracing female voice, the voice of your best friend.

'I was the voice of something that happened in the culture, the rites of passage for a generation, and my fictional alter-ego articulated it in a way people could relate to,' she says. It was one of those books that can only have been written in the afterbirth of feminism. Jong hit it: women's power lay in discovering their sexuality and unleashing that force.

Jong's revolution, liberation and motivation has always been sexual. That's always where she saw the power base. As feminist polemic moved and splintered and the banner-carriers were Dworkinesque-style dykes with bullet heads and dungarees, Jong's blondeness, lipstick and heels became fabulously un-P.C.

In *Fear of Flying*, she invented a sexual philosophy and called it the 'zipless fuck' – sex without guilt. Today, if you quote it back at her, her smile flickers nostalgia, but not quite remorse.

To quote from the book: 'The zipless fuck was more than a fuck. It was a platonic ideal. Zipless because when you came together, zippers fell away like rose petals, underwear blew off in one breath like dandelion fluff. For the true, ultimate, A1 zipless fuck, it was necessary that you never got to know the man very well . . . So another condition of the zipless fuck was brevity. And anonymity made it even better . . . The zipless fuck is absolutely pure. The man is not "taking" and the woman is not "giving". And it is rarer than the unicorn.'

These days it's even rarer. The zipless fuck is a sad anachronism. There is no such thing as guiltless sex and there probably never was. It seemed to be an ideal to cleave to at the time because it was new and freeing and self-affirming.

'My generation was born into a world where women wore white gloves, where a college pregnancy could destroy your entire life, there was no access to choice, no abortion, and now we are raising our daughters in the age of Aids. Having gone through the 1960s, the 1970s and the filthy 1980s, women have been expected to modify themselves every half decade. First there was freedom, then there was backlash. It's very confusing.' Free sex is no longer in the *Zeitgeist*.

'Now, if you meet a man and immediately go to bed with him, he's going to think you have Aids,' she says. 'Men are terrified. The propaganda of that whole Aids thing frightens people to death and has brought back a new puritanism. The zipless fuck can exist as a fantasy. It always existed as a fantasy.'

Did it ever really exist? 'No, I don't think so, because we don't understand sex. The ancients had a better notion of the stuff than we do. They understood that sex was very dangerous and risky, edgy stuff, that it deals with matters of life and death. They understood that sex was not always about establishing a home and family. It's about communing with that other side of human nature. That other side is there but we still don't recognize it.

'It has nothing to do with hanging the curtains and having babies. As a matter of fact, the two are antithetical. Passion and harmony can never exist at the same moment. I'm a great believer in allowing that wild side of human nature a place in your life, but not to determine everything else about your life.'

Her current husband – her fourth – is attorney Ken Burroughs. 'I don't think Ken and I would ever have worked twenty years ago. It is the relationship that is most like my parents' marriage. We give each other hell about everything, but we are totally upfront, no hidden anger or resentment. We have tremendous companionship. If I wake him up in the middle of the night with a joke, he'll laugh at it.

'It wasn't love at first sight. It was bonding, but it wasn't love. I didn't want love. I was sick of people falling into bed and then it becoming horrific and destroying. It was at least a month before I went to bed with him. That's very long if you're seeing someone every day. But I wanted to know that he was something that I wanted to bother with before I went to bed with him. I was sick of going to bed with someone and then getting to know them later.'

So, the complete opposite of how you started out on the Holy Grail for the zipless fuck. 'Absolutely,' she laughs, delighting in her own irony. She says that you work out a lot of paradoxes when you hit 50.

Jong is a small sharp woman, primmed into a pin-striped jacket, blonde, wiggly tresses and pink, pillowy mouth. She's just finishing her memoirs, it's called *Fear of Fifty*. It deals with the political, the personal: what has happened to her feminism and her sexuality. Within a half-hour of talking to her, you see that part of her power still lies within her sexuality, part of it is still kind of a spiritual abandon. Henry Miller, the author – whatever one thinks of him, prophet or pervert, sexual enslaver or liberator – once told her that she was a female version of him, and he intended it as the highest compliment (a compliment she recently returned with her memoir of him, *The Devil at Large*, to be published this spring.) Without his novel *Tropic of Cancer* coming out in the 1960s, she says, a whole gaggle of sexy books, such as John Updike's *Couples* in 1968 and Phillip Roth's *Portnoy's Complaint* in 1969, could never have been written.

In the 1990s however, she says, she has seen enlightenment turn dark.

'My generation thought, "Put a little LSD in the water supply and you have sex without consequence." Well, sex is never without consequence. We were also the generation that had children and then got divorced. We were going to live together in these amicable post-divorce settlements, and then we grew up and discovered our children were incredibly damaged and wounded by these divorces. It is not easy to go from Mummy's house to Daddy's house and never know where your favourite toy is, and never know whether you've left your underwear or your hairband at Daddy's house.

'We thought because our hearts were pure that everything would be OK. We didn't anticipate what our children needed. Or that, if you have a child with someone, you are with that someone for the rest of your life, whether you get along with them or not. Now, all these things have come home to roost.'

Jong's life has been both literally and emotionally prolific. There have been seven novels, numerous award-winning collections of poetry and a study of witches and witchcraft.

And there have been four husbands, all of whom have been woven into her novels.

Born and brought up in Manhattan, she is the daughter of an artist mother and a songwriter father turned successful businessman. When she was growing up, every time she wrote a poem, her mother would tell her to send it to the *New Yorker*. 'It wasn't enough to have written a poem,' she says.

She was the second daughter, the one who was meant to be a son. 'I had to be a star, no question about it. There were no limits placed on me. My parents thought I was a genius.' She found that her limits came from the outside world and from within her own spirit. She often thought it would have been easier to have been a man. As a teenager, she became anorexic for a time and stopped menstruating, as if she were punishing her body for being female.

She touches on this in a Channel Four documentary about body fascism; how women's body shape is defined by a patriarchal culture and what a torment this is. Then, with typical Jong panache, she'll deliver me sticks of carrot crudité for lunch. 'They're healthy.' She is at her best when uncovering paradoxes within herself.

She originally wanted to be a doctor, enrolling at the University of New York, but changed her mind when she entered the dissection room and was confronted with a foetal pig. She switched to English instead. During this time she met her first husband. It was 1963, she remembers, when you married the first man you slept with. She split with him after he suffered a mental breakdown.

Husband number two was Alan Jong, a Chinese American who was a Freudian psychiatrist. She took his name because he wanted a commitment from her. 'We were totally unsuited,' she says. 'I was 23 and I'd been through an incredibly traumatic experience with my first husband who had had a schizophrenic breakdown. So at the age of 22 I was taking care of someone who thought he was Jesus Christ, and then I married this nice, serene, older, Freudian shrink and had this fantasy that he would keep me from craziness.'

Instead he encouraged her to deal with her conflicts about being an artist and a woman and encouraged her to be a writer. The experiences of those two marriages led her to sit down and write the heavily autobiographical *Fear of Flying*.

Then, at 35, she met and fell madly in love with Jonathan Fast, son of the American novelist, Howard Fast. 'From the moment I met him, I knew he was the father of my child to be; there was that kind of connection. He already felt like family, a soulmate. We had both grown up in the same kind of left-wing Jewish bohemia.' Their daughter Molly is now 15, framed photos of her seen-it-all eyes and lazy smile, constant in various stages of babyhood to puberty, haunt every corner.

Fast was artistic, clever, funny, and six years younger. 'I don't think the marriage could have survived because of the competitive element. He had a famous writer father and a famous writer wife and his own literary career did not pan out as he had hoped. The pressure of that became so great that the marriage couldn't stand it.

'The ending was a bereavement so deep, probably the worst thing I ever went through in my life. We had fought constantly about everything. I joined my life with his, heart and soul. My daughter (Molly) was 2, it was the third divorce, and at the end of that marriage, I had a headache for six months like a steel band around my head.'

It was motherhood, she believes, that helped her political development along. 'Having Molly radicalized me,' she says. 'It made me want to make the world a better place; and she's a fierce feminist, much more so than I, much less forgiving. If Molly and I go into a store and the guy is acting flirtatious, she'll turn to me and say "Mom, you shouldn't do that. He's disempowering you."

Perhaps Molly is one of the politically correct feminists who disapprove of mini-*maîtresse* boots with high heels? Jong flexes her ankles approvingly. 'Yes, but she's working through her own thing of having a sexy mother or a mother who's famous for writing sexy books. She's at an age where you have to define the bond between yourself and your mother. So if I'm going to be A, she's naturally going to be Z.

'I am very forgiving,' she muses. 'I give people chances, perhaps too many. Maybe I've been too forgiving. Did I stay too long? I ask myself that.' She's asked herself that several times, that's for sure. She tried to answer the question in her last novel, *Any Woman's Blues*, which was about being addicted to a bad boy who provides good sex. It was written in a period that she calls the most important in her life, when she was alone, but falling in and out of various obsessive relationships. She wrote poetry that was almost Plath-like in its bleakness.

'I went through a period when I wanted to sleep with men who had bodies like Michelangelo's David. And of course, wonderful hip muscles aren't going to make up for a man being brain dead. But if a man was a good fuck, I was certainly more forgiving.

'I've never been with a man who abused me, but there's such a thin line between mental and physical abuse. There is such a lot of passive aggression in me, you don't know where the boundaries are. When women are trod on, they don't feel trod on soon enough.'

Feminism and emotional masochism don't really seem like kissing cousins, yet Jong has had a relationship with both. She has said that all men worth having in bed are partly beast. Why then would she deplore the beast then want it?

'There is the whole issue of women's submission and no one has addressed this in the feminist movement. They say we can't deal with this, we're going to be lesbians. That's the aversion response. Who in literature has dealt with the way women get hooked on men who satisfy them? Other feminists got mad at me in *Any Woman's Blues* when I tried to deal with a woman having a relationship with a man who mistreated her and gave her good sex but no self-esteem. But what about sado-masochism? What about dominance and submission in a love relationship? You can't pretend it doesn't happen. What about the turn-on of being submissive?

'Some men like women who are powerful. But the paradox is this: the strongest feminists, the most powerful, passionate, independent women have always been the biggest fools for love. Once you recognize that and look at it in history, it's very comforting – Colette, Mary Wollstonecraft, Mary Shelley, George Sand. The women who were the most fierce, the most intellectual, the most in love with revolution, freedom and the right of women, always fell over backwards to some asshole.

'But, as hard as it is to give up good sex, there always comes a point where the abuse is not worth the sex. Then you keep going back for one last time. Then you reach a point where it's no longer worth it because you feel so bad about yourself you've got to stop. That bad trip, smoking that joint that makes you paranoid, so paranoid you say you'll never get stoned again, there's that moment when you say your self-esteem is in the toilet and you say you'll never do this again.

'Men are frightened by women's insatiable sexuality, frightened by women's ability to create life in their bodies, frightened by women's enormous creative force. Why would they have spent so much time putting women down if they didn't fear them? They are afraid of being controlled by us and our sexuality; like the myth of Circe, they will turn into swine because of their physical desire. I see this as the time of the endangered erection. We've had a huge change between men and women in this century and men and women have not come to grips with it yet. The price that smart women often pay is not to find a partner, and men, they lose their erections. It's a metaphor that says they are the weaker sex.

'Within each person, there are male and female characteristics and for a woman who is bright to discover that opposite in herself is very freeing. The more self-empowering you are, the more you are going to desire submission, so you are more vulnerable to it,' she says, all at once admitting me into her coven, 'than those dress-for-success women who tune out their sexuality.'

The backlash to the sexual liberation of the 1960s worries

her. She sees it as unhealthy repression. The answer, says Jong, is not to deny your sexuality, but to confront it every day.

'Monogamy is not possible among interesting people,' she asserts. 'You can be monogamous one day at a time. I don't believe, that just because you're married to someone, that person has the right to tell you what to do with your body at every moment of your life. You may make the choice to be monogamous because you feel more centred and you feel solidarity and union with someone. But I don't think you can marry someone and say, "I will never have a relationship with anyone else."'

When she speaks it's quiet and mellifluous. She says words like cock and fuck with such elegance and confidence because she's made them her own. She's continuing to claim the new territory to be sexual and an older woman in *Fear of Fifty*.

She feels the new book is the best thing she's ever written. It's another landmark in feminist literature, but for different reasons. I asked her if she's become tired of the word feminism. Does it really mean anything anymore?

'I define it as a woman who is self-empowered and wishes other women to be self-empowering. Unfortunately, it's a word that's been associated with one branch of the women's movement. I want to address why we've feuded among ourselves. There should be no divisions between Betty Freidan and Gloria Steinem, but it's a subject that the P.C. feminists refuse to let us address. There is an official denial that this problem exists. It's not men's fault. It's women's. We see power is still male and see women as weak and vicious. Powerful women denounce their femininity. You had a prime example of that in Mrs Thatcher, the third sex. It's the women who are angry at other women. If you come into the board-room wearing a filmy blouse and have a baby at home that you are nursing, and your breasts are leaking milk, who is going to enforce that you can't come into the boardroom? Not the men, who might be slightly turned on, but the other women.' Other women have often attacked her work. This hurts because women are narrowed in their expectations.

'You are not allowed to be funny, sexy, clever, and a mother all at the same time. The fact that men still think this is bad enough. That women think it is a tragedy.

'In a way, I'm typecast. For the outer world, I will always be Erica "zipless fuck" Jong. But what matters is what you think of yourself, not what other people think of you. You embrace who you are, and I always wanted to be a woman of letters. I thought writers were next to God. I always wanted to be a woman of letters, to have written a shelf of books by the time I'm 80.'

She says she was recently asked to move to California to be a screenwriter. 'I had problems with the tax people,' she says. 'At one point, I owed them $1 million. Moving there would have made me enormously rich and enormously frustrated because you write movies that are never produced and your work is changed. But they are just beaten people with huge jacuzzis. Despite all my problems I couldn't go to Hollywood. That isn't who I am ... And I still want that shelf.'

Erica's words have no doubt shaped my psyche. I was the generation of women that read Fear of Flying *and thought that I was entitled to sex without guilt, lust without love and I was confused when life didn't represent art in the way that I had hoped. I wanted to know, how can it work out. I am still so moved by her. I took it as a sign when I turned up for the interview wearing a Botticelli print blouse which she also owned because, of course, I wanted to occupy the same space as her. Of all the people I have ever interviewed, this was the person with whom I didn't want it to end after the interview. I didn't just think, 'Oh, it would be nice to be her friend,' I needed to be her friend. Somehow we bonded in a way that made me hope, anyway, I could give something back to her. And of all the people I have ever interviewed, she is one of two with whom I have an ongoing relationship.*

Passion's Contract Killers: Zipless Sex
31 October 1993

It was a fortieth birthday party, quite a swinging affair. I was introduced to this man described as a Polish Dreamboat who was unmarried and rich. He looked like a sub-Martin Amis type, small boy's leather jacket, pouting lips and baby eyes, don't know what colour. We'd been chit-chatting for a while when he produced his party piece.

He explained how, in view of these dreadful date-rape cases and the business with Diggle and the business with Donnellan, it was impossible to pick girls up at parties without protection, and he didn't mean a packet of three. He pulled out a folded, typed paper which he called a contract, the gist of which was that you were *compos mentis* when you consented to (and you had to tick off from the list): kissing/stroking of breasts/clitoral stimulation/manual-lingual/vaginal penetration/manual-lingual-penile.

No doubt every girl at the party got the same trick. I think it was designed to break the ice. It was delivered in such a way that, if you thought it was funny, it was a joke. If, however, you thought it was interesting, it was a way to get you to talk about sex within five minutes of knowing him. It was one of those jokes that he hoped was going to get him taken seriously. Because it was supposed to be a joke, he no doubt felt that it validated his intent, which was to pick up somebody at a party and have uncommitted, unrepeated one-off sex.

I listened sleepily as he wove pictures of his perfect sexual encounters. The best sex he'd ever had had been with strangers. The excitement of knowing you were never going to meet them again, that everything existed in the moment he cliched on. I moved off to find a more interesting conversation with a 21-year-old gatecrasher. I felt sickened by the man's insidious fear of women that led him to crave revenge-coated romance. If a woman thinks sex is wonderful, of course, she wants to do it again with that person. For a man, it seemed, this need not apply.

All this happened in the wake of the cumulative effect of recent rape cases, in one of which the woman claimed to be drunk and changed her mind half-way through. The case involving the accused, but acquitted, student Austen Donnellan, has had a more pungent and confusing effect on sexual mores than the film *Fatal Attraction*. There are some men who as a result, perhaps conveniently, suspect women of being 'tauntresses', as the MP Sir Nicholas Fairbairn last week so memorably referred to those involved in rape cases.

The Polish Dreamboat was one. Later on, at home time, this man who hoped to have a contract on my libido sidled up to me again and asked me, hopefully, if I'd be interested in anything on his list. He seemed to think it was a very Now way of doing things. Not liking or fancying him in the least, I asked him if he carried condoms, knowing he would not. He didn't. He said he thought all women were on the Pill. I told him that I didn't know any woman on the Pill. He gave up. It all seemed to prove a point.

Mr Polish Dreamboat was in a little time warp, part of the zipless, clueless, hapless generation. At 42, he fitted perfectly into that group of men who were weaned on the preachings of early feminism – those interesting theories about a sexual freedom that turned out to be sexual slavery. When Erica Jong, then, extolled the wonderment of the zipless fuck, it was supposed to be the beauty of sex without guilt, without responsibility, without love. (Now it's probably called rape, and very dull it is, too.)

But the men of the zipless generation knew how to cling on to a good idea when they had it. Sex with a contract is a neat-over-and-done-with affair. It's the way they've been conditioned. Men one generation older or one generation younger are more considerate. This group of men in their forties are not only grappling with their menopause, but with the changing *Zeitgeist*. They often have sex with the same person, although she comes in different bodies.

And now the 1990s equivalent of the zipless fuck novel has finally come around again, and it is the irksome *The Bridges Of Madison County*. It was written by Robert James Waller. *The Bridges Of Madison County* is the ultimate Males and Boon, a monument to male selfishness disguised as a metaphysical romance. It's been on the *New York Times'* bestseller list for over a year.

It is about this Marlboro Man type, who goes to take pictures of some boring bridges in his pick-up truck, and picks up a woman whose cattle-brained husband is off buying livestock. He's the best lover she's ever had, and she has him for four days, virtually without stopping. It is an elongated one-night stand, a four-day zipless fuck.

'He was an animal. A graceful, hard, male animal who did nothing overtly to dominate yet dominated her completely . . .' Everything's fantastic, but they split up because, as she says, she thinks he is on the road, 'your old knapsacks and a truck named Harry . . . I cannot think of restraining you, to do that would be to kill the wild magnificent animal that is you . . .'

She conveniently goes away to pine forever, and they think of each other every day, although they never speak again. He told her they had ceased being separate beings, and had instead become a third being that was left to wander. 'To the universe four days is no different from four billion light years,' says one of them. It's all very well to delve into the parallel universe, but what it really means is being too lily-livered to hang around. This brute-force romanticism amounts to the same thing as a man with a contract. Their twin detachment encompasses the form of male cowardice first enjoyed by the zipless generation, and here we see it coming around again. Sexual slavery posing as sexual awakening.

Karl Marx described how history had a nature of repeating itself, 'the first time as tragedy, the second as farce.' History, in fact, burps. We taste again the gentleman's relish that we swallowed a couple of decades ago.

Joel Schumacher
Sunday Times Culture
22 June 1997

His last three movies banked over $100 million. He took Tim
Burton's gloomy *Batman* and made it hipper, faster, sexier,
bigger box-office with *Batman Forever*. He followed it up
with *The Client* and *A Time to Kill*, both by America's law-
court drama uber-author John Grisham. Now he's back in
Gotham City with *Batman and Robin*.

You can spot a Joel Schumacher movie. There's always a
dip that dives just the right side of schmaltz. There's usually a
pumping, yee-ha-ha sound-track. Remember *St Elmo's Fire*,
The Lost Boys. The sets for the new *Batman and Robin* shim-
mer like the most extravagant Christmas windows you ever
saw on Fifth Avenue. That's because he began life as a
window designer for Bendel's. His costumes are always slick,
sexy – sheeny rubber, sheeny hair. Poison Ivy is the look for
the summer. Barney's has already sold out of the venom-
green, glitter lip paint as pouted by Uma Thurman.

I went to his house, a huge ship rambling with – would you
believe – indoor creeping ivy. Heady scented wild flowers,
belladonna angel trumpets drip alongside candles and giant
rosaries. He looks *de rigueur* director. Director's hair – salt
and peppery flowing to shoulders – and one wrist dripping in
silver bangles, but he is not pretentious, alienated
Hollywood. He's warm and real and funny. Success hasn't
soured him. He's Jewish but the images all over his house are
exotically Catholic because he finds them ravishing and sexually tortured. 'Perhaps it's a self-description. Although I'm
just oversexed and tortured. You can take out the ravishing.
We're all tortured. It's tough to be a human being. We're insecure. We want love, approval. We want to have passed
through here and have someone notice. We fall in love and get
rejected. Sometimes we fall in love and wish we were rejected

because it turns into torture.'

He's 57 and thinks that men base self-worth on what you do for a living and how much money you make. Women, he thinks, can get self-esteem from being a good mother. You can see how this kind of thought process might lead him to being mystified and tortured. Anyway, the more tortured one is, the more one has to prove oneself and express that torture. The more you express it, the more you need to be validated. That's his motivating force. Not that his movies are dark and grimy – far from it. Think hot and racy, think heartfelt, think gasping and sighing. *St. Elmo's Fire*, *The Lost Boys*, *Flatliners*, *Dying Young*, *The Client*, *Falling Down*. All epics in their own way.

His own life sounds like a movie he might have made. He was born in 1939 in New York, a poor neighbourhood, an only child. His father, a soda jerk who was studying to be a pharmacist, died suddenly when he was 4 and his mother was out at work six days a week and three nights. ' As an only child, you're pretty used to running the show. When you have no father and your mother's out, you have loneliness but you learn self-dependence very young. By the time I was 7, I was out on the streets, the mean streets of Gotham city. It was a tough immigrant area. Poor people always have room for one more. Only rich people are selfish. By the time I was 7, I had decided I wanted to make films. I needed to make money because I wanted to take care of my mother. That was my dream. And also, not to be invisible, to be somebody. I'd see photos of people at parties in black tie and I thought they were happy people, beautiful people and I wanted to be one of those. It wanted me as much as I wanted it.

'I had developed quite a taste for alcohol. I started drinking when I was 9, smoking when I was 10 and experimenting with sex when I was 11. With little boys and little girls. I put myself through art school and made a name for myself doing the windows at Bendel's which was a very hip department store in the 1960s.'

It was 1965, New York. He hung out with Andy Warhol and Diana Vreeland and was offered a job by Charles Revson who owned Revlon and wanted two clothing companies revitalized. His salary was to be $75,000 a year. Big money. 'More importantly I wanted to get my mother out of the building she was living in and to buy her a fur coat because fur coats were still part of the American dream. I signed the deal with Revlon and the same week my mother had a fall at work. She broke her hip. She had diabetes, but no one knew because she was the type that would never have gone to the doctor in case the doctor told her to take it easy. The fall gave her gangrene, but she didn't know it. She was rushed into the hospital. I said good-night to her and when I got home the phone was ringing. I picked it up and a stranger said, "Your mother, Marion Shumacher, is deceased" and then hung up.

'That was the beginning of a very catastrophic and destructive period in my life because I became a full blown drug addict. I was shooting speed from 1965 to 1970, six times a day. I was 130 pounds. I lost five teeth and was $50,000 in debt. I felt my mind and body hadn't connected since birth and I didn't know who I was. I was very guilty that my mother's death had happened in coincidence with my great success, that she never got her fur coat. I felt that God was punishing me. I was a bad person. My mother was very beautiful and very kind. If she had five dollars and you were broke, she would give you three.'

His debts were immense and he had gone back to Bendel's on a salary of $10,000 a year. 'But one day, I remembered what I really wanted to do as a child. I stood in front of the mirror and said, I'm to Hollywood to become a movie director.'

And that's what he did, at first living on $2 a day for a year and a half. He did costumes, sets, art direction and then decided to write a screenplay as a faster way to get into directing. His first was called *Sparkle*. It sold to Warner's. His second was *Carwash*, the surprise hit of its day the soundtrack to the 1970s. He was in, realizing his childhood dreams.

They offered him *The Incredible Shrinking Woman* with Lily Tomlin and that was his first break.

It almost sounds like a success story with a happy ending, but, although he stopped shooting up, he was still doing alcohol and drugs.

'If a very successful person in the movie business was doing drugs, then I had to do it for my career. I couldn't say no or they may not like me. If I was going to have sex with someone, well I had to be on the same level, so what the hell? I was never one of those falling down drunks. Before filming, I would stop everything. That's how I lived for many years. Work, party. Work, party. I didn't get sober until five and a half years ago when I was 52 because it stopped working. I got into a terrible depression and got suicidal.'

Now, it's just work, work. One obsession replacing another.

'Yes, but it's a good use of obsession. Believe me, there are mornings that I have to get up at 4 a.m. that I'm dragging myself out of bed with exhaustion. But then I remember there are people who do that and go to a coal-mine, who never get a pat on the back, who never get overpaid for doing what they would do for nothing.'

It's almost like he's guilty for making money. He gives some to those who can't afford college fees, some to Aids charities. He has an overstuffed house secluded in the Beverly Hills and an English butler who used to work for the Queen, but it doesn't smack of pretentious waste, and he certainly has made millions. I believe him when he says it wasn't his motivation. He said, 'I had a calling and I thought because I had a calling I was going to be a genius. And then I thought, "Oh my God. You're miserable at it." I think I had a little bit of a nervous breakdown over that. I always think I still don't know what I'm doing. I'm surrounded by people who are patting themselves on the back and I prefer being humble. I am not a genius. I am not a great artist. I have a long way to go as a director. However, I do think if you're not a great artist, you can still make an entertaining film artistically. I try to walk a thin tightrope. On one side there's art and on one side there's commerce. If you fall too heavily on the art side, you're pretentious and people will think it's a pile of rubbish.'

Batman would be heavily weighted in the commercial side. Its budget was $90 million. 'There's a humungous pressure to deliver something that has to be a great success all over the world. On the other hand, I had a huge playground. I think I've made something more humane, but also deliciously mischievous and a very eroticized *Batman*.'

The film is fun because it embellishes real life paranoias – George Clooney's problem with committment to women, Alicia Silverstone's potential political correctness, Chris O'Donnells perennial fresh-faced new kid on the block syndrome and Arnold Schwarzenegger's propensity to always utter clichés. It's very smart and visually a feast, and even if you don't like *Batman* movies, it's worth seeing George Clooney's charisma take over the big screen.

'George Clooney is my favourite Batman,' Schumacher says.

There were rumours that predecessor Val Kilmer did not get on as well as you and George Clooney.

'Those aren't rumours,' he cackles. 'We had a fight in his trailer because I had to discipline him about his shocking behaviour one day. He was screaming at the cinematographer and the first assistant. Val got carried away and grabbed me and threw me into the wall of the trailer. Much to my surprise I grabbed him and pushed him right back. I can't remember ever lifting a hand to anyone. So Val ordered me out of his trailer and I said, "Excuse me. I'm paying for this trailer. You're my guest. You cannot order me out." He said, "If you don't leave, I leave." So I threw open the door and said, "Be my guest." Then he stormed out and didn't speak to me for two weeks, which was bliss. People are always saying he's a difficult actor. The truth is, he is the most troubled.'

So it was very convenient when Val Kilmer wanted to do the Saint, because Shumacher already had his eye on George Clooney. He wanted him to be super-sexy in his Batman costume – and he is. He also wanted Alicia Silverstone to be super-sexy, and we all read the stories about too many pizzas and Fatgirl and Robin. Is it true that he sent her to a fat farm?

'*Batman* is very gruelling physically. The costumes are forty to fifty pounds, everyone does their own stunts. Everyone has to be super-fit. Alicia is tiny and she's young. She went on vacation and ate too much and she needed to be reminded that if she was going to continue to work in the movies, she has to understand that her face and figure are part of her assets.

'She lost the weight. She looks beautiful and it would have been fine if she wanted to stay heavier. She could also leave the movie business and go to college and do other things. I say to my friends in the movie business who complain, you see the guards at the gate of the studio? They're not there to keep you in. You can leave at any time. Go work at a bank. No one will bother you. I don't have the tolerance for "Poor me, I'm a movie star." The perks are phenomenal. Give back the money. Give back the fame. If you want the perks, accept the responsibility.'

Shumacher likes those old-fashioned values. He wants to be thought of as kind like his mother, but not weak. He says, 'The love you take is equal to the love you make. If you want friends, be a good friend. If you want respect, treat people with respect. If you want kindness, be kind. I've suffered a lot, but I don't have a licence on it. When you've suffered you either become a very angry person who wants to hurt others, or a compassionate one. If we're not compassionate, then we're nothing. Anyway, giving people massive amounts of money and attention doesn't clear up damage if there's a hole in the soul.'

Has his hole in his soul tightened up?

'It will always be there, but at least I'm no longer trying to fill it with drugs, alcohol and sex.'

The other thing that keeps him going, of course, is his own insecurity. 'I remember once ringing up Woody Allen on the eve of one of my movie's opening and I was in a panic and I said, "What if I've made the worst movie in the history of movies?" And Woody Allen said, "That would be a very important film. You haven't made that one."'

Joel Schumacher is the only person to have sent me a bouquet of flowers after an interview. Although Donna Karan did get me an orchid tree. Joel's note said, 'Thank you for printing all those fabulous lies about me.' You would never imagine that such a nice, funny and sweet guy is one of the most powerful men in Hollywood. He has a big generous spirit. He gives good interview. He gives good flowers.

Donna Karan
Sunday Times Magazine
15 September 1996

There is such a thing as clothesline surgery. You know, the skirt that magically slims the hips, the shirt that skims away flesh. The trousers that become like second skin because for some reason they make your legs look thinner and taller. Not as dangerous as cosmetic surgery – far more illusive. Finding these things, the perfect this or that, is a holy grail. And it's a holy grail to make yourself thinner, better, more sexy, more powerful. Donna Karan knows how to manipulate flesh like she was a surgeon, and she knows how to choose a fabric for its sensuousness. She can make you feel good – the ultimate retail therapist.

Women know this. They become devotees, quite evangelical. Addicts, in fact. Because of these addicts, Donna Karan is probably the richest female designer in the world and probably the most important. It's not just because of clothesline surgery that she's up there with Calvin Klein and Ralph Lauren. She has learnt how to sell you the whole lifestyle. If you can't afford the suit, maybe the travel candle or the control-top tights will do.

She has a knack for knowing what people want. She never wears clothes that she has not designed herself. She knows the self-consciousness of a mis-matched outfit, the discomfort of an ensemble that does not move seamlessly from office to dinner date.

She is wonderfully neurotic and has tapped into a particular female empathy. Not that she just does it for women. She does it for men too: the designs worked out on her husband's imperfect body also clothe the president. Clinton is another addict. She has constantly designed the best-selling men's suits in America.

She started off knowing what people wanted, selling clothes, advertising on whole outfits – this going with that – in a store in Long Island when she was 14. Now her company has gone public and it is valued at $275m. She got a $58m lump sum, and will inaugurate her flagship Donna Karan Collection Store in London, the first of its kind in the world, with a star-studded party on 26 September. Apart from this store, Donna Karan's boutiques nestle in the classier big department stores: Bergdorf Goodman, Saks and Bloomingdale's in New York and Harvey Nichols and Harrods in London.

She started off as a designer for Anne Klein, purveyor of Middle American chic. She became its chief designer in the mid-1970s. Anne Klein got cancer, Karan got pregnant. Klein died and Karan's baby was born in the same week as her first collection. Timing has never been her thing. Just before the company went public this summer, her husband, the sculptor Stephan Weiss, who was the chief executive officer, discovered he had cancer.

She had tried to go public in 1993, but the attempt was scuffled. She cited a bad climate in the market. In fact, it was a tense time for Karan. Things seemed to be slipping from her mistressful grasp. Temporarily, she stopped being the darling of the fashion world; there were rumbles that this woman who created the body and found a plethora of uses for lycra was falling off her pedestal. It seemed she was no longer the champion of the big-boned, stomachy women who once swayed down her runways. Kate Moss nymphed along instead. Karan's clothes, which had always been casually sensuous, became more obvious, certainly in DKNY, her modestly priced diffusion range.

She turned it all round though. She came back with collections that sold better than ever. Last year, the president of Saks said that DKNY was its biggest-selling success story. The Wall Street move seems well received. Going public – following the reinvention of Gucci, which itself went public and has been phenomenally successful – seemed inevitable.

Looking back at over a decade of her work, you see that her genius is making something revolutionary a uniform in everyone's wardrobe, like the one-piece body designed to create smooth lines. This season it's the unitard, the full-length body. She has worked with fabrics to restructure their fluidity, created several more uses for lycra. Her basic black silhouette for women was thought to define the 1980s the way that Quant had designed the 1960s and Biba the 1970s. Going public and expanding into home furnishings and cosmetics means that she wants to define the 1990s as well.

With the New York skyline almost exactly as it appears in the DKNY carrier bag as a backdrop, I meet Donna Karan the woman and the corporation and the lifestyle. It's always hard to meet someone whose work you admire. In fact it was an effort for me to meet her and try not to wear an item she had designed. Her skyline office on 7th Avenue is airy and ethnic. Modern and cluttered. There is a sandbox to doodle in, rocks everywhere and a framed picture of her husband on his Bugaci racing bike.

Like her office, she is packed tight with contradictions. She's in a sloppy, boxy, lineny jacket, h in an antique battenberg lace scarf. She's fondling the holes on the lace like a security blanket. Her face is an oval. Her eyebrows are perched in oval arcs. Her hair is in a Sumo knob. She is tense and her eyes dart at me suspiciously. She reverts to an insular kind of Donnaspeak. You can imagine the kind of thing, how the

Donna Karan flagship store is in London because 'it's the bridge between the United States and Europe. It's an embracing bridge that holds the whole thing together.'

DKNY is not simply a cheaper version of the Collection, although it is about half the price. The Collection is deeply personal, exquisitely finished, very expensive, perhaps £800 a suit. DKNY is more diverse and aimed at a younger urban woman. She says she likes to think they both embody her. 'Two parts of me. Collection is the quality and the refinement, the sensuality and the sophistication that I love. I perfected it. DKNY I love because it's an expression of creativity. It's a moment. It's a flash. Collection has something that establishes a lasting foreverness. Collection is more about sculpting the body. DKNY is more about freedom.'

Her hands cup a plain, black mug. 'It has a certain simplicity,' she raves in her Long Island drawl. 'It's black. It's clean. As opposed to a teacup. A teacup wouldn't be me. It doesn't have the guts. It doesn't have the substance of things that are instinctively me.'

She's so instinctively her that she defines herself every day in the exact same clothes, always in her own design.

'I like a uniform. I very rarely change my clothes because I don't want to think about it, so I try to establish what is the perfect thing that I can wear multiples of. For DKNY I might think what am I going to wear to the gym? What is my daughter going to wear? What are my nieces going to wear? It's like a private world for collection that evolves into a different energy for DKNY.'

Thus, with one swift sleight of hand, the private world is the whole world. Donna Karan, though, does embrace extremes, and when the esoteric, flighty Donnaspeak peels back, she is very solid, as solid as the rocks she loves.

At her beach house in the Hamptons she sits on her own personal rock for inspiration. The menswear this season 'every colour, every texture has been inspired sitting on this rock. It's wonderful for menswear, but I find rocks very female.'

'Like wombs,' I suggest.

'Exactly.' We had bonded at last. Suddenly, her whole face changes. Less long and tense. Now open and pretty. She's less self-conscious of her quirkiness.

The Donna Karan philosophy is not necessarily the most commercial. There is endless in-house experimenting. There's a whole floor given over to a kind of antique warehouse where clothes have been collected from all over the world and chosen for their detail – the weight of a lace, the texture of a linen, the fall of a velvet, the cut of a sleeve, the knit of a sock. Her quirkiness is part of that philosophy. 'She surrounds herself with on-the-edge people,' said one employee. 'Because that is how she can plug into a soulful quality.' Her employees are all devotees.

Designing for men is a different challenge. 'It's like fine-tuning something beautiful, and there's more to do to change men's attitudes to clothes.' Men's bodies, she thinks, are the perfect triangle the right way round.

'That perfect virile body of theirs. Who would not want to look like this? No hips! I'd rather work on that than try to figure out that lump lump lump. How to get from the round to the round to the round. I've covered so many different rounds.'

It was on the smoothing of the rounds that her empire was built. In the beginning, she was always popping into her instore boutiques, including the one in Browns on South Molton Street, and telling people how to wear her clothes. She loves to make the difference, to see that transformation on the woman's face. After mentioning a particular personal fashion dilemma, I find her urging me: 'You need my DKNY amazing white stretch jeans. They are fabulous. Do me a favour. We'll get them. You'll feel like a new person.'

Phone calls are made and people scurry, and I have serious doubts of the possibility of white stretch denim. She tells me, 'No one in the world can say, "God you look great" if you don't feel it. That confidence has to come from you, your-self.'

That confidence has been created out of Donna Karan's

own insecurity. 'I am always looking at myself in mirrors. Hourly, minutely. If I wasn't mirror-sensitive, I couldn't be doing what I was doing. My clothes are not about someone who's 5'9" and very perfect. Sometimes I put on the clothes and interestingly enough people say it looks better on me than it does on the models.'

Why then did she recently change from normal-sized models to superwaifs?

'When it comes to a runway show, the magazines, they want to see who they're photographing. We can fight this till I am deaf, dumb and blue in the face, but the clothes then go from runway to photo shoots. So you might as well put them on the girls that they want to shoot them on.'

I tell her that the latest survey says something like eight out of ten women suffer from some kind of eating disorder.

'They lie. It's ten out of ten.'

Do you think about food a lot?

'Oh no. Not at all. Just every second of the day. What diet am I on today?'

'We're doing no carbs,' says her assistant.

Donna Karan has spent a lifetime of energy doing what she calls 'problem-solving with clothes.' Yet one senses that there must have been problems at home that never got solved. 'It's hard. I've lived the guiltiest of lives. I was a very guilty mother and I still am to a certain extent, although I feel better about it today.'

Within days of giving birth to her daughter, Gabby, now 22, she was back at work.

'It was a horrible, horrible experience. Yet I felt that the entire company was depending on me. I feel like I'm a mother of this company and these are all of my children so I felt responsible.'

Her mother worked, though she didn't have to. She lived in suburban luxe. But the work ethic, and indeed the garment district itself, were bred in her bones.

'My mother was a working woman and that's why I am as sensitive as I am. I didn't like it. She was a very difficult woman and I knew she loved me. She showed it in her ways.'

Her mother's attitude mellowed with her daughter's success. But Karan still seems to find it painful to talk. 'I think that that generation was different and difficult. People were not open with their children. I don't believe that it was intentional. The fact that my father died when I was a baby had a lot to do with it. She lost the man that she loved very much. She was in mourning for that and grieved for it for a good amount of her lifetime. And I felt like "why me?" I don't think a child can understand the loss when a parent is taken away from them, or the loss she felt.'

Do you have any recollections of your father?

'I was only 3 years old ... I don't remember him, but I remember an event. Sitting watching the Thanksgiving Day parade on 7th Avenue and I got terrified watching the Indians so I hid under the bench. My father had a shop which manufactured custom-made suits for men. So it's kind of funny that I'm now in the menswear business. Talk about fate!'

It was fate, she feels, that drew her to her current husband, Stephan Weiss. Like how they met. She was 19 years old and engaged to be married to her best friend, Mr Karan. There was a snowstorm. She could not get home to Long Island. She was trapped in the city at a girlfriend's apartment and Stephan showed up. He was ten years older, achingly handsome, an artist, with a wife and two young children. The wife was on the way out. She spent the week with him. Then the snow thawed.

'It was in 1965, and although it seems ridiculous now, I was 19 and ... I thought you love a guy, he marries you – end of the line. I don't think my daughter would make this judgement, but I wanted more than anything to be married and I thought Stephan was cute, but he didn't want to marry me so I left. I was engaged to somebody else and prepared to be married. When I met this guy that I really loved and I said, Do you want to marry me? Except I didn't say it as bluntly as that, but he couldn't. He wasn't ready to move straight into another commitment.'

Ten years from the first meeting, Karan met the mutual friend and said if you see Stephan tell him to give me a call. Then it snowed again and Stephan called. Would she have dinner? They were back together just like that.

Weiss abandoned a lot of his sculpting to help his wife build a company. She admits to being very jealous of other women and for years their personal and business life was a blur. He was the president, often in charge of commercial and marketing decisions that were against the grain of the creative ones. His most known work was the penile-inspired bottle for the men's fragrance.

Then, in September last year, he decided to resume his career and announced his decision to semi-retire from the company. The same day, his doctor rang him to tell him he had lung cancer. He was whipped into hospital for an operation on his lungs which zapped the cancer. He has since resumed sculpting and intends to show his work.

There is an inner force that sweeps Karan along. Everything is important. Everything is catastrophically important. She is driven by wanting to please them. She began in a little suburban shop showing people how to coordinate outfits. Now she admits, 'Dressing is so hard, so hard to get right.' By getting it right she means making yourself feel comfortable and powerful when you spend the rest of your life feeling insecure and on edge.

All her talk of spirituality seems incongruous in the face of her ferociously competitive multi-million dollar company. Did she ever imagine this eye would be steering such a financially huge operation?

'No, it was never my goal. It was a creative process that got out of control. I just do things and then I like to top them. When we went into the beauty business, I just wanted to have the perfect moisturizer, so I created it. Now I'm obsessed with finding the perfect black pencil.'

She hails for the moisturizer to be found and continues, 'You're only as good as the people who are around you and it's not about me. It's about people who allow me to be the best. Creative power really does embrace so many different elements. It comes from a soulful place.

'I have learned to surrender control. I really don't think that it's me. It's just destined. I'm just a vehicle in the whole thing. There are so many things I want to do, but my biggest dream is not to do. I love not doing. I love to veg out. I go out walking and people try to find me and they can't. I love to be in nature and just float.'

There is not much floating going on this week as DKNY and the Collection prepare for the New York men's shows. A team of acolytes come in and whisk her to a rehearsal and she sends me over to the DKNY building for the white jeans.

'So how were the white jeans?' she says excitedly.

Actually, they were good.

Incredulously she roars, 'Did you doubt I was right?'

Well, yes.

Tangible panic flecks the faces of the entourage of three standing with her. There's a communal gasp. I could doubt Donna?

Well, much as I trust your judgment and vision, you have to know that I fear my stomach and bottom more.

The next day it's the DKNY men's show and then the Collection men's show. DKNY is well received, but the real angst is for the Collection. On the eve of the show, we attend a function at Saks, where she is treated like a goddess, and she says, 'It's hard to think of myself as a designer. It's something that I do and it's so personal to me. Sometimes I find it all so peculiar.' Her style is far removed from her roots. Her mother had wall-to-wall white carpeting. 'You never walked into the living-room because it was roped off. Now I've reversed. I'm very child-like.'

In a very child-like way, she says she wishes she could get her timing better. By this she means perhaps she could be on time once in her life. But some people are never going to be on time. Not just beacuse they have too much to do, but because it's an addiction. Controllers arrive late. She arrives for the party at Saks very later. Afterwards, we loll into her big black limo. She beckons the driver to drive around all of Saks' windows so she can examine how they've displayed her pieces. She's not very impressed so she must be further gratified. Bloomingdale's. We must go do Bloomingdale's windows. Each window has a single item of Karan displayed. Svelte-making trousers suspended in mid-air. A disjointed waistform slims itself into a jacket. Oh yes. This is very good. Karan is tangibly excited by what she calls retail and proudly re-informs me that she worked in a shop when she was 14. They loved her there. It was in the heart of suburbia where she managed to sell whole looks for kids to go to camp, whole schemes of casuals. They still have an early Karan drawing of a long-limbed girl walking a dog, because she started off wanting to be a fashion illustrator before she realized she could make more of a difference selling pieces that were like second skins. She loves the devoré evening gown that she's just designed. She still gets a childlike excitement, a huge thrill from pleasing herself.

After she's talked about the luxury of the fabrics we all want to wrap ourselves in, she luxuriates in the self-absorbing question, 'What did you think when you met me? Was I what you expected?'

I told her I felt I knew her from her clothes. She seemed to like the idea that she was already part of something that touched skin. It made her do one of her sloshy, throaty laughs. I've listened to it on the tape to think what possibly describes this noise. You think she might be choking, but you know she's happy.

The next day the artistry of the menswear is revealed. The couture is at once comfortable and glamorous with the kind of casual opulence that she specializes in. Once again, she is hailed as a goddess, a magician, and she's pronouncing to video cameras that her collection starts with sex.

'We shouldn't be afraid of it. The most important thing a man wants to feel in clothes is powerful.'

She probably told that to the president too. What she is most excited about is the first suit off the runway. A cunning black number that lengthens legs and tightens waists. She says she has at last created the perfect suit.

'My collection could begin and end just with that one suit.'

The thing is, she may talk of editing her life and her cupboards, and her ambitions to not do, but she is a compulsive. She will always find something more perfect.

I love Donna Karan's clothes and I feared very much that I would love her because it's always hard to write about somebody when you think you love them. Unadulterated adoration is boring. But she was such a mix of insecurity and power that made me identify with her and at least understand why I loved her. All love is narcissism, of course.

Sandra Bernhard
Sunday Times Magazine
15 August 1993

They used to gush over each other in purple-tinted sunglasses they bought for each other, cut-off Levis, bra tops. They declared their love on prime-time television – they kissed on *David Letterman*, America's most popular, hip chat show.

Sandra Bernhard was the prelude and inspiration for Madonna's orchestrated abandon, theatrical confusion and clichéd lesbian chic. The much-hyped friendship was to be a watershed for them both, but it was Madonna who broke all the wrong taboos, becoming somehow sexless, her shock value spent. For Bernhard, in spite of all her other achievements, her most powerful strut into the public imagination remains as Madonna's girl toy.

Their relationship, which caused a media sensation, turned sour when Bernhard felt her sexuality was used as a gimmick to promote Madonna. She also believed her life, her great lines and even snippets from her one-woman show, ironically titled *Without You I'm Nothing* were blatantly ripped off platinum big-time by Madonna. It was more than three years ago, but she can still barely bring herself to utter the singer's name.

'I can't say the experience with the M-word was the worst of my life, but it certainly was the most public. It frightened me. It scared me into a good place, to learn that you can't live your life on half-truth and hype. It takes so much away from what you're supposed to accomplish.

'It startled me. It was like walking in and seeing your love in an embrace with your best friend. You almost want to laugh so you don't say anything. The resentment builds up and up inside you. You're ready to strangle somebody. She did actually go off with a girlfriend, but it didn't matter, it wasn't about that. Everything was finished by then: the friend, her. What really hurt was thinking that I had allowed it to happen. I said to myself, how many times are you going to allow yourself to play second fiddle emotionally, whether it be love, friendship or work? I was depleted. Rock bottom.'

The experience was none the less evolutionary. Somewhere around this time Bernhard, famously fearless, infamously strident, stopped equating ultimate cruelty with ultimate tenderness. She stopped being fearless and allowed herself to be herself. She also stopped feeling guilty about needing to sleep with the comfort-noise and fickering screen of a television in the dark Los Angeles night.

'I found myself complete: this is me baby, this is what you are, this is what you look like, this is what you feel ... I stopped hoping I could sleep without the TV on. If I wake up I'm afraid to go out of my room. If I have to go to the bathroom at night I have to run there and back.

'I used to crave that other people would accept me. I stopped seeking out people who wouldn't, because I accepted myself.'

There is also an excruciatingly revealing book, part autobiographical, part fiction, called *Love, Love and Love*, a direct reaction, she says, to her time with Madonna. 'It's a reaction to that cold, ambitious, manipulative working the press, working each other, going out and looking hot, going home and being alone and dealing with the fact that you can't sleep at night, and dealing with the fact that you've got no fucking soul.

'Madonna's got one big choice. Take a couple of years off and become a human being. Take time to learn something new.'

In the book Bernhard tells us, 'Love is the only shocking act left on the face of the earth . . . Winding ourselves up into frenzies of fear and self-loathing we are tamed by a cocktail of hallucinogen, strange desert journeys, emptiness and abandonment. We flee from this most terrifying moment. In a warm room, in the quietest whispers of tenderness and trust penetrating the senses, control, power, anger are thrown aside and we bear witness to the only valid instant in the universe, love.'

The mouth is unfathomable, the squishy pillow lips hint that she is a sexual omnivore. Sandra Bernhard does not so much look at you as through you, with compassion, fear, scorn, indifference and intimacy all at once. It does not matter whether she is wired up on stage, dressed in sadistic heels and a couple of tassels, or slumped on her own sofa in a stripey T-shirt and forgettable slacks. She looks at you in a way that lingers between terrorism and seduction and touches something deep. She has always managed to look wounded and wounding. It stares out from portraits of herself on the walls of her home. There are the moody and the sleek shots by the photographer Robert Mapplethorpe, and shambolic, garish paintings where you see her red gash of a mouth and splayed-out skeleton fingers, reaching. But tucked into the corner of a frame in her guest bedroom is a small, square, photo-booth shot of Bernhard from another time, pubescent and all bad haircut, surprised eyes, tense erect neck and, of course, that great wedge of mouth. She looks like a frightened alien.

'If I wasn't an alien I was at least part of an experiment. I think you come into the world the way you are and you don't really change that much.'

Some things don't change, at least. She still has the same neo-erotic, paranoid fantasies she developed while growing up, first in Michigan and then Arizona, and that figured so large in her first book, *Confessions Of A Pretty Lady*. They involve sexual entrapment, torture and the director of a film that Bernhard had just finished shooting, *Dallas Doll*, in which she plays a manipulative golfer who sleeps with a husband, his wife and his daughter.

It is hard to imagine such lurid fantasies going on beneath the crisp white linen coverlets, on the twirly wrought-iron bedsteads and the smooth, dustless, twinkling floorboards of her L.A. home, not high in the star-studded Hollywood hills but in the detached suburbia of the Valley. She is intriguingly houseproud. There are flowered pillows to fall back on. Only a spattering of trinkets, all of them dust free. Inside the wardrobes all her clothing hangs in polythene covers.

'Is my house as obsessively clean as you imagined it would be? I do wander around in the afternoons adjusting the angles of things,' she says, apparently fearful that an untidy household will further tangle her mind.

Bernhard continues, wickedly, 'I've got a new book, *Neurotica*. It features me on my hands and knees cleaning the toilet and getting into small crevices.' The joke is on Madonna and her Erotica album, but it does not have the edge on real bitterness any more. Bernhard is the kind of person who believes you have to be disappointed to learn. She says she bought her home, which she has just painted eau-de-Nil green outside, long-stemmed roses around the door, for its black and art-deco-green tiled bathroom. The bath is so cute and so dinky that one wonders how those long-dripping limbs actually fit into it. Absolutely a surburban girl at heart, she loves living there, among the 'real' people. She has always been a financial pragmatist, saving her money in tidy amounts to move 'on to the next stage. It's the first time I've allowed myself to spend money on my house. I'm an organizational fanatic with money. Conservatism is inherited in my nature.

The free-spirit part of my life has been saved for relationships and emotional things. If I was pissing my money away the way I've pissed myself away through relationships I'd be bankrupt.'

She had always felt a misfit, growing up in Scottsdale, Arizona, with her mother, an abstract artist, her Jewish father, a proctologist (specialist in the rectum, anus and colon), and the constant traumas of three older brothers. Her parents had wanted her to become a dental hygienist, but at 19 she left home for Hollywood. By day she pedicured the once-famous and nearly-famous in a Beverly Hills salon, but at night she did stand-up on the cabaret club circuit, with varying degrees of success.

Her only friend in Arizona was Daniel Chick, tall, elegant and the first soul to which she ever connected. They met in high school when they went to Cat Stevens' concerts together. He followed her to a kibbutz in Israel, where he declared his love. Not knowing how to respond she threw a tantrum of irritation, which somehow subsided into Chick becoming her absolute best friend. Three years ago he died of Aids, and there is in Bernhard some vestige of guilt that they could not be lovers and that he took a different path.

'My parents never once asked me, is Dan your boyfriend? It was like they were in complete denial that I existed as a sexual being,' she says. Chick was the only person to laugh, big loud laughs, at her jokes. 'I needed that validation. My father never laughed at my jokes, but I laughed at his. They were Dad jokes, not funny, but I laughed because I loved my Dad, I wanted him to love me.'

Bernhard felt an almost ridiculous admiration for her father. Inspired by his distance, she imbued him with all kinds of god-like personality traits. In *Confessions Of A Pretty Lady* she wrote, 'I think of my Dad as vulnerable, lying on his back with deep feelings stirring in his heart, a heart he never imagined, with feelings never admitted to anyone.' When she was 8 and had an outbreak of hives, he hypnotized them away. He was always hypnotizing her mother, who was a depressive. 'My mother thought that he was trying to take her pain away: he probably caused it in the first place.' Eventually he stopped hypnotizing and, after thirty-eight years, decided they were incompatible and divorced. 'After the split he felt I took my mother's side. We didn't speak for a few years. We made it up again until I made a documentary where I said my father was a proctologist, but also a GP. I was trying to protect him because I didn't want him to be a joke. He thought I was insulting him, that I was diminishing his years of training.' She yawns, affecting nonchalance, but it clearly disturbs her.

'He has forbidden me from talking about him in public. He's mad at me because I discussed his hypno-analysis. He says I was defaming him. Actually I said he was the biggest hero I ever had.'

Who knows what hand the father-figure has played in the mangling of the Bernhard psyche? In her book *Love, Love and Love* she writes with bruised knowingness about men. 'I can't say it was the best sex I ever had, but then again sometimes the look in a man's eyes that betrays his deepest fears makes up for the quickness with which everything happens.'

Sexual awareness came early. 'From a very young age I always found sexiness in both men and women. If ever I came into contact with exciting, powerful, intriguing people, I found myself sexually excited no matter what sex they were. There was never any question of a sexual turning-point of female role model. I never decided to give men up. In a perfect world it would be great to continue experimenting. This is not the right time.'

At 22 she had an abortion, acknowledging today that had she had the baby she would probably not have had the career. She refused an anaesthetic because she wanted to know what was going on, to be in complete control of her body despite the pain. The father was one of her first boyfriends. He was very sweet but she hardly knew him. She didn't seem to know any of her boyfriends in those days: 'I didn't have relationships, I was sleeping with a lot of men, usually only once.

Thank God Aids wasn't around. Herpes was, and I got that, and I vowed I'd never again have sex with a stranger.

'Nobody wanted to date me. I was this weird girl, a fag-hag from Arizona. I'd just meet people, fall in love with them and go to bed with them. I'd hate it that I never got to go on a date.'

It was always in the back of her mind that her partners didn't like her enough to buy her dinner. 'Breakfast just didn't cut it, but in a way there was no time for dates. Because of Arizona and the absolute loneliness, crawling-out-of-my-skin loneliness, I had a very strong fantasy life,' she says. 'So I already knew them, I knew what I wanted to know about them, there was no need for the date. If the sex was bad it was a big waste of time. If the sex was good then it was an even bigger waste of time because then you were stuck with them. They were still hideous to you but because the sex was good you have to fool yourself that it was worth it.

'I was already projecting personalities on to people I didn't know, only to be hopelessly disappointed. I gave too much of myself away to all the wrong people and when someone did love me I was scared and overwhelmed.'

The Bernhard voice curls, languid. She slouches with feminine arrogance into the muted floral cushions of her den, the neck still erect, long hands wafting. 'I used to have the same relationship over and over again with different lovers. I was attracted to unhealthy people, borderline addictive, usually to drugs and then to the relationship. They get totally involved, give up their life for you, then they resent you, do you over, you feel hurt.'

Because she was lonely and frightened a lot of the time, she knew how to terrify her audience. Her big break came in 1984 when she was unnerving as the maniacal and clingy fan in Martin Scorsese's film *King Of Comedy*. She was intense in her one-woman show *Giving Till It Hurts* which toured Britain last year. She shocked the audience by searing them with a torchlight, outing individuals from their appearance, profession or their voices as homosexual, bisexual or, that

111

least interesting category, heterosexual, before stripping to a fishnet and heels, limbs and breasts shuddering, teetering, grinding.

All this is marginal, cultish, off-centre, but the Bernhard evolution also means mainstream. She is starring in the Australian movie *Dallas Doll*, and she has been written into the television series, *Roseanne*, America's highest-rating comedy show, as Morgan Fairchild's girlfriend. She has swapped her tag of supervixen, dismissed her long-time collaborator John Boskovich in favour of planning her own sitcoms with Roseanne Barr's production company.

In spite of the unhappiness, the disappointment and the hurt, it is love itself that has touched, seeped through and softened Bernhard. 'Once you see that someone is consistent in your life and they're not going to leave you, it's not a constant threat, everything else falls into place, you can allow goodness into your life. You get rid of the false mythology that you always have to be suffering, in pain and in transition and, of course, in a terrible relationship, to be a good artist. I have drawn an incredible amount from my disappointments, but I don't have to keep living it.

'When I met my present lover something happened. I saw such good in this person. It was not the typical way I meet people or the typical things I used to find attractive. This person is healthy and complete. It was spirituality at first sight. I sensed amazing calm and beauty.'

Bernhard uses the word 'lover' with purposeful sexual ambiguity. 'I've never been one for putting all my cards on the table. I always want to leave my options open. That is why the gay community have a hard time with me, they don't like my mixed bag of emotions and sexuality. They would prefer brainwashed and marginalized,' she says.

The cards may not be on the table, but an entire book on the table shows us the lover, a model named Patricia. She is there in her full voluptuous slinkiness, dark-eyed, perfect breasts popping out of sheets of water. It is a charity book to raise money for Aids. 'The very opposite of the M-word book,' muses Bernhard, referring to Madonna's indulgent metal covered volume, *Sex*. Pictures of Patricia also hang on the walls alongside those of Bernhard, and various magazines featuring her are placed just so.

Bernhard is now 38 and hungry for a baby. 'It's a big dilemma. There's nothing wrong with adopting a baby. Wonderful babies need homes. But I want to have my own baby. I am looking for a suitable father or donor. I'm not opposed to some man popping in once in a while to play with the kid but I'm not going to have sex with somebody. Sex is sex, it involves feelings. And if that somebody is not your lover, and you already have a lover, you can't do it.

'It's all very *Brave New World*, the idea of a donor. I don't feel good about it. But I don't want to miss out on one of the essential opportunities of womanhood. Am I supposed to put an ad out? If I think about it too much it will drive me crazy.'

Comfortable at last with her own image and what she now sees as beauty, Bernhard knows that her sexual appeal is still ambiguous. 'I did the *Playboy* shots (dusted in gold body make-up, patting her gilded pudendum, among others) because I wanted to be a showcase of alternative beauty for heterosexual men. But without all those socio-political reasons it was great and fulfilling for me.

'I grew up in a male-dominated family. I learned to understand men emotionally but not sexually, therefore I am always comfortable being buddies with men. I have a bigger problem being seductive with men. What I would really like is for men to find me appealing as me. It's irritating that women can't be themselves with men. I watch them playing the *femme fatale* and it nauseates me. Women are much crueller than men. Men just don't have it in them.'

This she knows for sure. All the really menacing, personal, savaging reviews come from women. Uncomfortable interviews result when some women meet her, and Bernhard thinks she knows why.

'I am not a sexual cliché and certain gay women resent that. There's nothing worse than a dry, didactic, colourless, humourless dyke who feels they've put on a nun's habit. They resent me. I don't understand k.d. lang's thing.' She puts up her hands in *diva* horror. 'The cover of *Vanity Fair* where she was being shaved by Cindy Crawford. What was that about? It totally baffles me. These girls are saying, "Oh she's so cute, she looks like Chris Isaak." I just don't get it. Given the choice I'll take the penis. I'll take Chris Isaak any day.'

She finds it obscene that women get excited over a woman who looks like a man. 'Some gay women are angry they don't fit in with the beautiful people and take it out on me personally.'

Bernhard is undoubtedly a phenomenon, both despite and because of these women – designer dykes, lipstick lesbians – many of whom make up her most loyal and devoted audiences. There is a seething new sexual revolution for women. Everyone wants at least a vicarious thrill and Bernhard is all too aware of it. 'Sometimes I feel that I am a conduit to their sexual liberation. Amanda de Cadenet goes around saying, "If I'm going to sleep with a woman I want it to be Sandra Bernhard." Please, I don't want to deal with that girl. Please, can they work this out, but not on me. Not for free anyway, not without a 1-900 number.'

When Sandra Bernhard told me she'd had the same relationship over and over again, but with many different people, it was a seminal moment. I realized that we all do that and it also works in reverse. I've had all of the relationships in this book with the same person.

She also proves my mouth theory. How she's got one of the best mouths; all voluptuous, and voluptuous words come out of it. Now, go and look at Kenneth Branagh. Which one would you rather have dinner with?

Burt Bacharach
Sunday Times Style
18 February 1996

Burt. Burt, I've always ached with Burt. Always been in love with him. Long before his irony-free re-evaluation. Before comfy clubbing and easy listening became hip. Before the Brothers Gallagher placed his picture like an icon on their C.D. cover for 'Definitely Maybe.'

When I was a very little girl I used to sing 'What's It All About Alfie' – or anyone else that could tell me the answer. I assumed it was what both me and Burt always wanted to know. 'Is it just for the moment we live? Are we meant to take more than we give?' At least now I get to ask him in person in Florida in Boca Raton where he's rehearsing with the Boca Raton Pops Orchestra.

The 1960s may have been his decade but the 1990s have rediscovered his sonic opulence. The unforgettable hooks have not been forgotten. Unexpectedly, they still touch, smooth and sear.

Three-and-a-half-minute mini-movies, he called his songs. They're all momentous, distinctively dramatic. A very big picture of making up and breaking up, of stopped souls and reconstructed hearts, unashamedly confused and vulnerable. And there is Burt, by the pool on a lounger, applying sunscreen. He asks me 'Would you like some?' Clumsily I apply it, but he has to rub it in for me because I've left blobs on my nose.

Burt is slight, defined, handsome. But he's never been confident about his physicality. If he had, he wouldn't be who he is. Britain discovered him first and the British are leading the re-evaluation. 'What does it all mean?' he says. 'Maybe the English have great taste but I'm not sure I agree with the terminology "Easy Listening," the way you describe my music.'

He was right. Listening to his new compilation, 'The Look of Love', I cried all the way through it.

'It's what I've always been comfortable with, writing songs of heartbreak. That's one of the great things about writing music. It's always very solitary and I'm hard on myself. If things come too easily, I don't think they're any good. And then you find out years later that you've affected people. That a particular song had this huge impact in somebody's life.'

'I remember taking a plane trip from Los Angeles to New York, sitting with a girl I didn't know and she told me about her boyfriend. She told me she couldn't have sex without having my music on and I thought, 'Well, that's great Burt. You've played some part in a facet of this woman's life.'

A part in so many lives. How often does one not wake up and put on one's make-up and not want to say a little prayer? Or want to know the way to San José and vow to never fall in love again?

Noel Gallagher recently said, 'If I could write a song half as good as "This Guy's in Love with You" or "Anyone Who Had a Heart", I'd die happy.'

Perhaps his wish will be granted as next month Burt has been wooed to write a duet with him and has been driving around L.A. with Oasis surging from his car radio. Michael Stipe, Jarvis Cocker, Paul Weller and Massive Attack have all recently covered Burt songs. He's also writing with Elvis Costello. But where do the songs come from?

'Did I go through one of those things? Did I have my heart broken? Did I love passionately? The way I write is not related to specific incidents or a relationship. I think it's just the stockpile of who I am. I am sponge-like.'

Does he feel that he writes better when he's in an intense relationship? He is, after all, a savage romantic, now happily married to his fourth wife. She's called Jane and she's a ski instructor. Seven weeks ago she gave birth to their second baby. She is 35. He is 67. They have been together for five years and married for three.

'I think when you're happy, your energy is at a high level.

It's like when you're in love you can get three hours sleep at night and still function and be at a high charge. When you're feeling like that, I don't know how much writing you get done, but that would affect my life, and maybe it's used later. I've written well in down periods when I haven't had anyone in my life. Things just go into your system, your stockpile.'

He never felt born with a great musical longing. His mother forced him to keep practising the piano.

'She was strict. I hated it. I thought I had absolutely no talent. I had a small drum set, but I couldn't keep time with the radio. My mother stayed with it and bought me a Steinway Grand. After a period of time my mother came into the room and said, 'We've exhausted our patience. It's your call. Do you want to continue the lessons or stop?' I thought that I would continue because I didn't want to hurt her feelings, not out of love for the piano.'

His strong mother terrified him and adored him and coloured his relationships with women. If women are too strong, he runs, thinking 'they are just like my mother.' The fear comes back. But he likes them self-sufficient too.

'It's a hard one because I want them not too close, and not too far. You want to abandon and you don't want to be abandoned yourself. But as for a woman who's intensely needy, I could never handle that too well. I don't think most men can. I think there's something really wrong with the guys who thrive on it. Maybe they had weak mothers.'

He was born in Kansas City and raised in New York. After studying music at McGill University, and after his stint in the US Army, playing Boogie Woogie piano in Germany to Korean War casualties, he was offered a gig with the singer Vic Damone. He had thought he would probably go into the menswear business. But finally he became musical director of Marlene Dietrich's nightclub act.

Like all the best creative minds, he was an only child: this often makes for a longing to communicate juxtaposed with a need to be alone, because there's such a lot of headspace that's your own when you're little. Growing up, Burt had no friends; this was partly, he says, because he was so small. 'I was the smallest person in a high school of 3,000. There wasn't a girl that I was taller than. Playing the piano in a little band was a good outlet. It helped me get some dates. I never have been confident around women.'

'But you've had such a lot of them.'

'But that doesn't mean that you ever get it or you feel sure of yourself. I look back at pictures of myself twenty years ago and say, "Shit, I looked pretty damn good." But at the time I didn't think so. I was never confident about my work. I never understood why people were giving me money. Money to stand up and conduct an orchestra.'

In those early days, the recording studio people would try and regulate his work and he would get crazily protective. 'I can get down to the smallest pimples that no one would ever see. What the drummer played on the thirty-first bar.'

The gorgeous hits of the 1960s ('I Say a Little Prayer', 'Anyone Who Had a Heart' and 'Alfie') were all written with the help of lyricist Hal David.

Burt has always implied that the partnership came to a tetchy but organized end. He hates to talk about it. He usually doesn't. But for some reason, because we were bonded, he was a little more specific.

'The breakup of the relationship between Hal and myself really came about because of the devastating process and results of *Lost Horizon* (The 1973 film, a musical for which they wrote the score, was a huge and expensive flop.) The picture was a disaster. I didn't want to write anymore. I didn't want to see anybody. When it collapsed, I felt, "Wow, we were partners in this picture and I did all of the work in the last year and a half." Teaching the singers, auditioning, and I felt like I really worked my tail off and he played tennis in Acapulco, and he shouldn't have been able to.

'We could have been running out of gas anyway. If we couldn't write together, we couldn't perform our commitment to Dionne Warwick (he and David had written a string of hits for the singer since 1963). I had to say to her, "I have trouble sitting in a room with Hal." It wound up with lawyers. It was very messy and nasty and foolish. I should have seen what it would become and said, "Hold on" but those things come and go.'

He's back speaking with Hal and even trying to write a song with him. And certainly, first getting back together with Dionne, which he did in the early 1980s, was a big relief. 'That's What Friends Are For', the first song that he and songwriter Carol Bayer-Sager (who became his third wife in 1982; he was previously married to the singer Paula Stewart and the actress Angie Dickinson) wrote for Dionne was about putting the past behind them.

These days, he's comfortable with Sager, from whom he split in 1991. They have a ten-year-old son, Christopher, whom he sees almost every day in L.A.

He puts the success of Jane down to her self-sufficiency. He told her she could have a baby if she wanted, but he wasn't going to have his sleep disturbed with her 'having an alarm every two hours to pump. She asked me to be her breathing-coach and I thought about it. But I didn't feel comfortable with it. I don't want the responsibility. I don't want to learn that process at my stage of life. And she respects that.

'I think anybody's OK as long as you're clear with them. And I've spent a whole life ducking and diving, subterfuge. You try to be what people want you to be for them. You try to be a good boy. It all comes back to the mother thing. If you behave like that, you're basically living a lot of lies. You wind up being unfaithful with the woman you're with. You've got to come up with an excuse. One lie breeds another. It's a mess.'

This is a conclusion that has not come from serial monogamy, but from serious therapy. He used to go five times a week. Brutal honesty is not easy for an incorrigible romantic, who has spent his most heightened moments in self-delusion.

His love of self-sufficiency sits rather uncomfortably with all the yearning and hurt that is the sound of anyone who has a heart. This is trauma transferred into gorgeous, desperate music. The transition could not have been easy. He used to fall in love all the time.

'First impacts, they can dupe you. And I've been duped. We all have. There's a lot of camouflage that goes on in the first week of a relationship. Self-deception is practised. You think you're in love. It's like a cold. It lasts for three or five days, then you get over the cold and you may have lingering effects, like a cough.

'I've done things like seen a girl on a street in Copenhagen and gone back to that street corner the next day at the same time, hoping I'll see her again. In the meantime, in that twenty-four hour period, what I did in my head ... I've got to find her. God, she's the girl for me. You do these insane numbers ...'

We bond more. He sings advice about my love life. I hang on his every word about calling and not calling, about fooling oneself.

Burt is looking right at me. 'You have this piece of food stuck to your tooth,' he says. 'The one that sticks out. I used to have that.' He points his finger helpfully. 'And I'll bet you bite your lip at night. I know about lips and teeth.' And of course, that's not all he knows about.

Music and horses, he gets obsessive with. But not women. Not anymore, anyway.

'With horses, you can't be protective because it's out of your hands. You have no control and that's one of the reasons it's so appealing.' He owns a string of world-class racers and is very emotional about them.

He doesn't think about the age difference in terms of Jane and himself, but he thinks about having a six-week-old baby and a three-year-old son. He thinks, 'How long will they know me? Sometimes you think you're indestructible. Sometimes I think it will go on forever.'

And in a way, something always will. That night, Burt's limousine took me to the concert at the Florida University. He teased and twitched the Boca Raton Pops Orchestra in an unbelievably sexy way. And as the first strains of 'This Guy' came over, I was crying. It was the lush and swampy terrain of my childhood, my lost lovers, and the one of the moment. It was every emotion I'd ever felt, packed and essenced. I thought that I wouldn't mind if I died now, and then I understood about the *petit mort* – why they call it that. And as Burt told us, 'Without true love, we just exist.' Just for that moment, we in the audience all knew what it was about.

I've often considered what it would be like to be married to Burt. But I think Burt can empathize and write music sprung from the heart of neurosis. He doesn't want to live with it. I would be too much for him. I flew in from L.A. to London to see him play at the Albert Hall. Afterwards he said, 'I put suntan lotion on your nose.' And I said, 'You can put lotion on my nose any time.' And we all laughed. And that's as far as it's going to go with Burt.

MAD LOVE

Relationship of the Week
Daniel Day Lewis and Isabelle Adjani
26 February 1995

She once said it would be wonderful to have a relationship with a man who would be like a twin, then she met Daniel Day Lewis. It's not only that they look like each other: dark with implacable faces, stern lips and bruised and bruising eyes. In many ways Daniel Day Lewis and Isabelle Adjani ARE each other. Both tragedians, secretive, exotic, destructive, elusive. When he is asked where he lives, he answers, 'in transit.' Her reply to the same question is, 'I'm a nomad.' And this was during the past five years when they had been on and off with each other in Paris, in Los Angeles, in London, and when she rode pillion on his motorcycle across Italy and also conceived his child, a son.

They were not usually in the same country together for long. Peripatetic souls never settle, they prefer to keep love in their heart rather than in their house. Perfect for an uncommitted passion, but when a child was involved Day Lewis appears to have feared the stabilizing or possibly stagnating effect. He feared fatherhood and last week broke off their relationship *allegedly* by fax. Faxes and telephones have been important in their relationship. She has always been a telephone maniac without respect for hours and distance, all her life she's been a three or four times a night girl. It didn't matter if she was in Paris, New York, L.A., Japan. For dislocated souls it is easier, more bitter, more sweet to deal with the machine.

Both were born in one country but feel rooted in another. He feels his soul is Irish and although she lives in France, a few years ago she fled to Algeria to give her support to a youth movement. Both are warriors, showing courage on screen. There's madness in his method acting, asking to be beaten up to understand Gerry Conlan, the imprisoned char-

124

acter in *In The Name Of The Father*, living as a paraplegic to play Christy Brown, using only his left foot and asking actors to spoon-feed him. And then suddenly he wants to throw it all away, give it all up, to be a cabinet-maker.

She fought passionately for the movie *Camille Claudel*. She financed it and seized on the part of Claudel as if her life depended on it – Claudel was the mistress and muse and doomed passion of Rodin. After the sculptor left his mistress she, in a paranoid struggle to survive his huge and brooding shadow, destroyed her work and herself and spent the rest of her days in a lunatic asylum. Adjani got Bruno Nuytton, her ex-lover and father of her teenage son Barnaby, to direct it. He took some persuading. 'I would never ask Isabelle to jump from a plane in a film. She is quite capable of not opening the parachute just to annoy me,' he said. It is not emotional bravery that makes her not open parachutes, it's not even a risk, it's narcissism. She has often talked of love's dramas as a way of feeling alive with the only proof of love destructive proof.

People who find it easy to throw themselves outside of themselves so passionately and aggressively are often emotional cowards. But this is only the epidermis. Laced into their core is a similar dybbuk, a fixation where dead fathers howl at them and commune with them like ghosts. He fell apart when playing Hamlet at the National Theatre because it is said that, rather than the ghost of the King of Denmark, his own father visited him and told him awful things. His father, the Poet Laureate Cecil Day Lewis, was sickly, stern and distant, and therefore awe inspiring. He died just after his son's fifteenth birthday and Daniel was undone, went into self-destruct mode with a bottle of migraine pills. He has been haunted by the father he couldn't really love because he never really knew him. Both of them talk of longing to please their fathers. With Adjani this was a lifelong quest, an impossibility.

She had a father who was obsessed with her. His love was claustrophobic, a destructive force that became love as she knew it. She describes him as the love of her life. When she was a small girl her father forbade her to look at herself in mirrors. Her time in the bathroom was carefully rationed because he feared her contemplating her body. He managed to convince her that she was ugly and that when she went out into the world she would be rejected, never be loved by anyone except him.

She's still funny peculiar about mirrors. She describes the camera's mirroring lens in photographs as face rape, in movies it's okay because she's moving and therefore more in control. But what about looking into the mirror that shows her twin, the twin tortured soul. She must have seen the despair of her life in his eyes, the parallel universe, an abyss. Not just his pain and her pain folded into each others souls, but weakness and everything they knew and loathed about themselves.

Like minds are meshed together out of self-interest and self-absorption. Scientifically, as with magnets, like repels like. In relationships what is emotionally compelling can also be repulsive. Which is probably why Day Lewis and Adjani had short spurts of living together before redesigning the relationship in their own heads in another country. It could have wandered on forever if she had not thrown in the wild card, the pregnancy. Which makes her altogether less wild, more smothering, yet perhaps reckless in an unpleasant way.

Although Adjani has been called the French Garbo because of her reclusiveness, he is even more of a lone soul. 'I am alone, but I prefer it that way. I don't go in search of new people.' One gets a feeling that it was she who was the more erotically assertive. His sexuality is colder while her emotions are brittle. Once they snap she's hot.

Day Lewis has been romantically linked with Winona Rider, Sinead O'Connor and Julia Roberts, but doesn't ever seem to have had a substantial proper relationship. Several of his friends have commented on how he likes to keep his distance from women, how he flirts without intent, often keeps them in other countries. Adjani, although skittish, is much more assertive and more obviously needy.

In the past she has been receptive to father figures, mentors, directors, and a longstanding romance with Warren Beatty who is eighteen years her senior. But it is her actual father and the conflicting fear and love she felt for him that informs her every emotional urge. She was so besotted with him as a little girl she wanted to 'save, rescue, nurse, change him.' She was already condemned because the man she wanted and the men to whom she is attracted are by her own admission 'unfinished characters', characters 'in which the child still lives, this is what moves me. Finished characters are of no interest to me.'

The trouble is that unfinished characters are children who do not necessarily want to be nurtured. Children quite often want to run away from other children, especially those they have fathered. It was frightening enough when they looked in the mirror and saw each other. For Day Lewis to look in the mirror and see a further replication was just too much for him to bear.

Day Lewis decamped to New York where he was living with his personal fitness trainer until she discovered he was engaged to Arthur Miller's daughter. It was the family and the breeding, and more to the point, it seems like it was the father he wanted to marry into. He met Rebecca Miller on the set of The Crucible. *He was reported to have written to Arthur Miller saying that he might show up on his doorstep 'with adoption papers.' He explained his letter to her father saying, 'There is something about Arthur Miller that makes you wish he was your father.' And now he is.*

Never trust a person who likes to fax.

It means they're passive aggressive, can't say what they think, mean what they say, and say it when they feel it. It's for people who need an excuse never to say yes, never to say no. Instead they say put it on a fax. Faxes can't be passionate. They are used sometimes to end relationships when the emotion is dried out like an old leaf. They can't be angry, they can't be demanding, because they are sent to a vacuum. They are very narcissistic.

Kirsty used to use the fax all of the time to end relationships. She used to spend not just a lot of time, but a lot of working-out in the emotional gymnasium to hone perfect, brilliant words and phrases, to tell them exactly what she thought of them. And it was always cruel and witty and brilliant, and no one could interfere with the perfection of the statement. No one could ever stop her from getting the last word in. Faxes are for people who love the last word, but usually the last word is not what you really want. You want a response. Otherwise, you're sending all of that energy, all that heart, into the unfathomable.

Sometimes you really do want the last word, but because it was a fax you'll never know whether you really got it. For instance, recently, I telephoned my agent. My agent was notorious for not calling me back. He's been waiting for the manuscript of my novel for years, but in the meantime, because he was my agent, I thought it a prerequisite of an agent that they deal with all your literary output. As I had been offered a deal for this book, I felt I should allow him to negotiate it. After he hadn't called me back three times, I told his assistant that I'd gone ahead and done the deal myself, therefore I supposed that was the end of our relationship. And what happened? He tried to fax me back the next day, pronto. I lied and said I didn't have a fax machine or number because I hate faxes so much. But the assistant read the fax, which wished me luck. The final line said, 'call me old fashioned, but I just couldn't wait any longer.' Now he couldn't speak to me and say this. No. Because by faxing it, he has turned around the rejection.

A fax is not a conversation. I find that my language becomes stilted, clumsy, especially reduced to fit on the page, a page that's going somewhere completely uncovered and you don't know who will see it, so you speak differently than with the spontaneity of a telephone or the intimacy of a letter. Hannah says that she has developed an entirely different language for faxes which involves a lot of exclamation marks.

Somehow, the very reason the fax was invented, speed, is avoided. There is only *faux* immediacy. For instance, where you now make a professional fax to request something, you used to just make a phone call and then you'd get a call back. Now, you make a call and they tell you to fax. This is because no one wants to say, 'I'm not interested in your idea, treatment, proposal' in case they change their minds or simply because they haven't got the guts to say no. A publicist friend of mine, says, 'They use technology because they can't deal with people. The faxee likes power and likes to waste other people's time. They like to give you hope when there is none. They are people who can't decide, so they keep you hanging on. Sometimes they say, "Oh I never got your fax." Blaming technology for human error and human frailty is cruel.'

Danny said that he sent his CV seven times, phobic that it never arrived at the other end. Now he feels an idiot. He also says he hates the noise that they make. I hate them also because they're like doorbells. The telephone, you can screen that with a machine. A fax is unsolicited and irritating. And a stupid menu is always coming though just at the time when you want to send things out.

When I'm forced to send faxes for, say, an interview request, I know I can never be as passionate or as persuasive. You feel forced to address potential problems, fully realizing you could be inventing them. Technology does not move as fast and intuitively as the human brain. Danny got a fax which said 'Danger Fax.' Then it churned out another fax which said 'Let's have lunch.' What a waste of time. And how self-conscious to think that that was funny.

Liam, of course, loves faxes. He says it's because 'I can make my point without having a conversation, when I don't feel like having one. Very practical.'

I didn't bother to tell him that when other people made their point to him via a fax machine, his was always spilling with demands for overdue money, sensitivity or chores to be attended, and he let them pile up in curls in the fax room and never even read them.

Never trust a person who doesn't leave a message on the answer machine.

They do it when they want to talk so much they can't speak. They can't identify themselves in case they are rejected. They think you might not call back. When you hear the sound of someone hanging up on your answering machine, it is a sign that they love you more than you love them but they don't want to admit they need you. Their silence is the emotional proof that they are terrified of any reaction. I used to have an announcement on my machine that said, 'Hello. This is Chrissy. Please leave a message unless you're a neurotic needy obsessive, in which case you'll hang up.' This was when I was getting five hang-ups a day. At least two of them could be counted as PRs who had already left two messages that were unreturned. But, with three of them, you could tell by the time of day and the way the phone was hung up that it was Him. I had this relationship that mostly took place on the phone. You know, phone boys; men who are emotionally castrated, so they need the telephone as their tool. Their weapon, their 'ego. They can say anything on the phone because it doesn't blush. It's always hard and shiny and it doesn't show the dark panic in one's eyes. But the very boys who love long phone conversations are also the ones who most often sigh and hang up when they get the machine. My rows with this particular man were always on the phone. They ended in one of us slamming the phone down and his only way of apologizing was to ring and not leave a message. This was years ago. I expect new technology, the arrival of 1471 and 141 has ruined all his fun. It has certainly ruined the life of my friend Kirsty. 'I feel like the gun-club people must do, having had their hand guns taken away from them. The hang-up is my favorite hobby' she says. 'In spite of 1471, I still do about ten a week. I do it because I want to check up on them. I want to know if they are where they say they're going to be. The person you want to call most you shouldn't. But you still have to. Usually I 141 so when he dials 1471 to find out who's called last, he finds my number has been with-held. It's addictive.'

Another friend of mine is plagued with calls from a needy ex-boyfriend. He never leaves a message and always uses 141. But he always calls at 8.30a.m. so she knows it's him. There's nothing wrong with leaving a bunch of messages. It's endear-ing. No shame in that. But if someone doesn't leave a message it's because they're ashamed of their need.

My friend Liam, who always has some kind of catatonic crush on someone, is always not leaving messages on the object of his desire's voice mail. I think this is because he fears she will do to him what he does to her. Whenever she calls, any friend who happens to be passing by is subjected to listening to the tape. There follows a half-hour discussion on the emotional significance of the intonation of the words 'Hello, it's me. I'll call you later.' There's something crazed and stalker-like about ringing someone's answering machine and then hanging up. Nobody who is in a healthy relation-ship would indulge in such a practice. Either they wouldn't bother calling at all or they would simply leave a message like any normal person. Kirsty knows this, but she still persists. Since the advent of 1471, she has press-ganged her friends into dialling the person she is involved with from their home numbers. It's less embarassing for her. Unfortunately, they are not all naturals. 'My advice is to rehearse first in case they answer. You'd be surprised how they do a simple sorry-wrong-number wrong. Once, this friend of mine started up a whole conversation about surnames and chatted for so long that I could never introduce her to my boyfriend in case he recognizes her voice.' Hang-up people may think that 141 protects them, but it doesn't. I mean who else, except for an involved person would be ringing at 2 a.m.? Everyone has a time of day when their phone-need matches their spare moments, and if you are a constant screener, you know the number of seconds your regular caller takes listening to your voice before putting the phone down. Anyway, don't kid yourself. The domain of those who consistently hang up is restricted to lovers, would-be lovers, or ex-lovers.

Relationship of the Week
Liam Gallagher and Patsy Kensit
31 March 1996

The more I know about Liam Gallagher, the less I like him. For a start, never trust a man who checks into a hotel, code-name: Lucifer. Dull. Never trust a man who said his band is bigger than Jesus. You know he's not original. Never trust a man who talks about Paul McCartney all the time. Never trust a man who mixes his icons – God, the Devil, Lennon – and also copies Pete Townsend. He said that he expects to die before he gets old. Actually, before he gets to thirty. He's twenty-three, full of boast, and used to call Patsy Kensit his dove. Never trust a man who says, 'A fit bird is a fit bird. That's why I like Americans.' Never trust a man whose eyebrows meet in the middle, who doesn't have the guts to be wolf on the inside because he's too busy being a dog on the out.

Liam is not attractive, yet he's been invested with attractiveness because he is more attractive than his brother, who writes the songs he sings, and he is a famous pop star. But he seems to be a cartoon pop star with no real verve, and barely an original thought in his head. He behaves badly, as he thinks rock stars should behave. He swears a lot, talks about pulling a lot. He and Patsy Kensit have reputedly split up now after a few months together. Last week he was accused of flirting with former *Brookside* actress Anna Friel at a party and refusing to let poor Patsy join their conversation. She apparently ran off back to London blubbering, hormones a go-go, reportedly saying that she had just told him she was expecting his child. 'The last thing I need is a little Liam,' he says. Never trust a man who assumes his first-born will be a boy and named after him.

There has been some dispute as to whether the two are still having a relationship and there is also some dispute as to whether or not there is really a baby. All I can say is, Patsy, I know you like to be validated by pop stars, and when Big Audio Dynamite were hip you married the band's keyboard player Dan Donovan. But that was because you were young and frail. And I know you later married Jim Kerr, but that was when Simple Minds were big and you needed a Dad and a friend. And I know you said that because Jim was your only friend, you turned him into a mother, father, therapist and left him behind as a husband. God I know you must have been lonely, desperate, and Liam seemed like fun, because I know you like lads, because it reminds you of your dad, the heady cocktail of machismo and sentimentality. And I know Liam seems so fearless, and you are so afraid. But he's not. He's just scared and bolshy. In fact, he's the biggest mistake that any woman could make.

He's not as attractive as Damon from Blur. And if he weren't famous, he wouldn't be attractive at all. Patsy once said that she wanted to be famous more than anything else. She was 17 when she said it, and it keeps coming back to haunt her. 'Please God make me a star,' she said. But actually, that's OK. I was just saying to somebody the other day, 'We all want to be stars, don't we? And those who don't want it badly enough don't get it'.

But this is just it. If Patsy Kensit would only rate herself as an actress, as a human being, she wouldn't have to try to plug into being famous by being some pop star's muse. She's done some very bad movies. Lots of pouty-pouty, breasts and blondeness because she doesn't rate herself as an actress very much. Often, her clothes have been off because other people rate her body a lot. And she knows only too well what men like. Long blonde hair that smells fragrant, slim thighs, adoring eyes and no dirt behind the fingernails. On the whole, laddish men are threatened by clever women. Following her latest film, *Angels and Insects*, A.S. Byatt remarked that Patsy displayed stupidity in a clever way, that she put incredible intelligence into playing unintelligent women.

That's because she's spent her life doing that. These lads that she goes for are based on her father, Jimmy the Dip, an antique dealer who ran a nightclub, a friend of the Krays who spent time in prison, absent and adored and called 'Jimmy the Dip.' That's what lads want. It's hard to resist something you have a fatal attraction for. But perhaps, she thinks, out there, there's a man who's brute enough, clever enough and romantic enough for her. Lads are always the romantic ones. The more civilized the psyche, the more cynical the mind.

Jim Kerr was probably much better for her, but the relationship must have got boring. Apparently, they used to watch a lot of *Match of the Day*, drinking lager and eating take-away curry. I can see how Liam might have seemed more glamorous, more dramatic. In a way, there's nothing that makes you feel more alive than hurling your boyfriend's clothes out of a hotel window as she reportedly did a few days ago in Dublin.

Patsy, now 28, is torn between being a wild thing and a cosy thing. Her Catholicism, her loneliness, the deaths of her mother and her father have made her want to recreate snuggled-up suburban family love. She has always wanted lots of babies. She and Jim Kerr have a three-year-old son James. But she wants this fame thing too, because she equates being famous with the same kind of love. Public adulation is more comforting, less demanding than personal commitment.

In a way, hers and Liam's relationship is very public. Every day this week, there have been reports. On or off? Who dumped whom? Baby or no baby? And before that there were reams of public snogging pictures. Overkill on the public snogging front – it means the couple are more concerned with being validated by who they're with than with kissing them. They feel good that they've got someone whom other people want, but they don't question how much they want them.

A few weeks ago, Liam bayed at a pretty waitress for her phone number. When she gave it to him he allegedly screwed up the piece of paper without looking at it and flung it in front of her to humiliate her. How can anyone ever trust a pop star who has to score points off a waitress like this?

He grew up in a brawling family. Last time he saw his father, a decade ago, it was when his older brother hit him and put him into hospital, allegedly in return for violence inflicted. Who knows what Liam is trying to inflict on the world in return for his own grievances. Liam, who didn't have many jobs before he was a pop star, sometimes valeting cars for Manchester City, is graceless and takes himself too seriously. Patsy Kensit is achingly self-mocking and extremely gracious. I've written terrible things about her and she smiles at me so sweetly and knowingly whenever I run into her. She doesn't deserve Liam, but one hopes that he is merely a stepping stone out of a marriage that had become cavernous. Patsy Kensit can do much better than Liam Gallagher, but Liam Gallagher could never do better than Patsy Kensit.

Unfortunately, they remained snogging and screaming in public. Their marrage was on, it was off. It was the worst kept secret wedding in the history of the marriage ceremony. They blamed the media for Patsy taking a turn and checking into a clinic for tired people. We don't have to ask Mystic Meg to know that by the time he's 30, he may not be dead, but he'll most surely be single.

Never trust a person who asks too many questions.

They're always stupid questions because they're questions to which they already know the answer and they want to get a different one. They are insecure people who want to be made more insecure. They might tell themselves they want to be reassured but, actually, they provoke insult and abandonment. The kind of questions I am talking about are, 'Will you miss me? Do you love me? Do you think I look fat? Are you having an affair?' And if you're having an affair, 'What did you buy your wife for your birthday? Does she know about me?' All these questions already contain the answers. Do you love me means I love you and will you please tell me you love me back right now? Are you asleep means wake up.

My assistant Julia lives in a separate time-zone to her boyfriend Anthony. When she calls him at 3.30 in the morning or 6 a.m. or whatever completely inappropriate time, she says she has to ask, 'Did I wake you?' because she can't quite manage 'I'm sort of sorry to have woken you, but not enough to not want to have a telephone conversation.' He always says, 'No, you didn't wake me,' even though she always does and she finds this exceptionally chivalrous.

Julia is always very demonstrative with her bad moods. A black cloud hovers over her and her mouth inverts and falls into sullen. She looks like Shiksa, my black and white cat, angry to be trapped behind the window when she sees an imaginary bug or bird. It is pointless and futile to ask, 'Are you OK?' but I fall for it every time. It doesn't matter if she says yes or no. She clearly isn't. And about 50 per cent of the time, it's my fault.

It is extremely stupid to ask questions where you know the answer will stab you with pain or the answer will be a lie. Anna had this long-time boyfriend. 'Who is this woman you work with? What is she like? And why do you have a mobile phone for which only she has the number?' He described his secretary as big and hairy. She thought it meant armpits, legs, fat. It actually meant she had a mane of wild red hair and she was big in the breast department. He left Anna for his secretary and stopped needing the mobile phone.

Men's insecurities show when they get obsessed, not only that you might be unfaithful, but that you might have a past. It sort of counts as infidelity to them. They want to know how long did you go out with him? What was he like? Was it great sex? They want to know was it better than me? Because they're terrified that the previous boyfriend was better or bigger or could manage it for longer.

I know this woman Ruth, a crunchie, earthy sort. Lowers her eyes when she speaks to you, always a straight 'A' student. She's now 25, but by the time she was 18, she'd slept with 10 boys, then became sexually quiet until she fell passionately in love with Josh two years ago. The relationship was cosy-wosy until he started needling for details of former bed conquests. She told him. He was practically hurling himself at the ceiling and howling. She told him it meant nothing. That only made him worse. He left her and wishes that he had never asked the questions that he feared the answer to.

Men tend to ask more questions about the past. It's all part of their detached, compartmentalized minds, and then they'll thrust it into the present when they decide that they can't handle it, when they want to be masochists. Women, unfortunately are more concerned with asking stupid questions about the present.

I know you should ask no questions, and then you'll be told no lies but, only last week, I committed a fatality. I said, 'Will you miss me?' in a moment of cruel vulnerability. For one blink of a minisecond, I thought he might say, 'Of course.' But he said what I knew he would say. 'No. Why should I?' This is double-edged because if he'd just said no, I might have believed him, but 'Why should I?' is is a bit over-emphatic, therefore it's ambiguous.

A lawyer I know has had a successful affair for seven years. He has a very rich wife who he's never going to leave and before that, he was a serial heart-breaker. So how come it works with Rosa? 'She never asks me any questions so there are no bones of contention. I talk about Marcia (his wife) quite freely, but if she asked me, "What present did you buy her? Do you still sleep with her?" I would never tell her. As she never asks, there's never angst and that's why it's such an agreeable relationship. In the past, when girlfriends ask me questions about my wife, I felt like they were bunny-boilers. They wanted to know about her so they could hurt her, and it made me feel protective of her and wary that she was going to chop the arms off my suits, start dialing transatlantic speaking clocks and appear with a box of grass seeds, what-ever mad mistresses do. The very moment they know they're not getting what they want is when they ask you for it. Whenever they would say, "Do you still sleep with her?" is when I would end it.'

A person who asks too many questions is a person who has no understanding of the sacredness of personal space. The place you go to with one person is never the same as the place that person goes to with someone else. If you don't respect that, you don't respect yourself. When anyone has started to ask me too many questions, I can't be trusted not to hit them or not to walk away.

Relationship of the Week
Gillian Taylforth and Geoff Knights
5 February 1995

I have learnt to be wary of men who call their women babe. Often it is because they have so many women on the go it is safer, in case they confuse their names while making love to them. Whether it is true or not, I think if you use babe as a term of endearment it is quintessential barrow-boy language. It suggests you want psychologically to disempower your woman and make her as defenceless and small as a little baby.

Could this latter reason perhaps be why Geoff Knights is alleged to be fond of the word 'babe'? Sometimes this psychological submission process is tortuous. Certainly in Knights' case it has amounted to a form of public torture. Ever since he, former roofer, fax magnate, and property developer, started dating Gillian Taylforth, *EastEnders'* Kathy Beale, five years ago, their relationship has been a sensational public property. The most developed property he ever managed.

The most recent incident was Knight's cautioning by the police over what seemed to be a bit of oral sex in the back of a Range Rover. His and Taylforth's decision to sue the *Sun* over reporting the incident was to become the most titillating, salacious and degrading libel action of 1994. Having lost the case, they must have forked out something close to £500,000 in legal costs. It cost her much of her dignity and went to the very core of her sexual nature, a private area open to debate and abuse. This can only have left her feeling emotionally scarred, devastated and somewhat slutty. The pressure made the cracks in the relationship scream loudly.

Ten days ago, Knights tore her down publicly after she had crashed her new BMW with their young daughter Jessica in the back seat. Taylforth had been at an *EastEnders'* party and was charged with drink driving. Although she was stricken with remorse and fears for her daughter, Knights appears not to have minced his words, accusing her of drinking too much and accusing her family, Islington working class stock with whom Taylforth is close, of not being all there.

It seems as if he was half-auditioning for an unfit mother custody case. Meanwhile, the child pictured last week at her third birthday party at a North London restaurant, while her parents vowed to stay together for the sake of her, has eyes of hollow wonderment, disappointment and panic. If that weren't enough, one can imagine how Knights might use the very libel action, which he largely caused and which he was supposed to have encouraged to clean Taylforth's name, to make it dirty. 'Sex crazed mother, unfit.'

Like all womanizers Knights is brutal in his romanticism. Sugar spun sweet and then a verbal lashing from which it is hard to recover. Sometimes the lashing is even physical. Last year, after a bust-up with Knights, Taylforth had to wear shades to conceal a shiny black eye.

He now seems more than ready to blacken the soul and psyche of Taylforth. Breaking her and then breaking up and then making up again, usually in public. They have long since destroyed the intimacy that may have existed in their relationship, in the way that relationships typically degrade themselves. First of all you think nasty thoughts, then you say them to the person, then you say them to your friends.

He likes control, men of that kind usually do. She likes that too. It's been emotionally ingrained there. Her late father Ronnie, a printer, is supposed to have ruled his four daughters with a rod of iron. Taylforth lived at home until she was 28 and she had to be home before midnight every night. She disliked his control, often rowed, but loved him deeply and was devastated when he died. She is, it seems, repeating a similar pattern.

Knights has said on occasion that he would like her to choose between *EastEnders* or him. She says she resents it, but she is still there with him. And what exactly is it about *EastEnders* that makes her in any way an unfit partner? He admits she is a good actress. Because she occasionally goes out for a drink after work with her on-screen boyfriend Steve McFadden? That she socializes with Tony Jordan, the *EastEnders* scriptwriter? Knights publicly slates Jordan whenever he gets the chance.

This is a man with a hole in his pocket and a purdah problem. He now does not seem to like his girlfriend working, although she is probably the more regular breadwinner. He was often touted as a millionaire businessman. He promoted this, dealt in that. He was and is a man with too much time on his hands and probably too much envy in his heart. Perhaps the car accident incident ended up as an excuse for him to fume because really he doesn't want her even to be driving in her own car, therefore she should be banned from it like a proper purdah partner.

They first met in a bar. They both liked each other because they were both wearing the same gold bracelet. Was it fate or just that they both came from the same place, a hard background, shrunken in its ideals that somehow made this pair aspirational? It is sometimes easy to confuse her with her screen character, Kathy Beale. She herself has said that she is not as tough, she sees herself more as Princess Di, having a catalogue of terrible things happen to her. In other words she sees herself as a victim.

She is the star, she has the power. He was attracted to that yet now he seems to want to diminish it. These are the actions of a broken man. He has seemed even more emasculated since he's had to sell his Ferrari to help pay the libel costs, and you know what they say about men who own Ferraris.

Problems are easily traced, right back to base. And that's certainly where he wants to be. Last week when they are back together for the sake of Jessica he decides to be openly contrite saying, 'The poor girl (Taylforth) is on her knees at the moment and I want her to know there's someone there for her.' That kind of submission probably makes them both feel better. That's why the relationship doesn't simply end, that's why the abuse is compelling. They also see it as some strange

141

romantic transcendence of love. High drama means high adrenalin. High rage is often a substitute for passionate sex although sometimes one fuels the other.

It is hard to know whether Knights prefers sex or the ego gratification that often comes with it. In their five-year on-off relationship he has not been wholly faithful. Perhaps that is why he can be suspicious and jealous of his fiancée. She has been a fiancée for four years. Men who makes their girlfriends fiancées often do so because they want control without commitment. They feel they can behave badly and still have approval. Not making a decision is a weakness, but they see it as a strength, something to make their girl strive for, work for. That old treat 'em mean and keep 'em keen maxim.

She must know about the women who have kissed and told. But no matter how badly he sometimes behaves she's caught up in the forgiveness syndrome. She will not release him.

Even though he exudes a primitive kind of love, part of her even seems to admire it, and the more beastly he is the more sweet she is. She seems to see his brutish behaviour as a strength because it controls her, and the submission to it must make her feel small and womanly, and wrapped in a great passion. She has compared their relationship with the Richard Burton/Elizabeth Taylor romance. But actually Taylforth and Knights are icons in themselves, not in passion but in spiritual weakness, desperation, wincing manhood and an element of victimhood.

SAD LOVE

Relationship of the Week
The Maxwells
16 June 1996

During the 131 days of her husband's trial for fraud, Laura Maxwell, a willowy blonde, showed up every day. She said that she and her husband 'were like two old pack horses, leaning on each other when the load got too heavy.' Such a thin thing to be leaned on, but she became steely with dignity, enabling her husband, the older Maxwell brother Ian, to affect disinterest in the proceedings, to lie back, his eyelids often drooping, reclining in full nonchalance. Outside the court, their hands clenched and gripped each other. Inside themselves there was a passionate kernel. She said, 'No matter what these people do, they can never get inside us, they can never take away what matters most to us: our love for each other, our sense of ourselves.' Sadly, it seems that it was in fact the trauma of the court case which gave them a sense of themselves.

Their relationship became rigid in its role playing. Without passionate intensity provided by impending humiliation and destruction, there was no relationship. With customary dignity, Laura announced last week, 'While we remain close and share a strong mutual affection, we are no longer living together.' In fact, her husband is supper-dating a racy young brunette, a polo-playing City bonds trader called Dalit Cohen who has a very rich father and not much to be insecure about. Ian Maxwell is attracted to extremes, attracted to the kind of detachment afforded by submerging himself into something totally alien. This comes from his close and simultaneously distant relationship with his father who is said to have alternated love with the most dreadful bullying. Blood bond intimacy with intricate secrecy. I really believe that Maxwell's power was to tell nobody what he was doing. Of course, both his sons could suspect, but could they really know about exactly what was happening to the £22 million of pension funds? The trial acquitted them, but somehow it was not a glorious victory. There was no jubilation. There was simply a sense that something terrible had been worked through. When the intensity was over, it was like a bereavement. There was a barrenness. I've heard stories of women who have had miscarriages and suffered dreadfully. For a while, the suffering unites them with their partners. Then they can only identify their partners with a pain that won't go away. This metaphor comes to me because Laura said many times how she specifically put off having children until their future was more certain. It is as if the trial became their monstrous baby. The only way they could find a release was by escaping from each other. Their relationship was not like knitting a family, not like Kevin and Pandora. Hoards of kids, the bondings of practicality to keep them going. Ian and Laura Maxwell were much more intense. The reason she's so calm now is that the release was cathartic.

They were married for five years. He was hard-working, clever but weak, had the joint forces of arrogance and a need to please working within him. He always had the ability to detach himself, which is alluring and dangerous, and basically shifty. But what you can't trust about him is that he chose to marry her on his birthday, as if she was a present to him. Never trust anyone who has to buy themselves their own birthday present. It means they've got no friends.

She was a small-town American girl, a basketball player, whose height made her a successful catwalk model, whose strength made her loyal, and whose loyalty made her stronger. She was quiet but articulate, shelved a television career which she later took up again when circumstances changed. Six months into the glittering life in the millionaire tycoon dynasty, Robert Maxwell drowned. The glitter was smashed into smithereens. She was turfed out of her smart house and on to a moped which she drove to court. At the time, when she was asked how she coped, how she was so steadfast, she said, 'I didn't consider it exceptional.' Once you consider the exceptional commonplace, the commonplace becomes unnattainable and suddenly, in the topsy-turvy world, she found she had married him for poorer, not richer, for worse, not better. Laura saw herself as Ian's lover, not ever a mother figure, as if it was just the two of them and the world. He had never experienced loyalty like this. His own father had depended on him, then sacked him for not collecting him from the airport, then hired him again two months later. How could he know what was real? Ian Maxwell was frightened of his father. Both boys were. In his presence, they were nervous and silent, always waiting to see which way the wind would blow. They questioned nothing outwardly. Yet, on the inside, they must have questioned everything. This kind of scenario probably means that if you have a wife who is out there, does everything for you, gives you no need to question anything, you are inherently mistrustful. Not at her or the relationship, but that such loyalty and straightforwardness could ever be given to you. Those who are bullied equate humiliation with love. During the humiliation of the trial, the love could nestle nicely. Their love could have grown, but only in relation to the trauma of the trial and the need for basic survival. With this kind of pressure, it would have been disloyal to examine the relationship in any other way. With the pressure gone, a new mirror comes into play. Who knows what they saw? Perhaps an ugly reminder of a past they'd rather forget. Robert Maxwell had approved whole-heartedly of Laura. Perhaps, though, Ian Maxwell didn't want to have his approval, or anything that he approved of. There is a sense that she, who would never have left him, feels released from the fairy tale that turned into a nightmare. There is a sense that the role she played of pack-horse overcame her until there was nothing left of her. That the relationship couldn't move because it was only about surviving pain. Ian and Laura had forgotten the principles of pleasure. To find them again, they must leave their relationship behind.

Relationship of the Week
John Major and Jean Kierans
19 February 1995

I have always been suspicious of men who kept hamsters. For a start people in some way always *are* the animals they keep. Hamsters are a pet with no status; something kept in a cage, hidden away, nothing to show off about. John Major used to keep a hamster. Things are so easy to control in a cage. A love of things caged seems to me synonymous with putting passion in a box.

Jean Kierans, his first love, his inspirational, sentimental, older-woman love. Thirteen years older, she was the one who encouraged in him a political dream that she could never be part of. She was an unsuitable consort, not a quiet, mousey arm-piece, she was a vibrant, sexy, cream of skin and dark of hair divorcee with two children. She seemed womanly in a way that it is difficult to imagine the young John Major matching with manliness.

At first examination the revelations about the affair in the *Daily Mail* seemed a massive puff for Major. The idea that he could be capable of passion of any sort, even stifled and quaint, seemed an improvement. But after examining Jean Kierans' sad, docile account of their affair that was the love of her life, that turned her inside out, that had her watching resignedly, watching him leave his flat, almost opposite from where she lived, and walk down the street to work every day for three and a half years, we see Major as sanctimonious and sentimental and a brutish coward.

It all began rather sweetly. They met at a church meeting, a Saturday night somewhere to which John had wanted to wear his new Burtons suit. It was 1965 but things in the young Tory's head were hardly swinging. He was never capable of radical thought. It was almost like pursuing a schoolboy fantasy, seducing the glamorous older woman neighbour.

She was a remedial teacher, a carer, seemingly attracted to a young man in the special needs division of life. She was 35 and he was 22. After a few weeks their affair was consummated. She, and of course the times, demanded discretion. It was the 1960s, yes, but in that hushed-up Brixton suburbia world of Conservative association cheese and wines, school concerts and vicars popping in and out, it may as well have been the 1930s.

She says that he was even more fanatical about discretion. For discretion read discomfort, possible paranoia, the hiding of all things true and basic and darkly seated in the sexual psyche and soul. For discretion read shame. Yet at the same time for Jean it was a blissful physical, mental and spiritual mingling. It was cosy, supportive and loving in every way. It lasted five years during which time he hardly ever stayed the night. It was rumpy-pumpy when the children were in bed and then usually he left.

After passing his banking exams he had been sent to work for a branch of the Standard Chartered in Nigeria where he was involved in a horrible car crash. It was Jean who arranged his homecoming, and he elected to stay with her in Kevin's room instead of with his family. Jean's was a shared bathroom and he had to be helped in and out of the bath with his leg injury. He bathed therefore in his swimming trunks. Whatever was going on was deep and conveniently hidden. But how deep?

The ambiguity of his passion seemed to have Jean rapt. There were many sublime suburban days, cycling, watching cricket, going to the football, her school concerts, where they were accepted as a total couple. Yet the stability was shadowed by his hardly ever staying the night, a ghastly premonition surely that he was not likely to stay the relationship.

Her mother wondered when they would get engaged and she hoped he would marry her, but she didn't hope too hard. All the time she thought that no other two could be as happy as they. Generally women feel that their power is in the present whereas men plan for their future, no matter how

they are enthralled. It wasn't just the age difference, it was the
two children, Kevin and Siobhan. He was good with them,
but they did not fit, the package was always going to be an
encumbrance.

She had divorced her husband. He went to Australia,
didn't pay maintenance. She was by all accounts self-reliant
and self-effacing, sadly all too glad she had anybody, which
built up the Major ego into one that told him she was lucky
to have him, when in fact it was clearly the other way round.

She has been talked of as a Mrs Madrigal figure in
Armistead Maupin's *Tales of the City* series, fussing and
mothering, giving out rooms in her house, a carer. In fact
pretty much close to the archetypal maternal icon for
thwarted Tory passion. Warm, strong, undemanding, always
there when you need her and cleanly disposable when you
don't. Major seemed to be completely controlled by his own
mother who was appalled by Jean when she learnt of the age
difference. They planned a holiday in Spain. His mother
insisted she came with them and plonked herself down in the
middle of three single beds in their boarding-room. What
kind of a woman would accept this spineless behaviour? A
foolish one perhaps, but one who was blighted by her big, big
love for him. He once told her she was too much of an 'accep-
tavist'. She says looking back it's just as well she was.

She would tell him all the time, as he scooped her in his
arms and carried her up the street, that she loved him. He told
her he would never say that to a woman unless he could add
the words and I want to marry you. Crazily she admired this
as a strength. He usually kept his glasses on when he made
love to her and was excessively paranoid about making her
pregnant. She didn't think this was odd. Undue care taken
over contraception can be massively unsexy and a kind of
rejection. Still, his glasses were on and her vision was blurred.

She recounts many presents he gave her, a picture of a
church from Amsterdam, an umbrella, an antique pendant
that later she had to remorsefully sell, a blue glass bowl from
Sweden days before he ended the affair. If a person is over-

active in the present department it is often suspicious – providing materialistic jollies to substitute the love that cannot come out of his heart, or at best a language of his heart that he cannot articulate.

Once she opened the fridge and found a toy suede dog they called Plute. He had said that the dog was to look after her when he couldn't be there. Such a callous sentimentality. Why couldn't he be there? She wasn't married to anyone else and neither was he. He couldn't be there because he didn't want to be there.

She pet-named him Rover, a dog's name. In her dreams he was a faithful lapping thing, but in reality he was calculating and didn't like telling the full truth. His valediction was controlled and cowardly. He told her that he wanted to be an MP, there was to be no more making love, then there was to be no more kissing and then there was to be no holding hands. In his small mind he could not equate making himself happy with the thought of making himself successful. Or else he thought he was a boxer and surmised that the political sparring could be enhanced if he retained his energy by not spilling his seed.

Then he seemed to return to her arms for a six-week Indian summer. They were hand in hand walking in the blossom in the dusk and the physical relationship did resume, but it was only his compartmentalized way of saying goodbye because he had already decided he could not see her again. He did a trip to Sweden and did not call her as promised the night of his return. Eventually he came round acting awkward and said he'd met a girl called Norma, 'and I am going to marry her. She looks just like you.' Like this was some carrion comfort, and he expected her to be flattered. And because she so adored him she mistook his cowardice for control although her heart was broken.

For many years she has written to him without signing her name, knowing he'll recognize her handwriting. It is an extra-ordinary blend of self-effacement and self-confidence. She may take some pleasure in the theory that all men are cowards and they never marry the woman they really love, always the second best, always the duplicate, because they hate being controlled by passion. When it came down to it, he simply wasn't up to it. He didn't deserve her.

I wonder if she was happy or sad when he lost the election so spectacularly. She clearly doesn't have a resentful bone in her body, so she was probably pleased that now he could relax while there was still time for him to become the person he always could have been.

Relationship of the Week
Michael and Cheryl Barrymore
21 May 1995

I've always thought that Cheryl Barrymore looks something like a drag queen, vulnerable and brassy, Tizer-haired with those massive and mobile lips. There's something high camp and highly unreal about her. Theatrical family, an adored dancing child, all the hallmarks for that kind of larger than life that is so unworldly. Everything is extreme.

Thin as a wire but a powerhouse of strength, a stalwart. Not just Michael's wife of eighteen years but his manager since she met him on stage at a tangy revue and decided she would make him.

Sure he made it from bankruptcy, a Bermondsey council flat to the brink of super-stardom and alcoholic disaster, yet managed to remain more or less the same – hypersensitive and lizard-tongue fast, funny, edgy, and super self-critical. What changed in his life is that he famously and painfully quit his addiction to booze. Booze blots, booze blurs.

This is a man whose psychological turmoil reeks through his comedy. He didn't necessarily turn to booze through pressure and stress – he flung himself into his work, also to blot. The terror of what he is blotting must be huge. It's to do with who he is and why he is. Last week he was still running – out the door and a three-day disappearance after a demented row with Cheryl. Eighteen years in and it's still high drama, high passion, intense. Another addiction. Now they're back cosy cute.

The whole issue of his relationship with Cheryl is not so much fudged in his autobiography, but smeared to death by chocolate sauce. The postcards she wrote him, that sing, 'I'm going to love you like nobody's loved you, come rain or come shine. Happy together, unhappy together, won't it be fine.' The people at the rehab centre said he was addicted to alcohol and she was addicted to him. Perhaps to her that was fine.

She loved him enough for all the people who hadn't loved him. The drunken gambling father who in a stupor tried to shoot him, pointing a gun through the letter box. The mother he feels let him down that day by not standing in front, protecting fiercely. Cheryl protects fiercely enough for the both of them. Since marrying her his relationship with his mother, a hardy little matriarch, undemonstrative and unpraising became gradually more and more distanced.

From day one Cheryl was the predator who wanted the best for her boy. He lapped it up. She was lithe and forceful and, he said in his book, paid him attention like no other person had ever done before.

Sure there's the odd reference to you always hurt the one you love. But it's not quite as explicit as their former writing partner Ricky Green was in the *Daily Mirror* earlier this year, where Barrymore was described as calling his wife an old has-been cow and she would scream back, 'You stayed with me because I made you.'

And yes, yes, she did have a lot to do with the making of the man. He's dyslexic. She read his scripts. Screamed at directors she didn't think treated him right. Provided him with a ready-made family. Her dad Eddie was his father substitute and he was welcomed so overwhelmingly by her mother Kitty that it was a whole other world, an escape from being unloved.

She chose his clothes. Packed his suitcases. Did so much for him that if the phone rang he never thought of answering it, she would always do that for him. He is dismayed with himself that he can't pack his own suitcase 'but it suits Cheryl because I muck things up.'

When this sort of thing first happens to an unloved person it's comforting. After a while it's controlling, smothering. And then it's totally debilitating. You can't do anything for yourself and feel more worthless than you did in the first place. All you can do is provide yourself with a secret life where everything feels different. And Michael Barrymore did just this. He drank secretly. Kept hidden bottles in the car-boot and would pop down to the garage of their home. Wherever it was that he was running to, heading into alcoholic bleariness, or last week, away to friends, it must seem as though he can never really run from Cheryl.

Living together and working together must always be a pressure cooker, particularly when you know your wife made a contract. If ever you separate, she'll still be your manager.

The lying about the drink excluded her. Obviously she must have felt bad about that. She was mummy and daddy's dancing darling, a spoilt controlling child. They don't have children. She can't. 'Simple as that,' he says, in the way you know it isn't simple. With their spaghetti limbs and haunted looks they've kind of coalesced. They are each other's child. And they parent a white westie. I've always thought that long men who walk little square westies are in denial. Westies are sweet and sentimental and bright. There is something so sombre about Barrymore.

I feel the sex life of people who can't have children is somehow diminished, if procreating isn't an ultimate option. It's as if that sexual creative urge was totally sublimated into her ambition for him. She was nurturing the vortex, being sucked into his fears and insecurities, constantly demanded of, constantly urging him to new goals. It can't have been very satisfying for her. Even if she did make life happen for him, it is she who is the real addict. She consumes him and is consumed by him.

When the people from the rehab centre wanted to counsel her she tossed them off as jargonistic Americans. They tried to tell her that she was an individual and he was an individual and that they should live separate lives. 'They pulled you apart to rebuild you. We didn't need rebuilding. It was that simple.' She said it in the way that makes you know it isn't simple.

She found it difficult to adjust to the fact that someone else had tried to heal her boy. She seemed jealous. 'Once I got him back that was it. They had no chance.' How sad to be in competition with rehab people. Perhaps jealousy also lurked when she saw recent newspaper photographs of Michael spontaneously embracing a fellow AA member in the street after driving him home. Feeling so purposeless can't be good for her, or him. They both protest so much that nothing is wrong. It must be. It's that simple. He describes her as eclipsing all else around her, which is a shady compliment. Who wants to be eclipsed by their wife? Who wants to be lessened by anybody? Yet those two seemed compelled to diminish each other – Cheryl because she is addicted to being diminished and Michael because he needs it so she can build him up again. She is still tantalized by him, and predatory. I feel that this is because even in intense closeness, he is also distanced from the world and from himself. That encourages her to submerge herself as if she is diving to find him. But he has purposefully lost himself. He likes the camera and he likes the audience because they don't talk back. They don't ask questions. He hates interviews, wants to control everything that's said about him.

When his mother and brother did some revelatory stuff in the tabloids, he felt 'suicidal.' Sure, be angry, be bewildered, but suicidal because your mother said you had a sad life? Humour is of course a way of releasing anxiety. The process of converting fear to funny is well-trodden ground. For Barrymore, the more he tried to convert terror to laughter, the more it reverberates, redoubling its echoey power. He always has to find somewhere new to run. If he could only bear to face who he is, perhaps he might be able to pick up his own telephone.

Since I wrote this piece, heavily hinting that certain things were being blotted out and suggesting that you never trust a person who says 'it was that simple', we have learned what it was that he was blotting. He came out. Cheryl perhaps realized that she couldn't love him enough for all the people who didn't love him because, in one vital way, she was the wrong person doing the loving. However, I'm sure they both still sing to each other, 'I'm going to love you like nobody loves you, come rain or come shine.'

Relationship of the Week
Elizabeth Taylor and Her Looks
19 May 1996

Elizabeth Taylor has survived many husbands. Some have died; some have abandoned her; some loves have turned her inside out with pain. She has survived two hip replacements, back pain, colitis, sciatica, pneumonia, even alcoholism and pain-killer addiction. She has lived through fat and thin, through diamonds and divorce. The number of serious operations she has undergone outnumber her marriages – all eight of them – at least two to one. And yet she's still standing.

Sure she's an actress, but she's much bigger than that. A legend that wouldn't lie down. She is her own Oprah Winfrey show, her own grand opera. So when we see her as a woman in a dressing-gown, as we did last week after she was snapped in the garden of her villa in Cannes, it's arresting. We stare at her pinkness, her plumpness, her pin-eyes, her sadness. We stare, searching for the physical beauty we thought was innate, yet at the same time experiencing a cruel, voyeuristic thrill. It hurts to look at this picture. We feel we are somewhere we shouldn't be because we are seeing a 64-year-old woman with no make-up. A woman we might once have felt jealous of. After all, she could get any man she wanted. Ah, we think, but look at her now.

It makes me feel the way I did as I watched the recent documentary about Marlene Dietrich. Marlene hid herself, masked her whole body and face. Her legs were festering under plaster because she had fallen over so many times drunk but, even so, she covered the reality in a shimmering sequinned sheath because that's what stars were supposed to do. Marilyn and James Dean died before they had to worry about carrying the baggage of years on their faces, and Taylor could have died so many times and nearly did. She might have abused her ballooning body, felt like hell, drunk too much, eaten too much. But, above all, she wanted to survive. And living meant eating, serious eating, the scary kind that builds fleshy buffers against disappointment.

This made her weight see-saw, sometimes as much as 40lbs in one year. But she would rather live in pain than die. I felt guilty when I first saw the snatched picture of her last week. Guilty because Taylor always arouses such conflicting emotions. Words can't hurt her, but pictures can. I felt dirtied to be looking at this picture in a way that, for instance, the pictures of the Princess of Wales not sweating very much in the gym did not make me feel.

Here we see Portrait of an Icon in a Dressing-Gown. I remember a 1960s black-and-white film called *Woman in a Dressing-Gown*, and my Aunt Tiger telling me dressing-gowns should never be worn after 10.00a.m., otherwise you were a slut, you were louche. Still, whatever you were, you weren't the airbrushed-like smoulder that appears in the ads for the scent White Diamonds.

But, after you get over the shock (and it is a shock to see one of the world's most enduringly alluring figures so pink and bleary) you think, well, the skin looks soft and nice, and the famous tadpole eyebrows are still there, it's just that there are a few pounds of misery weighing her down, and the kaftan looks synthetic (her fatal flaw was always kaftans).

And, for God's sake, the woman has just got up. She has been photographed in morning light and no woman over 23 is going to look that great shot first thing in the morning, and no woman looks exactly like her photograph. Real-life Liz may be as different from the pink kaftan as she is from the White Diamonds. Rather cruelly, she has been described as looking like a resident of an old peoples' home with overtones of Roseanne.

Well, let me tell you something about Roseanne. Once I was in L.A. and I was asked for my autograph. As I am often mistaken for Shannen Doherty, the former Beverly Hills 90210 star, I smiled. But the woman in the restaurant looked horrified when I told her I wasn't Shannen because she had mistaken me for Roseanne. She thought I would be complimented. But I almost threw my pasta in her face. Yet, Roseanne doesn't mind being Roseanne. She even took all her clothes off for a magazine.

Body fascism is a wicked thing, and it is hard to rise above it. The scales are our manacles and our mantra is thin equals gorgeous, fat equals ugly, and don't even mention old. Fortunately, Elizabeth Taylor has always looked upon her looks as a 'genetic gift'. 'What you are affects the way you look. If you are a selfish, hard person you can obliterate perfect features,' she once said in her book, about self-esteem and comfort-eating. Of course, she knows that if you like yourself enough you don't crave for that chocolate truffle to like you, too.

But with severe physical pain, fears for her life in January, and the idea that she has finally given up marriage with the departure of Larry Fortensky, eating must be one of the few pleasures left. Why should she feel guilty? Because pictures such as these punish her. We can all feel an empathetic sting. We have all seen unflattering pictures of ourselves.

The thing about Elizabeth Taylor is she touches you. She

always has. You do not remember her for her great acting. Sure, you remember the BC eyeliner she wore in *Cleopatra*. But you remember the rows and the tantrums with Richard Burton more. You remember him saying, 'I bred her in my bones', and you wish that had been said about you. But because she has lived through the same traumas of love and fatness as the rest of us, and then some, in a way we do think we are part of her. And she is a part of us. It's this transfiguration that makes her a goddess. And in a dressing-gown, she is still a goddess.

Liz managed to turn it all around with the bleached-out, shaven-headed look. By facing such a brutal crop, she dazzles as well as disconcerts.

Relationship of the week
John Osborne and Anthony Creighton
29 January 1995

John Osborne was sick when his father told him the facts of life. He told us in his autobiography, but it's only now that we know why. There were facts he didn't like, facts he felt alienated from. His work turned out to pivot around his sexuality, and it is this sexuality that may well have provoked him to unleash that famous anger.

In his life, he ostentatiously loathed four of his five wives: he repeatedly reviled homosexuals, called them cadging, called them criminals, he said he had been hag-ridden by poofs.

And only now do we begin to understand why he may have been so angry. Only now do we learn that one of the rare love affairs of his life was happy and stable, it withstood two marriages and did not finish in bile – a love affair in which he showed complete vulnerability and tenderness, the kind of loyalty and sweetness that has never been generally associated with him, was in fact with a man. A man he called Mouse because he was a small thing.

His name was Anthony Creighton and they collaborated on two plays when Osborne was in his twenties, *Epitaph for George Dillon* and *Personal Enemy* (the latter, being set in the McCarthyite 1950s, when Communists could be accused of being homosexual, was censored heftily).

Now we know that the playwright's anger was not merely anger, but a place to put his self-hatred. The revelation of his bisexuality, a month after his death at 65, throws everything into place. His prurient fascination with homosexuals, yet outward show of loathing for them, was a classic projection away from himself, by reviling other people. He found most disturbing in others what he found most disgusting in himself.

Osborne and Creighton (who revealed the relationship in an interview last week: 'It was a love affair, a good, happy, mutually supportive and enduring relationship') lived together while they were young actors in rep. Osborne, he said, did not even like to go to the postbox without him. When Creighton went away on tour, Osborne was almost maudlin in his pining. Creighton kept the love-letters: 'My love for you is deeper than I can bear to tell you to your face, it is so strong and indestructible. Never be in doubt about either this or my loyalty.'

At the end of last week, Osborne's widow, Helen, described the revelation as 'absolute tosh . . . there is no truth in it whatsoever'. But if we are to accept Creighton's account, Osborne was not looking back on anger but on lies. If you are living a lie loyalty turns itself inside out. He later wrote in his *Notebook* of 1964, 'Whatever else, I have been blessed with God's two greatest gifts, to be born English and heterosexual.'

Because of this one big lie, his whole life became riddled with contradictions. He dressed in velvet jackets and pink ties and two-tone shoes – incredibly camp, yet spewed out open disgust for gays. He drank only champagne while pleading poverty. He became a magazine columnist, yet reviled the

Press. Hating criticism, he doled it out big time: he claimed to be a socialist and ended up a bigot, despised suburbia and ended up telling Lynda Lee Potter of the *Daily Mail* that his neat acreage in Shropshire was 'the provincial life I've always wanted'.

Most contradictorily of all, he was a serial marrier while claiming to despise most of the women in his life. In his auto-biographies he was completely vile about all of his past wives except for the fifth, Helen. When his fourth, Jill Bennett, with whom he had lived for nine years, committed suicide, he applauded it as the one original act of her life, saying that his only regret was his inability to 'look down upon her open coffin and drop a large mess in her eye'.

His third wife, the film writer Penelope Gilliatt, was 'the grotesque adult embodiment of that properly despised school-boy creature of fretful, incontinent ambition, a swot'. She died of cancer. She was the mother of his daughter, Nolan, whom he said he despised. He never spoke to her past 16 and wrote that he used to fantazise so hard about hitting her that he had to take his big signet ring off when she came into the room. The charismatic Mary Ure, his wife from 1957-63, choked on her own vomit after she'd left him, and he seemed relieved. Pamela Lane, his first wife, (1951-57) was said to be the reviled prototype for Alison in *Look Back In Anger*.

Helen he seemed contented with. People who know them say it was not an overly sexual relationship. She would be strict with him, and fuss over him. She gave up work on the *Observer* to be the playwright's wife and formed a luncheon club called The Washouts where she would lunch with other 'washed-out' women. She seemed proud of that.

It is as if Osborne used his anger and his bitchiness as a cocoon. He stopped speaking to his mother – she was stupid and selfish, he said, and never loved him. She said he didn't even send Christmas cards, and that he had been bitter since he was 12, when his father, to whom he was devoted, died of tuberculosis.

We know that Osborne's misogyny started with his

mother, and his demonstrative, sweet devotion started with his father. We know that he was uncomfortable with waves of love, saying, 'I can only confirm that rollers of hate can be a most warming and stimulating dose of salts.' So here is a man who came to be so comfortable with hate that he wallowed in it. Maybe his tumultuous braggings of hatred were his only way of expressing affection, in which case he didn't really want to open the coffin and mess in Bennett's eye, but open the coffin and kiss her.

His plays show men being tortured by women and, like Archie Rice, the character Laurence Olivier immortalized in *The Entertainer*, being vituperative about women in soliloquies that are almost sonnets of hatred.

The only person, it seems, for whom he was able to express love as love was Creighton. His letters are as slushy and self-conscious and vulnerable as any other love-letter. Osborne sent him £20 a week when he was working and his Mousie was not. He came straight back to Creighton after the first marriage broke up, and the relationship was a catalyst in the break-up of the second. He told Ure that Creighton had had a bike accident so he needed to go on holiday with him, to look after him. He even managed to contain his huge ego when they collaborated in their writing. Each would discuss what was going to happen and write the same scene: whoever's worked better made the script, they did not argue.

Yet in his autobiography Osborne outed his old friend with contempt, calling him a 'cadging homosexual drunk'. While Osborne mouthed off, Creighton said nothing, and would not do so while Osborne was alive. Creighton was angry but not vengeful, for he was not an unfulfilled and tortured soul. He was not a hypocrite.

He was persuaded by the theatre critic Nicholas de Jongh to speak about the relationship because it had a considerable bearing on Osborne's works, particularly *A Patriot For Me*, which stigmatizes homosexuality. The truth about the playwright's sexuality was crucial to the understanding of Osborne and what haunted him. The pair had met a few months before Osborne died to discuss a royalties matter, but Osborne had been pretty incoherent, through drink or his illness. A diabetic and heavy drinker, he died in December last year.

There is no sense of spite about Creighton, now 72, as he discusses the old days: he is not lonely or sad. 'I prefer to remember the good times.' When he looks back on Osborne, he says, it is with love.

A love that's implied is more powerful than a love that's explored and a love that's shrunken from has to be expressed in another way.

Relationship of the Week
Tina Purser
8 September 1996

She was 26 and he was 12. She wrote him sick-notes so he could stay off school so that he could stay in bed with her. He probably learned a lot more from her than he could have done from his schoolteachers. It's classic. It's Mrs Robinson, except this woman's name was Tina Purser. She's now 28, vulnerable, used, divorced, dumped. Possibly desperate. Unemployed nurse. Maybe her only way of achieving a thrilling empowerment, her only hope of a successful seduction, was with a boy who hadn't learned men's wicked games. What she gave him was exquisite experience. He got there further and faster than any of his friends. What she gave him was pleasure. It seemed to be a mutually beneficial relationship. It's hardly a first. Upper-class fathers often took their sons straight from boarding school to be initiated with this kind of experience. Far from ruining the boy, Purser, who last week pleaded guilty to two charges of indecent assault, has probably sexually matured him. Yet such a *brouhaha*. She got two years' probation. The boy says that, despite the fact that he fell in love with her after she gave him his first proper kiss, he feels that she took his boyhood away. He says that he felt like he had to act like a 'grown up' – to be mature when he was with her. 'Now I just want to be a boy again,' he says.

Please. You can't take adolescence out of a male. They pass straight from puberty to menopause, hardly with a hormone-changing pace. This is a line I feel was fed to him by his mother, freaked that her son, her 'baby son', who is now 14 and has a girlfriend of his own age should have been looking forward to his first kiss and was having full sex with this 'experienced woman.' Perhaps she feels she is in competition. Perhaps she's jealous, as Purser is closer to her own age, 36. Oedipus did not give his name to a complex for nothing.

I have learned from a poll of my male friends, 100 per cent of whom had experiences with considerably older women when they were pubescents/adolescents, that this sort of thing happens time and time again. I learned that these experiences were with the mothers of friends. Apparently 25 per cent of teenagers under age 15 have sex. It may as well be good sex where somebody knows what they're doing. Otherwise you just get that failure smell. Purser's estranged husband, who now has custody of their four children, is also feigning big shock/horror, yet he apparently got her pregnant when she was 16.

Sex is interesting. Human beings want to know about it. It strikes me as rather sad that this woman should be so ashamed. After all, a woman can't actually rape a boy. There's a thing called an erection that gets in the way. She wanted to marry him, even putting her own wedding ring on his finger in a mock ceremony which suggests that she might have been somewhat deluded. But also, tragically, lonely and alone. But one thing she isn't alone in being is someone's older lover.

It seems a given that boys have a fascination for older women. The very sexy Neil Norman recently wrote, 'sex with an older woman is the best sex you'll ever have. The older woman is a walking, talking encyclopaedia of sexual etiquette.'

Inevitable as the thrill of a first credit card, a feeling of power, of experience, of potency. All of my men friends can recall their particular older woman. They use words like teacher, sexually demanding, direct and grateful. Men fear women and they fear sex. They like to be told what to do, and a girl of their own age doesn't usually like to do that. 'Puberty is a new toy that boys don't know to handle,' said one man I know. 'It's like a Meccano set. You need someone to help you put it together. It doesn't matter if they assemble it correctly because you will believe that they do. You're attracted to the unknown, to the darker side of experimentation. It's better than *The X Files*.'

He says that he had his first experience with his mother's best friend when he was 13 and it was stunning. He felt adult. 'Every kid wants to grow up fast,' he told me. 'They are desperate to please. But girls their own age are like sisters. Someone you don't want in your bedroom. Someone you don't particularly like. The only experience of a woman is through mothers. So it seems logical; a mother's friend you'd be desperate to please, and then addicted to it.'

It seems as though the kind of women who become involved in these scenarios are desperate for devotion of some kind. They don't want someone who'll stray, someone who'll go out with the lads drinking. They want virgin territory, everything fresh and malleable. It's a way the vulnerable can take control. It's a psychological dildo.

Another man I know was 17 and had a two-year thing with a 33-year-old divorced woman. They had nothing in common except what he wanted to know and what she had to instruct. 'She was kind of slutty and glamorous. It was naughty and there was no commitment necessary.' She frequently made hundred-mile trips to visit him after he went to university. She got predatory and he got bored.

While I have no moral objection to this, and even an understanding that youth, potency, happy hormones, a need to learn without embarrassment, coupled with a female's natural instinct to seduce is a reasonable swap, the idea of having an affair with a boy has never appealed to me. I think only weak women want to control something so easy and eager. I have never had sex or wanted to have sex with anyone younger than me. One of my best friends thinks that this is because I am sick. She has done the boy thing many times. She says she likes them pert, lean, taut; puppy dogs, enthusiastic for sex and her; biddable with no bad habits or previous owners. Whereas I prefer enthusiasm to come with interesting bad habits and twisted experience. Taking control of that combination is exciting. So what if it comes with grizzled flesh? For me there would be no point to seducing anything that's so easily controlled. My friend says that this is because I trade off looking like a winsome little girl, and I have a ridiculous Daddy thing. Soon, she says, this is going to look really hideous because no man would be taken in by it. Besides, you can't do winsome over 30.

This is perhaps what happens to some other women. They reach a point where they decide they have to be a grown up, decide they are so sad and vulnerable they can't deal with men anymore and it's at this point that they feel it's more interesting for them to take and to teach rather than to learn. They become Mrs Robinsons in all their seedy splendour, fulfilling the needs of all these young graduates, and then they probably get dumped. I always think that there's something really tragic about being dumped by something you moulded. You created the boy that discarded you. To be rejected by something you love, respect, admire is one of the most hideous tortures on the planet. But to be rejected by something you created as a safety mechanism, your key to empowerment, is the ultimate humiliation. To be rejected by a 12-year-old boy that you'd promised to marry, like Tina Purser, is a very scary insult indeed.

The older woman/younger boy is always seen as a scary outrage. The Lolita syndrome gets made into a movie, but when it's the reverse scenario, the woman gets ridiculed, which is worse than reviled. A girl can say 'no' and a man might think she means 'yes', but an erection is consent. It means please.

UNLOVELY LOVE

Relationship of the Week
Catherine and David Bailey
30 April 1995

David Bailey used to keep parrots. So many used to sit and scream at him that he caught a disease specific to those who inhale the fumes from parrot diarrhoea. I find this a cosy metaphor for Bailey's life and loves. He says he loves parrots and he says he loves women. I'm sure he loves women most when they are most like a parrot. Caged maybe. Talking parrot fashion, repeating whatever he says.

Those who know her say his wife Catherine is such a siphon she opens her mouth and his words come out. To justify a collection of rancid, cold-slab photographs of her in the book published this week, *The Lady is a Tramp*, she uses the word 'honest'.

Tramps are hot, sexy, dirty. Tramps move. Tramps make pages shudder. Tramp she is not. And I don't really understand what honest means in connection with a photograph. Photographs are about telling a story, telling a lie.

Bailey is a man who said on countless occasions that his pictures of trussed up women, mummified women with only the pubic triangle showing, hard-looking women, unfortunately naked or ruined, do not denigrate women. No, no, no. 'I don't want to degrade women, just the opposite,' he has said. Perhaps he is lying to himself, just misjudging the pungency of his own work. He 'loves women.' And we all know about men who say they love women. They love so many of them so much of the time that they can't help upsetting some women in particular.

In fact a journalist that I know once did an in-depth interview with him. He loved it so much he bought 12 copies of the paper. The first half of it was all about how he wouldn't necessarily consider it unfaithful if he was sleeping with someone else. It wouldn't be necessarily treating your wife badly. 'There's nothing to say that this marriage won't last. There's nothing to say that it will. I've never understood what marriage means. It's never meant anything to me,' he had chirruped in that bluff wheeze of his.

The interviewer is known to be meticulous, and when she met his wife Catherine she was slightly nervous that she might have been upset by the callous attitude he had revealed. Catherine said without rancour, 'I know you made it all up, he told me.' Ah, how she stands by him. How easily she is placated. She stands by without irony.

The book is a very unattractive package. It has text by Fay Weldon which is repetitive drivel. I couldn't understand it. I could understand the pictures though. A man so totally out of touch with himself and his sexuality, had got his wife to do things he thought were sexy. The photographs were not raw and evocative, but rather vulgar in their staleness.

Catherine is smooth and flat with a column of a neck, big eyes and a small neck. Never trust a woman with a small head, it means she's got a small brain, that's what I always say. And never trust a man who marries a model.

Of course not all models are stupid just as not all nuclear scientists are clever. Yet they can be both clever and stupid in the same way – not an interesting way.

Men who marry models are not deep. They do not have an edge. They are easily modified control freaks.

He used to frighten women and make them cry just because he could. He met Catherine when she was 18 and he was 44. She missed out on that development process, child to woman. He simply took her and formed her. She was greedy to learn everything, everything from him, how gratifying.

So then, it is a woman with no sense of self that must look at this book and say she is flattered. Without self-knowledge there can be no intensity in a chemistry.

There's a plethora of shots where she is covered in plaster looking frail, hollow, discarded mannequin. In some she's fondling mannequins. There are a couple of crotch shots where she's opened out on a rock. All through, there's the metaphor of cold and implacable. Maybe this is what Bailey admires? Maybe this makes him hot?'

He once said he needs a woman to maintain mystery. Maybe for him, this icy obedience is intriguing.

Then there's the book's lesbian phase where she's obediently lingeried up and licking some other girl's nipple, or having a girl press parched looking lips on hers. They both wear studded dog collars.

It's Readers Wives without the charm and freshness. There's another chapter called Fashion which includes a picture of her sitting on the toilet. Then one called pregnancy where we see the birth of Fenton in ludicrous detail – baby slime, rolling eyes and hospital tubes – for that trussed up look he so enjoys.

There have been three other wives – Rosemary Bramble, Catherine Deneuve and Marie Helvin – and two long-term girls, Jean Shrimpton and Penelope Tree. They were all probably a bit too exciting and nervous for him. They never gave him children. This one's the bearer of three, Paloma, Fenton and Sascha.

Bailey may once have seemed vivid, bohemian, and free. But that's all part of being a leftover icon of that frivolous, sad sixties era. His background was grim, working class, rigid, East End, born into the war. He's not a complex man. To have an unambitious woman who didn't threaten him, who loved her garden and her children, a woman who would let him photograph her digging her garden with her tits out. Well that's the best yet. It's simple mother/madonna/whore. It's what simple boys like.

He loved his mother, she looked like a gypsy and smelled sweet. Hated his father. He said, 'I wasn't formed by men, my mother made me.' His father was cruel, unappreciative, never there, out with other women, a philanderer. It's the classic. On that long journey looking for mummy he turned into daddy.

Bailey used to always flit from woman to woman with the attitude that they were lucky to have him, that big rude boy, brusque and vivid. Now he's just brusque and bid. But he's conned Catherine by keeping the same attitude.

He always managed to photograph Jean Shrimpton like a trapped butterfly, a bruised dancer, a child, a kitten, a bambi. Never just a woman. She commented once she had to leave him in order to find herself.

Because Catherine was formed by him she never made the leap from girl to woman on her own. It was girl to image to fantasy. She delights in these caricatures of motherhood. This is how Catherine is trying to find herself.

Real women do not run through corn fields with their babes in tow or fling themselves at their children on beaches in the sunset, as she is photographed doing. Real women do not need to record the experiences of the labour ward to check that it happened. The pictures are passionless. An acquaintance of theirs and mine says, 'She is a cod. A big dark-eyed unmoveable cod.' Nonetheless, she is a supportive cod and won't have a word said against him.

She lets him do anything he likes with her photographically and he once said, 'I do find photography a sexual act.' He even made a film, which was a recent South Bank Show, which depicted her in childbirth in all its gory glory. She didn't seem to do it like she felt it was a sacrifice, she did it perkily, or as perky as one can be in gruelling labour. He likes to push things because he has a low boredom threshold whereas hers is obviously very high. She has done so much tedious stuff simply because he wanted her to. That's the way he likes and she doesn't know any better.

I'm especially fond of this piece. Not just because the photographer/model relationship acts as a cruel metaphor for real life but because the editors of the Sunday Times *inspired and encouraged me to write in such an undiluted way, although in this edit I've changed the word lavatory to toilet, the word breast to tit and the words spread eagled to crotch shot.*

Relationship of the Week
Brad Pitt and Gwyneth Paltrow
8 December 1996

I'm engaged. What a funny expression. I've always thought that. It makes you sound like a telephone or a toilet. Brad Pitt and Gwyneth Paltrow are engaged. Engaged to be? Something they're not already? Engagements are so proper, so old-fashioned, so romantic, but as we all know, romance is brutal. Promises are made to be broken and lies to be spoken. Brad Pitt must have spoken them before to his other long-term loves. And guess what? Both Juliette Lewis and Geena Davis he met on set. They too were his co-stars. We all know about the drama, the intoxication of the shared endeavour. They meet, they burn, they smoulder, then finally they fizzle out because there's always going to be another co-star, another movie. Brad Pitt, 32 – they tout him as James Dean. He is what girls like. He looks like a wolf, he ripples in the right places and the script usually says he should be topless at some point.

He met Gwyneth when she played his wife in the thriller *Seven*. Gwyneth is 24 with long, blonde hair, an antiseptically pleasing face. She's 5'10" and pin-thin. And we all know what boys like. They like the long, blonde hair, the long limbs and the innoffensive prettiness. I bet she smells clean. Good genes, Gwyneth Paltrow. Mother is the actress Blythe Danner – a mature version of the same clean spirit – and father is Bruce Paltrow – producer of the long-running schmaltzy *St Elsewhere*. Gwyneth cooks cordon bleu. That's her hobby. She wants children. She got the part in *Seven* by answering a casting notice which said they were looking for 'the most beautiful woman in the world – drop-dead gorgeous.' So what kind of girl would imagine she would be eligible for this role? One whose self-esteem is obviously even bigger than her big, fat, vacant-looking smile. The part was to play the role of a devoted wife, a robowoman. OK. So if she's innoffensive, why wouldn't Brad want her? He has been pegged as this daring free spirit as if that's supposed to be sexy. Well, what did he do that is so daring? He left college two weeks before graduating. He left the Midwest and came to L.A. for a walk-on crowd scene in that yuppie dilemma *Less than Zero*. Daring? Free? Sounds pretty regular to me.

I was talking with my friend the other day, discussing the nature of true love and, out of nowhere, he started quoting metaphysical poetry which I will summarize as 'Love is begotten on despair and impossibility.' Sure. That's the way love goes. That's how you know it's real. But this walk-on wife, this relationship, seems to be more of a love begat of convenience, expedience and cheerfulness. It's not love as I know it, but then I can't cook cordon bleu, I don't have that smile, and I'm not dating Mr. Robosex. Although of course Brad Pitt himself shuns the sexy image – well, he didn't shun it when he needed it to make his mark playing the trickster in *Thelma and Louise* who seduces Geena Davis, but now he is announcing, 'I'm average in bed.' I have noticed that men who have a girl with a healthy sexual appreciation for them or have legions of female admirers often feel that these are nasty predatory women and they want to be wanted for who they are – whatever that might be. They want to be wanted for their souls or their intelligence or something like that. The reason I have never thought that Brad Pitt was particularly sexy was that I have never, no matter how hard I have tried, been able to invest him with any kind of original intelligence. I feel the same way about Gwyneth. When she talks about her work, which she did quite a lot when she was publicizing *Emma*, one had the sense of words learned rather than felt, although for that part she did do a brilliant English accent, and apparently she does a great Texan one too. You can never trust a woman who does great accents. Too chameleon; so busy being less of themselves so they can be someone else.

Now, some people around Hollywood are saying that Brad put the proposal on her because he was in a panic: while she is the cover girl, the shimmering star, the new hot babe, he feels he is slipping down the A-list. I doubt that this timing had anything to do with it. He's asked her three times because she's a nice, well-brought-up, doesn't stuff herself with dinner type of girl who would feel most obliged to refuse until the third attempt. She's not insecure. She doesn't believe in instant gratification. She doesn't need to go to Las Vegas right now this minute. She'd rather wait to see if the feelings of wanting to cook and have children with this person remain, because she probably believes marriage is forever. Besides, she learned all about delayed gratification from Jane Austen.

Now, when they first met, he had had his eye on her because she did a good audition tape for *Legends of the Fall*, even though Julia Ormond got the part. She however insists her interest was far more innocent. 'It would never occur to me to flirt with someone even if I have a crush on them,' she explained. 'And I wouldn't know if someone was flirting with me. I had no idea. I thought Brad was just being really friendly.' Well, there you are. Obviously the words of a truly dynamic, incisive, perceptive woman, a perfect match for Brad.

It was over as soon as he made her get her hair cut so from the back they looked identical. If she looked like him, why would he need her? Apparently, he read something I'd written about him in the British Airways Magazine. *It seemed like I'd committed blasphemy. His publicist inferred that I'd never even get as far as eating breakfast in this town again and I'm banned from her client list. But I was right. I knew he was a serial fiancé.*

Relationship of the Week
Kenneth Branagh and Emma Thompson
12 November 1995

Friends. They say they are, they were and always will remain the greatest of friends. But that friends malarkey, when two people have just torn each other's heart and soul inside out, has always bothered me.

People become friends when things are really over and there's no longer a flicker of manipulation, control, revenge, heat, between them. Anyway, it's Kenneth Branagh who made the friends speech. Emma Thompson may go along with it, but she's too much of a volcano to support it whole-heartedly.

In fact the way she has expressed her most profound feelings for her estranged husband was in the revenge fling with the brooding-eyed, nicely-bottomed, great-in-breeches actor Greg Wise, with whom she worked on *Sense and Sensibility*. Friends of hers said that this affair reeked of her distress, her need for ego-reupholstering after Branagh became increasingly distant and involved in what has been labelled 'a private and complicated arrangement' with Helena Bonham Carter.

The official reason for their split was the old too-much-time-apart lark. Indeed they have both been prodigiously busy. The more glitz-rated Thompson became, the more Branagh drilled himself into project after project. He's just directed the award-winning, arty, bleak, black and white *The Bleak Midwinter*. It's supposed to be a comedy, but it's rather self-conscious, as indeed you'd expect from this Irish working-class boy. He seems to still have a brickie's hod on his shoulder which has informed his every gesture – to conquer and control the luvvie world, the sophisticated, complicated relationships that as a boy he thought he'd never belong to.

He met Emma Thompson in 1986 when they were filming the TV series *Fortunes of War*. She was impeccably pedigreed, arty family, actress mother Phyllida Law and daddy Eric who wrote and spoke *The Magic Roundabout*. Before her Branagh had gone for the other dynastic great, Joely Richardson. And Emma, insatiable Emma, boasted of her joy of experiencing the pre-Aids generation, where she 'had everyone' before she married in 1989.

Essentially, we have a clash of backgrounds. Branagh has always been irritatingly aspirational, and Thompson absolutely middle-class Hampsteadesque. And we also have a clash of sexual drive. Branagh comes over cold, detached.

But look at him. He's almost gingery, self-consciously serious. He wrote his autobiography by the time he was 30, enjoyed a friendship with Prince Charles, and loves control. Sure he wants to be admired by everybody, either sex. But that thin little slit of a mouth, you can just tell he's not generous of spirit. I think he likes relationships to be in his head. It's easier that way. Rather complacently he said, 'Life is easier if Em and I are together. I relax when I'm with her.' Whereas Emma is always flickering with tension. She is hot, a volcano. She has said, 'I'm a very sexual being and I have always been driven that way. I'm always looking for adventure.'

She was also particularly struck by Michelle Pfeiffer. 'So delicious. I have never met another woman who made me feel sexually for her, but I have no problem imagining it. I've always longed for it to happen to me.'

Thompson likes sex, no doubt about it. She is a full-mouthed sexual omnivore. It's always in the mouths, believe it. She is capable of great passion. The passion she feels for her husband however has probably been forced to be folded up, otherwise it would fold her up. She once moaned that despite her tick-tock biological clock, 'Ken's sperm are on crutches.'

And there again they never saw each other. Appetites had to be feasted elsewhere. It was all rather too brazen, too brash, the way she was so public about Greg Wise. It was obviously a physical passion, but perhaps inspired by hurt. Branagh didn't bother to come to the première of her last movie, *Carrington*. And over the past year she's always been booking into health farms claiming to be exhausted and looking wretched.

He on the other hand has always looked frighteningly smug. She is interested in coming over the strong, sexy one. At the time of getting married to Branagh she said that she could never handle infidelity. In fact the wedding was almost called off when she found a selection of letters preserved from an ex-girlfriend. She stormed off to New York in a fury – her own behaviour the complete opposite of her saying that Hugh Grant's behaviour on Sunset Boulevard was reasonable and that she wouldn't have had any problems with Branagh if he'd done something like that.

It could mean all lust is spent with Branagh if she really doesn't care what he gets up to. Or it could mean she'd rather he hired the services of a street-stranger in another country than have a private and complicated deal with Helena Bonham Carter. How irksome to be superseded by a woman with no neck, a woman who resembles the love child of Denis Healey's eyebrows and one of those Victorian ornamental dolls that are advertised in the trashier Sunday supplements. They struck up with each other when she played Elizabeth the corseted damsel in his version of *Frankenstein* that flopped. Critics described her and Branagh's performances as having the sexual chemistry of a potato salad, but we know how orgasmic Branagh gets over breeding. Bonham Carter is the great-granddaughter of the Liberal Prime Minister Asquith. She is completely marbles-in-mouth posh. She fled to him in Italy where he was filming *Othello*, saying someone in Paris had messed up her hair and she had to go to the set in Italy to have her hair done by the only person who could deal with her hair. Bonham Carter's hair seems never to have changed in years, and she is one of those irritating characters without vanity. She wears horrible clothes purposefully she thinks so much of herself.

Now, maybe she seemed a good idea at the time. After all he was safely married to someone else. But recently he has claimed that they phone each other five times a day although they avoid being photographed together. To my knowledge those who phone a lot have sex a lot, but only in their minds. Why should that be? Because Branagh is a sexual narcissist and that's probably good enough for him. Also, five times a day sounds a bit obsessed, no wonder he's backing off. Now there are rumours of a reconciliation with Thompson, because despite how ravishingly complicated she is to the rest of the world, she is known territory, a fantastic Oscar-winning actress always on hand to front his luvvie lacklustre films. Bit of a great combo to give up for an ambitious man.

Let's face it, who would want to swap the child-bearing lips of Emma Thompson for the child hips of Helena Bonham Carter. The girl is 29 and still lives at home with her parents. She is a stunted thing, I mean emotionally, not just because she's five foot two, who seems constantly on the point of sexual discovery in every bodice ripper she pops out of. Only recently has she decided it's OK to wear jeans. She used to find them too revealing. Only after playing opposite Branagh in *Frankenstein* did she say, 'At last I've been allowed to act my age.' I wonder who she thought stopped her. Anyway, she seems to think Branagh has released her, and a released woman must seem dangerous to him. He doesn't like danger, he likes easy.

All I can say is, never trust a man who doesn't have a top lip.

Relationship of the Week
Imogen Stubbs and Trevor Nunn
27 October 1996

I always used to think about ways to tell a man. You know, you can tell a man by his shoes, the contents of his wallet, the shape of his beard, if he owns any Prefab Sprouts records or too many clothes made in denim. But the most precise way to tell a man is by his choice of woman. So, what can we tell about millionaire theatre-director Trevor Nunn, the man who brought a million tour buses to Cambridge Circus to sing along to *Les Mis*, the man who put big *Cats* all over the world, a man who likes a sure thing like Shakespeare – what can we tell about him by his woman, Imogen Stubbs?

We can tell he's not a risk-taker. She has a composite beauty. You know, good hair, good eyes, good mouth, milk skin; but somehow, put together, they are meaningless, unengaging. They try, but not too hard and not in an interesting way. She talks in educated clichés. She doesn't say anything inanely stupid. She does dishevelled girlie.

She plays dippy yet she's fiercely organized. She is a boyish girl, a child-woman. These things cancel each other out. She almost doesn't exist. Imogen Stubbs, you think. Which one is she? No, she's not the one that's funny. That's Imelda something. No, she's not the one who's clever. That's Emma Something. Ah yes. She's the one married to Trevor Nunn. That's how you define her. And what does it say about a man who has a composite girly, who can't be defined unless he draws her?

She's starring, if star is the word, in *Twelfth Night*, the film. He directed it. He met her when he was coaxing her into Desdemona in his 1989 *Othello*. It's a one-dimensional role. She played it brilliantly.

I think I would have felt happier about him had he not traded in Janet Suzman, his first wife. Her rasping haughtiness, her nobility, her rawness probably diminished him. He divorced his second wife, Sharon Lee Hill, weeks after Imogen had given birth to Ellie, their first child, who is now 5 and has a baby brother Jesse. Imogen is not too anything. She's not too glamorous, but works on that natural effect. Has a first from Oxford, but says herself it's because she has a good memory and knows how to pass exams. She speaks lines as though she's looking for approval, as if she's playing some part.

Imogen has had a sad life. Her father died when she was 13, her mother when she was 25. They both had cancer, but she doesn't get too hysterical or bitter. She doesn't do the victim. She's far too into the glorification of normalcy for that. She talks a lot about being normal and says that she didn't marry Trevor because of his money, although it's nice to have the 'luxury of taxis.' The man is a millionaire. He could buy a fleet of taxis. Riding in one is not exactly taking Concorde. 'I do lead a normal life with the privilege of having a Marks and Spencer charge card.' This is not a privilege. This is an essential. But she's not of the real world and apparently doesn't know that you can never trust a woman without an M&S charge card. Now that would be really bizarre.

She tends to play classical roles and talks with a learned intelligence about their authors. I have always felt she does not have enough of herself to bring any real quirkiness or vibrancy to these women. She is perhaps most famous for playing the pantomime boy/bimboesque television detective Anna Lee. She appeared wooden, clearly uncomfortable and turned down a second series. 'I must do something that has street credibility, like *Prime Suspect*,' she said. 'I haven't shown I have guts as an actress. I end up playing roles where the dominant interest is what I look like.'

Unfortunately, that is because the dominant interest is what she looks like. I always find it embarrassing when pretty people complain that they're not taken seriously. There are plenty of gorgeous women who are taken very seriously. Helen Mirren, for instance. That is because they have a *grav-*

nefarious
decadent

itas, a presence. They often incur serious criticism because they are slightly threatening. Imogen Stubbs is rarely criticized. Why? Because she threatens nobody. And that must be why Trevor Nunn chose her. All her sadness covered up so nicely makes her easy-peasy lemon squeezy. Also, she says lovely things about him, how fantastic a director he is and how marvellously thrilling it is to work for him, although when discussing his new job as director of the National Theatre, she said ruefully, 'I'll never never be able to work there because people will cry nepotism.' Hmm.... that's hardly stopped her before.

Is it that good old credibility she's after? The pair of them seem to have a symbiotic naffness and they are both way overdrawn in the credibility bank. She says it's not his money or his power that she was attracted to and he's the love of her life anyway. I really do believe that they suit each other. They have the same kind of anoraks in their souls. He has a square, ordered little beard, while her dressing rooms are apparently as organized as a TV dinner. He's 21 years older than her so one can't help but be slightly Freudian. She lost her father when she was 13 and needed an older authority figure to replace him. He's 56. She's 35 and agrees that she tends to 'latch on to wise figures.' 'I think I have retained some of my girlishness because unconsciously I didn't want my childhood to end. I didn't want to become a woman,' she has said. I think she was fairly successful there, and I think Trevor Nunn is more at ease with a girl than a woman.

I don't know if something, too much pain, too much money, too much theatre for the masses has in some way limited Trevor Nunn's appetite for a passionate response. The only thing he seems to be passionate about is writing letters to newspapers.

Now what kind of person gets to be Mr Angry with a bee in his bonnet? A bored person. Never trust anyone who writes complaining letters to newspapers. It is themselves they are dissatisfied with. Recently he was most passionate about the word 'lovey.' He said it is as abhorrent and perjorative as any racist word. Well, obviously it isn't. He says that being called a lovey categorizes you as hysterical, trivial and self-indulgent. I never knew that was what it meant. I don't think you can compare that to the hideous prejudice that can be associated with colour or race. That is the prejudice that tortures, the prejudice that kills, and I think it is entirely self-indulgent and hysterical to compare the two.

Imogen once wrote to this newspaper. I remember the letter because it was about me. I can't remember exactly what she said, but I don't think she likes me which is a pity because Trevor Nunn once bought a picture of my bottom. Of course he didn't know it was my bottom. It was a group of delicately painted lovelies, one of which has a bare bottom, and was painted by the artist David Remfry, my then-boyfriend, from memory. It must have cost Trevor a pretty penny. I bet he feels like tossing it away now.

As David Remfry no longer owns the rights to this picture, sadly, it cannot be reproduced here, but I'll bet if someone wants it, it will be going very cheap.

Never trust a man who wants to go Dutch.

Going Dutch establishes a date as *faux*-casual, as a place where nobody owes anybody anything – emotionally, sexually or financially. Nobody gives and nobody receives. Men who carry purses, wear last year's racing-green wind-cheater, and whose idea of a nice car is a Volvo go Dutch. They have horrid hair and use 'wash and not sure if I should go' shampoo.

Imagine going through a bill and thinking, 'How Dutch do we go?' Do you have a discussion about who had dessert, who had an extra glass of wine and who had chocolate on their cappucino? Men who want to go Dutch are selfish and meagre with their emotions. They give only what they think might be required. Never more.

I recall going Dutch. It was back in my student days, when I thought that men with no manners and no money were acceptable. I remember back then the stupid notion that if you paid your way for dinner, you wouldn't have to visit the sexual favours department. Well, for a start, why bother going on a date with someone if all you're interested in is how not to become embroiled with them? Besides, does anybody really value themselves as being worth, say, half a pizza?

But I soon learned that the kind of man who thinks he can get away with not buying me dinner also believes he can get away with other liberties. The most strikingly selfish relationship I've ever had was with a painter. I was mesmerized. I let him do anything, including the Dutch thing. He said that he couldn't afford to pay for me because he already had a wife that he was paying for. The women that men want to pay for, or feel the need to pay for, are the ones they return to. Sure enough, he left me to go back to her. And he's still paying for that.

With most of my platonic friends, we take it in turns to pay, then you always have the pleasure of giving or of receiving. But if you're on a date it's a different kind of deal. The interesting part is when do they bring it up? I don't know which is worse: when they call to make the arrangement and say 'And we'll go Dutch' or when they spring it on you at the end of the meal. If they do it before, it's a code for, 'I don't fancy you, but I'm not doing anything Thursday and I have to eat.'

My friend Sarah, who works in the theatre, recently got asked out to dinner by someone she met through work. She was interested in him, but she didn't know whether it was a date. The word Dutch had not been mentioned at all until after the armagnacs had been downed. 'He wanted me to take my cash and put it with his so it looked like he was paying,' she says. 'But I didn't have the cash, so we gave credit cards and the waiter looked at me as much as to say, "You idiot" and looked at my date as much as to say, "You schmuck."'

People who don't want to pay for you don't want you

enough. It has nothing to do with poverty. It has to do with generosity of spirit. If you are mean with money, you are retentive, obsessed with your calorie intake and pernickety with your emotions. There is nothing more repulsive than watching a man totting up a bill and asking you for money. It's demeaning.

Another friend of mine, Eric, doesn't think going Dutch should be dismissed entirely. 'I have no problem with going Dutch except I wouldn't do it on a first date,' he says. 'I wouldn't do it if I was trying to impress either.' But who wants to go out with someone who doesn't want to impress, whatever the context?

I do know one girl who still says she likes to go Dutch because she believes it means she doesn't have to, as she puts it, 'put out.' How very old-fashioned. The Rules, an American guide to winning and keeping a man 1990s-style is not a bestseller for nothing. It says men should call you and pay for you. That 1970s state of affairs when girls used to ask to go Dutch in order to make a misguided statement of independence just meant that they ended up giving him his cake and paying for half of it. Free love, but expensive meals? Now who wants that?

Relationship of the Week
Naomi Campbell and Jaoquin Cortez
19 January 1997

He speaks very little English and she certainly speaks very little Spanish. Just what kind of relationship can Jaoquin Cortez and Naomi Campbell have? I suppose the sort you'd expect. No one expects Campbell to be wanted purely for her conversational skills and Cortez has managed perfectly well to communicate with all that stomping and stamping, his legs flicking like whips at thousands of hormonally excited women throughout the world. He doesn't like to be called a flamenco dancer. He likes to be credited with flamenco fusion, a sexual combination of flamenco and ballet. Naomi likes to think of herself as not just a model but an actress, a singer – a writer even. Of course, how she sees herself is not necessarily how other people see her. We now see her as a beautiful trophy again, with a non-speaking part in a possible melodrama involving Jaoquin Cortez. It could be the undoing of her. In the past, it has been said that she's gone for trophy men: De Niro, Stallone, U2's Adam Clayton. But of course they go for her. They think of her as the perfect trophy accessory, available to make pictures, babies or trouble depending on whether or not she's stamping her tantrum feet. She has always said she likes macho men, that she prefers the Latinate sensuality and heat. But she's always had a problem. No one believes she's smart and has a heart that doesn't deserve breaking. All models suffer that problem. People think they're stupid. You know, the way the human mind doesn't allow for a woman to be clever and gorgeous. Unfortunately, sometimes, your insecurites become a self-fulfilling prophecy.

Jaoquin Cortez, who is 27, is certainly macho a million times cubed. Who will believe in Campbell's intellectual capacity now she appears quite happy to conduct a relationship virtually without speech? Cortez also likes to stamp his feet, although not in a babyish tantrum, more like a storm. Onstage, he sweats so much he has been called a human fountain. He apparently put an end to his former girlfriend Maria Pineda's career as a model because, she says, he didn't like to see her 'wearing clothes where my neck's too low or my skirt's too short.' He dispatched her to run part of his business.They split just a few months ago and she told *Hello!* there was no third party. 'We simply decided to let it go.' I don't know what kind of grand gypsy passion you do that with. Anyway, as she still works with him, they see each other all of the time. In fact, he was recently spotted in Madrid airport on a double run: seeing off Naomi and welcoming Maria back from her Christmas stay with Gloria Estefan in

Miami. He was clutching a large white fluffy toy for her. Never trust a man who gives you a large white fluffy toy. It means he thinks that that is demanding enough and securing enough for you to play with. And for that matter, never trust a woman who says, 'We've decided to let go' in a calm and manicured tone. It usually means they have decided to hold on, wait it out and stick by the mantra 'the looser the grip, the tighter the hold.' Maria Pineda, subservient to him yet strong-willed, in with his family, running his business, she is the kind of matriarch he would respect. It was she who got him the deal with Pino Sagliocco, the manager-promoter responsible for bringing Michael Jackson and the Rolling Stones to Spain and for teaming Freddie Mercury with Monserrat Cabale. He is a kind of Spanish version of Harvey Goldsmith. She set about moving him from interesting cult figure to international idol. How will Naomi, with her lingering legs and kisses and her giggling, match this kind of drive and solidarity?

Maybe Cortez doesn't respect drive and solidarity. His view of women is distorted by his own machismo. Of course he loves women, but he loves them in a way that means he loves to toy, to have, to hold, to dump, to move on from, to be in awe of and then afraid of and despise them. He also probably has a mother fixation. He says that he loves his mother more than anything, likes to spend as much time with her as he can, probably because he was brought up by his grandparents. He sees her as some kind of detached angelic force, but also one who has the power to abandon him. Sounds pretty dangerous to me. He says that when he falls in love, there is no stopping him. But at the same time, he also admitted to this game of sitting on sidewalk cafés awarding points to women as they walk by. Oh yes, he loves women. And in return women love him back. My friend who met him said that although he's smaller than you think and his features are quite ordinary, he has this way of making women feel very sexy. She said although she doesn't speak Spanish, he found ways of communicating with his eyes, his face, his body. He's very into face communication. He knows what to do with his smile. My friend said that he did all of this intense-looking stuff and eyebrow-raising, making out that he was frisking her for her soul.

I gather Cortez and Campbell met in New York last September when his show opened there. Armani threw a party for him which Naomi also attended. They both like clothes and they know how to move in and out of them. She was very struck by him. Her eyes sparkled in that way that most women's do, and he was on his way out of the relationship with Pineda. There were several meetings all over Europe in that globe-trotting way that beautiful people like. They communicated in a few phrases of broken Italian, but basically through an assistant. An acquaintance of mine, and also of his, says how difficult it was for the assistant to be the broker of the love chat. Their verbal skills were so sparse, it seemed like she had to be like an omnipresent chaperon. Could it be that these people are so used to being in the public glare, they become unused to one-to-one intimacy? I suppose the whole point of being a dancer, or a model for that matter, is that you speak with how you move, and when they move, they fall over each other, giggling like schoolkids, says our mutual friend. Before Christmas, she apparently chartered a plane to get to Madrid to meet him because she had a spare six hours and obviously a need. I wonder about the symbiosis here. Obviously, together they maximize each other's publicity potential and radiate an image of ultra-cool. They have each other as trophies. But I don't think either of them have thought about it like that. Apparently, he doesn't make publicity decisions like that, and even though his dancing is precise and intricate, it is unorthodox and passionate. He talks a lot about great souls and she talks a lot about great hearts. She has always said she wanted a sensitive bull, and he is a Spanish bull, even using the bull's head as his logo. However, in finding what she thinks she wants, she may soon feel too reduced by it. It's typically macho and typically him to pursue, to pamper, to say, 'once I fall in love there's no stopping me,' and then it stops, it all cools. And if it cools and you can't even have a conversation, it's going to be into the freezer time.

It cooled. There were reports of her reaching into the fridge for champagne and barbiturates. She denies it was anything to do with a love meltdown. Just an accident. And another non-speaking part in a big melodrama.

Relationship of the Week
Paul Merton and Caroline Quentin
12 February 1995

There they were, him with his fleecy-lined, tactile metaphors, her with her nanny-like, cosy sternness, both of them in brushed-cotton pyjama stripes for *The Live Bed Show*, which is really about dead sex. In real life Mr and Mrs Merton often wear clothes that look like pyjamas. Baggy, shapeless things are second skins to them. The play weaves in and out of a very unspecial relationship. It is a rambling, shambling interruptus with no coitus. It is quite an old-fashioned examination of the minutiae of seduction, how things get together and how things fall apart.

I was quite transfixed. Not because their performances were so compelling, but by wondering whether they were comfortable, casual old slippers off stage as much as they are on.

People who know them say they are splendidly suburban. I think that perhaps they are so at ease with each other they have eased into each other. Paul Merton is Chambourcy-skinned with sweetly kinking hair, baby-girlie, and gentle, while his wife Caroline Quentin is hard-jawed with bloke's floppy hair, big strides that make her husband look coquettish. Here they are, Mr and Mrs Showpersonality, so conspicuously happy to love together, live together, work together.

They have been married three years and are often vignetting in and out of each other's shows. Before this epic the most notable was Granada TV's *An Evening with Gary Lineker* written by the same author as *The Live Bed Show*, their friend, Arthur Smith.

As I watched the bed show the thought that was gnawing at me was, I wonder what kind of sex these two have. I cannot imagine that their relationship is particularly sexually embroiling. They have grown to look alike and inhabit each other's worlds so totally they are the kind of couple who can finish each other's sentences. Often this is the kind of couple that does not yearn for each other's bodies. There is no tension of opposition, they seem to have nothing to surrender, nothing to strive for, nothing to need to know, nothing to explore. They have already become each other, bonded by a nannying kind of love. It's a co-dependence and transmutation of personality that is beyond sex.

He says, 'She can sort of keep me in order.' She says, 'I understand him completely, therefore he'll listen to me when I say I think you should go to bed dear. Similarly he's very good at organizing me.'

You just can't imagine them doing it because they seem so sexless. They weren't born sexless, sexless is a thing that you achieve. You achieve it through fear of being destroyed and by sentimentality and romanticism clogging the arteries of passion.

They met on a train and he flirted with her forcefully. Not having been very good at anything much made him try very hard. He was a loser at school and while on the alternative comedy circuit he worked in the Tooting Employment Office in south London. His humour is not on-the-edge nervy, it's something that comes from underneath and seeps in. It's the shared embarrassment of minutiae.

He is also moral, in a Roman Catholic way. After they had met a few times he ended the relationship he was already in and a few days later moved into her house. At this point they'd scarcely kissed, but it didn't feel strange: 'It was just fine. The minute he arrived it was as though he should have always been there,' she says. Three months later he diverted a taxi to Piccadilly Circus so he could propose to her under Eros. The wedding was at the Grand Hall, Battersea. They sat at a tiny table for two while their guests, most of whom already had a series on Channel Four, supped Guinness and champagne.

Merton is of Irish stock. His mother was a nurse. Perhaps he had always been looking for a stand-in. I notice during the play that he has a lisp, I haven't noticed it before. Has he developed it as he's recoiled into a new babyhood?

Quentin has often stropped that her husband didn't have a proper girlfriend until he was 27 and then added that she finds this fumbling *naïvety* with women part of his appeal. I don't believe that any real women are attracted by *naïvety* in a man. It is the single biggest turn-off because it gives you too much power, so that there is no erotic tension in the relationship.

Perhaps Quentin had had enough of tension. Her life before Merton was miserable and lived too much in the pain dimension. Her father, an RAF pilot, and her French Canadian mother, separated when she was 15. Shortly after, her mother had a stroke, couldn't speak or feed herself. Quentin abandoned her ballet training to be with her mother. Suddenly she was all sequins and sacrifice, hoofing summer-season, end-of-the-pier shows. The father vanished from her life for ten years. It was traumatic, she was angry. She concedes, 'I think it must have affected my attitude towards men a lot because when I was younger I was needy. I went into completely unsuitable relationships with men who used to run away.'

Before Merton she has said that she was demoralized by men. It is still a needy relationship. But her needs are so enveloped by the smugness and glory of being suburban, successful, secure, it's hard to know where the needs are buried. Certainly one senses that she might have been sexy once. She is a little overweight and although she makes a point of protesting she isn't bothered she seems to me not comfortable in the way she carries herself. Some people who carry weight do so because it thickens their skin against repressed pain and mutes their emotional wires.

Merton describes her as 'a talented actress, a very good cook, someone who is very funny and occasionally very attractive.' Interesting that order, food before looks. Of course he looks terrible all the time with his shambolic ill-matching outfits and horrible too-small T-shirts. She says she finds his lack of vanity refreshing. But lack of vanity is so near to lack of self-respect.

He was ten years trudging the circuit before he hit the TV screen and suddenly his linear wit made girls say to him any time any place any position. He can't quite believe in his own sexuality, you can see that. And Quentin would have no fears that he would ever go off with any of these admirers. He is collie-dog loyal, absolutely faithful. No infidelity pattern whatsoever, not in his nature. But she's so insecure it probably comforts her that he never makes an effort to be attractive.

He admires her, he wanted her to be on every sketch in the Channel Four *Paul Merton* series. When she guested on BBC2's *Have I Got News For You?* she outperformed him, took a wincing delight in putting him down in public, only teasing of course, but there again there's no such thing as a tease. His love for her seems cradled in fear of her. She intimidates him, but he probably likes that, for a while anyway.

Nothing so conspicuously lovey-dovey is without suspicion. She says she doesn't want children. That is because she already has one, him.

What does he nurture? Probably sucks his thumb. I'm sure they cuddle each other all the time. They are each other's insecurity blanket. They are a very ordinary couple and their aspirations are very ordinary. His success as a comic depends on that. He thinks for the fumbling world of the pink-skinned Anglo-Saxon male. In *The Live Bed Show*, they joke that boringness personified might be a weekend in Solihull with Richard and Judy. What they don't know is they almost are Richard and Judy, except that Judy is far more sexy, interestingly neurotic and perceptive. There is an erotic tension between Richard and Judy that could never exist in the ‧mollycoddled world of the Mertons.

Well, they didn't manage this nannying kind of love for very long. Earlier this year, they split up.

FAT

Relationship of the Week
Chubby Chasers
4 August 1996

When I feel fat I don't want to be with a thin man. It would make me feel self-conscious, uncomfortable and like a big dollop. It's not that I feel sexually attracted to great mountains of wobble, but the odd vulnerable, grabbable fleshy bit can make me feel at home. Who wants a man who does aerobics or measures out his fat grams or eats reduced-fat blueberry muffin? It's far too feminine a preoccupation. And it's a repulsive preoccupation that we do not want to be reminded of. However, all love is narcissism. You fall in love with either who you are or who you'd like to be. This is why more often than not you see a visibly indulged, emotionally out-of-control man with a thin, sunken woman who perhaps was once a model and has had a history of food disorders. The more upset about her food problems she might be, the more he would contemptuously eat. The more she tries to control her intake, the less he cares. And, in a masochistic way, she might enjoy this voyeurism.

Earl Spencer had an anorexic, suppressed-looking, hoovered soul of a wife, Victoria. Now he's swapped her for a look-alike, Chantal Collopy, who is equally thin and involved in the fashion business. He was named by Don Collopy in the divorce papers. Although under South African rule this was not necessary, Mr Collopy wished to stab at him, seeking damages for his broken heart. Not a very restrained, dignified thing to do. But there again, Mr Don Collopy is not a thin man. Not used to self-control either. He lets it all spill out while his wife Chantal remains fractious and poised.

Not only has Earl Spencer gone for a similar love type, but so has she. She likes, it would seem, that love handle zone. People who don't feel comfortable with their own bodies like to be with bodies who are comfortable. No, I'm not talking

194

obese. No one wants to be crushed by that. But in order for a woman to feel womanly, there has to be a point where you surrender to something enormous and powerful in order to feel who you are. You can't surrender to something scrawny. It just doesn't make sense. When you think about it, there are very few thin men who are powerful – not in that aphrodisiac way. You don't get a mafia boss ordering the steamed vegetable plate, black coffee and a cracker. No, they eat pasta because pasta is sexy. Nicoletta Mantovani even finds Pavorotti sexy, although personally I think his size has less to do with it. Nonetheless, they're obviously doing it.

Men who cook are sexy because they are sensates. I've always found that if you know someone's taste in food, you know someone's taste in sex. Oddly, I think, Chantal Collopy cited that the chief bonding experience between her and Spencer was that they like to talk about the same things; cooking and design. So you can imagine them talking endlessly about recipes, calories, and then cunning little suits that will slim away the pounds that they just ate. Somehow if a man cooks, it validates a woman to eat without guilt. I think that's why I've always found being in a room with Marco Pierre White both comforting and exciting. Of course it's unfair that love handles are held so much better on a man than a woman. It may be a tyranny that men might like to go to bed with fat women but they don't want to be seen with one on their arm, and there are special 'Big Girl' clubs devoted to this tawdry pursuit. But that's the way it is. On the whole, men carry fat better than women because they feel less ashamed of it. It doesn't spread all over them, but comes out as a neat little pouch. If a man knows how to carry his fat properly, it can be smouldering and protective. Actually, I don't think Earl Spencer does carry his fat that well. It looks kind of separate to him, as if perhaps he has the mindset of his food-disordered sister, but not the body. Therefore maybe he lived out his eating disorder vicariously through his last wife.

It's a well-known theory that fat is an emotional buffer, a

barrier that assists the process of denial, of blot-out, which makes me sense that fat people who don't know how to carry their fat are using it as a buffer. For instance, Don Collopy announced, 'I had a happy marriage until he came along.' If the marriage was that happy and sexually fulfilling, there would not have been that extra car-park space in her heart. And Spencer said he was going to South Africa to give his wife a breathing space when he was already seeing Chantal. According to one report, she was already coming over to the house that cricketer Alan Lamb had lent him to cook him breakfast, lunch and dinner.

I don't think human beings are just blatant hypocrites, I think they actually don't know the cruelty and pungency of the double standard. Anyway, interesting that she came to cook.

On the whole, I would say that people with imperfect bodies are more interesting. This is necessarily so because they are less acceptable. Being acceptable is boring. Also, I would make the same observation about those who work out in the gym. They control their anger, their insecurities. They diffuse the power of these. Those who do not go to the gym need the gymnasium of the mind for the same process. I feel this produces a more interesting, more communicative, less narcissistic result. Fat people are often funny because they spent a lifetime limbering up on how to laugh at themselves and how to be liked for their wit, not their fat stomachs. People who go to the gym too much are like people who used to go to therapists and the therapists would never speak, just let them talk. It makes for a selfish breed.

Of course women often make the mistake of feeling that they can perform with more abandon with a fat man because they feel it's easier to have empathy and it's a more comfortable ride. Fat people often have an inverted sense of high esteem, a superiority complex, a huge sense of entitlement because they've often been rejected because of their lumpiness. Resentment is quite an ugly quality. Sometimes you find a fat man's ego is both more sensitive and more brutal; an interesting mixture of very soft and very hard. Just the kind of cruelty and vulnerability that Earl Spencer has always shown his women. He is always riding the scales between shame and regret and plush pleasure-seeking.

Relationship of the Week
Duchess of York and Her Weight
15 October 1995

Fat has always been a Fergie issue. There have always been several Fergies. She comes out like a set of Russian dolls, sometimes weeny Fergie and sometimes blobby Fergie. Her wardrobe apparently includes both size 18s and size 10s. But then what kind of a robowoman, what kind of Stepford wife is a solid size 10 only? Every warm-blooded woman must allow herself to be occasionally plump and occasionally toned. In Fergie's case, dress-size swings with her self-esteem, and with who's been calling her a big frump, with who's been disappointing her, disillusioning her.

Fergie was once wildly optimistic. She was a size 14 when she met Prince Andrew and unused to the harsh paparazzi lenses. She thought that was fine. She said, 'It's nice to be big up top. I do not diet'.

Then she became huge. She became Duchess of Pork. She became humiliated as her waist got thicker and her skin thinner and the insults wore out what was once a rhinoceros hide of self-regard. Actually, she became a wreck.

There was the painful purging with colonic irrigation. Then there were thermal blankets and freezing cold, sloppy clay, mummifying treatments. There was Joe Corvo and his zone therapy, where nerve endings had to be agitated. There were slimming pills that caused mind-altering states. There were blue pyramids. There was Paul McKenna hypnotizing her, and her hair being analysed so she could know what food she was allergic to. Indeed, she even endorsed the Callanetics woman, Callan Pinckney.

But of course, just like any woman, she's allergic to all foods if she eats too much of them. You know, hungry for love, but in the meantime she'll just settle for chips. You know, wanting that emotional nurturing that comes only from fantastic sex, but somehow being convinced that an orgasm can be reached through ice-cream.

Over the years, each of these gurus (this time it's the turn of her personal trainer, Josh Salzmann) like to claim that she has lost four stone in five months and it's all down to them.

The thing is, if she'd actually lost all this weight within this particular time span and never put it back on she'd weigh less than a budgie by now. Sure she gains it back again and she loses a bit, but her real weight is the one thing that will be known only to her and her scales.

I doubt that she was ever fifteen stone. But she couldn't come out and say she wasn't because she'd have to come out and say what she really did weigh. What has changed about her is the public perception of her.

Incredibly, faced with nine years of Fergie press cuttings I noticed that the photograph – a seated Fergie in a suit with big brass buttons – which was used in one tabloid newspaper last week to illustrate how fat she once was, was also once used by the same paper to illustrate how thin she was; how much weight she had lost.

Anyway, over the past year she has been exercising and eating sensibly and now there is no doubt she is looking fairly gaunt. And we are supposed to like this because fat equals ugly equals greedy. Fat is about not being able to shut your face up. Fat is about needing instant gratification, having no control. Fat is about overstepping the mark. Fat is about wanting that chocolate now, not wanting to wait until you're half a stone thinner, a dress size smaller, and that prince can come right on back from round the corner and everything will be lovely again.

Being thin is somehow being clean and neat and disciplined. When she lost twelve pounds in a week after a particularly bad heffalump period following the birth of Princess Beatrice, she said, 'This shows I have discipline'.

During her next pregnancy, as a result of all the cruel pictures and taunts, she decided that she would not eat for two. She dieted throughout and didn't even show until she was seven months. Instead of thinking this was sick, she said approvingly, 'I had to do it.' And she was complimented.

Of course, fat isn't a feminist issue, fat is a competitive issue. It is about who in the class can look the best, get the most attention and get the best boy. It's woman against woman. And now she's been pitted against Princess Diana it is not just that Fergie is thin, this time she is thinner than Di.

Now that Diana has fallen foul in the public eye, portrayed as a cruel Jezebel who tempts men, only to cast them aside after her ego has been gratified, the Duchess of York has, by default, won esteem. And all those lovely adjectives that go with thin: confident, proud, dazzling, lustrous are being applied to her as if she really is this other person that stepped out of the fatty shackles of the old Fergie.

But sadly, or perhaps happily, she will become fat again because the pendulum will swing back, she'll do something gauche, and even though she may still be a similar size, she'll be called fat. I saw her two and a half months ago looking sleek and leggy, dining in Le Caprice, and that was when she was supposed to be fat.

Also, it is likely she will go on a comfort binge the next time she is distressed. Until she has learned all that stuff about it's not what you eat, it's why you have the need to eat it, to indulge in it, she'll always be a size-changer.

The year she learned so many distressing facts about John Bryant, she was big. The year that her marriage was under pressure, and she was under public scrutiny she was bulging. Now, she seems relatively happy and contented, and she is thin for the time being.

Fergie says that she hates exercising and that losing weight was 'a nightmare'. She daydreamed about 'juicy steak and creamed potatoes', which is food-combination hell and absolutely not allowed. Where was the big Fergie with the big appetite for life who could deal with anything that was put on her plate? Swallowed up by thin Fergie, the one who pleases the public more, the one who isn't such an easy target.

Both Fergies, fat and thin, are the targets of body fascism, of a life swinging between cheekbones and double chins, of self-esteem being manipulated by dress-size. How hurtful it must be when the womens' magazines say 'relax girls, voluptuousness and curves are back' and you know they are not talking about you, they are talking about how to be a pipe-cleaner with implants.

Sad Fergie, you do not need to have other peoples' ideals imposed upon you. Have the strength to be who you are. Fat.

Well, she's still hired by Weight Watchers, so I guess it's an ongoing relationship.

Statistics Can Be Vital: Big-Breasted Women 15 May 1994

Some men dress to the left, some to the right, and some women dress right, left, up and down. Elizabeth Hurley clearly didn't want to be an accessory dangled from the arm of her now very famous and very dashing consort, Hugh Grant, at the première party for his box-office smash, *Four Weddings and a Funeral*.

Inappropriately, she thought to upstage him. She pouted out her breasts – they were pneumatic, they were Russ Meyeresque. It wasn't her that got the attention, it was her breasts. She is a competent actress, yet she has since been described as a veritable Bond girl because she has chosen to hide her light under a bosom. Maybe she felt insecure and it was the quickest way to get a front-page flash. But it's not her smile that flashes, it's not her face we look at, it's her breasts. Therefore she's diminished by them, and has become the very trophy wife she wanted not to be.

Big breasts carry big prejudices in the 'This Woman is Stupid, This Woman is a Slut' department, and it can be very tempting to hide behind them. I know this because I have them. Although I'm very fond of them, other people aren't.

Women are jealous of them and men are scared of them, scared because they can't have them, scared because they can.

I was recently told, rather hurtfully, that I might get on better if I dressed less provocatively. You know, try and put them away. But they are a distraction that is not easily disguised. The slinky Chanel suit is not an option; it's not built for me. At an early age, I discovered I had a choice to wear baggy clothes and look like a sack of jumping bunnies, or to throw them forward on a couture platter. I thought that the latter option would get me lots of attention, but this was a confusion; it got my breasts a lot of attention.

When I got my first job on a national newspaper, word was that I was hired because the then associate editor couldn't take his eyes out of my bosoms; this was not good. True, he couldn't be in the same room as me without turning a blustering shade of purple. Rather than control his intense reaction to me, he found it easier to control me by simply avoiding me.

My suspicions that my breasts held me back professionally have been borne out by a report in the latest issue of *Good Housekeeping* magazine that suggests women with small breasts are more likely to end up in the boardroom, because small-breasted women are deemed brighter, more competent, more moral and more modest.

It advises big-breasted women to choose clothes aimed at concealing their most visible assets. If they want to be one of the boys, they have to hush up their girls. Gennifer Flowers says that Bill Clinton used to call hers 'girls', but I think of mine as babies. But who wants to suffocate their sexuality?

As a damage limitation exercise, strapping them down works. The 1920s and the 1960s were among the most empowering time for women, and also the time when breasts sat like two fried eggs.

If I take a look down the corridors of power I do not see breasts. I see breasts on check-out tills, massive. I see breasts on secretaries, massive. But the female executive cup size runneth not over.

My gynaecologist, who counts a bevy of media starlets as his clients, and also boasts a brain that is a computer file filled with the proportions of every breast he has examined, notes, 'All the most successful of the career girls have the smallest breasts.' There are several theories for this:

Number one: it's a class thing. You could never be too rich, too thin or too well-educated if middle class. Working-class women eat fatty food and are not so narcissistic. Big breasts, they go with barmaids, wenches, wet-nurses and the woman who does. Delicate breasts are for the delicate, conniving mind.

Number two: lean and hungry is ambitious. Testosterone makes for a competitive, ambitious streak. Women with thrusting ambitions have small breasts and a lot of testosterone, which is a masculinizing hormone, which it seems may reduce the breast size.

Richard Lynn, professor of psychology at the University of Ulster, says, 'People differ in their hormonal output and this affects their psychological drive. Women who have a larger amount of testosterone are more status-seeking and this reduces their breast growth. It could be that it has a reciprocal effect.'

If this is so it is a symbiotic thing; one recharges the other.

If you combine the hormone theory and the class theory, even in a loose way, you slip into the prejudice theory – the prejudice is that oestrogen-inspired, big-breasted women want sex and babies, not great jobs. Prejudice is the wicked thing that really escalates the action. And while we're in the prejudice department, we find that blondes are fun and brunettes are not, and we find that you cannot be lusty, busty and in the boardroom.

For similar reasons, women comediennes cannot be sexy and funny at the same time, because men can't laugh at as well as fancy something – it's simply too awesome. The new, chicken-chested Cleo Rocos claimed she dieted her boobs away because she didn't want to be thought of as 'bimbonic'.

A woman can be beautiful and successful, a pretty face is, after all, arbitrary, but sexiness is insidious; it gets you. There have been studies that indicate certain types of men like certain types of body shape.

Intellectual men prefer small breasts and this has led us to the equation that small breasts equal big brain. But there is another equation lurking. People often describe me with a smirk, because the equation they've made is: big breasts also equals 'slut'. This is because I do not hide my breasts. As one friend said, I gift-wrap them, I dress them up. I refuse to put them away because they are a perfect litmus test. Men who are confident of their own sexuality don't feel threatened by me, they feel lucky. Men who are uncomfortable with themselves don't want to cope with me, because they believe that women with large breasts are all sexual experience and demands, and they are not up to it.

Women who think I'm slutty are probably jealous of me. At least with my breasts, size 36D out there, it means I have no truck with such characters. I don't want to think of my breasts as my problem. I would much rather know it was someone else's.

Never trust a man who tells you you don't have to go on a diet.

It means they are viciously possessive and they want you to get fat so no other man will want you. They want to appear to not be tapping into your insecurities. They don't want you to go on a diet and talk about calorie intake, food-combining, a carb day, a protein day. No. That interferes with them eating what they want to eat. They don't want to make you verbalize your neuroses. They want you to have all your distorted feelings about your own body in private, never so that it would interfere with their enjoyment of it. All men want an easy life. They want food and sex on demand. They want a medium-thin, medium-attractive woman. Anything too big or too beautiful disturbs them. All men fear women and fear losing them.

Sarah told me about when she was 17 and about to go off to college. She had this boyfriend who was fretting: 'He knew I was going away and would probably leave him eventually. But he'd stuff my face. He'd bring me cakes and Ben and Jerry's ice cream. I said to him, "Do you want me to get fat?" and he'd say "I love you the way you are." But then we'd be out in public, and he'd be staring at these really thin girls. I noticed this and said, "I thought you liked hips and curves . . ." He said, "Don't worry. You're the one that I want." I said, "Yeah. I can tell by the drool sliding down your face for those stick insects."'

Sasha is a Russian artist that I know. He was obsessed by this one very brilliant pupil. He let her live in his studio, have his tutoring free for the occasional life-modelling. The more brilliant she became, the more obsessed he was about her. He was an emaciated thing and she had a history of bulimia, low self-esteem and was ravenously insecure. But not as insecure as him. He began spending more and more time in the studio, monitoring her every move and her every meal. He began cooking blintzes and knishes for her and, he confessed, 'Eat, eat' he told her. 'I want you to be so fat that no other man will want you.'

The problem with becoming so fat that no other man wants you is that the first man doesn't want you either.

I know this man who has a really fat wife. He's a New York lawyer. He can tell anybody anything, except to tell his wife to go on a diet, yet he talks to me about little else but her fatness and says that her obesity is why they don't have sex anymore. I always say it can't just be because she's gained weight and he says, 'Yes, yes. It is.' So then, when she begs you to pay her some attention and she's becoming more and more neurotic and feisty when you roll over and refuse, why don't you tell her to go on a diet? 'I can't.' Perhaps if she was thin, you wouldn't have an excuse to have affairs with all those nubiles. 'Yes. In a way, keeping her fat and unappetizing, I feel justified in my other carnal pursuits. Anyway, I don't want to see my wife as a sex thing. I never want to leave her. We work too well together. If she lost weight, I'd have no excuse not to have sex with her.'

I'm afraid this all comes down to men's compartmentalization problem. The woman they want to live with is rarely the woman they feel the high voltage stuff for because it would be unliveable and not easy, not comforting. I've seen women in stable relationships get fatter and fatter, not necessarily because they're cosier and cosier, but because they've been conned into thinking they don't need to diet. Then they get dumped. I'm sure Paul Merton and his wife Caroline Quentin split up because they both got too podgy.

Sometimes they say, 'You don't need to diet. Exercise is what you need.' Yeah. That's because they want to torture you and drag you out on four-mile runs because men have this ridiculous belief that they can have their cake and work it off. The only way to get thin is to not eat and to not have an emotional relationship with food. Men like you to have an emotional relationship with food because they prefer it to having a sexual release with other men.

Saying you don't need to diet is a way of keeping you in your place because every woman always thinks they need to diet. It's a way of keeping you indoors when you feel too fat to go out of the house. It's disempowering. The man who will spend months telling you what he thinks you want to hear – 'you're not fat' – will choose his time. When you're having a huge row and the woman is winning, he'll play his final winning card of devastation. He'll tell you that no man wants you anyway – you're too fat.

Eschewing the Fat: Men and Diets
3 October 1993

Fat men can be sexy. Svelte men can be sexy. But there's something deeply unsexy about the thought of Men Who Diet. That is partly why men who start to diet are so furtive. Women are programmed to diet from the day they are born. By the time they are teenagers they are chucking up everything they've ever eaten and studying for a degree in calorie-counting.

Men don't think about diets until they have to. They do not have the same sort of relationship with their bodies. Self-examination is not a way of life until someone points out to them that they have a little 'pot'. This might not happen until they are 40. They are shocked. They do not know what to do. There is no male diet role model, no 'Mr Rosemary Conley's paunch and bottom diet', so they retreat into a quiet, calorie-controlled Hell, and don't tell anyone about it. They are ashamed not only of their fat, but of their dieting.

I didn't know my friend Ben was on a diet. For the seven years I have known him he has swept restaurants clean, ordered double portions of vegetables, and up to fifteen starters from a Chinese menu. And only last weekend he couldn't pass the butchers without being tempted by a particularly succulent leg of lamb.

'But darling, we're not having any people round', said his wife. 'I know', said Ben. He stuffed it with garlic and rosemary, then stuffed it down himself. He spent the next day hugely guilty and had to reaquaint himself with 'that Ovaltiney stuff'. He meant Slimfast. 'Did your wife get you that?' I asked. After all, most men don't like buying diet products because you have to go to Boots, look beyond the tampons and the Immac to find the pastel-coloured, whimsically boxed diets.

'My wife?' he yelled. 'If she knew she would be merciless. I keep it in my desk and wait until she's gone to bed to drink it'.

Another acquaintance, Graham, said, 'You never tell another bloke you're on a diet, because that will mean they have to look at you and compare bodies. You don't buy diet products, just cut out things. I'd never dare ask how many calories there are in anything. If a man found out they would laugh at you. It's displaying a vulnerability'.

Diets for men can be very lonely regimes. First-time dieters are like born-again virgins. They are embarrassed. They take a stab in the dark, read the back of a glossy magazine that advises them to go to a Harley Street clinic, where a man will stick a needle in their bottom like an inoculation against yellow fever. They do not see dieting as a way of life, at first. It is a rather nasty disease that must have a rather nasty cure.

Robbie Coltrane, who has just lost six stone (although, like Meatloaf or the recently slimmed Pavarotti he seems much the same size because he is probably a man who is supposed to look like a blown-up chunky cherub) did it by mail-order 'NutriSystem'.

Most men don't know about diets, and are ashamed of their ignorance, but fear that gaining knowledge in this department would have sinister implications: that they are not sufficiently macho. Playing on this knowledge, Pepsi has marketed a new Pepsi for men, called Pepsi Max. It does not contain the word Diet. And a woman from the American marketing office that created it says, 'We say it's got no sugar. We don't say 'calories' because men don't like that. Men think diet drinks are sissy, yet the diet drinks market has a robust growth'.

Diet cola represents 40 per cent of the cola market. That's because once a woman starts a diet she's always on a diet. Fat people use diet products. Thin women and men drink regular cola, or they used to. It's Pepsi's idea to tempt the men into the sugar-free zone. But, as Pepsi knows, men don't diet, they get 'health conscious', they get fit, they live life to the Max.

The accompanying commercial shows a bunch of men who look like they could be former rappers with Marky Mark, surfing down a waterfall and parascending off a cliff, thus plugging home the message 'I'm not really on a diet'.

The first stage of 'men on diets' is full of sixth-form sophistry and pre-pubescent silliness. It's not long before the virgin dieter becomes over-confident and boastful of his exploits. Thus, I have discovered among my men-friends men-who-diet tips for dieting:

Adam: 'Kick-start it with a week's package holiday in West Africa'.

Graham: 'Never wear a jumper because it makes your pot show'.

Sean: 'Eat three prunes a day, they've got nine grams of fibre per 100 grams. That's more than a bowl of All Bran'.

After a while, men who are on diets are like men who are having affairs, sordid unspeakable affairs, breaking the last taboo. Then some of them reach a point where, yes, they are comfortable with who they are and the fact that they diet. They can talk about it. In fact, they can talk about little else. The secret obsession is revealed, they are out and proud and, like new-found evangelists or homosexuals, like attracts like. A secret support network spiders out.

A newspaper editor used to diet in secret with wheat bars tucked away in his top drawer. Then during one editorial conference he came out, saying, 'Our readers don't need to know about the recession, they need to know they can win battles'. The paper's slimming editor was duly summoned. Every few weeks she would devise a special new diet for her boss, like the 'all red-meat diet'. But he was allowed chunks of fruit during the morning. He took up power-walking and now everyone knows he is always on a diet.

Simon, a publisher, has a similar story. 'I went to W.H. Smith's and bought a calorie-counting book for 60p. I read it in the toilet and learned it. I starved. I did Slimfast. They gave you special Slimfast cups, but I would cover the name of the cup and go to the bathroom to mix it up. My daughter caught me, so I was forced to confess. Then people started to notice my different shape. I have lost three stone in six months and I have proved to myself that I can make a change in my life. Very few men have asked me about it, but those who have enquired have been intrigued and asked me to explain my success'.

Other men in Simon's office say that he is their guru, and men who diet need gurus. When male dieters hit the news, it's usually because they've failed. John Smith lost weight but gained it back, and Neil Kinnock simply looks faded. Pavarotti lost weight, more than three stones, but for all the wrong reasons – he was in love. Marlon Brando became bloated because he wasn't.

In November the first all-male slimming seminar will take place. Its creator is Paul Goldin, who is a hypnotist and who has worked successfully with women slimmers simply by 'placing a thin person's belief system into a fat person's mind'.

'The reason we eat is 5 per cent hunger, 95 per cent emotional craving', he says. 'It's the same for men and women but the fat doesn't usually hit men until they reach a certain age'.

Goldin's seminars throughout Britain used to be 90 per cent female, but when he opened up a clinic in Knapton Court, Dun Laoghaire, the figure rose to 40 per cent men – the Irish being less inhibited than the English. Next time round, the men's seminars will be almost the same as the womens: Goldin will brainwash them to simply eat less, and never go on a diet 'because once you start you will be on a diet for life, just like most women'. Be warned.

BLOKES

Never trust a man who calls you baby.

Who wants to be likened to a mewling, puking, pink, wet, screaming thing? Why is it supposed to be endearing to be a little something? And if you're going to be little, at least be a kitten – fluffy with claws. Babies are such dumb things.

The two biggest brutes of my life both called me baby. Baby this and baby that. It's a terrifying habit. They call you baby and then you end up calling them baby back, reinforcing the infantile behaviour. If he calls you baby, he wants you to become one: inarticulate and dealable with.

One of these brutes came from the East End of London. Babe used to roll off his tongue. Everyone was babe, and sometimes, if I was lucky, it was 'oooh, baby.' He thought he was Frank Sinatra.

People in mob movies call their women 'baby', and then they go and saw off someone's feet and put them in binliners in the Hudson River. The word is also popular with men stuck in the 1970s, and characters featured in pop songs are always calling each other baby. Even British boy bands – boys you would never expect to use the word in real life – litter their lyrics with 'baby' and 'babe.'

An acquaintance of mine, John Campbell, from the band It's Immaterial, recently put together a tape loop for a museum installation in Liverpool consisting of ninety-six different versions of 'baby' plucked from pop songs. It began 'oooh baby, baby' sung by Karen Carpenter. 'Baby means nothing and everything,' says Campbell, who is intrigued by its popularity among musicians. 'It's two syllables, it's androgynous, and "b" is good for singing. But in real life, you would never . . . You just wouldn't call anybody "baby". It's a ridiculous concept.'

My friend Sarah used to go out with a well-known magician. 'Hey, babe,' he would often say to her. She said that he said it with such sarcasm that she was never sure whether it was tender or ironic. 'The way he said the "b" it was like a bullet coming at you,' she says. 'The "b" was an anger thing. It scared you. I never felt love from it. It was as if he hated the fact that he loved me and this was how it came out.

Baby often has a violent undercurrent. This is where extremes meet – one reason why it's so popular in soap operas, where you get the full emotional range all at once. Frank Butcher of *EastEnders* was fond of saying, 'oooh, babe,' as is *Brookside*'s Jimmy Corkhill. 'I'm getting you your dream house, Jackie, baby,' he'd say. 'I love the bones of you, Jackie babe.' And that was at the peak of his heroin-dealing career.

The *Honeymooners*, the long running 1950s American sitcom, drew on a relationship where the two characters were always fighting. The female was a feisty piece. She had the upper hand, but the man always had to diminish her. Every episode ended with: 'Baby, you're the greatest.' Baby is diminishment territory. Like the line between love and hate, terms of endearment and abuse can often become blurred.

Then, of course, there's sex. There are only two names that people use during sex: baby and God. I prefer to be called the latter. My husband says that he has used the name 'baby' during sex just in case he used the wrong name. It's safer that way. Fortunately, he's never called me baby in his life.

Another ex-boyfriend of mine never dared call me it unless I was in tears, as in waterbaby, which was just about permissible. But he did use it, unashamedly, as a 'term of endearment' for anyone else who was female. 'I use it for people I feel responsible for,' he claims now. 'Especially if I am having a disagreement. I call them "baby" to show that I am still fond of them and want to remain friends.' In other words, he wishes to patronize them, although he refuses to admit that this is so. When I told him how unappetizing the word is when used to address a fully grown woman, he said, 'I think women who get worked up about things like that should get a life.' Never trust a man who says 'get a life.' It means he hasn't got one. But that's another story.

If you don't want a confrontation, there's an easy way to stop a man calling you baby. Next time he says it, ask him if he's using the term because he actually wants to have a real one.

Relationship of the Week
David Baddeil and Frank Skinner
3 November 1996

I could always imagine them together. There was something Walter Matthau and Jack Lemmon about them, impeccable chemistry, impeccable timing. They could talk about Shakespeare and football, be sensitive then brutal. Sure, David Baddeil and Frank Skinner were laddish together, but there was never anything vulgar. It's hard to share a TV programme and then share a flat, but they did so for three-and-a-half years. It was David's flat in Hampstead. Frank moved in for a week, and never moved out. The cleaner was never allowed into his bedroom. It was like a 14-year-old's. It really was a mess, but David didn't mind. Frank was allowed to let the bread get mouldy and they never had an argument, which was particularly amazing because Frank apparently used to put everything into sandwiches, including steak and kidney pies and jacket potatoes.

Now you think that that would be enough to drive a person mad, but no. They were strange and kindred spirits, David with his double first from Cambridge, middle-class Jewishness, and Frank, 38, a devout Catholic from a working-class area in Oldbury. His was the kind of family that was sometimes so poor the electric got cut off, but his parents always used to tell him never to put the candles in the windows where the neighbours might see them.

It's sad when things you thought were forever come to an end. David is to move out to live with his girfriend Sarah

Bowden, even though she had been living with them there for most of the past year or so. It's somehow not the same thing though. I'm not sure the change will be good for any of them. Frank says that there's never anyone he's got on with so consistently well in his life. He described it as a very successful marriage. 'I think if you had marriage with the sex removed, it would be ideal. If you're not sexually attracted to someone then the tension is out of the way so you can be yourself.' And that's what they were. Themselves, but more so. They indulged and cosseted, reinvented football as an art rather than a sport. Frank and David together fitted perfectly in the *Zeitgeist* of *Men Behaving Badly*, but actually they behaved rather nicely. Frank doesn't drink. He stopped that several years ago after a binge of pernod and home brew in the same glass. They had a cleaner. It was blokishly intimate, but not vulgar, not crass. You could imagine them at home, spiritedly discussing football, or pornography. David likes pornography. His girlfriend is very understanding about it, but I don't think she understands the way Frank does. Frank said, 'One thing we have a frightening affinity for is sexual taste. I bought a book, quite arty erotic photographs, by Kroll for his birthday, and the inscription I put was, "The sad thing is, I know which photos you'll like best." Although we like different women, we like them to do very similar things.'

To be so sexually in tune, but not want to have sex with each other is a very interesting place to be. On the whole, the basic claustrophobia of domesticity kills passion in a sexual relationship. It enhances a platonic one. It is same-sex harmony. Frank and David are blokes – post-modernist blokes – but still blokes. They are comfortable with the masculine mind.

Whereas David is happy to get out his little electronic chin gym, and sleek cheeks in front of Frank, and it feels cosy, doing that stuff with Sarah brings a kind of unpleasant comfortableness. It is the equivalent to a girl not bothering to put on make-up and slouching about in track suit bottoms in front of her boyfriend. Something is being lost here, not found. But if you're a man letting yourself go in front of another man, it is the complete reverse. It's vulnerable in an exciting way, in a way that says you don't have to know who was the only Port Vale player to be capped for England, to prove how big a bloke you are.

I get the impression that Frank has a kind of awkwardness with girls. His longest relationship was for six years with someone from college, and although he was married once to a very nice woman called Lisa, it barely lasted a year. He says he was lonely and sad after his parents' death. He was the youngest son, the favourite baby boy, and his parents died. The father died soon after his mother, he thinks of a broken heart. His father was robust and strong and dwindled away in the space of a year. 'The whole notion of a marriage is that two become one and that's what happened. His other half had gone and he couldn't go on living.' Perhaps if you watch that happen to your parents, you don't want a replica relationship.

I know change is supposed to be welcome, it's supposed to mean we move and grow. There is something so natural and so sweet about the fantasy football couple together. It is as if the season has suddenly changed and you don't know what clothes to put together. It's uncomfortable. It's disorientating. If they have to grow up, will it make them less funny or less fun? I wonder. Rather worryingly for Sarah, David has just written a comedy for Hollywood. He says, 'Like all romantic comedies, it ends where the marriage starts. Those comedies are all about euphoria, and euphoria doesn't exist in a long-term relationship. You have mild epiphanies over a long period of time, and that's so much more complicated to do.' More complicated and more stimulating, but I'm not sure which relationship he's talking about – Frank or Sarah. He says, 'Monogamy isn't natural. My affections are drawn to it, but my groin isn't.' I think he's trying to apply the same hopeless honesty that works when he's talking to Frank, to Sarah. Sarah will be blokish about it, be *faux* casual, but really, what woman wouldn't worry as she planned to set up *à deux* with a man who's talking about the affections of his groin? Of course you might think, well, he was only being honest, and that's the whole point. Men can be honest with other men. That's fine. But if they start this kind of honesty with women, they can only expect to be manipulated and hurt and relearn the discomfort on the soles of the feet when you have to walk on eggshells all of the time.

Blokes
10 October 1993

I had drunk too much vodka. I had said too much. I was desperate to go to bed. But my then-consort had just been bought a drink by the then-editor of the *Daily Sport*. He had to buy him one back. It was two in the morning and I was cross. Why did you have to do that? 'It's a blokes' thing,' he said. At the time I didn't understand or care what he meant by this weird male etiquette.

Bloke isn't a word I use. Blokes aren't people I know. Bloke isn't a word I had heard much until recently. This week I have been drowning in the concept of blokeism.

Jeremy Paxman on *Newsnight*, Monday night, showed us the empty blue conference hall soon to be filled by 'Major and his brand of blokeism'. He actually referred to Major as a bloke. Of course, the reconstructed Tory is just that. Just look at Clarke, he's a bloke and like attracts like.

At the same time every literary review page I scanned seemed to be talking about Martin Amis being a bloke. Reviews of his new book, *Visiting Mrs Nabokov and Other Excursions* were celebrating his excursions into blokeishness, his love of darts, his playing of snooker with Julian Barnes and poker with David Mamet. And as Nick Hornby put it, 'He did not invent that combination of blokeishness and cerebrality of course, but his emergence seems to have validated it.'

Go to the movies and it's all blokevision. There's Harrison, there's Clint, but the cult film is *Reservoir Dogs*, exalted into a bloke landmark. John Woo has been making films for twenty years, but it's only now that his stylish killer-movies have been wooed by Hollywood. They are defined by blokes' simple morality – the good guys kill the bad guys, rescue the women and observe the code of honour by trusting their friends and extinguishing their enemies.

Turn on the television, and it's bloke-in-a-box, Danny Baker, all laddish camaraderie. He has been on the peripheries of television for ten years, and look what's happening now – he's hailed as the most innovative chat show host ever, when he has actually been scripting other people's shows for years. There is no doubt this is the era of the bloke.

What, you might ask, exactly is a bloke, in the sense that the word is now being used?

It wasn't always a term of praise. The bloke – wasn't he an ordinary sort of man? Now he probably, though not necessarily, works in the media, like Baker, or writes, like Amis, and as such can afford the costliest watering-holes, but makes appearances in his local, with other blokes.

His conditioning and background may have fitted him for pastimes such as rugby or chess, but the New Bloke will protest his affection for darts or even the dogs at Walthamstow. He kits himself out in chain stores, Woodhouse, Next or especially by mail order. He loves Racing Green because blokes hate to shop. Blokes hate to cook, so they eat fast-food burgers, spaghetti, and curry that isn't a korma. What's in their fridge? A few beers, Cracker Barrel and something else that used to be cheese.

In search of the New Bloke, I went to Paul Ross, the editor of that after-the-pub Friday television slot *The Word*, and the presenter of *Crime Monthly*. He seemed blokeish enough. He seemed chuffed to be so referred to. Why?

'It is the most I can hope to be,' he said modestly. 'Post-feminism has forced men to try out many impossible roles – the caring New Man, the New Lad, and surely we can't really be doing that bonding "Iron John" thing? The idea of being a good bloke is such a low target that you can actually achieve it.'

A good bloke is, indeed, something to be. But what exactly is it?

Ross defines: 'Blokeness is something that is thrust upon one. It can't happen until your early to mid-thirties, until you grow into your dad.'

'Blokes have a sense of reliability and a whiff of sulphur. You don't go out with a bloke, you go out with his brother. A good bloke would lie for you and hide you from a rampaging virago, and lend you money and never ask any questions.'

'When blokes are in an emotional crisis they go to a pub to meet other blokes and talk about anything except the thing that is bothering them.'

'They do not reveal themselves to other blokes, and, of course, not to women, because they think that women are either inferior, superior or on another planet. They talk about football, money or women.'

Blokes, says Ross, like old songs and equally old movies. They are nostalgic creatures, and therein, I think, lies part of the problem with blokeishness.

It's about looking back and therefore tends to stagnation. John Major's speeches conjure up the paradigms of the England the war was won for. He is Oval-visioned, impassioned about the freedom to clunk a cricket bat. Blokes are not innovators, they do not have a lot of imagination, and it is the out-and-proud bloke Ross who admits that blokeism is about 'settling for less'. It's about a return to your earliest passions.

When you're a young blade, you might want to wear designer labels and pretend you're not interested in Dennis Law, but when you're a bloke you no longer need to impress. You think life's too short to listen to a Husker Du record or read that Kathy Acker novel, so you slip on your video of Oliver Stone's *Salvador*, and you listen to Rod Stewart again.

Stewart, along with Mickey Rourke, are the great bloke icons. Neither are number ones in their field, but then blokeism is about survival. Blokes are not casualties. They do not go out of control, they are not dope fiends, alcoholics or 'bird bandits'. They have a quiet desperation which they control, because they are a bloke.

Blokes and women are another problem area. They call you 'Baby'. They think women are another species, and eventually merge all their experiences into the one that got away. As the blokeish Ernest Hemingway said, 'We all had a girlfriend and her name was Nostalgia'.

This is the ultimate blokespeak, combining brutal romanticism and helpless backward yearning. How do blokes like their women? Never more than three feet away when they want them, and not on the planet when they don't.

Sadly, these non-aspirational creatures have collected a gaggle of wannabe blokes. Ben Elton is an aspirant bloke, as is Robbie Coltrane.

Blokeism has nothing to do with class. Linley is a bloke, Prince Andrew, with his golf, is a bloke, but Prince Charles and Edward are not. Although Princess Anne gets near to being a girl-bloke.

Blokes do not exercise. They might sit in a steam room, but they'd never go to a gym, and thirty sit-ups a day belong in the 'life's too short' department. It's about the elevation of ordinariness bringing its own reward to its own kind, and thus bringing another glimpse of the dark underbelly of cheery blokedom. Jobs for the boys.

An executive bloke whom I know confided, 'If someone comes recommended as a good bloke, it's shorthand for a lot of things. It's a commendation much greater than an impressive c.v.' Blokes will employ and promote their own. They have to. Blokes work hard, but have no ambition.

For blokes, in the end, are sad, sated things. They realize that they will never change their lives. They accept cowardice, lust, hunger, failure and a loss of ambition and nerve. Blokes measure their lives in potential freedom. They will sit in the pub at six, and believe that they are footloose, free men who can stay there all night. Until it is all of eight o'clock and, with a quiet desperation, they go home to what they've settled for.

Relationship of the Week
Damon Albarn and Justine Frischmann
11 June 1995

He is the archetypal sensitive lager lout. Deliciously bony, frail, even girlie in that pop star sort of way. He is thought of as a babe and says he is 'a bored housewife.' Does lots of hoovering. But Blur write boys' lyrics. Cerebral. Important, trivial. They are arguably Britain's most successful pop band, did a clean sweep with the Brit Awards.

She is languid, detached in a regal sort of way. Handsome, hair in that floppy crop. She has been called 'sir' in shops. Her band Elastica, one boy, three girls brandishing guitars that thrash out jaded, ironic, sexual energy. Their recent album went straight in at Number One in the charts.

Together Damon Albarn and Justine Frischmann are the cult king and queen of pop. A more emotionally stoic, more honed, more middle-class, more violence-on-the-inside-only type of pop couple. A constructive version of Kurt and Courtney. The Sindy and Paul of post-grunge pop music. He gets drunk, she gets practical. He keeps their house clean and she thinks dirty thoughts. He cries at yellow-pages adverts, she doesn't believe in emotional excess.

She likes to be thought of as a good bloke, as opposed to a sex symbol. She is incredibly modern like that. They met four-and-a-half years ago. Justine was in the band Suede and going out with its *chanteur* Brett Anderson. Blur supported them a couple of times on the gig circuit. Damon rang up one day and said he was coming round. 'I was very forward and I just said this is what's happening. I think you can do that once or twice in your life if it's right. I don't make a habit of it,' he said. She left Brett for Damon, then Suede got terribly famous and Blur were mainly known for Damon's vitriol about Brett and vice versa. Then Suede faded and Blur became an indie supergroup.

Damon has been described by *Select* magazine as Britain's most shaggable boy. And she has been described by the same magazine as one of the few people who is 'on a permanent cool.' Naturally a lot of people would like to think they don't deserve each other. And would positively trill at the idea of pop's perfect duo going solo.

Last week Damon was pictured in a tabloid bleary-eyed in Stringfellows with a platinum blonde with Bjorkesque squiggly, horned hair. Justine is on tour in America. Much could be made of this except it turns out the girl is called Jo and is a friend who went to school with the band in Colchester. A couple of days later Damon left with Blur for their own North American tour which kicked off with both Blur and Elastica playing in Toronto.

The thing that snuffles any shock-horror infidelity, treachery, betrayal, bust-up scenario, is the permanent cool of Justine herself. She has said publicly, 'Luckily I am not sexually possessive.' It's not that they have an open relationship exactly, it's just he's on tour, she's on tour. If she finds out he's slept with someone she hits him on the head, gives him a hard time for half an hour, and that's it. She says she's snogged people, but has never done anything to jeopardize their relationship.

Her lack of sexual jealousy is either magnificently realistic, practical and self-assured – or deeply clever. A friend of hers confided, 'She says all that to wind him up and to keep him in his place. You know, the looser the grip the tighter the hold.'

Of course there is another possibility. That the bonds that bind them are beyond or below sex. She says, 'He's a boy but he's not that sexually motivated. He's more attention-motivated. I find he has the lowest sex drive of any boy I have ever met.' This would all seem palatable and cosy if she did not give herself 'ten out of ten' for sex drive. Although Damon doesn't write about sex that much and says, 'It's not a big issue in my life.' I believe he's just very English and middle-class about it all.

His father is a lecturer, mother was in theatre. She has a Scottish mother and Hungarian architect father who is chairman of the Pel Frischmann Group who constructed Centrepoint and the NatWest building in London. Justine herself qualified with a degree in architecture but used university life for getting bands together.

They are both of sensible stock. Neither of them are the kind of pop stars that spill guts and gore and throw themselves into unnecessary torture for the sake of a lyric.

Justine feels that that's why Blur are not big in America. They're too refined. Emotionally taut, not gushing and extreme.

Justine doesn't like sentimentality in songs, prefers dryness. Says that if things are open and over the top they lose their power. 'It's like how it's a lot sexier to see someone half-clothed than naked. Lyrically if you leave yourself really naked there's something quite uninteresting about it. Whereas if you write something that's got a négligé on it's more intriguing.'

I suspect Damon and Justine are completely a relationship in a négligé. And I would share the disbelief that she's not sexually possessive. She's just playing it right.

When she wakes up every morning she looks at Damon, who is like 'a small furry animal being disturbed.' Then he gets up and brings her coffee in bed. Then he might do some tidying up.

It's certainly a realignment of sex roles that doesn't seem to emasculate or defeminize. Justine buys *Loaded* magazine. She thinks it's funny to look at tits and bums. She thinks you can be a girl and you can be a lad. She thinks that 1990s babes have to be that way.

'Around the time of Debbie Harry women were less frightened of their sexuality. You could look glamorous and people wouldn't think you were a bimbo. It can't be that way now.'

So then she lets Damon pout and flirt, and he wears more jewellery than her. While she's sultry, angular, sardonic. She's glad she cut off her hair. 'The girl who looks boyish is the intelligent boy's choice.'

She's so eager to appear at home in this good-bloke mode I wonder if she protests too much and it's another négligé. If there was ever a point of pressure in their relationship it was that she couldn't stand to be the also-ran, the girlfriend who also had a band. That would be much too Courtney.

They say that their relationship is stimulating but not competitive. Yet it is she who has the greater musical knowledge. It has gratified her though that in America Damon has been described as 'Justine-from-Elastica's boyfriend.' The rawness of Elastica's sound is more to the American palate. And it is likely they will be the bigger success Stateside. Will the sensitive lager lout be able to handle it? I hope so.

She once said that when somebody tells you they love you every day it becomes meaningless, whereas if they tell you once a year it totally means something. I don't think they have to say it very often, but in a way they say it all the time. As the Blur lyric goes, 'Looking for girls who are boys/Who like boys to be girls/Who do boys like their girls/Who do girls like their boys/Always should be someone you really love.'

THIRD SEX

Robowoman
4 June 1995

I always understood that love could turn you inside out, but never that it could turn you into someone else. Even as a small child I had a notion of the malignancy of possession and control that so often pose as sweetness, protection and a life of no responsibility. The idea of changing the name you were born with just because you decided to be married to someone always seemed ridiculous.

Mine was the generation of women who took the spoils of feminism for granted. You know, the right to an interesting job, an independent life, being your own person, keeping your own name. Not having to be defined by a man unless you wanted to be. Watching the film *The Stepford Wives*, where husbands replaced their wives with acquiescent robots, for fun not for real.

Feminism is now of course a dank relic of a word that doesn't fit in its own skin comfortably. The same might be said of all the things it stood for. A survey last year in American demographics reported here last week confirmed that the pendulum was swinging back. More women wanted to be Mrs. Among my friends I notice a creeping trend of wilful submission.

The famously pneumatic Pamela Anderson has had a new contract drawn up that says in the next series of *Baywatch* she'll be known by her married name, Pamela Lee. She loves writing it on cheques. She thinks it's cute and rightful.

Jemima Goldsmith didn't only change her whole name – she is now known as Haiqa Khan – but her religion, her home, her clothes, her lifestyle too.

You can't escape the sad pictures of her in that drooping mustard outfit, claiming, 'I find the traditional shalwar kameez (tunic and trousers worn by most Pakistani women) far more elegant and feminine than anything in my wardrobe.' She says it in the same voice of the pleaser that Pamela uses when she reveals how she's going to serve Tommy, dinner, herself, and two babies very quickly.

They are of one voice because they are one woman – robowoman. Pamela, pouting her way around Cannes recently to promote *Barb Wire* – a film based on a cartoon character that she is to portray – was poured into a latex corset and was liquorice-legged in black boots. She was a cartoon of sexuality. She was in a uniform, therefore in her box, not threatening, not sexy for real. In the same way that the shalwar kameez is designed not to threaten. It is the same uniform, whether you overtly hide something or overtly display it, it demonstrates that you are conscious of the female form.

Both appear to be dressing for men, designed by men, controlled by men. Both are equally untantalizing. Both outfits spell submission.

Jemima issued a little speech which was printed in a newspaper. One had the sense that though it had come out of her, it was written by the robowoman that had taken over. Carefully worded it said, 'Religiously speaking there was absolutely no compulsion for me to convert to Islam.'

Robowomanization is a force stronger than religion. It makes you open your eyes and not see things. She boasts that she's visited Pakistan three times and seen that Islamic women have nice responsible jobs and are independent-minded. Asking the question, are the women of Islam male-dominated rather goes along the same lines as the Pope being Catholic and Dolly Parton sleeping on her back.

Jemima also said, 'It would seem a Western woman's happiness hinges largely upon her access to nightclubs, alcohol and revealing clothes.' How could she have forgotten that she met Imran in a nightclub (named after her mother Annabelle) wearing revealing clothes?

Men may package robotization very warmly and sweetly. Once the robotization process has been completed you're helpless and reviled. A spirit is only interesting till it is broken. Men want to make wild, untameable creatures homey. That's the thrill. Cartoon life becomes boring and they will go out in search of another drawing.

Robo nation does not stop at Jemima and Pamela. Nor did it even start there. It's always been around. Although it used to be disguised. Those hard blondes with pouting buttocks, pert lips, long blonde tresses, and bandage-size skirts, those bimbos with whims of iron who wielded their way through the 1980s so successfully, were a prototype.

Feminism wasn't quite dead then. And one could grudgingly admire a girl who knew how to get what she wanted out of a man and his wallet by wiggling and jiggling all the right bits.

Short-term manipulative success was a long-haul disaster. If the way to getting ahead was getting what you wanted out of him, it wasn't really getting it on your own terms. It was still a form of dependency. As the man paraded his trophy of cleavage and heels, it was difficult to know who was manipulating whom. For a while back there, bimboism was ironic, post-modern, fun. Then it gave birth to the emasculated man, who resorted to the gore of laddism. Laddism does not respect brains, it respects taut disposable flesh. Laddism swept into men's hearts like a football hooligan. Then things really started to move.

Instead of it being quirky for women to say, 'I hate female bosses,' it became the norm. Instead of it being amusing to boast, 'I'm tired of working. I want to be a full time wife,' it became too creepy, too true. Although more women than ever are working, and more women than ever are the main breadwinners, there is still a sense that robowoman is on-hand. They work for the money, not for the job. They work because the family unit likes the luxury of a secondary income, not because they need a life.

Some months ago a friend of mine got out the movie *The Stepford Wives* and said with a thrill, 'I want to be one. Just think how wonderful. No responsibility, no worries. Like a Tory wife. I want to cut off my long hair and wear a headscarf and swap recipes, go to step class. I get a thrill out of it.' I thought she said it with irony. But now I don't see her any more. She's too busy cooking and stepping and collecting headscarves.

Shirley Conran is an interesting litmus test. In the 1960s and 1970s she was out there on the edge of feminism writing those superwoman books about doing it all and having it all. This week, at 62, she's showing off her surgery – breast reduction and tummy tuck – posing topless in Monte Carlo waves for *OK* magazine. She didn't see the need, or no one saw the need of her, at 22, 32, 42 or 52, to pose topless. Why now?

Because she wants to prove that she can still please men. She may think she's showing sexiness. Instead she's showing surgery. She's showing herself to be a cartoon character called, of course, Robowoman. Somebody to be looked at merely as a physical entity. Whereas when she was younger and in a different climate she sought to survive on her writing skills and her wit.

Once again, women are not only a physical convenience for men, but a fiscal one. Recently, we have been treated to reports of top flight male executives shovelling over shares and putting them in their wives' names.

Mrs David Jefferies, whose husband is chairman of the National Grid, was quoted as saying, 'I am not even aware of how many shares I own.' Actually it was £334,000 worth, and a heftily reduced tax burden for her husband. Men like a woman who is tall, lean and voluptuous, but who takes up very little head space.

One only has to look at the fashion industry. Fashion used to be an interesting expressive force for women. Look how dull and samey and uniform and retro clothes are becoming. And look at the clothes-horses. Small-headed women with coat-hanger shoulders have become revered as a breed.

Jean-Paul Gaultier was wrong when he suggested last week that Claudia Schiffer was finished because she was too doll-like, too boring, too bland. He doesn't understand because he's a gay man with different requisites. It's OK to be funny and sexy if you step out with a gay friend – he doesn't understand that unchallenging Claudia, her Barbie doll bones, her blondeness, her unshakeable smilingness, her giggling at unfunny jokes, is exactly what men want. They want it in their bones. It comforts them because it doesn't challenge them or move them. Boring, yes. But you could always swap her for another model.

After Robowoman came Robogirl. Robogirl comes in ginger, posh, sporty, scary and baby. And it sings of girl power, which they think is the power to tease and to take, but is actually the power to please, make a lot of money and make a whole generation want to be robogirls just like you. They are the first pop band which are also a franchise.

Anne Widdecombe
News Review
21 January 1996

It's a thin, strangulated voice, militarily crisp yet sing-songy evangelical, brutish and babyish. The 's's come out like 'sh', as if her breath is always in shock. She is short, so short that I can look down on an inch of white root.

Ann Widdecombe, Home Office Minister, pro-life, pro-death penalty. A recent Catholic convert. An arch-Tory lost in that tricky territory of promoting personal freedom and obeying the harsh authoritarian doctrine of the church.

This week she apologized to the House for her mistakes. The policy of chaining women prisoners in hospitals when they are about to give birth has now been reversed. Hospitals had voiced their concerns about it to her, but in a mix-up the correspondence had never reached her. So let us be clear here what she was apologizing for. Not an error of judgment, but an administrative error.

'The mistake was very clear – that there was on the face of

the statement a very clear contention that the hospitals had not expressed concern and in fact it has come to light that they have.'

If they had not expressed concern, would she still have felt that the issue of security before dignity is a valid one? 'What I have said was that we have a balancing act to perform between security and dignity. It has never been our policy to restrain women in childbirth.'

So although she has apologized for being wrongly informed she seems strangely unrepentant and still untouched by the human depravity element of prisoners having to give birth supervised by a prison official. The *Daily Mirror* nicknamed her Doris Karloff.

'I can't get worked up about that. Occupational hazard. Your profile rises and you get more of this sort of treatment, one is used to it. On the whole this week has not been upsetting,' she clips.

Some of the attacks on her have, however, been misjudged. The notion that she's been unsympathetic to these mothers because she has never had the experience of giving birth is a ridiculous one. What she has not had, it appears to me, is the emotional experience of being a woman.

Sure, she may temper her Albanian hockey-team-goalie looks with dainty red fingernails, but mentally she is a secret sex. She doesn't seem to want to know herself as a woman. She doesn't take this extra flack and feel persecuted because that's 'whingeing and feeble' – which is appropriate. But what is more revealing is that she doesn't think that men and women are different creatures, thus she has none of the gallantry and protecting instincts of a man, or the vulnerability and power of a woman.

There's a stubborn refusal on her part to see any issue as a woman's issue. Of course she would be against positive discrimination, getting more female MPs in the house because she got there fairly and squarely.

She's square of figure, of face, of manner, of style, of haircut. And of course her anti-abortion stance means that she doesn't see abortion as a women's issue. 'Unborn children come both male and female, so it's not one just for women.'

She doesn't care to temper her views in accordance with how the rest of the world might react. She doesn't even care to get my name right and does not care about my opinion because hers is so absolute, so rooted, chanted mantra-like and spat out with fundamentalist zeal.

'Valuing life is for society, not just for women. I think that this rather diminishes the role of the father. It indeed suggests that the male could be completely irresponsible.'

In reality that's often the case. 'This may be your view, but my view is that it is not an ideal basis on which to run a social system, a basis in which half the society is completely irresponsible. You base your principles not on what happens but on what you want to see happen.'

This is only the first instance where the phrase 'reality check' pops into my head.

She studied Latin at Birmingham University before going on to Oxford to study politics. She speaks in the language of another England, you know, the one the war was won for. She says 'bunkum' and 'rot' a lot.

She has always been ambitious, wanting to go into politics since she was 16, suffered a series of knock-backs, like not being offered a safe seat the second time around and had to wait to get Maidstone at her third attempt. She enjoys saying, 'Life isn't about being easy.' She is pleased that she was not always top of the class at school. School was a convent, single sex, in bed by 7.30 p.m. on Saturday when she was 18.

No, she never rebelled, thought the discipline was a good basis, single sex schools a sound ideal. When challenged about the intense focus of her ambitions, she will reveal that she neither dwells on a past that might haunt her or dreams about a future that might disappoint. She simply seizes the day. Except she says it in Latin, '*Carpe diem*.'

Has she ever seen an image consultant? 'Most emphatically not. In the 1987 election there were four female candidates for Maidstone and an image consultant phoned and said as I was in competition with three other women, I would be judged on my appearence, could she give me advice? I said absolutely not, and my majority went up 60 per cent. The electorate is not swayed with an image.' What she means is she isn't swayed because such fleshy things never touch her.

Despite the fact that her clothes seem to be ill-fitting and always strangely-coloured synthetic materials she always has these nice manicured nails and she dyes her hair black. So there is, one imagines, a lurking concession to gender.

Why does she paint her nails? 'I happen to like it.' How does she feel about the way she looks? Does she ever think, 'I wish I looked like this or that?' 'No, I don't waste time on that.'

Has she ever worried about these things? 'When I was a teenager I had some model perfection in my mind. Teenagers do get terribly uptight about glamour and looks and all the rest and I'm sure that's probably true. But it's not something that's a serious consideration in my life.'

This frumpy thing was not always thus. There's a picture of her from the early 1970s where she looks almost babe. She's in a wench-like dress, low-cut, lace-up cleavage, a velvet choker and wild hair. Did she ever have an image that she aspired to? 'I don't recall it. The 1960s was a ghastly look. All those made-up eyes.'

Ask her anything to do with her being and the physical perception of it and she will blank and say, 'I can't remember.' It appears she nurtured her political ambitions at the cost of any emotional, physical ones.

She was utterly indifferent to boys while at school, she says. So she never worried, will he like me, will he not? 'That was never a phase I went through.' Have you never thought in your life, will he fancy me? 'No.' Did you never have a crush on a boy? 'No, this is going to be a barmy article. I honestly think I had better things to think about.'

Didn't she think she might be missing out? 'I never missed out on anything. I really think that individuals should be allowed to do their own thing.'

There was only ever one boyfriend, a three-year romance

while she was at Oxford, but she said, 'It didn't survive the transition into the real world.' I think perhaps it was she who never made the transition.

She had a cat for twenty-four years, it died, and she talks of 'taking it for disposal.' As a Catholic, does she believe animals have a soul? 'Absolute bunkum.' As for the man and her broken heart she declares, 'Absolute bunk. It was a very straightforward mixture of choice and chance that I never married.

'As far as I was concerned Mr Right never came along. I had other things to do.' But what about a Mr Wrong? 'I wouldn't have been interested in Mr Wrong. Because I wasn't looking for Mr Right, I never found Mr Wrong.' And does she feel lucky about that? 'No. Like I said, I regard it totally neutrally. I'm neutral on this issue.'

For a second I thought she said, 'I am neutered by this issue.'

I wonder if it was a fear of failure that prevented her from going headlong into a relationship. She assures me that if she had had a marriage it would not have failed and no failure in her life could ever be as painful as a marriage failure. Her bleakest moment was the defeat of the David Alton anti-abortion bill. She cried.

She is, curiously, romantic. Which fits with her unworldliness, but not with her 'bunkum' and 'rot' talk. Her favourite period of history is Charles II, ironically a notable rake.

Her other interest is Roman Catholicism. She left the Anglican Church over the ordination of women. She explains, 'At the point of consecration, a woman cannot be *persona Christi* with the Church as her bride. It's a bit like trying to have a man play the Virgin Mary.'

She seems more sure of the roles of the sexes and sexuality in the Church than in life. It reminds me of the metaphysical poets, John Donne's 'Batter my heart three-person'd God.'

Most of the issues she feels strongly about are free votes in the Commons. She's anti-hunting, but pro-hanging, justifying it in accordance with the catechism: it's all right to kill if you're protecting life. There's no point in getting into the argument with her that our justice system sometimes makes mistakes. Her beliefs are absolute, even believing that hospitals hadn't complained, when they got her into the mess from which she has not quite emerged.

The other thing that separates her from the rest of the world is that she doesn't own a TV set. She doesn't want to pay a licence to have 'a continual diet of filth and irregular living and pure rot that is turned out by the Beeb.' What does she mean, irregular living? 'I don't think I have to spell it out, that's slightly disingenuous.' Yes she does. What I consider irregular may not be the same thing. 'I think that if you have a programme that portrays drugs and wanton sex it portrays it so much so that it becomes the norm and this is institutionalizing irregular living.'

Yes, but people do take drugs, they do have sex. She seems allergic to it. 'I am not allergic to it. Just don't want to watch it.' Her hands flutter and she squirms in her seat. We have to agree to disagree. She does not shake my hand as I go. Who knows what or who ever touches her.

Well, we were never going to get on.

Never trust a woman with a bob haircut.

It means they are covert and corporate; bland but baleful. The bob is for women who have truncated themselves and hate you for it. Two of the most hateful women in my life had bobs. One was a commissioning editor on a magazine: 'Don't worry. Tell me all your ideas and I'll shape them up for you.' Yeah. Shape them up and pass them off as hers. People with bobs tell you: 'We women should stick together.' This is what this woman said, and then, after a cosy lunch, she spread the word that I was basically a tart.

Women with bobs are jealous if you have a boyfriend. Women with bobs steal husbands because theirs have already left them because they've had a bob and desexed themselves. After all, it's called a bob. And that's a man's name.

The other hateful woman I knew with a bob was very angry. Her husband had left her for me and she had a peculiar, bob-like, insidious torture routine. First of all, she spent all of their savings having me followed day and night by a private detective, just to spook me. Then she sent me all the love letters that the man had ever written her, including ones he'd written her while living with me. In fact, the ink had hardly dried. I still remember them. When this didn't split us up, she would empty the contents of my bin – cat sick and all – through the letter box. She should never have cut off her hair.

Bobs look innocent, but they are packed with aggression. My friend Ros, a psychic, once went for a bob and the minute it was cut she had a panic attack. 'I felt a nothing. I felt locked into it. I felt that I had given my power away and I started screaming,' she says. Ros immediately clipped it up and pulled it into a mess, which is where it stayed until it grew. 'I felt girlie in a pubescent way,' she says. 'It's OK to have girlie long hair. That's sexual. It has power. But the bob doesn't have any sexuality to it.'

I've asked men if they trust women with bobs. The painter says that his model, who is a dominatrix, has a bob and he trusts her implicitly, but he's the one who had the wife with the letter-box habit.

Another man, a writer, says, 'They're not overtly sexy. They come with women who are good at golf, who wear all-concealing sports bras.' His ex-wife had a bob. 'Bobs are not romantic,' he says. 'They are not showy. And there's always something invulnerable about people who don't need to show off. It's kind of a challenge to secretly believe that under the bob is a Farrah Fawcett waiting to get out.'

A bob often means there is an undercurrent of great passion. Or venom, as can happen when the passion is unrequited. Hair is an emotional barometer, and a bobbed head shows someone who has settled for less. It is hair in denial. It is masochistic, medieval. It's Joan of Arc. It's for women who have problems being women and unleash that on the rest of the world.

Once, in the 1920s, this hair was a symbol of rebellion, liberation and innovation and now it's just the opposite. It's the symbol of a woman who's tamed. Bobs are coming back into fashion, along with shoulder pads and power dressing. You must be on your guard.

A bob haircut looks easy, but it's very complicated. You have to maintain it every month at the hairdresser, although you don't do much to it yourself. You can't. You're stuck with it, so you're dependent on someone else – the hairdresser – the biggest control freak in the universe.

I asked one friend, a former hairdresser, what he thinks of women who have bobs. 'Very unsexy conformists. I've cut millions of them, but I've never gone out with a girl with a bob,' he says. But there again, you can never trust a hairdresser. They're responsible for them in the first place.

Never trust a woman who doesn't wear make-up.

It's such a horrible expression of vanity, self-assurance posing as timidity. It's *faux*-modesty that says, 'I don't need to be a tripped-up tart. I'm good enough *au naturel*. It looks cowering, but the subtext says, 'I'm so perfect my features speak for themselves.' It also says, 'I'm so brazen I don't need to hide.' I don't trust people who aren't insecure. They're aliens. Wearing no make-up is a definite mask in itself. It says, 'I'm serious. I'm too busy for fripperies.' Or, 'I'm too put upon and I'm a professional martyr.' Or, 'I've given up on myself.' Women who have given up on themselves smell bad in their soul. They're like a contagious disease. You don't want to be near them because they're jealous of you.

My friend Anna, the artist, likes lipstick and eyebrows a lot, but most of her friends don't wear make-up. They make her feel as if she isn't self-sufficient and confident enough not to wear it. But she is striking, with or without, actually, and her friends are mostly plain, make-up-less beings that seem to be in perpetual jealous agitation about her pulling-power. One of them, Ellen, 30 years old but still gets a rent cheque from her parents and has a lot of cats and lentils, will occasionally venture out to a dance club with Anna. She sneers while Anna's having a good time flaying her hair and limbs around. But if guys come over, she'll say something like, 'Oh Anna. You poor thing. That spot's looking really sore,' as if Anna didn't know that her concealer stick was not enough.

Then there's the third sex; those busy, busy women with large wardrobes of trouser suits. I had an editor like that. She would commission the kind of article that said a famous actress should have stood by her man even though he may or may not have been beating her up. These are women for whom the bond of female empathy has long lost its appeal.

Then there are women who are afraid to be seen as sexual

beings because they have not been a sexual being for so long, they think that make-up is tantamount to a leather basque. Not like the maintenance of brushing your teeth. They don't want to focus attention on themselves. You can't trust a woman who wants to disappear because then she'll only resent you when you are noticed.

Then, of course, there are the women who buy make-up to look like they're not wearing make-up. They are the Julia Carling wannabes that read somewhere that men like girls to look natural. Who hasn't had the boyfriend who's said, 'You look much better without make-up.' Yeah. Without make-up you look blemished, pink, virginal, innocent and owned, because no one else would want you looking plain. Men always get it wrong. They think it's vulnerable to look slightly chafed of skin and darkened of eyes and pale of lip. But it's not. If you feel bold enough to be seen like this, it's a kind of armour and it's deeply manipulative and covert. Of course there are times when I don't wear make-up: when I used to go to the gym, because big black lines running down my face, a sticky combo of mascara and sweat, looked really stupid, and to walk the dog first thing in the morning. But then as soon as I'm out, I'm ashamed of myself and don't give the dog enough time in case I'm going to run into somebody who knows me. Or, when I'm feeling so supremely confident that I don't mind waking up in the morning with someone looking on my slept-in face. I never take my make-up off at night, whoever I'm sleeping with, basically because I can't be bothered. Life's too short to get our face naked.

Then there's the type that doesn't know how to wear make-up and never really did. They say with gushing girlishness, 'I just am no good with eye shadows. I make myself look like a clown. Hee, hee.' If you can't manage dusting your eyes with a bit of powder, or you want to appear so helpless as to suggest this, there must really be something wrong with you. Most dangerous though are the martyrs, the 'I'm too put upon.' They're nearly always blonde, and there's the type that have inveigled themselves between me and my

various consorts over the years. They try to use their pathet-
icness as a weapon. They're the sort that get pregnant and
pretend they didn't understand the pill packet and their
names usually end in 'ie' or 'y'. Mia Farrow was a hoover for
sympathy. She never wore make-up. It would in some way
deflect from the plaintiveness of her eyes. She also wears
jumpers and T-shirts that she's had for years as a form of self-
confidence. Also, lesbians who are not lipstick lesbians don't
wear it. But there might be an exception to the rule here
which is 'Never trust a woman who doesn't wear make-up
unless she's called kd lang.'

CONTROL

Relationship of the Week
Nicky Clarke and His Clients
3 December 1995

Hair and sexuality are inextricably linked. Surrendering your head is to surrender the most intimate body part. Nicky Clarke, probably the most famous hairdresser in England knows this, he is empowered by it, thrives on it and is paid very well for it.

For some time now he's charged £150 a head. His telephone line opens at 8.30a.m. and by 8.45a.m. he's booked a week of hair appointments and there are another 350 women on the wait list. For God's sake why?

He's affable enough. Cuts a great soundbite. But look at the hair he cuts. Unbelievably, he was awarded hairdresser of the year again this week. The award presented by one of his clients whose hair has featured in the news this year more than ever before – Paula Yates.

We have had the inside scoop on her baldy bits, her greasy bits. And the tomato soup coloured pointed tufts that were her recent crowning glory. I wonder how many of his clients whoosh him into the *chaise d'amour* in the VIP room, all droolingly attentive and say, 'Make me look like Paula.'

He not only gets away with such mutilation, he is applauded for it. Oh, you've seen them time and time again, those before and after pictures where a reasonable-looking, long-haired model is the pretty one, and then we have another shot, her soul cut out of her, while she flashes a Stepford wife grin and gleams out of some truncated form, or worse, she's wearing a bob.

Clarke's hands are insured for £1 million, and indeed they are invested with extraordinary powers. After people have been to see him they often claim it was like an out-of-body experience. Indeed, they certainly look like they are visiting someone else's body.

Remember when Fergie was fashioned into a cheek-sweeping bouffant bob? She looked like she was visiting the ghost of the *Mary Tyler Moore Show*. Selena Scott, when she went from longish to crop, looked like Princess Diana. And Yasmin Le Bon, who went from a sensuous amount of dark, long hair to a stripy two-tone geometric crop, looked like Nick Rhodes.

Some women are addicted to having their hair cut. Some are sad and like the whole performance of the attention with which they are fêted. And they are famous by proxy, because his fingers that are touching your head have touched other more famous heads, thus they are validated. Some just like to be touched.

For Clarke himself, though, born a boy without a bathroom in a grim East End flat, four of them in one bedroom, it must be an incredible control thrill.

There are never famous women hairdressers. Even though hairdressing is populated by thousands of them. They can never snip their way through the glass hairdryer because men are more easily allowed to manipulate and recreate. Control, sex, hair – they are a triumvirate, a kind of reverse Samson syndrome. Women deprived of their hair are harmless as well as hairless. They become nearer the middle sex.

The thrill to be found in mutilation of hair is quite known as a fetish. It is not talked about much because hair can be savaged so rarely and dramatically because of the length of time it takes to re-grow. Submission and surrender are all part of basic S&M. And a form of this is replicated by Clarke and his clients. The more famous the woman the more exciting is the possibility of submission and humiliation. The brilliant joke is he convinces them that he has improved their looks.

Interesting that Nicky Clarke is famous for his own long, strawberry-blond locks. No one gets to cut him. Yet he is notorious for advising the chop. He's radically shortened the hair of Selena Scott, Yasmin Le Bon, Amanda de Cadanet, Lisa Butcher. And he has radically lessened the hair of Paula Yates, in that it has got thinner as well as shorter.

Short hair in itself is of course not uniformly unsexy, but almost always with the famous heads he has cut he has made them less sexy and more rigid-looking. This is especially curious because he's always saying hair should look natural. 'The best haircuts look like they haven't just come out of the hairdressers.' One might argue that for £150 one might want to look as though one had been to the hairdresser.

But this is Clarke's subterfuge. Saying that a new haircut should be almost unnoticeable is the exact opposite of what he really enacts. He loves the dramatic, the radical. He likes the haircut not to look like a hairdresser has touched it, but that he has touched it, that he has been there and is empowered thus. For years people talked about the Duchess of York's bob, in fact for the length of time it took her to grow it back. He says he is deeply affected by what a client thinks. Actually he is deeply affected by the attention it gives him.

He has his own pretentious brand of hair treatments that allege thickening and shining. They are called Hairomatherapy. His clients, largely female, although not always – his male clients uncannily include Bob Geldof – do seem to think that a visit to him is a kind of therapy, what you might call a head shrinking. If he can operate from inside the head, tell them he is spending two hours on a sculpture, tousle them, tinker with them, their egos will feel so puffed out it doesn't matter if their hair is.

Priests, shrinks, hairdressers, politicians – they all like power. Usually because someone somewhere tried to control them. Nicky Clarke is 36 and has been with his wife Lesley for 13 years. She is his business manager. Six years older than him. Orders his day. Takes his appointments. Takes his money. Doles it back out again. She is the woman he admires most and she stands for no nonsense.

He may take his clients and cosset them in his womb-like VIP room and adore them with his fingers, flirt with them with his smile, snap his lizard-skin cowboy heels at their feet. But watching over him, guiding, sometimes subtly, sometimes not, there's always Lesley. Lesley's a nice woman, jolly.

But somehow the more overly relaxed he is, the more shifty he steals within.

I went there once. He did drawings of the haircut he planned to give me – a tufty-looking thing. When I quibbled that it was shorter than I intended he urged that otherwise there was no point, I needed to make a difference, be transformed into this new, lighter, funnier thing. Trying to sell me the line that new hair means new head. So many unhappy people must buy that. He mentioned the phrase 'a cartoon sort of look,' which finally had me scuttling. But then there are certain buzz words, like 'short is practical' that the initiated know to run from.

Again it is a testament to his shamanistic reputation that makes Paula Yates say that she goes in looking like 'a sad testament to motherhood' and leaves 'looking able to stop the traffic.' Yes, but does she think she's stopping the traffic because she looks good?

He doesn't so much cut hair as blind people. He once said that he tends towards quietly sensual hair. He speaks like that, and nobody bothers to tell him that sensuous is loud. His greatest compliment is when something looks 'post-coital.' I wonder if perhaps he's not seen much post-coital. Why would anyone want to pay £150 to look like they've got hair that's just been fucked? Clearly he must bamboozle his clients with his wordplay by insinuating that his haircutting is a sexual experience.

Bad girls, fallen women who get tarred and feathered, also get a shaved head as a punishment. But I can't think of a worse punishment than having the hair of the stripy Yasmin or the orange Paula.

Never trust a person who wants to control your hair.

People who want to mess with your hair want to mess with your head. If a man says to a woman 'Grow it', it's like saying he wants you to be fluffy, more feminine, more controllable. And if a man says, 'I think you should cut it shorter' it's like he's threatened by its wildness and wants to make you less of yourself, more plain because he's worried about other people fancying you. If a woman wants to radically change the hair of her boyfriend, it's branding him as hers. Some people like hair control and they take it personally if a radical change occurs without their permission.

Julia's mother says, 'I used to have long, straight, brown hair in the seventies which I occasionally tucked behind my ears. My first husband was constantly taking my hair out from behind my ears so that it hung around my face. I looked like Cousin It, but I think he did it because I have a round face and he thought it made my face look thinner. On our honeymoon in Paris, I had just seen *Last Tango in Paris* and in it Maria Schreiber changes from a conservative girl into this wild, teased and tousled thing. One day during the honeymoon, I went out alone for a walk and decided to get my hair cut like her. I went back to the hotel to show my new husband. I had forgotten my room-key so I had to knock on the door. The door opened, then it closed and he said, "We don't need any maid service." He hated it and immediately stuck my head under a tap and changed it back to the way it was.'

But I have discovered that hair control is a hereditary trait. Julia herself was going out with this smoulderingly attractive boy, Evan. One of his best features was his wavy brown hair. He always got bad haircuts and she says, 'I couldn't stand seeing him at any less than his physical peak because looking at his beautiful image made me feel better about wasting my time with such a loser. One day, I arrived at his house to find him completely bald. I couldn't speak or move for about a minute. I felt like someone really close to me had died. I locked myself in his bathroom and couldn't stop crying for two hours. Soon after, we broke up.'

It is unclear whether it was because of the hair or because of the loss of control. Hair and sexuality are inextricably linked. Control, sex, hair – that's the Holy trinity. If you surrender your head, it's surrendering your whole body. It's submission. It's basic S&M, a shaved head as a punishment. It's not for nothing that nuns, when they marry Christ, relinquish their human sexuality. All their hair is cut off.

The person that I'm not having the relationship with was having this affair with this actress who had really nice hair. 'Her husband found out about me, so he pinned her to the bed with her hair and cut it all off.'

Many years ago, Sarah was a child bride to a controlling European. She had her hair done in braids like Bo Derek in *10*. 'He was very angry because my hair-style was analogous with the thing that made her a sex symbol. He called me a whore, got hold of me and ripped the braids out. He ripped my own hair out of my head. The pain was incredible and it was enough to make me rip him out of my head. I left him and chopped all of the hair so I was like a marine. This was because I didn't want men to look at me because I hated him so much.'

The other Sarah says, 'All my boyfriends were paranoid of an upcoming trim. They'd say, "Only half an inch, OK?" Because I'm so tall, they wanted to keep me non-threatening, they wanted to keep me a woman. Short hair might be too butch, too tough. This made me feel that I'm ugly without my long hair.'

Bill always had total control in his relationship with Becky. She was a manic depressive and he used to dress her. Select her underwear, her jeans, her blouse, and put them on her while she was still lying in bed. She had shoulder-length dark hair and he encouraged her to cut it. 'It looked so beautiful, and her face was more stunning than ever when it was cropped. It was a total transformation. My next girlfriend had shoulder-length brown hair, and I'm afraid I got a bit of a vertigo syndrome. I wanted her to cut it like the other girlfriend's'. So she too would be transformed, transformed into a replicant, branded, made his.

Meg Ryan
Sunday Times Style
5 September 1993

The hair is a cropped wheat bob. The skin's all made up to look like no make-up. The lips fleshier than flesh. And that nose. It screws itself up; rabbity twitch, rabbity twitch, hello, aren't I cuter than cute, safer than safe? This is Meg Ryan: baggy suit, white socks, sinking into the sofa at the Regent Hotel in London. But it could be L.A. There's an overdose on awe, an overdose on publicists.

This is the Hollywood interview. We are looking at big box-office. And if big box-office tried to be girlie, with magnificently controlled effervescence, it's because big box-office is an incredibly good actress, turns steel into fluid and angst into giggles. Ryan has been the conduit for Nora Ephron's cute but masterful one-liners in the character of the impossibly neurotic Sally in *When Harry Met Sally*, and now in the so-straight-she's-weird Annie in *Sleepless in Seattle*.

The plot is unlikely, ridiculous, made real by Ephron's clever manipulation of the minutiae of life, and the totally believable performances of Ryan and Tom Hanks. He plays an architect in Seattle who can't get over his wife's untimely death by cancer. She plays Annie, a Baltimore reporter who is touched by his story on the radio and is moved to do things that she has been least likely to do.

Ryan enthuses, 'Annie's a Republican who's never had an orgasm. She's never left home in her own mind. She's not a risk-taker. She doesn't know herself, what makes her happy, what it is that she needs, so she's moved to behaving totally out of control for the whole movie.'

She talks with such eloquence about Annie that I wonder how much of Annie is Meg. Meg uses longer words. Meg is not small-town. Meg lives in L.A. and Montana. There, home is the Yellowstone River, what they call testosterone country, in a beach-coloured ranch with her movie-face husband Dennis Quaid and 'expansive' baby Jack, 16 months.

'My friends always say it's so odd that I play these people because they're not like me at all.' She shuffles her long fingers through her wheat hair to denote complexity, thoughtfulness. 'I suppose I have certain dilemmas.'

Does she, like Annie, ever do anything totally out of character? 'Yes. I'm not happy when my life seems to be going in too linear a way. I like blowing up bridges.'

We're ten minutes into the interview, and the blowing up bridges stuff, I sense, is the truth. Unfortunately, when I ask her what bridges she has blown, she switches back into Hollywood interview mode. 'Having a baby, it changes your life. Getting married. Shuffling the deck with interesting movies. My next one, *Significant Other*, is about an alcoholic who recovers. Then she has to renegotiate the terms of her marriage because the roles shift.'

Ah, I say, has the dynamic of you and Dennis changed since you became so megastarry? 'Megastarry? What's that?' She pulls the rather stiff, overstuffed and not cuddly cushion towards her and picks at it. This is megastar gone coy. It's a brilliant disguise. You don't acknowledge that you're successful, you have no perception of yourself whatsoever. You talk intelligently, but vaguely, and never about specifics. This is Meg Ryan doing the Hollywood interview.

The era where stars sat down, spewed and spilled about their drug addiction, how their cousin who lived next door abused them as a child and exactly how their family was dysfunctional, is finished. Low self-esteem was a brilliant read, but these days, it's become old-fashioned. It went out with guts and gore. Just like sex and violence, it is politically uncool. The post-Oprah generation speaks with dignity, but not depth.

Ephron reminds us, 'Sex killed the romantic comedy.' And just like Meg's movie, where they don't even get to hold hands until the end titles and you have to imagine the big swirling emotions and sexual hurting, today's interview is running with an undercurrent. It's not what she says. It's what she doesn't say.

So . . . Meg and Dennis. Meg is happiest with gooey lovey-doveyness. 'Why, if it's really true that I'm what you say (she can't bring herself to say the word Megastar) our relationship wouldn't change because of it. He and I understand the vicissitudes of the business. If you're in it for the long run, sometimes you're more famous than at other times. You're not always going to match up. But our relationship is not rooted in any of that.' Of course not. No doubt, love at first sight.

They first met on the set of the film *Inner Space*. 'Somewhere in the back of my mind, I knew it was going to be a big something. He used to live a block away from me when I was in journalism school in New York, although I don't remember him. I remember a perfect autumn day in New York. It always stuck in my mind. What an amazing day, perfectly glorious. And I had on this strange sweater I got in a thrift store. Dennis says he remembers me walking up that street on that day wearing that sweater.' She shrugs and the nose twitches.

Big box-office Meg tells us about big romance. Why, along with labrador puppies and chocolate and raspberry crumble, it's her only weakness. She's 31 and has hips the size of an 8-year-old's. Her weakness for chocolate can't be that weak. A couple of birthdays ago, she had a plane fly with a banner 'Happy birthday Dennis, I love you' where he was filming. He responded by sending a singing band of majorettes on to the set of *The Presido*, where she was working with Sean

Connery. Yet there were also rumours that she threatened to call the marriage off.

Montana makes her happy. She watches Dennis beat trout he has fished and loves 'hiking in the vast landscape of Montana, it's terribly humbling. It gives you a perspective on yourself.' Perspective is what is sorely needed. She doesn't know she's sexy, she doesn't know she's starry. She's a perfect blank canvas, a director's dream.

The most brilliantly complicated actors always try to be simplistic. It's as though Meg Ryan is saving up every ounce of warmth and willingness in her being to pour into her craft. She tries to give conversation, it's just she doesn't know how to. Because she gets such a brilliant response as a female stereotype. 'A lot of women relate to me, to Annie, thinking is this relationship right? How much work is it supposed to be? It's the universal dilemma of women, the hope for romance. Someday, somehow, somewhere, there's going to be someone out there.' She behaves with me as if I am a female stereotype.

What is it that really makes her happy? 'It's Jack. He's so amazing, funny and expansive. I understand more. It's changed the way I approach life and everything has bigger stakes. I understand more because I'm in this club now.' She looks at me conspiratorially and the cushion is womb-surrogate. 'The club of mothers. It's such a sorority. I've rediscovered the women in my life. It amazes me that women have careers and children. It's so hard and great in a way.' She smiles and this is her attempt at female bonding.

She tells me that she's a very even-keeled person and when I ask her whether she's neurotic about anything, she puzzles: 'Neurotic? What makes a person neurotic?' Insecurities, I say. She tries with, 'I have mother worries because you imagine all of these disasters when you're away from your child. You start thinking wild things.'

Does she have mother worries about her own mother? She flashes me a blank. Meg doesn't talk to her mother. The story goes that after her parents divorce, when she was 15, her

251

mother moved out, leaving the children in the nice Connecticut house. Maybe Meg felt bitter and abandoned. Certainly their relationship was fragile. Who had done what to whom when she decided not to visit her mother in hospital when she had a mastectomy? There must have been a lot of hurt on both sides. The recent upshot is that Susan Jordan, her mother, is not allowed to ever see her grandchild.

When it all got too much for her, Susan gushed for attention in the tabloids. 'The image she has of the innocent, dizzy girl-next-door could not be further from the truth. In real life, she's a cold-hearted, cruel manipulator. She channels all her emotions into anger.' So it really comes as no surprise that Meg's mother is banned from any contact with Jack. And it is with some degree of dignity that Meg says, 'I don't care to talk about it.' Is she friends with her mother? 'No I am not.'

Does she see herself as this all-American homecoming queen? 'No, not remotely. I was a high-school homecoming queen. Gosh, it seems so weird to me. I don't really know what one is. There's like this football game or something and it's her job to wave in the parade. You know, I never feel like I'm in the centre. I feel I'm way off to the left or the right, not conventional like that. I don't know if I was popular at school. How do you know that?' She shrugs. Because you got elected. She screws up her nose.

Recently, she has posed in little vests with her little nipples poking out, while still claiming not to know that she's sexy. Men fantasize about her. First of all, they want to be looked after by her, and then they want to remove her prissy twin sets and sensible footwear and have her rampaging their backs with stilettos. You know the one: inside every good woman there's a whore. Finding it is the challenge. Finding anything about Ryan is a challenge. She's affable, to a point, and that point is carefully measured, just like the scripts, to which she often requests changes before accepting. She turned down *The Butcher's Wife*, which went to Demi Moore and *Housesitter*, which went to Goldie Hawn, because script changes were never delivered. *'Sleepless* was so terrifically written, you didn't want to change any of the words. I am very discriminating.'

Acting, why does she do it? 'I just fell into it.' She's looking almost foetal now, curled around the big cushion. And although she has ambitions to work with people she admires and will learn things from, there seems to be a great big open space in the motivation department. This seems a dramatic paradox: she has so very much controlled what it is she does – oh, she has no respect for those actresses who uncross their legs for an Oscar, she has said – and yet she seems to me to have no reason, no motivation for acting. At least not one that she will reveal to me. Big box-office person can go on that set, be anybody, be kooky, be touchy, be accessible, remote. Whether she does this consciously or subconsciously, she saves the core of herself for those moments. Here, today, she wants to be nobody.

It was a long time before I could watch another Meg Ryan movie. I found the experience of her very uncomfortable. Why did I feel like a piece of bubble-gum on the end of her shoe? She's very much used to the Hollywood celebrity syndrome and seemed surprised when you asked a real question and expected an answer. The interviewing process has to be about questions and answers, not about an obstacle course of avoiding the questions to get in maximum plugs for the movie. I'm sure she's used to the mutual-gratification society and what we ended up with was the mutual-humiliation society.

Presents
24 November 1996

It's not for nothing that sex and shopping are linked. Somewhere along the spectrum, buy me, want me, love me, pay for me is a more exquisite parallel. The way we make love is always similar to the way we shop. Some of us give so elaborately and ridiculously it can be embarrassing, it can be masochistic, it can be a thrill. Others don't buy, they receive. Among all of my friends, those who put themselves out, those who are sensitive and thoughtful, and want to give of themselves, who want to please, are invariably the ones who get dumped. None of my female friends are the ones who can sing with any conviction the words to 'Diamonds Are a Girl's Best Friend.' In fact, it was a 16-year-old, Molly Jong, the daughter of Erica, who once snapped at me, didn't I know there are only two sorts of women – those who have been bought expensive jewelery by men and those who hadn't?

She was talking good jewelery, stuff with rocks in it. She looked at my marquesite bracelet and silver charm bracelet. 'Ha! Too inexpensive and too good a taste. No man would have bought that.' But she was quite strict. 'The only way for a woman to be happy is to become the one who is bought for rather than the one who extravagantly buys,' she said.

So why do women, rather than men, buy superior gifts? It's not simply that they're more generous, take more time, show more thought. I think women look for that holy grail of presents. They have to have the best gift for the best boy or girl. They hope to touch the other person in a new way, to impress them with their cleverness of choice, to press that seduction button. Sometimes, they give of themselves so totally they give a present which is slightly narcissistic because they want so badly to be received. I once gave a dictionary to a man I knew, whose favourite phrase was 'Look up beautiful, sexy, clever, bed in the dictionary and there's your picture.' I cut out my picture and stuck it under all the appropriate words, a painstaking task. (Poignantly, it was a dictionary that another lover had given me. You see, that's the kind of presents I get.) Anyway, it didn't work because the relationship ended soon after Christmas and guess what I got? A big nothing.

There was another time I scoured New York for the perfect collection of knitted ties for a different man. Undaunted, it wasn't until after I bought this same man an Armani suit and still hadn't been given anything for my birthday or Christmas except some very compelling words and unkept promises, that I came to realize that the bigger the gift, the more extravagant the gesture, the more doomed the relationship. I put this down to growing up a material girl, where love and money often got confused. But I think now that any type of giving that involves an excessive gesture is bad news.

Sometimes we confuse giving with controlling. A friend of mine was desperate to please her boyfriend so much she would have done anything. For his birthday she was going to drive halfway across the country to the chocolate body paint wholesaler, thinking she would wrap herself as his gift. It was a wasted journey. The relationship ended before his birthday. You can only give yourself if it's you that was wanted.

Another friend, upon receipt of a Gucci watch, panicked that she'd nothing for her boyfriend for Christmas, quickly stripped some roses that were in a vase of all of their petals, threw them over her bed and told him he could come in and get his surprise. He is, of course, still buying her trophies. Sometimes she likes them. Sometimes she doesn't.

How much you like a present has nothing to do with how much your taste is similar to its giver's. If you adore the person and they give you some silly scrap – a drawing, a liquorice allsort, a card, hand-drawn, badly drawn, ugly or cute, it doesn't matter. There's a direct ratio. If you like the person, you view the gift with gorgeousness. And sadly the converse is true. I had one boyfriend who was not rich but who bought me the most fabulous array of presents, usually from Browns in South Molton Street. Romeo Gigli dresses, devoré scarves. Did it get him anywhere? It got him lunch, never dinner. Whereas another man donated to me a battered shirt so I could smell him in his absence. This, I thought, was highly charged.

You can't just tell yourself it's the thought that counts. Sometimes the thought counts too much and it's oppressive. Another girlfriend of mine, she of the extravagant giving school, has decided to stop present buying. She is the type of woman who is attracted to vulnerable losers that are really quite cool. Her two-year relationship recently ended. 'I had this thing that I wanted to make him feel loved. Every day, because he is sad, he would go to the local take-away and get a kebab and four Cokes. One day, I paid for them in advance. He was overjoyed. So then, I started to send him little presents in the post in jiffy bags until he eventually called me and said, 'You don't have to get me anything, you know. It's just that I'm never up when the postman comes and they make you go to the post office to collect it.' In the end, of course, it didn't matter what she was giving him. He didn't want it because he didn't want her.

The giving person has to be a balance, not an addiction, and I've always thought if you weren't going to give completely marvellous, over the top, exhilarating presents, then what was the point? As for receiving, in recent times I've been very strict. I never open presents in front of anyone because I never want to do an Oscar-winning 'it's lovely.' And in present receiving, as in life, you have to ask for what you want. Otherwise you won't get it. If you don't know what you want, you are doomed to disappointment. I learned this from years of forlorn gifts that stayed in their festive wrappings, or, if I was lucky, got taken back to Marks and Spencers and exchanged for gift tokens. Last year, I was the envy of all of my friends because my husband ordered a pair of metallic Gucci boots from New York, the last of my size in the world. OK. You don't really believe it was his idea?

Some men of course are hard to buy for, and I always think

if you find people hard to buy presents for that is because you find them dull and have no mutual understanding. I remember last year, one man was venomous because his wife bought him a hair-trimming nose-clipping set. But Max Clifford had the very same clippers given to him by his daughter. 'She knows I like a bit of a trim. Marvellous,' he said. So it just goes to show, one man's nose clippers is another man's festering dustbin.

That is not to say that taste doesn't count. We all grew up with Aunties that gave scratchy bathrobes, vulgar address books and stinky stuff from Boots. Of course we've all known the friend or lover who is eager to please and got it just slightly wrong. Underwear in an unflattering wrong size; how he would like you to be or how he sees you. Underwear in scratchy lace that's black or red. Never trust a man who buys you underwear. He's buying himself a good time and is to be avoided. Sometimes they try and buy you jewelery, and that's worse because it's a more expensive mistake. They often buy gold because it means something to them and nothing to women who only wear silver or platinum.

Women too can be thoughtless. The wife who bought boxer shorts for a man who only wears briefs shows she hasn't been thinking about that department properly. I hate presents that are nonchalant, that are presents for the sake of it. One of the best presents I ever had was made by my Auntie Dorris; Joan Collins as a crinoline toilet-roll holder – kitsch, ironic, painstakingly handmade for me. Now Auntie Doris is partially blind, and every time I look at it, it's more poignant. But I can't think of anyone else who would have appreciated that gift.

For some people it would be a selfless and wonderful gesture for their friend or lover to buy them an exotic holiday or even a relaxing break. I would find it a claustrophobic insult that someone could assume they could spend so much time with me. I would feel invaded. And yet, like most of us, I think I'm an incredibly easy person to buy for and, for the most part, my friends know that anything poodle, cherubic, or any books to do with sex and death are reasonable choices. Interesting footwear works too. And surely a key point to present-buying is the kind of bonding that comes when you show somebody you know them. You can respond to quirks they didn't know that you had noticed. When it's perfect, it's a kind of symbiosis that's symbolized in a gift that is something from the very depths of one person that has touched the depths of another. It's best when presents don't try to say 'we love you', but if they can say 'we know you', and get it right, it's fabulous. If on the other hand, people are telling you that they know you and they send you anything in nylon, hot pink or monogrammed, it says something very embarrassing about either you or them, depending on how much you like it.

Relationship of the Week
Caroline and Peter Hook
5 May 1996

On the whole, men don't like women who are truly funny. For a start, they can't tell the difference between funny ha-ha and funny peculiar. And there's also a huge chasm for them between laughing at and laughing with. So while they might be able to deal with the notion of a truly funny woman on the television, it's not easy for them to deal with the constant sharpness of wit and perception of a wife or girlfriend. They can't get away with anything. They don't get let off without a quip. Humour is about power. It's about catching a foible and making it winceable. Humour is discomfort. And what could be more discomforting for the ego than a once ladder-than-lad, first-generation, Manchester pop bloke who could have boasted a groupie in every port, then reinventing himself as a band-leader on a spoof chat show hosted by his wife dressed up as a pensioner? That chat show is, of course, the award-winning Mrs Merton show. And Mrs Merton, Caroline Hook, was married to Peter Hook, who was once more famous as New Order's low-slung bass guitarist. This week she announced they had split up, although she still says, 'I'll never love anyone else like I loved my Hookie.'

Caroline Hook was always sensationally plugged in. Before her incarnation as shrewdly proper Mrs Merton ('Tell me Debbie McGee, what attracted you to the millionaire Paul Daniels?') she toured successfully as the stand-up nun Sister Mary Immaculate.

All beings who project part of themselves in alter egos are more complex than even they would like to believe. She is perhaps cleverer, sexier, more extra-ordinary than even she aspires to be. When she moved into the rock star's house that was painted dark red, she complained that 'it hasn't got any nets.' Just as Dame Edna Everidge was created from being on the edge of average, Mrs. Merton was created from a similar edginess. A kind of barbed suburbanness that smacks you with its oven mitts. Even so, she had to be a Mrs. A wife. Caroline probably always was one of those girls people thought of as wild and strange, but longed to be Mrs.

Even though she had a successfulish career as Caroline Aherne the stand-up, she changed her name to Mrs Hook when she married in 1994. She said she and Hookie had a game of darts and the one that lost changed name. But still, changing a name that you are known by professionally is a risk. It is the combination of sharpness and devotion, being demanding and demanded of that can be a crippling dynamic.

Peter Hook was probably the most blokey out of the more broody New Order. But like attracts like and he would not have stuck it out with the destructive suicidal songs, particularly those from their previous incarnation Joy Division, had he not had at least a voyeuristic thrill in dark territory and chaos. Whenever she talked or wrote about their relationship, it was 'my charming husband', 'my genial husband', 'my-that's-why-I-love him husband' and 'we did this and we did that.' She described how he once bought her the loveliest birthday present of a wide-screen TV. The loveliest part of this was that it made everyone look fat, so she put on Hookie's Pamela Anderson video so she looked really fat and stocky. She also joked about how her husband hadn't wanted to go and visit her cousin who had just had a baby. But that when he got there, he had a wonderful time. Every time the baby cried, she said he kept suggesting it must be hungry, so he could ogle the cousin breast-feeding. Of course, these were all jokes. But, as we all know, there's no such thing as a joke.

Peter Hook's ex-significant other, Iris Bates, with whom he spent twelve years and with whom he has two children, alleged that he was a serious womanizer. Anyone in Manchester knew that Hookie was a bloke's bloke and enjoyed a kind of blokeish personality that made him both ambivalent and boastful about women.

They met in the Hacienda. Caroline was coy and cool, wouldn't give her phone number. She said he could find it if he really wanted it. So the dynamic of game-playing and one-upmanship was always there. She did this even though she was mad for him. Just as, now, she is saying she can't cope with living with him, even though she is mad for him. Whenever they were seen in public, their eyes shone. They seemed to delight in each other's company. But behind the net curtains that they didn't have, things were often tense. The kind of tension that humour can constantly divert until finally it turns back against itself and explodes. They were very possessive of each other. It stands to reason that she would be a little unnerved by him. After all, he came with a past, a history that was either going to keep her on the edge or send her over. But apparently they were very much a twosome. It's always a strain to wipe the slate clean. It destroys the future if you have to negate the past. It seems like Caroline fell into the trap that a lot of women do. They are attracted to a man because they want to change him. That is part of the pull, the challenge. That your man will allow himself to be cosseted, keeping his wildness for you and you alone. That is an incredibly suburban dream.

It is questionable whether it is weak or strong to tolerate the excesses of the crushed egos of moody men, especially ones who were once pop stars. It is perhaps stronger not to tolerate it. But in her case, it is also more self-destructive because she clearly still loves him. She just wants more control. And, as I've already said, that's what being funny is all about. Control.

Perhaps they were both a little wild for each other. On the surface, it looks as if Caroline is the apotheosis of normality. (That is almost a madness in itself.) She will only shop at chain stores, saying 'It's just not right buying dear clothes' in the same way she might feel that emotional indulgence is just not right, that being sucked into a love frustration is just not right. Her alter ego Mrs Merton would probably find it intolerable. She doesn't have much room for over-indulgence.

Caroline has gone home to her mother, who certainly doesn't have room for excess. When Caroline collapsed due to a near-fatal allergy to some antihistamine tablets, her co-writer Craig Cash saved her life by calling an ambulance. Caroline's mother showed her appreciation. She sent him £5 for his trouble.

As for Caroline, although she may have given Hookie more attention than he deserved, his catch-phrase to her was, 'There's something wrong with you.' But of course the only thing that was wrong with her was him.

Andy Harries, head of Comedy for Granada, discovered Caroline and is a kind of mentor. He said to me, 'How did I get everything so right? I was incredible.' When I went to interview her, she wouldn't explain exactly how this was the case. She is very much two people. She says you can always tell a convent girl. And I think what she's talking about is the dynamic of guilt, rigidity and self-criticism versus exuberance, gaucheness. In the bar of the casino one night, she wrote, 'I swallow' on my hand, so we could laugh when I reached for my roulette chips. And I don't know if she was laughing at or with me.

Never trust a person who thinks they can change another person.

It means reform, reinvent. It's a form of hubris and arrogance to think that I'm so fabulous that this person who's been this way, and never made an effort to change for anyone else, will do so for me. It's an exercise in power and self-validation that often ends in self-mutilation. But I think we all do it. Any relationship has a basis in conflict. You meet someone, you like them, you like them more, you want to change them. Sometimes it can be as superficial as you hate that bad jacket. So you buy them a different jacket. And then it's bad shoes, bad hair that have to be modified. And then it's bad habits. And those habits are the glue that holds it all together and the grease that makes it slide apart.

Sometimes, we are of course attracted to something that's going to destroy us and we may say we want to change it, but really, we don't. Otherwise, we wouldn't have been attracted to it in the first place. I remember a girlfriend, Cleo, who was heart-broken because the man she was in love with was kind to her, attentive, made her laugh, perfect in every way except he was gay. She'll admit now that this was partly because she didn't want a real sexual relationship and partly because the addiction was about power, how powerful I will be if I'm the only woman he's ever had.

Sarah has a friend Kim who was gorgeous and always dated the popular rich guys. 'There was this loser called Chris in a band – a 1980s frizzed out rocker wannabe, every sentence began and ended with dude. He was sleazy and he'd get on the piano and start jamming Rush and Journey. He was also mean. He had slept with 150 girls and literally carved notches in his bedpost. He had this chopped-up bed. Once Kim came home and caught him inside another girl and he said, 'Go away. I'm not done yet. I'll call you later.' Kim said, 'He's really sweet and I can change him. I can make him better than he knows how to be.' He said to her, 'Don't call me anymore. You make me sick.' She was a screwed up girl. However sick this story may be, I think we've all been there, or somewhere like it.

I have been not having a relationship with someone for over a year. I love everything about him except the way he treats me. If he was all brute, it would be easy. The addiction is the blend of kindness and callousness, of supersensitivity and heroic brutality, and of course my ridiculous blinkered belief that things will get better, when probably they will only get worse. A therapist once told me that in order to change their behaviour, you have to change yours and your reaction to them. So I've become passive aggressive, rage on the inside, never say what I think or think what I say – generally less of myself. Has this made any difference? No. Just makes us not know who we are.

My friend Amanda used to be married to an alcoholic drug-addicted rock star who cheated on her. It was she who told me that she followed this advice about no matter how they treat you, you don't react. It's not their responsibility to make you happy and, if you turn into a harridan, they will only blame you for making them what they are – in her husband's case, a drug-addicted womanizing alcoholic. You have to let them be the only one screaming. Then they'll feel stupid. She put this to the test herself when there was a proposed reconciliation. 'We planned a weekend in Monterray. I was treading eggshells. We arrived at the hotel for dinner and I smelt the bread was mouldy. It was making me feel sick but I said very politely to the waitress "Look at this bread. What is this blue in it?" "Ah," she said. "It's blue cheese and sourdough bread."

'It was really stinking, so I said, very politely, "Could you please remove it from the table and replace it with ordinary bread?" Rock-star husband was about to explode because he's very English, hates a scene, hates anyone to complain. So I was determined to be all smiley about this bread that was making me sick. But he blew up. He grabbed a nearby knife, stabbed it into the centre of the bread and brandished it in the air before shoving it up my nose. I was still smiling politely and he was standing up, arms flaying, screaming "You always have to make a fuss." I said, "excuse me", went to the ladies room, and let him scream on his own for a bit. Afterwards he apologized and was very sweet for the weekend.'

He has since given up drugs and alcohol, and Amanda. She says it's because a relationship that worked in sickness doesn't necessarily work in health. And now that he is a perfectly decent, sober, nice person, they still can't have a relationship. Why is that? Because he changed too much and she didn't have to nurture him? No. Because, even sober, he was still insensitive. He still shouted first thing in the morning and said everything that she said that was funny louder, thus claiming a laugh for the joke, thus proving the stuff about tigers and stripes and leopards and spots and about taking the man out of Essex but not the Essex out of the man.

Never trust a man who doesn't give you his home phone number and tries to fob you off with office or mobile.

It means you never know where he's living and he wants total control. It means that he wants to talk to you on his cue, never yours. Any person who thinks that the phone ringing in his own home is some kind of missile of invasion that they can't cope with, is terrified of something; intimacy, their consort, girlfriend, boyfriend, mother or themselves.

First of all, mobile man. What kind of person only gives you a mobile phone number? The kind of person that gives you his pager in L.A., his business managers's number and his secretary's number. The kind of man who you think perhaps doesn't have a home. A kind of club-class gypsy – emotional vagrant, more like. Sarah had a man who only gave her the mobile. She found out later that he lived in a squat. Another boy I know does it because he lives with his mother and he's embarrassed if questioned, she might ask about potential new conquests. They need to be screened before they're allowed to talk to his mother, and his mother has to be screened away from them. It's about control. It's about hiding.

Traditionally, the man who calls you three times a day, first call before ten, always eager, always openly yearning, stops the phone call both ends of the commuting-time-zone-belt. He does this because he is married or domestically otherwise engaged. The same stuff doesn't work in reverse because women are less compartmentalized about their lives. I've been there in mobile land. In mobile land, there's always an excuse. When the conversation got sticky– whoops! The batteries are running out. That particular man with a mobile never switched his mobile on, so it was pointless having the number at all. He only used it to call out. Once having grasped that the mobile was the only means of communication, my imagination narrowed and thought, 'Oh. No mobile on. No means of contact. I'll just have to wait.' How demeaning.

What is really tricky though is the man with whom you are not having an affair, but who still doesn't give you his home phone number. The other day, a man I have known for nine years rang me out of the blue. We were really happy to hear each other. He'd moved to a new city. I asked him for his phone number and he said, 'I don't know my home phone number. I mean, you don't do you? You never call yourself up.' He gave me office and mobile. How shifty, I thought. What doesn't he want me to know? I have never been romantically involved with this man, but a girlfriend of mine has, so I suspect he's worried I'm going to tell her if a new female voice answers the phone. She ended the relationship four years ago on the day they were due to have two weeks holiday in Antigua. She woke up to find him gone. Later that day he tried to call, reverse charges, from Istanbul where it seems another girlfriend had booked him for the same two weeks.

One of my closest male friends may think I haven't noticed, but whenever he calls me and I'm at home and he calls me on call waiting and I say, 'I'll call you back', he says, 'No. I'll call you back.' This is because I have never had this man's home phone number. I never mention it and neither does he. Strange, that.

Then of course there is William. I have known him for six years. He used to call me every day, except weekends. I could never call him at home because his wife was extremely paranoid and hysterical and, anyway, once he had a nasty incident with a bunny-boiler type. So he liked to keep things separate. What kind of man is too afraid to have their spouse take a phone call from a woman with whom they are not having an affair? A kind of man who is having an affair with someone else. A kind of man who fears his wife. Anyway, the paranoid wife turned out to be not paranoid, but correct in her suspicions. They split up. Did he give me his new bachelor phone number? He did not.

Then there's is the man who used to say that he liked shopping for women as if they were items on a supermarket shelf. One day in your trolley, the next day you didn't feel like eating them. I have had this man's home number for five years. I've just never rung it because I never wanted to be in that supermarket in which he shops. Julia has stopped me from including the digits of the number in this piece. I'll only say that the very last number is 6.

Relationship of the Week
The Princess of Wales and the Press
2 April 1995

Princess Diana is reported to have whimpered angrily last week – whimpering angrily is the thing she knows best – 'They're raping me.' According to this assertion in a British tabloid, she was referring to the nasty thrusting reporters and poking paparazzi who were following her around the ski resort of Lech in Austria. One of them, Mike Lloyd, an ITN cameraman, was subsequently fired.

Rape is such an emotive word. It makes haunting headlines and movies. I still wince at the thought of Jodie Foster as the rape victim in *The Accused*. The basic stance of the men in the movie was that a tarty, dancing blonde who was ravaged didn't have a case. She was, as they say, asking for it. Perhaps the Princess of Wales, who in the past has been such a bewitching manipulator of the world's press, was asking for the attention she has received.

What Diana asks for is complete control: the media at her beck and call, snap, snap, snapping and a big shoulder for her to cry on when she needs attention, affirmation or to leak something, such as, for example, her side of the marriage split.

There was the time when, in 1993, following allegations in the Calcutt Report that Press intrusion had played a part in the break-up of the Royal marriage, Lord MacGregor, then the Chairman of the Press Complaints Commission, was forced to conclude that the intrusions into 'the private lives of the Prince and Princess of Wales were intrusions contrived by the Princess herself and her entourage'. He also pointed out that: 'The princess had, in practice, invaded her own privacy.'

There was the time when, after ostentatiously retiring from public life in December 1993, Diana attended a charity event for runaway children the very next day, conspicuously hiding behind her handbag to avoid the press. Oh, and the time she allegedly asked her detective, Ken Wharfe, while holidaying in the Caribbean, to make an informal ring around to make sure that the photographers could all see her happily splashing in the waves and thus splash her on their pages.

And yet, when she wants to be red-eyed, water-retentive, cross, sad, alone, or in oh-so-protective-mother mode, those who fête her are suddenly her tormentors. Like all hysterical people, she is contradictory about what she wants. Almost all her adult life has been lived in a state of tacit collusion with newspapers and photographers. She has spoken to them, leaked to them, performed for them, usually been adored by them, sometimes been picked apart by them. If they didn't exist, she wouldn't – not as an icon of victimhood, anyway.

She courts attention, any attention. In fact, she is more comfortable with negative attention. How many times has she posed, head cocked, eyes sad, to confirm her in her role as sufferer? Most effectively so when sitting sad and alone in front of the Taj Mahal in February 1992. It suited her to have the world believe she was ill-treated by Charles and Camilla, and that her alleged extra-marital exploits were a desperate need for love in such a lonely world.

It worked. She's a smooth operator, except when she says she does not know how to use parking meters, let alone a pay phone for those alleged hang-up phone calls to the handsome, married and kindly Oliver Hoare.

She had to explain all this to the handsome and kindly Richard Kay, the *Daily Mail* Royal reporter, in his car, in private, where she could pour out her troubled heart, so that it could be displayed in the kindly *Daily Mail* last August.

She is not clever, so 'poor thing' is the best she can command. Right from the start she got attention for suffering, from the moment when the paparazzi first chased her along the Brompton Road when she was the heavy-fringed, shy Lady Di. She leapt out of her Metro screaming. The hacks shoved a bunch of flowers through her letterbox with a note saying, 'Sorry. We love you.'

She was comfortable with the 'Feel sorry for me, I'm a

bulimic' label. She seemed to condone all that was written about her in Andrew Morton's book, *Her True Story*, by publicly visiting her friend Carolyn Bartholomew, one of its main, named sources shortly after its publication. This, despite the fact that she was officially supposed to be furious and feeling invaded by it.

Bulimics want control, it's their thing. They like to have their cake and eat it. This is what she wants over the Press. Like an over-indulged child, she has a strong sense of her own power and her own helplessness, and she exploits this. When she does not want photos taken she has been known to lie on the floor of her car and walk with her back to the photographers. And yet the next day she'll be posing for a photo spread in *Vogue*.

Nigel Evans, *Majesty* magazine's editor, recognizes the contradictory behaviour: 'She's the most famous woman in the world and she wants to go out in the street. Madonna, who is possibly the second most famous, doesn't go out without bodyguards. Diana wants to be photographed because she wants affirmation of the way she looks, but it's a double-edged sword. She thinks it's a violation when she doesn't want it.'

What are princesses for? To be photographed. Diana knew the deal ever since, as a shy kindergarten teacher, she wore the see-through skirt. She does not acknowledge the gargantuan telephoto lens a yard from her cheek, but every movement is designed for its greedy gaze: head to the left so, a shrug so, a compassionate clutch of the child or afflicted one. As slick as a supermodel strut.

Over the last decade and a half she has appeared on more covers worldwide than anybody else. She has a set of six skillfully chosen expressions. There's one that is small-mouthed, the head cocked and with big whites of eyes gazing upwards, like the Madonna look; there's one narrow-eyed, flash-of-teeth pose; there's one coy, teeth-clutching bottom-lip, naughty one; there's the grim, defiant photograph-me-why-don't-you expression; there's the 'I'm not noticing the camera but resist me if you can, I'm wearing my new Catherine Walker' look; and finally there's the very small-mouthed, cheeks sucked with distress, brittle one, which also comes with big whites of eyes gazing upwards.

In the flesh she is unmoving. Her hair static, lacquered. But she sets fire to film emulsion and she knows it and she needs it. Perhaps this is why, subconsciously or otherwise, she goes on holiday to public places. There are private, sheltered spots all over the world that she could go to as, sometimes, she does. Then what was the point of going to the Costa del Sol in April last year and expecting not to be noticed when she took her top off? And then there was the débâcle about the leotard shot taken in the L.A. Fitness Centre in south-west London. Why would a woman who can afford a private gym and a personal trainer go there?

It may not be the first time she has used the rape metaphor in connection with the paparazzi. She is not referring to the regular Royal watchers, with whom she has rather a cosy relationship, but those scummy stalkers, usually the foreign ones. Essentially they are a truculent breed, contemptuous of their quarry, and yet willing to be humiliated by daily rejection. Desiring control, and yet masochistic. It is the chemistry of like attracting like.

The day Diana died I thought perhaps I should remove this piece. But that seems convictionless, as if she, or I, had become a different person because of her death.

There was a three way collusion; Diana, the Press, the public. She had a contradictory relationship with the Press because one minute she was demanding attention, the next 'wanting to dissolve like a disprin.'

Why do the paparazzi exist? They exist because of the concept of the voyeuristic thrill. Should we blame ourselves for buying these papers when Diana often courted publicity?

As any good bulimic will tell you, what you desire to control most controls you.

Relationship of the Week
David Copperfield and Claudia Schiffer
28 July 1996

I've always had a problem with magicians. After all, who wants to be fooled by somebody? If you believe in something that is pretend you will soon see that illusion equals disillusion and disappointment. But just what exactly is the illusion here? One report says that David Copperfield and Claudia Schiffer are splitting up. But were they ever really together? Another tabloid comes back with her saying, 'He's still flying all over the world to see me.' What happens when he gets there? They play chequers?

If indeed the romance is off, I cannot hear the tearing out of hair. For a start, there's something about both of them that's a little unreal. She's all piano lessons and he's all piano teeth. She's all pneumatic breasts and he's all clenched buttocks in his spray-on black Levis to create the illusion of rock star as he prances darkly around, amongst swirly-whirly music, girls who fly and amputated limbs. There was something unreal about the notion of the romance. Sure, he's rich, but with those jumping-around eyebrows, the American-tan-tights-coloured face and the stiff, quiffed hair, he's kind of sexless. Claudia bakes a good chocolate cake. She could have done better than this.

I remember when they first got together. I was part of a jamboree organized by the irrepressible Max Clifford that went to San Francisco to watch him. At that time, Copperfield was unknown in Europe and did not wish to remain so. Schiffer was also said to be aware of the model's shelf life and hoping to get into American television, which she achieved by fronting some of his TV specials. Speculation on the junket was that Max had planned the whole thing. 'No, no, no,' says Clifford. 'The fact that they found each other and enjoyed true romance gave us loads of column inches,' says Max. When I interviewed Copperfield, two tables and two PR's with walkie-talkies were placed in between us. Granted, in the circumstances, Copperfield must have felt a little strange. But I felt him wooden, churning out the same old line about his lower-middle-class upbringing in New Jersey, where being an only child encouraged self-focus and made him very goal orientated. He was a lonely, peaky boy who at first turned to a ventriloquist's dummy to make friends. Enjoying this kind of personality dislocation could have probably lasted a lifetime, but the dummy didn't because Copperfield couldn't throw his voice. So, instead, he made friends by playing tricks. He probably still sees himself as ugly, no matter how much money and fame he has. Applause can stroke him but he can only ever be validated by a woman everyone else thinks is beautiful. He's very keen on validation, talks about it a lot. He once said he knew he appeared to have a good deal. People think of a good deal as money, fame and the girl and the possibility of an effigy in Madame Tussauds but Copperfield said you have to keep 'figuring out something else to give you validation.' The quest is what drives him but he keeps on being driven. For a while, Schiffer shimmered in instant headlines of £3-million diamond engagement rings and a yacht on which Kennedy seduced his mistresses, which was another present. All of these things are huge gestures. It's like people who kiss in public. If you have to show it's real, it's just an illusion. Personally, I can't imagine anything more creepy than the huge dramatic gesture of hiring an island in the Caribbean for four days for the purpose of the proposal. You knew it then, didn't you? The eternal fiancé syndrome. Reports from restaurants in Monte Carlo, bookings for a supposed bridal banquet appeared all too often and disappeared. You knew they were in trouble when they gave an interview in which they made up all of the questions to ask each other, and Claudia informed us that he definitely wasn't gay. In fact he was 'very heterosexual, trust me I know.' She also said, 'And he's a magician in more ways than one.' Another time she said, 'He's a magician in every sense of the word.' Now, is this real? Do people really open their mouths and talk in tabloid soundbites? Even for a 24-year-old super-model, this does not seem a very good command of the English language to me. There's also a tell-tale sign in Claudia's autobiography. She failed to mention him, that suggests that she had forgotten the plot. Let us assume though that the illusion was real and they were seeing each other in that very unreal way of flying halfway across the world. We don't know who decided they no longer had use for the other. After all, Copperfield had said she was the most important thing in his life. She relieved his stress but the new home they were going to finally have in Vegas, when the two of them decided to opt for the quiet life, has reportedly been put on the market. Did she just open her eyes one day and find out what she was seeing wasn't really there?

Well, believe it or not, I have a friend who actually had a long-term relationship with Copperfield several years ago. I'd only known him as a picture on my girlfriend's New York wall. I'd only known him as some man who broke her heart, or she broke his, I couldn't remember which. She predicted that it wouldn't last with Claudia. She split with him because of his constant need to flirt and be approved of by other women. She told me once that he used to carry a framed picture of her and put it up at every hotel he stayed at. One day, she arrived unexpectedly in Vegas and he panicked. His knee jerk reaction was to slap the photo in his bedside drawer. My friend was angry, assuming it was some other girl's picture that he was trying to hide. But he was giggling because it was hers he was trying to conceal. 'I didn't realize it was you,' he told her. He thought she was some other girl coming in and, ever hopeful, wanted to hide his real girl-friend's picture. I wonder whether he's put the one of Claudia back in the drawer.

Since this, it has been reported again that David Copperfield and Claudia Schiffer are a symbiotic PR arrangement. He hotly denies it.

Never trust a man who wears a tight polo-neck.

They want to cover themselves, hide away even. And at the same time, they want to show off their bodies. Vain men who tell lies wear polo-necks. A man in a polo-neck hates confrontation. A great male friend of mine has a collection of figure-hugging polos. He is the Copperfield type of man who changes the picture on his mantelpiece according to whichever girlfriend is due round. Once, one arrived unexpectedly while the other was upstairs. He is so charming and so clever that neither of them suspected a thing. Then they both found out about each other and he had to start again with another two girlfriends. Always, his girlfriends came in pairs. One that liked him more than he liked her and one he liked more than she liked him. It's because he hates confrontation that he can never tell either of them the truth about what he feels, so he ends up defending a man's right to lie by omission – a very polo-neck gesture. The polo-neck epitomizes his character. It tells the world what he wants, that he's been to the gym and that he's also a bit shy.

I had a boyfriend once who thought he was Richard Burton and did that rugged polo-neck thing. You know, so macho you can carry off a garment that is actually completely camp. I know you can't trust men who wear polo-necks because I did trust this man implicitly. He gave me high-voltage compliments and declarations of adoration, but continued to lie like a rug. Once, he appeared two days late. 'I'm sorry I couldn't call you, but my mobile phone was in my briefcase and someone crashed into the back of my car and I couldn't open it for two days and my filofax was in there with it.' But polo-neck man, we've been seeing each other for six months. How come you didn't know my number? 'Because it's number one on automatic dial. I've never learned it.' The last time I saw him he was wearing his polo-neck, a purple one which he obviously thought matched the blue in his eyes. He thought it was casual, but it was specific. Anyway, I invited him to my birthday party. He said he wanted to be by my side as I received my guests and opened my gifts. He never came, he never called, and when I called to scream at him he avoided my call for weeks because he didn't want the confrontation. He wanted his head in his shell.

There's something very reptilian about a polo-neck. That's why its cousin is called a turtle-neck. It looks like some fold of skin that a head can poke in or out of. Roger Moore used to wear one as The Saint and Val Kilmer has reinitiated the trend. Michael Caine wore one for *Alfie* and look how that *faux* vulnerable barrow boy came unstuck as a duplicitous, can't-help-himself womanizer.

Men who wear polo-necks hold their stomachs in and consequently have a special walk. I know this man Bobby. He's always shimmying himself into polo-necks and asking his friends to call him Robert when a business associate or contact enters the room. Polo-necks are shifty. Bobby used to be in the army and now he wants to be an actor and he likes to pretend that his army career never happened. He says, 'I put on my polo-neck and it's insta-suave. It shows off my chest. They're very flattering. They're tight so you show off all your body contours and wear them with tight pants. Or I can look like a beat professor.' Yeah, can look like anything except an ex-army boy trying to act.

They are ambiguous and androgynous, like the Calvin Klein scent. David Bowie wears a lot of them. My friend Eric wears them because he thinks they're pretentious. His girlfriend Bethany says, 'I like him in polo-necks because they're androgynous. I could be wearing the same outfit. I suppose it's because I'm attracted to myself.'

Women who wear polos often have long necks and small heads. Sometimes they tug on them and chew on them and go little-girlie, and pull them as if they are embarrassed by their tightness and they want to distort what they started off wanting to reveal. Then it's as if they are ashamed of their shape and they want to be androgynous. It's hard to reconcile something that used to be worn to cover up love bites with a catwalk 'must', the retro-chic employed recently by Gucci and Versace. Any man who is ultra-fashion-conscious probably measures his mueslis and is definitely not to be trusted. Besides, I like necks. I once read in a psychic's memoirs that if you look at someone's neck and gaze right into it comfortably for seventeen seconds, it means they will open their heart to you. And of course I always trust a psychic.

Camille Paglia
Sunday Times Style
16 January 1994

If Camille Paglia reminds me of anyone I'd say that she is the love-child of Quentin Crisp and Dame Edna Everage. Small and navy, skinny and lumpy, she is all regal posturing as she holds court at the Basil Hotel in London. The hotel has 1950s wiring and smells of scones. It matches her brittle splendour.

But whereas Crisp was an alien in New York , Paglia is just an alien, trading on sexual dyslexia. She grew up not wanting to wash her face, wanting to do street-fighting: she says that if a sex change operation had been available, she would have been obsessed with having it. She says that, instead of the operation, she wrote her book, *Sexual Personae*.

It was a book that took ten years to write and made the Professor of Humanities at the University of the Arts, Philadelphia, very famous. It was contrary, literary, anthropological and mythological. It was about sex being a darker power than feminism had admitted.

Here she was, this ordinary-looking lesbian, spouting the extraordinary, iconizing men and masculinity. 'Masculinity is aggressive, combustible, unstable. It is also the most creative cultural force in history.' Her range of focus is wide. She takes her inspiration from Genet, Katharine Hepburn, pigeons who mate out of her window, soap operas and the Discovery Channel, girlfriends, boyfriends, chats on the phone.

'I have been called anti-woman, pro-rape,' she says. (She once said of date rape, 'We cannot legislate what happens on a date. Sex is a dangerous sport.') '*Sexual Personae* was compared to *Mein Kampf*,' she continues. 'You can't knock people's belief systems without paying the price, but I am an Amazon. And all these pathetic little feminists' attempts to suppress issues simply produced me. The revenge is me.' Her bony hands beat her bosom, she is desperately theatrical. 'And I'm dangerous because I'm out of control and I can stereotype these little caricature things into cartoons. . . '

She looks so conventional, secretarial, but she carries a flick knife in the form of a silver pen. She calls herself a battleship, heavy artillery. Her father taught her street-fighting, Latin and how to be an independent thinker. Then, when her thoughts no longer mirrored his own, when she was about 12, he tried, she says, to suppress her opinions. The result was a steaming, bursting, angry thing. She speaks in a rat-tat-tat splatter gun of vendetta, put-down, and soundbite.

She is eloquent but unstoppable, and in my hour with her I was hardly able to get a word in edgeways. She will talk about what she wants to talk about, the same things she always talks about and in that way of the newly famous and those in love with fame for its own sake, she constantly refers back to when, 'I said such and such to the *L.A. Times*,' which pretty much amounts to intellectual terrorism. You sit, she speaks.

She will tell you that there are hardly any books in the twentieth century that matter. She mentions Simone de Beauvoir's *The Second Sex* and, of course, her own. All the time she's telling you she is the only pure feminist. She's ludicrous, heroic and sweet in a way that I have often found very ordinary people to be who chisel away at themselves to produce a beautiful bulimic brain. It gorges, purges, vomits. It is an extraordinary mind and a very female mind.

She says she can only fall in love with women's minds, but

had a problem when she was 12 and her 'hormones kicked in'. Then, against her better judgement, she found herself drawn to men.

She is here to promote her book, a paperback version of her essay collection, *Sex, Art and American Culture*, herself and her two new documentaries for Channel Four, to be screened next month – *Lesbians Unclothed* and *The Penis Unclothed*. She loves pornography, says she has a gay man's appreciation of it.

'I get so sick and tired of Andrea Dworkin's attitude towards the penis as an agent of mutilation. I'm sick and tired of the negativity. When I was here last time I went to see the comedian Robin Tyler. It's an all-gay audience, and she's talking about 'this guy took me out and there was this ugly thing, what do you expect me to do with that?' All the women were laughing hysterically, and here is my point. This is profoundly sexist. If a man made such a remark about a woman's genitals he'd be lynched. 'Dworkin has found an audience in Britain. She is a type – the girl at school with the eternal cold who never has a Kleenex and sits with a toilet-roll on her lap.

'I have lived most of my life as an open lesbian. I don't get involved with men but I enjoy men's bodies. The erect penis is the ultimate symbol of sexual desire, there is no female equivalent, nothing that shows complete excitation. If you live your life as a lesbian and don't react erotically to the penis, you are closed down. And I have always said that I couldn't really be involved with a woman that couldn't understand this.' Consequently, she's lived her life in an emotional and sexual drought, blabbing, 'I'm a lesbian, I'm a lesbian,' all through Yale but having nobody to be a lesbian with until recently.

'I've been involved for eight months with a woman who is an artist and a curator. My girlfriend's name is Alison Maddex.' And she spells it out for me very proudly. Alison is 27, which makes her nineteen years younger than Paglia, and very stylish.

Paglia's second documentary is about lesbians. 'Of course I am biased because my experience of the lesbian world is not pleasant. Neither was my girlfriend's. That is why we were drawn together. She sought me out. All this great talk about how wonderful and liberating lesbianism is, I am saying it is a disaster.

'No great art, great thought, great book has come out of it in the last twenty years. If it was so fabulous, and so sexual and so hip, why couldn't I get a date for years?

'Male homosexuality is not encumbered by the ideology that lesbian feminism is. I don't believe that you are born gay, it is a ridiculous, absurd statement. More women are bisexual, they can succeed bisexually in a way that men can't. As a child I was so completely drawn to women, madly in love with them.

'I think lesbian sex can be wonderful, but it's lacking in many ways. There's a brute animal quality, OK. Bodies fit together in heterosexuality. There's some frustration involved in the life of the lesbian. Of course, lesbians will want to hang me for saying this, they say we're fulfilled. Pardon me. Excuse me. I don't believe it.

'Man and woman can have wild primitive sex. You don't get that with lesbians, there's something lacking. It's so tiring making love with women, it takes forever. I'm too lazy to be a lesbian. Let me get a little air.'

She swivels round to open the window, still not stopping her speech. Not noticing if I'm there or if I'm responding as a woman, man, lesbian or eunuch. She talks a lot about her own alienation. With all her mewling and spewling she remains alienated, because she never picked up the knack of trying to empathize or even trying to listen to what anyone else was saying. Nobody taught her manners and she taught herself how to be a 'megaself'. That is why she reminds me of Dame Edna.

'My entire life has been very frustrating. I used to hang around with my gay male friends and the only lesbians were these working-class butch-fem things. They did not hate men, they liked men and men liked them because they were like men. They would drink like men, they had grandeur: they were lions to be served. But I had little in common with them and a relationship didn't develop. Oh, oh, this is good. I've never said this before. I had one date with an Afro-American woman. She was a soldier, home on leave and when I emerged with this black woman in the morning, in her combat fatigues and duffle-bags, the eyebrows of the neighbours shot up. I never saw her again. One night stands don't happen in the lesbian world because there are too many snivelling, white, middle-class feminists.

'I can analyse lesbianism in America, it's to do with the mother. They have a passive-aggressive mother who is sedate, withdrawn, doesn't like men, but one of the daughters becomes a vehicle for her suppressed rage against the father and enacts the rebellion that the mother never did. That is why lesbian-feminist rhetoric is filled with ideology about how terrible men are.

'Everything I thought about men when I was 13, and I saw women serving them and I didn't know how to handle them, is what current feminist thinking is about. It's so naïve. Then I saw that many women can be successful with men once they know how to control them. I had a lot of resentments towards men that were based on misapprehensions and bizarre distortions. If I knew then what I know now, my dating would have improved. I would have still ended up a lesbian probably.

'I despise self-pity, and women of this generation have sought victimhood. Woman complex, man simple, OK.' She goes on to a diatribe about Jesus starting off as a speck of plasma in a woman's womb, the old mistress-appropriation stuff and pigeons performing on the Discovery Channel.

From all of this she deduces that men are not using women but women are using men. Susan Faludi is snivelling and Naomi Wolf is a little twit 'because of the illusion that feminism has fostered. Men have died for women, they are the disposable sex.'

'They have the dirtiest, riskiest jobs and they bring their pay-cheque back to the women. Feminism is stuck in thinking it wants to view the career woman with her attaché case as the ultimate model of female power. But mistress of birth is the ultimate role', she says.

'I'm an egomaniac and the idea of allowing my body to be a vehicle for another entity seems to me repellent,' she adds as an aside.

'Feminists have overstated the way men objectify women and turn them into meat. It's actually the other way round. Men are haunted by sexual anxiety their whole lives. This is what pornography is all about. It's trying to understand the enormity of female sexual power.

'Male sexual function depends on women theatrically miming a momentary subordination. What's going on is an elaborate sexual game, an international conspiracy to keep men from the knowledge of their own frailty. Men never share secrets about relationships in the way women do. Women talk about men as puppets to be managed.

'Oh, oh,' she clasps herself. 'There are men in the room.' The photographer has just entered, and she explains to him that she will not be photographed in a bedroom and she has written a discourse on why. But before she can deliver it, the PR lady begs her not to.

Instead, she wants to do her own wrap-up to remind me how famous she is. 'If you close your eyes while I'm on stage you may think I am a gay man. I have copied their manners, I do not move like a woman.' She does some extra-queenly flouncing and continues, 'I have no rivals. I was asking the most basic questions before feminism provided pat answers. My work is based on anthropology, sociology, psychology. I watch TV, I watch talk shows, I watch real people.'

Then she's on about how everyone hates her and the *New York Times Book Review* doesn't want to use her, but when she goes to the University of Texas 'there was a thousand kids out there screaming like I was Madonna'.

Yes, she thinks she's like Madonna. And she is. Self-styled, self-hyped, with one-liners that make her hackademia read like the lyrics of a pop song.

She set herself up as an icon. She grasped her moment.

Relationship of the Week
Madonna and Carlos Leon
21 April 1996

I can't imagine anything less sexy than having a relationship with my personal trainer. But I'm not Madonna and my muscles don't have to shudder in front of Carlos 'The Tackle' Leon, thus named because he's big in all the right places. The female line on unzipping with a fitness instructor seems to me one step worse than intimacy with your hairdresser. Sure, it's a time when you confess all because you have nothing better to do, but workout clothes are the most deeply unsexy things on the planet, sweaty and tight or chunky and sack-like. You don't wear make-up, you bead out and you look a fright. How could this possibly be sexually enhancing?

The male line is that men love to see bodies at work. They love women vulnerable, reduced, their complexion red, throbbing and exhausted. And if they have the power to do this to them, it works the muscles in their mind as well as their body. Remove the equipment, the location, the leotards, and you've got Rhett Butler and Scarlett O'Hara.

High Romance, control and submission have always been Madonna's agenda. Every relationship she's had has been about her lusting either for control ('I like to do things to take power away from men') or submission, all those photos in warm leatherette for that book she did where she dribbled about rape fantasies. So, where it may seem a simple case of another of Madonna's toy boys, selected from the park for his looks and body to train her eighteen months ago, he has now been selected for his genes. He is the father of the much longed-for Madonna bambino.

Madonna is, of course, a woman of extremes. Latinate, passionate, sweet and power-crazed. Predatory. She's used to calling up men, famous men she fancies, via their agents and requesting them for dates as if they were a home shopping catalogue. She did it recently with byronic man Rufus Sewell who didn't stay for the second course of dinner at Le Caprice. And before that, it was the raw and strange, but very sexy singer poet Henry Rollins. But all while she was really involved with Carlos Leon. I'm sure she's not obsessed with him but nevertheless the dynamic works. He is her master in the gymnasium, possibly even the bedroom. She can feel 'the real Madonna', the full flush of vulnerability, the rush that submission gives, the delight in his ordinariness. 'He's the kind of man who can fix washing machines.' she says. But at the same time as being macho, he appeals to the extreme in Madonna because ultimately she's the dominatrix. She's the wilful girl who's got what she wants at last.

The baby thing has long been an obsession. A few years ago, she had an affair with the towering basketball player Dennis Rodman. She sent him stealthy, demanding faxes, including one that allegedly said, 'in three weeks time you have to be in this hotel in Vegas to make me pregnant.'

Madonna fears abandonment by all men. She suffered a distant, dislocated relationship with her father, of course. As a result, Madonna wants a boy who will not abandon her and she seems to want to insure this will not happen by reportedly asking her boyfriend to sign an agreement to give up all rights to their unborn child in the event of their split. Luckily for her, he was all too biddable, saying that he would never seek custody. After all, she has all of the money. He seems slightly too uninterested. Is he really ready for fatherhood when he seems so delighted to be excused of any commitment?

Leon seems a conduit to the emotional sanctuary Madonna has said she always longed for. As soon as the workouts stop then the dynamic of the relationship will have to change, and

I'm not sure it's flexible enough or powerful enough to surv-
vive outside the contained environment of the gym. He's 29.
She's normally only mentally hooked in to men her own age,
37, or older.

Personally I never trust a man with a body – because
they're always more interested in it than you. Big body, small
mind. Also, they start seeing bodies as detached things to be
worked on. Such graphic familiarity with the territory of the
flesh is not a turn-on.

'A baby would be better then money and fame,' she once
said at the peak of her popularity. Madonna, though, gets
what she wants. And it was hardly as if her main aim in life
was to try out every fertility treatment going, and on the way
to the clinic she thrust herself into a few bad films, bustiers
and sang a few songs. One of which, 'Like a Virgin', she
won't be able to sing anymore once the baby arrives – unless,
of course, she thinks she's the real Madonna, which she might
do. She actually seems caught up in that Holy Trinity of
mother, Madonna and whore. Maybe the whips, the studs,
the body that was to be the vehicle for public adulation, the
fame and approval she yearned for were all just displacement
activities for being loved, wanted. When fame wearied of her,
she realized public adulation was something she could no
longer control. She said, 'You're only allowed to be famous
with public approval. Sooner or later, you run out.' She talked
then of withdrawal. No one took her seriously. 'My whole
life is in a constant state of disarray and the one thing that
doesn't change is the workout,' she said. 'If I have nothing to
do, I will stay in the gym forever.' Convenient, then, that she
has become entangled with the one person she can stay in the
gym forever with.

All love is narcissism. She sees herself in someone who has
made his life his body. It's not only convenient, it's essential.
She'll need to attend and tune that body during pregnancy so
that the baby slips out more easily and she can get back as
soon as possible into that regime that has become an addiction
and a mainstay of her life. She has not got where she is by

looking grotesque. She needs someone to trust and encourage this process. It's not so much a relationship she has with Carlos Leon, but yet another vehicle for her own self-absorption, ditto her unborn child. She doesn't want a girl. 'Only room for one little Madonna.' She wants a boy. She is under the misconception, perhaps because she is Italian, that blood relatives give unconditional love. Although, given the difficult relationship with her father, she should really know better. Madonna's workouts have been so addictive because they are the place where she can unload a subcurrent of tension and unhappiness in her life. If the person causing the tension is also releasing it, then that makes a mess. If she had really wanted unconditional love, she should have bought a puppy.

Well, Madonna didn't get a boy. She got a girl and she got rid of the man. She got a whole new persona as Madonna the mother, Madonna the Evita, Madonna the grown-up. Carlos Leon got a job in the Crunch Gym on Sunset and Crescent Heights.

Relationship of the Week
Pamela Harriman and Winston Churchill
7 May 1995

When Winston Churchill was at Eton, one of the boys in his house asked if the fantastically beautiful redhead he was out with was his girlfriend. It was his mother. That is the moment he noticed that heads turned whenever he was out with her.

He liked to be his mother's escort. He and she always worked better like that. As young as 8, he'd put on the smart suit and charm-school smile and listened to other people being witty and tried to learn how.

Today they wear that same smile. She could still be his girlfriend. She's 74 but could easily pass for twenty years younger. As a mother, though, she was apparently pretty useless, hardly ever there. He mentions her only eighteen times in his autobiography, and only in passing, and never with emotion. The impact after all was psychological. He couldn't have her so he wanted to be like her.

They seem parallel emotional beings. Certainly they are very similar; money comes fortuitously to them when things seem bleak. Just look at how lucky he got with the lottery, a possible £12 million for his grandfather's archive letters coming to him and he's telling us National Heritage has got a bargain. That'll help him through any nasty divorce. After thirty years he and his wife Minnie are to split. They announced the news in March.

He had a bit of trouble with money he lost at Lloyd's. His mother had a bit of a squabble too. Her third husband, Averell, had left her a £20-million fortune in trust funds for his heirs and relatives. She's being sued by his children, the other Harriman heirs, who claim that she lost millions of dollars on bad investments since only a fraction is left. She still retains pictures by Picasso, Renoir and Matisse, not to mention real estate, but pleads she is part of the *nouveau pauvre*.

Still, they don't sweat, they don't get miserable, they know how to trade on a name. They are pragmatists who bask in the attention of the opposite sex without looking like they need it. They don't know about need, they've never really needed each other, but that comes from a lifetime of defying dependency for both of them. He is 54 and doesn't remember having a childhood. He says he never had any friends to play with and preferred to be alone in Hyde Park.

He learned to be drawn into his mother from a distance, as most people indeed did. Pamela Digby Churchill Hayward Harriman is the most acclaimed *saloniste* of the century. Now the American ambassador in Paris, she has spectacularly played for rich and powerful men.

She loved to flirt with power by proxy and then make it her own. She met Randolph Churchill on a blind date in 1939 and three days later was engaged to him. His father was running the war for God's sake, that smelt good to her. Randolph was a beautiful drunk, and a bully, but she liked the name.

During the war when she was 21 and he was 49, she first met Averell Harriman. He was Roosevelt's special emissary. Their two-year affair gave extra meaning to the special relationship that bound America and Britain. After the war she didn't meet Harriman again until 1971 when her second husband, the Broadway impresario Leland Hayward, died. She still found him sexy at almost 80. She married him.

Pamela was dazzling in the way that only a few of the women of that kind of breeding can be. More focused than the Mitfords and more manipulative than Lady Astor, she drew men to her by attending them. Being adored made them needy. Their needs, her power.

She was born into a tight, bluff, hunting and shooting, crusty old family where affection was displayed as discipline and routine. And that routine was carried out by a nanny who, years later, allegedly couldn't be bothered to take Winston down the several flights of stairs from the nursery in Chequers when the air raid sirens clanged.

She was never around much during the war. She acquired herself a small post in the Foreign Office. She needed to work to pay off Randolph's gambling debts. Then, she loved to work because it was an entrée to that vibrant new dating arena, mixing with men who mattered. It meant she'd matter too. He could never find a woman who could live up to that, that's why he is renowned as a womanizer, he never gave up trying.

Winston could not get huggy-feely-touchy with his mother, but he could admire her so absolutely. Although he seems quieter, women are compelled to him as men have been to Mummy.

Soraya Khashoggi had a hot time with him for five years in the 1970s. She said, 'He was a super lover. His loving was so passionate that no woman would feel a need for any other man.' And those are exactly the principles that his mother worked on. It's not that she liked sex that much, she has said that she didn't. What was enjoyable to her, she has confided, is that it was important for her to please her partners so that they would adore her and need her. She liked the way Wallace Simpson pulled things off, she doted and watched her husband constantly.

Thus she used sex as a means to feel loved. And if it wasn't love she got, it was power and dependency. The more other people depended on her the less she was dependent. Winston is a serial flirt. When he met the curvaceously gorgeous four-times-married American socialite Jan Cushing in Venice they all but consumed each other on the dance floor. They began an affair. She was in love with him, he proposed to her even though he was still married.

Suddenly Mummy came into the fray, incensed. Maybe she thought Cushing was too similar. She was suspicious of the female predator because she was reminded of herself. She felt threatened and for the first time reacted in a violent emotional outburst to her son. She was always used to being the youngest and most charismatic girl on the block. Maybe that's why she always went for much older men, so she'd always seem vivid. Now, more than ever, she acted more like a love rival than a mother. She forbade the relationship going any further saying it would end his political career, which has hardly been glittering. His most memorable moments were proposing a bill that regulated coloured immigration and a private member's bill to stop obscenity on TV. He did break off the relationship with Cushing in 1992, because he was caught by a paparazzo, he said.

He is a keen skier, and I am always suspicious of men who ski. It's a replacement activity, they know nothing of emotional peaks and plummeting. Winston was never particularly sharp and neither was his mother, despite her achievements. That's why so many men liked her, they were not threatened by her. Taki most famously remarked that she 'knows more about rich men's ceilings than anyone else.' She was all glittering eyes and throaty champagne bubble voice.

His eyes glitter too, and he has been described as so marvellously attentive to any new woman, even when his current escort, Belgian blonde Luce Danielson, is at his side. He has no manners because he was born with a sense of entitlement, and that's the best thing his mother ever gave him.

Her death means that now the movies can be made. I hear Sharon Stone is being sought to play her.

Peter Mandelson
News Review
3 March 1996

When I mentioned to friends, colleagues that I hoped to interview Peter Mandelson, their eyes invariably rolled. Their reaction was extreme. Some laughed in a cackling way, as if it were to be some blooded mud-wrestling scene – single white female meets snake. One man actually salivated and smacked his lips as if the combative exchange was going to be pornographic. Mandelson is a visionary, a one-off. He has been called mockingly, jealously, and realistically the Deputy Leader of the Labour Party. He and Tony Blair are sock and shoe. The one thinks, the other does. The title of his new book is *The Blair Revolution: Can New Labour Deliver?*

Previously, he was Neil Kinnock's Campaigns Director and creator of the Red Rose symbol; glamorous, thorny, British. Red, but could be any colour. Excessively moderate, despised by the old-fashioned Labour left, and pilloried by the Tories.

It is in my nature to warm to characters who provoke. But would he deliver himself to me? Politicians don't want to take unnecessary risks or ridicule. They like to vet, to control. His assistant had me checked out. Three separate sources said to meet me would be a very unwise move. Everyone said no.

Only Mandelson said yes. He said later that he thought I sounded exotic. I think he's generally contrary. But more than that, he is fiercely instinctive, and his instinct, he says, over-rules any kind of procedure or process or any rules.

So we meet for lunch. He looks rather long and waxy, shining eyes in a long face. Quite snakey. But he has a shimmering presence. It seems that often when he meets people they are in awe of him, and he can't help being irritated by that. 'Arrogant, I'm not. When people feel they are uncomfortable, they say the person they are with is arrogant.'

He's a maverick and a moderate. He's plain speaking and devious. He's confiding and secretive. Seductive, yet feisty. Inspirational and ordinary. Such a divergence of energies, and he's got them all under control. He has a brain like a nail. He remembers everything. What press cutting in what year gave what misquote. He makes things happen. He makes a difference. He is excessive, but only in his middle ground. Still, it's his ground, and he's claiming it.

'In politics it's often-times easier to make your way up the greasy pole by keeping your powder dry, your head down and buttering up as many people as possible, and that's not the way I choose forward in politics. I think that makes me different from other politicians and people don't feel comfortable with that. They don't really understand me. They don't know what makes me tick, and I think that produces nervousness.' We'll come to the ticking later, but for now there's the 'Why people are jealous of Peter Mandelson?' question.

He has of course, been integral to the 'modernize or die' beat of the drum. 'There are those who don't feel part of the changes being swept through the Labour Party. There is an anxiety there. And that nervousness attaches itself very swiftly and rather strongly to me. What I have to do is make myself better understood.'

There's a sense of that needing to be understood in the book, a sense of placation and appeasement. He says the book was the biggest risk of his life. Dull life, you think. Why was it such a risk?

'Just think about it. Controversial person, vulnerable person. Vulnerable to plentiful attack and criticism from outside the party and within. As I said in the preface, you put your head above the parapet. Did I not quote the *Book of Job*?'

And that brings us neatly to one of the problems that I find in the book. He says he is not religious. Both his parents were atheists, though his father sold adverts to the *Jewish Chronicle*. But that book, written with his longtime friend, Roger Liddle, has got a wholemeal Hovis fleck of Christianity chipping through it. It's not so much preachy, but solid, righteous, full of care. Shadowing the leader himself. The controversy is that it's the unriskiest book imaginable.

Roger Liddle, the co-author, is pink and snuffly; the Madge Alsop to his Dame Edna Everage. Dame Edna started off as Dame Edna Average, because she aspired to everything average, a middle-class clone. And in the process of making Labour an electable proposition, invariably intellectual breadth is sacrificed for the middle ground, the middle-brow, middle-class middle Britain. New Labour stands for ordinary families who work hard and play by the rules.

In all his astuteness and acuteness, Mandelson doesn't have a strong sense of himself. He would never aspire to the ordinary, so why can't people who join the Labour Party want to believe that they are special and that it is a special place? The place the Labour Party is going is centre.

'The SDP divided the left of centre and separated the centre from the left. The Blair revolution unites the left to the centre. The strongest possible alternative.'

The book is very readable. It provides passion and a structure. The book contains case histories for various stereotypes and charts their woes. They're slightly too stereotyped, one dimensional, but it's an innovation to put fiction in philosophy. It's kind of 'Our friends From Kennington.' It's suburban, family-orientated, and I tell him that I think this is a mistake because the family policy Back to Basics, traditional ground of the right, has a smarting bad taste.

It's dodgy ground, strengthening the family. He tells me I think that because I'm a Southerner. But I come from the north-east of England, the same as his constituency. 'The overwhelming mass of people choose to live their lives as a family. The government is not going to bring up children or parents. It's not going to be a substitute for families. Social services is not going to do the job for them – so support families.'

Now I can see why the Tories don't like him. They can accuse him of plagiarism. I tell him I'm too Bohemian for his policies and he looks startled and lifts his nose high from his tuna fish as if he were searching for smell of Bohemia.

'The object of government policy must be to enable parents to do a better job of parenthood so that the benefits are received by their children. And the same goes for schools and local communities, from which many children have opted out altogether. I think they ought to be brought back into a relationship to society, rather than feel like it owes them something, has given them nothing, which they just want to kick against and take out their frustrations on. I want them to have a stake in society through a strong family life and the most fulfilling education.'

Much has been made of the tax-free loan of £5,000 he plans as an idea for newly-marrieds starting up. He says it's for people who have made a commitment to each other. They don't have to be married, but 'there has to be some test of eligibility for this, and marriage is simplest. Chrissy,' he says conspiratorially, 'that's how most people, the overwhelming majority, choose to start their lives and bring up a family.'

But that's not what you did? 'Fine. Nobody's saying that I have to. Nobody's punishing me for not doing so. My motivation is simple. I know young people in my own town' (he means Hartlepool, his constituency) 'who do not have a start in life ... I want young people who are putting their home together to do so with less financial pressure. It's called redistribution.'

What if they want to make a commitment, but can't or don't want to get married? Can they get the loan?

'That's a matter for future government. Marriage, I'm afraid, is the most practical, and also what the majority find will fit in with their lives. Look, no policy is without its complexities.'

'Your body language is going all defensive.' He's lounging back and his arms are folded.

'I'm not.'

'You are.'

'That's how I choose to sit, and I'll sit any way I like, if you don't mind.'

He's slightly petulant, but if this is as bad as Prince of Darkness gets, it's perfectly bearable.

He is both spiky and confiding, which is an intoxicating cocktail. He can look through you, searingly, which alternatively makes you agog and surrender, or want to jerk away. The instincts that he talks about, the risks that he took to drop his television career at London Weekend when he was a producer, to campaign for a by-election for Brecon, are indeed fierce. He brings you in, wins you over. You feel he knows you. Incredible focus in a short time. He could actually have been Dame Edna Everage, pulling out the unfortunates from the front row as they smile, look simple, and feel caressed as parts of their lives and coat pockets are turned over.

Of course this is about control, about power. The power to move or make a difference. Comedians, priests and politicians share that inkling.

But how did he get to be this startling creature? He grew up in Hampstead Gardens suburb. At school he always came top of everything except maths. Which of his parents was he most like?

'I've got them both. I've got my mother's reserve, her caution, and my father was very outgoing. He died in 1988. He was an ardent conservationist and used to stalk the suburbs fending off conservation terrorists. He didn't have the opportunity to enjoy his retirement.'

He has one brother, a clinical psychologist. Tragically, his son, his nephew, died September before last at the age of 20. 'He was also Peter. He was a star.' He feels very emotional about this.

He does have a genuine love for children. He is a constant Godfather. It was children of friends, while on holiday, who took a style vote and demanded his moustache be wiped. His grandfather was Herbert Morrison, who organized Labour's 1945 campaign. Politics are in his genes. What makes him happy?

'Sitting at home, eating ice-cream, watching television with the answering machine on. Doing things well. If I've written a speech or a television appearance, I'm terribly self-critical and too easily discouraged.'

He inspires a fierce loyalty in friends and colleagues. If you believe in him, he seems so grateful, he'll never let you down. 'I am incredibly hard-working. I am an organizer as a person. I organize ideas. I organize my time. I organize others. Is that very boring?' he says, keeping all the details in check.

He says he never totters and turns in the night and wakes in a panic. However, 'I am an anxious person.'

He talks about how nervous he was when he first entered the Commons. How uncomfortable he was at first. He is both anxious and fearless. How does that work?

'I take risks because I am fearless. I am not a rebel, but I am fearless. I don't really hunt with packs. I don't go with convenient passions, but really I am a standard, conventional fellow.'

'That's what you fear, unconventionality, bohemia.'

'I'm slightly envious of that, but not frightened. I lead such a structured, organized life. Any politician does. I think there's a little bit in anyone. That they want to escape.'

I don't know if he really believes he's conventional. It was once written that PM wants to be PM. He said that someone made that up because it was a good soundbite, but does admit that he wants a ministerial career. But a Cabinet post has a price of towing the party line. He agrees. 'I will play by the rules, speak when spoken to. That is the nature of the collective.' Such a contrary good boy.

At the party for his book launch, he was effortlessly attentive, but on edge. He seemed to have no idea how he was commanding the room. Peter York, the 1980s guru for whom he once worked, was there and called him the Laurence Harvey of our time.

He seemed fretful, not of the celebrity count, but of people enjoying themselves. The regular bourgeois host. He gave up caffeine, doesn't want to be addicted to anything. Such a nice boy. Doesn't drink, doesn't smoke, doesn't fool around with women.

The next day, he called me to thank me for lunch. Tony Blair was reported to have once said, 'My project will be complete when the Labour Party learns to love Peter Mandelson.'

Does Peter Mandelson want to be loved? Or doesn't he care?

'Everyone cares about being loved and to love. And no, I don't fear it.'

So, does he fall in love easily?

'Sometimes I have in the past. But the truth is, now a love would have to be shared with my passion for New Labour, my work. Life is full of conflict. But this hasn't caused much conflict to date. I like warmth, intelligence, humour, in equal parts. But I'm not going to tell you anymore. My job is saving people from stepping on banana skins, not slipping on them myself.'

But Peter, there isn't a bowl of fruit around.

You can't dance like a snake unless you know how to be the charmer. And Peter Mandelson is very charming.

Relationship of the Week
Tony Blair and Cherie Booth
6 October 1996

Imagine Tony and Cherie in bed. I bet she sleeps in satin-viscose, peter pan collar pyjamas. The material sweats, but she probably doesn't. He I imagine striped. Striped boxer shorts and a fruit of the loom T-shirt. Definitely not naked, I imagine, although she might occasionally venture to wear a La Perla slip nightie. There's an awkwardness, an embarassed air about both of them. He can make swirly emotional speeches, but I can't see him doing intimacy.

I know power is supposed to be an aphrodisiac, but I've never really found it to be one. It depends what you mean by power. One person having power over another person in a relationship creates a frisson that matures into an interesting dynamic. But this is missing from their relationship, as they are both competent in different, separate ways. Sometimes I think people pursue power instead of sex. But what you end up with is something quivering on the inside, a vortex that is never shared.

They don't do warmth well either. They rarely seem go out *à deux* unless it's a public thing. And although she is said to make a decent fish pie, I wonder whether they entertain at home. These are clever people, they have a cerebral relationship. But, in public at least, they are clumsy with each other as demonstrated this week with that kiss at the Labour Party conference. She, rather theatrically, over-submissively flung her arms around him and closed her eyes adoringly. And his were pop-eyed open and looked out from the podium. As Matthew Parris put it, 'she's looking to him and he's looking to Britain.'

It was the kiss of people who don't, I imagine, fall into each other's bodies like they fall into their own skin. But then I have always thought of Mr. Blair having a surprised look of a

296

snake that has just shed an old skin, while his wife looks slightly perplexed at where the old skin went and what she should be doing with it.

I think they are people who don't know each other at all. I once had a dream they had reptile sex. She laid an egg and he came along afterwards and fertilized it. She probably doesn't even clip her toenails in front of him. Apparently, she thinks it's a bad idea to empty out the contents of your handbag in front of your husband. If you've never spilled out your handbag, it probably means you've never spilled your emotional entrails, never said, for instance, how awkward it was when that famous actor father left the family home when she was a baby and then came back later in a grand reunion after years of abandonment, alcohol and a torturous relationship with Pat Phoenix who played Elsie Tanner in *Coronation Street*.

The big, dramatic, emotional panorama can often create an emotional awkwardness in a girl. It is an awkwardness that sometimes comes over as a coolness, compartmentalized and clean, but quite endangered. If the compartment split, the psyche would be out of control and dirty.

While much has been made of there being two Cheries – Mrs Blair and Mrs Booth, the latter being the high-flying, £200,000 per annum QC and would-be judge but going for civil not criminal, I don't think she wants to cause any controversy or be a danger to her husband. She doesn't want to damage the Mrs Blair part of her, the little woman, considered to the point of frightened, who wears the right expensive clothes, even if they don't look it, who feels she must dance and kiss at party conferences. She is cleverer than her husband, more complex than him, yet, Mrs Blair must be defined by him. Always somebody's wife or somebody's daughter. Not easy when you're clever and complex. That makes you an awkward consort.

But then Blair is also two people. I'm not talking devil-dog and kindly Christian. I'm talking about that guileless school-boy who looks about 12, who receives an Oasis platinum disc as if he is an ancient alderman. There's always been a thrusting, a thwarting going on with Cherie. In 1983, she stood as a Labour candidate for an impossible seat, Thanet North, while her husband stood for the safe seat, Sedgefield. She lost but she talked of her commitment and her beliefs being defined by two Tonys. Tony Booth, her glamorous absentee father, and Tony Benn, the glitteringly left-wing radical, neither of whom think like Tony Blair. I don't think Tony Blair is a visionary. He just knows how to speak soundbites. His brain is simpler and he knows how to make his vision shiny – a shiny vision for shiny people. He has made Labour as shiny as Cherie's shiny hair.

Remember when she used to have that too-high-up spiky fringe affair reminiscent of Kate Bush's 'Wuthering Heights' period? Well, she is not good at being the shadow, the also-ran, the first lady, so she has allowed herself to be groomed. Outwardly she is much more palatable with the fashion *faux pas* of the thigh-length boots, or the Michael Jackson military-style jacket. Last month she edited *Prima*, a woman's magazine, and discussed knitting patterns and was pictured all cosy in an expensively cabled art-work knit. It all rather smacked of yarn spun by the spin doctors. What should Cherie do?

She's politically committed and politically sophisticated, but the idea of a Clinton-esque two-in-one package would be horrific to the British electorate. How can it be that a woman who seems more astute than her husband should appear to work through him or under him rather than over him? We cannot accept the idea of a non-elected political force, so her force must be played down again. That's why you rarely see her laughing, although sometimes she has a smile pinned on. Sometimes she looks rather miserable. And who wouldn't be with that tight-eyed, gloopy-looking kiss plastered all over the tabloids while her husband was busy being messianic? It was as if he didn't even notice her. But, as a political partnership, it will do. You cannot have love, sex, money, power all at once for more than one lunchtime. Political power is about expediency and if that means that she has to pretend to knit a jumper, she'll do that. She'll stand by her party, and that means she'll stand by her man. So, on one level, the relationship works but I doubt it's the kind of relationship where they sigh for each other or laugh with uncontrollable spirit. They are a partnership, but a partnership in which one half probably doesn't shave its legs in front of the other is not one to cry for. That is why when they move to look into each other's eyes they occasionally miss.

They became the essential shiny-people package. They could never lose each other now, not even if they wanted to.

SWEET

Mike Judge
Sunday Times Magazine
4 May 1997

It was hard to picture what kind of man had created Beavis and Butthead. For a start, there is no visual evidence, no pictures of him. We know his voice. He is infantile snickering Beavis and the moronically hard Butthead, the tattoos of stupidity that etch out the so-called MTV generation. We know all about their cultural validity, that they're supposed to symbolize the dumbing-down of America. We know that the man must be clever because he's created something that penetrates. You don't know if you're laughing at it or with it, and just when you hate it, and think that it's unbelievably stupid, Butthead will say something that cuts, that's so stupid it's clever.

At first you think Butthead is stupid and Beavis is stupider. Butthead talks more, in a demanding, deranged way, filled with half-assembled thoughts and ridiculous prejudices that are sometimes accumulated by hormonally challenged teenagers who don't quite fit in the world. Beavis has this unworldly droning cackle of a laugh, his answer to every-thing. You wonder why Butthead puts up with him. He has nothing to say for himself. You wonder why Beavis takes it, all that Butthead grouchiness and bossing him about. But who else would put up with either of them, except each other? The very nature of this relationship – one who is silent and inane and the other who is loud-mouthed and abrasive exemplifies the way so many teenage boy pals relate.

Beavis and Butthead started their existence reviewing videos on MTV. In their reviews they were cruel, casually cruel, and they tried to look hard. They invented couch violence. They sit there watching the videos and they never leave their couch, and people who never leave their couch watch them watching the videos. The show has been blamed for starting a fire which killed a toddler who, it is said, got the idea of burning himself and his mother's trailer from the one time catch-phrase of Beavis, 'Fire! Fire!' Actually the trailer park didn't even have cable, but it all helped inflame their appeal. Even so, you'd think their appeal would be limited to tweaking the teenage testosterone of acned yobs.

The movie *Beavis and Butthead do America* was made for $10 million, grossed $20 in its first weekend, knocking out the expensive Tom Cruise vehicle *Jerry Maguire*, to take the number one slot. The basic premise of the movie is Beavis and Butthead have their television stolen. Life cannot go on. It must be recovered. A tempting prospect? Bruce Willis and Demi Moore thought so. They did the voices of two supporting villain characters for scale. Their agents stressed that they must do no publicity, keep schtum about it, otherwise it could ruin their rates. It is actually the most successful movie that Demi Moore has been involved in for years.

It turned out not to need their publicity leg-up. It broke the Hollywood law that says don't do an animated movie unless it's a family movie because all animated movies that weren't family movies have bombed. Mike Judge, creator, writer and director of *Beavis and Butthead* has proved that they bombed for reasons other than that they were animated. The movie has grossed about $80 million across America and will no doubt do more when Beavis and Butthead do Britain. It means that the *Beavis and Butthead* audience is not just grossed out teenagers. Now everyone in America knows Butthead is the mean one, the one that talks, and Beavis is the weird one, who just has the mesmerizing, unrelating and unrelenting snicker-snicker-snicker. But what you don't know is, is Judge being subtle or is he just like them? And when they name their likes and dislikes and talk about 'things that are cool' and 'things that suck', you don't exactly know whether their creator is being ridiculously simplistic or focused on to the way it is.

You think that you can't possibly imagine or know any character who could assimilate randomly gathered pieces of non-information so stupidly. You imagine that he must have hung out with these people. So you imagine him to be pretty scary. I imagined him tattooed with something gross, maybe even a swastika. I imagined him shaven-headed or with a greasy ponytail. I imagined him burger-bellied. It disturbed me that there were no pictures of him. Perhaps it was like he was an evil ventriloquist whose voices had consumed him so he was a disjointed mouth which only ever said that things were cool or that things sucked.

He lives and works in Austin, Texas. Beavis and Butthead were created in that very extreme scenario of redneck suburbia where the cult hit movie *Suburbia* was filmed. He chooses to remain cosseted there. Parts of its landscape have desperation in their ugliness. It's the kind of ugliness that lurks in mini-malls, posing garishly under brand names like K-Mart and Target, places essential to the fabric of Beavis and Butthead. I pictured Mike Judge as crass, unsophisticated, leery. I mean, he provided the sexual agenda for his characters, their very basic instincts.

My plane had arrived late and I had been lost in the seaminess of the quaint streets. I was on his doorstep and there was a shuffling of the blinds, eyes poking angrily, head cocked. A Texas-drawled assistant was very sweet but said that we were very late. He was in one of his back offices, perhaps the one with the pool table, perhaps the one with the antique Hammond organ collected from a church. We heard only the noises of disgruntledness. We could almost hear the lip-curling. The sweet assistant said that Mike wasn't sure if he had time at all for us. There had been some mix-up and he had expected us several hours earlier and now he had to go to collect his tuxedo to wear to the Oscars. We heard more shuffling and then he appeared, tanned, toned in jeans, T-shirt and darting eyes; a face that is an uncaricatured Butthead, pleasantly chiselled, a face that has no idea of its own strength, a look which is totally and absolutely unassuming. Unassuming but angry.

But just like he doesn't know his face is handsome, he

doesn't know what to do with his anger. You can see it. He would absolutely like to tell us to go away. You're too late. Because what he's really concerned about is his tuxedo fitting. He's at the same time fidgety with himself because he can't quite say that. He's too polite, too shy. Beavis and Butthead were what he did with his anger. Beavis and Butthead is how he expresses a lifetime of rage against stupidity.

As he paced with his chin jutting out, he was Butthead. As he paced back again, he was as bland as whipped butter. 'All right' he conceded. 'We'll do some pictures now and then you can come with me to the tuxedo-fitting.' He posed excruciatingly self-consciously and nervously for the first set of pictures. He got over it by very occasionally emitting a low 'eh eh eh eh eh' Beavis snickering noise, like he was a naughty boy that had to do voices to distract, to amuse, to smooth things over. And of course he is.

He says I can drive with him in his car. He has a very nice car. Metallic pearl-blue BMW convertible. 'It's cute,' I tell him. 'MTV gave it to me as a present', he says. 'I didn't buy it.' He's very endearing in his car, which as he and Butthead agree is a very cool car. But he's also self-conscious in it, as if he feels it's kind of a fluke that he's actually driving it, as if he's not good enough for it. But the longer he's in his car, the more relaxed he becomes and he almost starts to fit into his own skin.

He then got very excited at the thought of taking pictures at the mini-mall, the mini-mall where the film *Suburbia* was shot, and he was going to collect his tuxedo. 'It's really ugly,' he said, his eyes igniting. Then he was totally inspired by the disused K-Mart because 'That's America right there.' he said, like he just churned a pearl from a shell. Mike Judge's and Beavis and Butthead's America is very much about the ugly and the damned. It's very much about K-Mart.

We drive to the tuxedo shop next to a Chinese take-away. He waits in line with a couple of grooms and their ushers and he's quickly in and out of the hired tux. He says he hates awards dinners, but Beavis and Butthead were presenting a technical Oscar and he had to be there. He shows me round the mini-mall and into the branch of Target that put K-Mart out of business, as if he is an excitable new boy freshly hired at the Victoria and Albert Museum. He looks at a video, a brand of dog food or a garish Easter bunny as if he were looking at a historic exhibit, and he tells me how he'd like to shoot a live-action movie. He's working on a script. He talks about it being about the kind of corporate life that would exist in a middle America business park inspired by his own miserable life as an engineer.

The studio, meanwhile, is of course screaming for the next Beavis and Butthead. Maybe he's ready to deal with real people. He hopes so. But he's an equal mixture of self-doubt and ambition. He can't get rid of the self-doubt in case it means he won't have the need to prove himself. He's had moments where his script was crippling him, but it was the same with Beavis and Butthead and that turned out a virtual phenomenon. He's in such a good mood after the tour and so excited by Fergus photographing him in a manhole outside the disused K-Mart, he seems to think that we might be getting to the core of him and what he's about, so he wants to go back to his office to talk more.

It's like he's spent his life as an outsider, his cartoons being the only way he can communicate. When someone sees in, he's grateful. He was born in 1962 in Albuquerque, New Mexico, which he says similarly inspired him. 'Beavis and Butthead come from somewhere in between Albuquerque and Austin, from the same kind of world I'm from. When I was a kid back there, we would go ride our bikes for hours outside K-Mart. In the front there was a place with game machines, but it would be a hundred degrees outside so we'd go inside K-Mart to cool off. I always imagined Beavis and Butthead living in this endless hot area. They're always in shorts and T-shirts. It's actually nice in the winter here, although in Albuquerque it snows, but Beavis and Butthead come from the summer.

'I was thinking of when I was a kid and bored. There's nothing to do. That's when kids start blowing up lizards.

You're this 14-year-old guy with no car. You just have a bike and testosterone. It's a dangerous situation. You're too old to act like a kid and go out and play, but you're too young to be doing anything. When we were cavemen, you'd get married then. But now we've evolved into where you have to be going to school until you're 22. There's something basically wrong with being 14 today.'

It would be wrong, though, to assume that the young Mike Judge was the class Butthead. He was actually quite the opposite. His family were lower-middle-class intellectuals. They were not struggling, but they weren't rich. He says he grew up hating all rich people. His father was an archaeologist who now teaches at Fort Louis College in Colorado and his mother was a librarian at an elementary school. He was studious, academic and an outsider. 'I didn't even go out with girls until I was 17. I was scared to death of talking to girls. I was a really geeky, quiet kid. I was very different from Beavis and Butthead. Although I was a loser like them, I actually got good grades. The good grades made me a loser. In my junior high school, if you were doing well in math, it was something to keep quiet about. My junior high was so awful. I was worried about my safety. People got stabbed and stuff. By the time you get to high school a lot of the scary people have dropped out. I would hate to go back there because it's the same gene pool of violent people and now they all have guns.'

When he was living in New York, working for MTV, he came across two other guys – one a writer for *Details* magazine, the other a big-wig at an advertising agency – who went to his junior high school.

'We confessed to one another that we were all scared to go to school. It was mostly hispanic, about 70 per cent, and we were the white guys, the gringos. And it was violent. We were scared. You'd be walking down the halls and they'd shake you down for money. It was like going through the gauntlet, this gauntlet of 'Give me some money, fucking gringo.' There's something about that place that makes you want to go away and . . .' Recreate it? 'Yes, I suppose.'

At school he never felt like writing or drawing, not until the end of high school where he did a few caricatures of teachers. That, he concedes, made him more popular than he had ever been before.

He went on to study physics at the University of California, San Diego. He graduated with an excellent degree and worked as an engineer for a government contracting company on the F-18 Electronic Test System until one day he decided he didn't want to learn how to kill people. I didn't have him down as a pacifist, but he's certainly emerging as a man with a conscience, which seems to me odd, considering his first animation short was called *Frog Baseball*, where innocent amphibians were squashed. He used the noise of baseball bats breaking water-melons and ox liver smashing against a chopping board to make the squelch of death.

Frog Baseball was the kind of violence that made him, but when he talks about it, it's as if all the squelching is in some place he is detached from. The way he detaches himself is through a geeky enthusiasm for detail. He made *Frog Baseball*, in which the Beavis and Butthead characters first appeared, with $250 out of his savings. He describes: 'I shot it on a Bolex. I took the film to a place where you transfer home movies to videos for $14, then I took the VHS tape and hooked up my cassette player. I timed the track out with a stop-watch. It took me forever.'

Animation was not something that had burned inside him. After he quit the engineering job, he started doing music for a living. That was in the mid-1980s. We're not talking metal-head Beavis and Butthead music, but playing bass with respectable bands. It seems there was something sick and twisted within him that wasn't coming out twanging his bass. 'I was playing music for a living and had been for five years and I didn't like it anymore. I don't know that I ever did. So one of the things I was thinking about was teaching. But the reason that I didn't want to teach at high school was that I know those characters. Those characters were just like, you can't teach them anything.

'Beavis and Butthead are like, here's my argument: they are a ridiculous exaggeration of a certain type of person. No two guys in particular. They came from a lot of different places. Maybe that Beavis-Butthead type relationship is one that all friends experience, like I was Beavis to my brother's Butthead. And another friend that I grew up with, who actually became the voice for Beavis's dad, was Beavis to my Butthead. There's no one defining, but there's a few instances, like we had this writing teacher who was actually a nun and she was reading this really bad poem by this like, honour student. And she was reading it real dramatically. The last line was "and the moon screams." She set the paper down and looked up and went, "Wasn't that beautiful?" This kid in the back of the class goes, "No." It was really funny and he got into trouble, but he was actually right.'

Judge relates this to when Beavis and Butthead were reviewing pretentious, artsy videos and it sounded really funny to have Beavis and Butthead be really stupid and also be right. It's a real put-down if even Beavis and Butthead can tell your video is bad. The future of Beavis and Butthead will inevitably be trapped in the same hormonal rush of the past because they cannot grow up. He says they are never going to get a girlfriend and he has a hard time imagining them with driving licences. But their relationship and their personas have evolved.

'Originally I thought I was more Butthead, because I wasn't sure what to do with Beavis. He just sort of cackles. He's one of these scary kind of guys because you don't know what he's going to do because his brains are fried out. Beavis may get smacked around by Butthead, but it's the price he pays. Who else would hang out with him?'

In his physics class he went through a phase of putting the word butt into everything. 'Why don't you look up that equation? Why don't you look up my butt. Let's go to ButtDonalds and get some Chicken McButt. So that's where the actual name came from. The attitude is, 'Me and my friend and my brother watching TV. You just get into that state, I don't know what it is. You want to turn off the smart part of your brain and just be stupid.'

Girls don't really get that way, I tell him.

'Yes, it's definitely a guy thing. Some women find it funny. I don't know why. Although most of the women I get letters from are in their fifties saying how the show helped them break ice with their sons and helped them talk about sex without awkwardness.'

Judge himself of course cannot talk about sex without awkwardness. But he knows this about himself and is rather self-mocking. 'Beavis and Butthead is definitely making fun of guys because they're losers. They're never going to get anywhere with a woman.'

Although it would seem more obviously a boy zone, as the box-office numbers testify, it is not exclusively male. This surprises Judge somewhat, probably because he thinks he's not good at communicating with women. He concedes that in the creative process, 'I do think, will my wife think it's funny?'

He met Francesca at University. She was his first serious girlfriend. He'd only ever gone out with other girls for two to three months. He has been with her over ten years. He says, 'I wasn't a real smooth single guy, you know. It was looking for a while back there like I wasn't going to have much of a future.' Do Beavis and Butthead, with their 'Hey, chicks' and endless discussions about masturbation and breasts reflect in *any* way his attitude towards women? Truly shocked, he says, 'I never talk to or about women the way they do. But I think the way Butthead approaches women is what I'm most afraid I would sound like.' Does he have Butthead's taste in women? 'Beavis and Butthead want to see Snow White naked. They figure if she'd do a dwarf, she must be easy. But it will never happen. That would be like letting Charlie Brown kick the football. They also are very impressed with Prince Charles when he told Camilla Parker Bowles he wanted to be her tampon. "We thought that guy was a wuss," they said. "But he's pretty smooth." '

When Judge laughs, or when he's nervous or angry, he

makes the Beavis noise, 'eh eh eh' coming muffled and mocking from way back inside the throat. The reason Butthead talks in that tight and slurping way is because that's the noise you make when your mouth is wired in braces, like the ones Judge wore. 'I had braces when I was 14 and the wires that stick out, they scrape on your cheeks when you're talking so the corners of your mouth don't go up when you smile. You smile *down*, which is what I do with Butthead. I used to see 13-year-olds in the mall in their badass Megadeth T-shirts, these guys who wanted to be heavy-metal rebels but first had to get their braces tightened.' Judge doesn't listen to Megadeth but he listens to AC/DC as a real treat.

Not surprisingly, it took him a long time before he had the guts to do comedy. It had taken him until his late twenties before he realized he was seriously funny. He still doesn't think he can draw. But out of this strange state of no confidence comes an almost naïve sense of self-esteem.

One of the most interesting things about him is that he knew no one in the film business. He just mailed the tapes of his first cartoon, *Inbred Jed*, which he made in 1991, to the addresses he found listed in the phone book. 'I had no connections. But I got the number for Comedy Central from information and, within a week, they called me. And the Festival of Animation called me and I thought, 'God. Why didn't I do this when I was 22?' In the first year of animation he had done four animated shorts and made $2000 from each of them. In 1992, *Frog Baseball* appeared on MTV, and the channel then commissioned the *Beavis and Butthead* series, which began in 1993.

Playing in the band, he made $26,000, which is roughly how much his father made as an archaeologist. He still has the head-set of a person who earns $26,000. Do you know how much money you make now? He blushes as he says, 'I've gotten to the million mark in what I have in the bank and what I own.'

Do you still hate rich people? 'That's where it's rough. I probably would have hated someone driving around in that car a few years ago. I've always hated rich kids and now my kids are going to be rich kids,' he says sheepishly.

He has two little girls, Julia, 5 and Lilly, 2. 'My older daughter, if I'm channel-fishing and she comes into the room and sees anything animated, I shut it off and she whines and says, 'I want to watch that.' But if I'm watching *Beavis and Butthead*, she never wants to see that. I think kids have a natural instinct that anything your parents are doing can't be very interesting. When I was a kid, people would ask what my dad did. I would say, "He's an archaeologist". They'd say, "That's interesting." And I'd go, "No it's not." '

He shows me the pictures on his wall. Julia looks like her mother, but Lilly looks like a cartoon version, a replica of Daddy. That same Butthead little mouth and beady eyes. He acknowledges this and seems especially pleased. He is very protective and strict with them. Ironically, it was the 'Fire! Fire!' brou ha-ha over the death of the toddler that made him a household name. He says, 'That was kind of scary, but you know there are a lot of important details that didn't get recorded.' His story is that the woman, a single mother, went out on a date. 'She left her five-year-old and two-year-old unattended. She literally left the trailer. This kid had started fires when he was 3 years old, before Beavis and Butthead were even on the air. And she just left lighters around the house. She should have been arrested for child abandonment.' Instead, he got the blame and reaped the rewards of the national publicity. 'She said to the cops, "It's that *Beavis and Butthead*." It later turned out that they didn't get cable in that trailer park and the kid hadn't even seen the show. After that, people at MTV took the word 'fire' out of every single episode. We had a Christmas special where Beavis and Butthead were sitting with Christmas carols playing, watching a yule log on TV. We had to use an animated fireplace because they said we can't have real fire in the fireplace like it was going to make people go out and start fires in their fireplaces.'

In America, much has been made of how MTV has not

really treated Mike Judge as a genius of his generation. They were, in fact, reported to be financially stingy, and I can imagine Judge taking that. He is not at ease with his own success. He wanted to go out to dinner. Not anywhere flash, but a local eatery that's reasonably healthy. He tends to avoid the fry-ups that are ubiquitously on offer in Texas. At night, he'll listen to a band play sometimes, but mostly he's working, writing or perhaps toying with his Hammond Organ. He's proud of that and he shows me how to make all the notes shiver and quiver.

After dinner, Fergus wants to take photographs of him at the gas station with his shimmering vehicle. Suddenly, the Mike Judge who had been ultra-compliant is getting edgy because people are looking. People are looking at him and his car and he's self-conscious about the association. 'Come on now,' he says and goes into a Beavis laugh. Inside the gas station shop, we go to pay. The boy at the counter says, 'That's a really cool car.' 'I didn't buy it,' snaps Judge. 'Oh, you're just test-driving it,' says the boy. 'No. It was a present.' 'Oh,' says the boy, looking askance and looking at me like I'm a mobsters' moll and suddenly the mafia are infiltrating Texas. Judge says, 'That was a stupid thing to say, that it was a present, wasn't it? I don't know why I can't just admit to owning it. It must be that thing that I have about rich people.'

Mike Judge is, literally speaking, the voice of a generation. Yet he's very unchartered territory when you ask him to speak for himself. If you close your eyes, he's still Butthead taken over by some super-intelligent, innovative force. He doesn't talk in soundbites, he doesn't want to impress. Unpromising material, you think, until you realize that everything normal is neurotic and everything neurotic is normal. There's the frisson.

Clare Short
News Review
12 November 1995

I'd imagined her brutalized and brutish, like a big old neutered cat with bits of her torn off in frays and the claws still out. Her office said, 'Don't talk about cannabis, otherwise she'll walk.'

And there she is, breathless, passionately excited about some minutiae of transport detail. She's tall, bosomy and on a diet. She's in purple and sexy. I mean really sexy. The kind of sexiness that you get with people who are both warm and fearless, a kind of velvety combative spirit. Not the person the *Sun* said was too ugly to rape, when she most famously campaigned against Page Three, believing its objectifying of women made us all up for violent grabs.

Clare Short doesn't really need the protection that her office wants to offer to her.

Does she think she's too hot and forthright to be a good politician? 'I refuse to accept you can't be a politician and be straight. It would be tragic for democracy. I do want to be honest and sincere about my politics, and I am.'

Her sincerity about speaking her personal views on the legalization of cannabis in a recent David Frost television interview means that she ignored her collective responsibility as a newly elected member of the Shadow Cabinet. Time and time again she has said how she hated compromise. Twice she's resigned from Front Bench positions under the Kinnock leadership when she felt at odds with the party line on the Gulf War and anti-terrorism legislation.

So what's going on? Is she now ready to sacrifice a passionate intensity for a powerful 'I can change the world' position? Or has she just got to stop saying what she thinks?

'I think it means that what I say will go under more scrutiny and I need to be aware of that and . . .' she bursts out laughing and says she can't resist talking about the subject she is not supposed to.

'In the famous Frost interview, personally what I did was wrong. He asked why I signed a motion in 1984 and I explained why. But I should have said, "But Jack Straw had reached the conclusion that there shouldn't be any change."

'There's a two-way trade with me and the Shadow Cabinet. No one thinks that everyone thinks the same. But what collective responsibility means is everyone has the chance to have a say and then you have to accept the decision. I accept that no one can have their own way all the time. But I do like very much to have my say.'

So isn't this going to be hard for you? 'No. I'm in an easier position than when I was a junior front-bencher because then you are bound by a decision that is made when you are not there. At least now I will be there when the decisions are taken.' So what about compromise? 'You have to compromise, it's part of democracy.'

This is a woman who can get passionate about everything. Who says that she's sometimes worn out by her own intensity. She holds her opinions strongly. 'I'm made like that,' she says.

So then, what if the rest of the cabinet decided on a policy that was against everything she believed in?

'We have to think, Do we have any bottom lines? And I have lots of bottom lines. It doesn't mean there won't be differences between us but we're coming from the same sort of space.'

Do you think you're coming from the same space as Tony Blair? 'It's funny, I do.' Yes, that is very funny. She laughs one of her naughty laughs. 'I didn't support Tony for leadership. I couldn't imagine him as leader of the Labour Party and we had a fall-out before he stood.' This is where you allegedly called him poisonous. 'No. I never thought of him as poisonous. I didn't think of him as . . .'

She's searching for some circumspect words and the face she's pulling seems to say that she didn't rate him enough to be poisonous. Her big, open face says everything. 'I just didn't think of him as being a leader. I couldn't have supported him, and then he was elected, overwhelmingly. Back to this democracy thing, and I'm surprised and I'm thinking, well here am I and I consider myself essentially Labour. I'm in tune with the party and its values, and look at this. The overwhelming bulk of them have voted for this bloke. And I don't think it's the right person. So I thought, you have to respect that Clare, it's their judgement.

'So we start and all this woman stuff was going on' (she argued for a 50 per cent quota of candidates). 'We had a few arguments and it was brilliant. We have a really straight relationship. I tell him exactly what I think. If we make an agreement we stick to it. I know it surprises people. But funnily enough I like him, and he . . .'

Do you think he's scared of you? The big cat that has the cream smile reappears. 'I think he'd rather have me on his side than against him.'

She was supposed to have received quite a carpeting for her cannabis indiscretion, yet she appears to have shrugged it off completely, quoting the piece of Mark Twain she's got on her toilet wall. 'Loyalty to a petrified opinion never broke a chain or fired a human soul.'

Does she often change her mind? 'Not likely, but if you never change your mind about anything what's the point of being alive, and I changed my mind about Tony Blair.'

She accepts that her kind of socialism, the people she reaches, are different to the ones he will touch. She, like many other more passionately hardcore members of the party have been exhausted into pragmatism by the desperation that there must be a Labour government, almost at any cost, even if the leader appears rather like a Tory.

Interestingly, Mr Blair and Mr Portillo were born on exactly the same day in exactly the same year, making them astral twins. She says she doesn't believe in astrology.

Growing up a Catholic, one of seven, informs her politics, a yearning for goodness, moral order. I had always thought of her as a dogmatist, dulled by political correctness, a puritan. 'I'm ruthlessly puritan when it comes to any kind of cheating or corruption, but I'm not in any way against pleasure.'

I had the idea that when she said, 'Going shopping is not a way of life,' she didn't know how to shop. Now I think her soul does a lot of shopping.

She says all her passions flow around politics: that it squeezes out the personal life. 'Anyway, my personal life has been a bit blighted and unlucky.'

Her second husband, Alex Lyon, was a Labour minister sacked by Callaghan. He lost his seat the same election she won her Birmingham Ladywood constituency. 'It meant everything to him, but he was not bitter or jealous.' She admits it would have been difficult to cope if it had been the other way round.

He was proud of her and passionate about her. They met while she was working for him in Whitehall as his private secretary. Eroticism of the shared endeavour and all that. He was married, and she was just falling out of marriage – someone she married when she was 17, and, even though mutual, her divorce was painful. She said that she and Lyon shouldn't have fallen in love. They had a hundred endings but could never stay away.

Lyon got Alzheimer's disease, he died two years ago, but was dead in his head long before his body. She watched a brilliant mind crumble, disintegrate into a man who wanted to make bonfires around the house until he had to be put into a home for his own safety. He didn't know her anymore. She felt angry at that, and angry that his dignity died before him.

Just how did she cope? 'That's what life is like. You have to cope, so I did.' Did she ever think she was not going to? 'No. I knew it was hard but I knew I could cope, I do cope, I'm that kind of person.' She says this almost sadly with the kind of resignation that seems to indicate that maybe just once she might have liked to have tried petulance or hysteria.

'Women deal with the tragedies better because they deal with emotions better. Women are expected to nurture, care and look after. They live more comfortably in those emotional spaces of pain and hurt. And despite inequalities I think women are happier than men, and it doesn't mean to say they don't have hurt. They deal with hurt, they feel for other people hurting. All women feel terribly happy and clucky and think it's lovely when people fall in love. They are so terribly romantic.'

And is she? 'All women really want is to grow up, fall in love and live happily ever after. Everybody does, I did, I still do.'

Is Clare Short still looking for Mr Right? Yes she is, even though she's been blighted. Before Lyon there was the disappointing first love who, years later, was tempted to sell lingerie shots of her to the *Sun*, and another lover who was a 'bad lot' who was killed in a gangland shoot-out.

She believes that only one in 3,000 relationships work, yet she still wants one, and is a passionate, generous person. She would have been a clucking and lovely mother, she longs for kids, but it didn't fall that way and now it never will.

Although she seems still that heart bleeding romantic, she says she dreads being hostage to her hormones, dreads to be consumed. 'I want it all really, and I want to make the world a better place.

'I think women want to love people, and one of the answers is for women not to give their love so lightly. They think, if you love someone enough, they'll be nice and you can change them. They should be more fussy about who they give their hearts to.

'This is my conclusion from my life's experience and I'm nearly fifty, so I apply it to myself as well as other people. It's better not to be in a relationship if you can't have a kind man.'

But love is so disillusioning, you see them as kind. 'Yes,' she says, looking right at me for the first time after an hour of arching her neck into space. For the moment that kindness is eluding her. She wants, rather purely and sweetly, to be kind to the rest of the world, excited at the possibility of ending world hunger, she wants to be round that table. I don't feel she has been thwarted or compromised. Her aim is still true and she's quite a pussycat.

At the time I didn't understand the potency of her longing for children. Since then it has been revealed that she did, in fact, have a child who she gave up for adoption and with whom she has recently and joyfully been reunited.

Her advice to me was, 'You've got to find a man who's going to be kind to you. That's the most important thing.' I often think about that.

Kathy Lette
Hot Air Magazine
October 1996

She's warm, keen, talks like her books. She's a good read and a fabulous *cappucino* companion – and she knows how to froth a soundbite. You go, you turn on the tape recorder. She does the rest.

The first time I met Kathy Lette, it was at one of those dreadful lunches that Andrew Neil, the then editor of the *Sunday Times*, used to have for bright young things. Well, women he thought were smart, sassy and suitable for his pages. Kathy Lette radiated wit. She shimmered with the kind of stuff that probably she would say had to be registered at the police station as a lethal weapon. I never opened my mouth for three hours except to put in some toffee ice-cream. My silence was as extraordinary as her verbosity, and it's a fair enough summary of how we respond to pressure. She auditions, she fights, she grabs the space, whereas I don't want to play the game. At the end of the lunch, someone asked me why I hadn't spoken and I said that I was too bored – which, had it not been for Kathy Lette, would have been the case. I think we respected each other's reaction. In the interim few years she has produced two babies and two novels: *Foetal Attraction* and *Mad Cows*. For this, I can only respect her more.

Kathy Lette is small and Australian, although small seems to be an inappropriate word because everything about her is grand-scale, dramatic, and she always wears heels. Heels and ear-rings with wit and panache. That's her thing. That's how she decorates herself. Big witty ear-rings are for insecure people who like to distract from their face, from who they are. And just for a while, the Australian-ness, the brash wisdom of this woman, makes you feel she's vastly confident. But then you know that someone who learned how to be that funny learned the hard way, learned from stuff that hurt her, and it must have really hurt her deeply because this woman is brilliantly funny from a very deep place.

She has a sharp tongue and a very wide mouth, and words come out honed and toned like a gymnastic routine. You can drown in her own sea, in what she calls punnilingus. She is very much the voice of her own novels and the voice has grown up with them. In *Girl's Night Out* she was one of those girls sharing a flat, dealing with men and evolving from the cameraderie of women, women who can be stripped down to their emotional underwear in seconds. She was one of those searching girls. In *Foetal Attraction*, she was still searching, but she'd lost the Australian girl gang, embroiled herself in an affair with a married TV personality and got pregnant by accident. In *Mad Cows*, she got into jail by accident – jail and other inventions being analagous of single mothers' second-division status and how they are discarded by society. Despite the verbal onslaught and the visual impact – she had the boys in Little Italy gawking when we met for coffee – and the fact that she has so many projects going (*Girls Night Out* is being made into a film by Miramax, *Foetal Attraction* is being made into a film by the BBC) despite the full-on Australian brashness, rawness that you'd expect, she's oddly self-effacing, dismissive of her own achievements, and kept saying, 'I'd much rather talk about you. I hate talking about myself.'

Maybe that's because she's all done with talking about herself, because she's sublimated it. She says 'on the one hand, people who write write because they can't do anything else, and then it's the best therapy. I don't have to visit couch canyon and, of all my bad experiences, at least I can say I can turn them into novels.'

And that's basically what she did do. The Australian men that she raged against really did exist. When she was a surfie waxing boards for her boy and generally lackeying around like a corgie, she and her girlfriends would rather masochistically make tan tattoos from their boyfriends' names by writing the name in tape and tanning all around it. She says that if she gets a melenoma, its name will be Bruce and she'll have to consider a Bruce-ectomy. Bruce was probably not very nice to Kathy, who grew up in that rather op-perfect suburban haven of Sylvania waters. She took the emotional masochism for a while, and then vacillated to the opposite extreme of mohair-legged feminism. Having embraced both, she is the writer and indeed the woman she is. She says that even though Australian men are 'emotional bonsais, they have a sense of humour dryer than an AA clinic, and that is pretty irresistable. And they have beautiful bodies. They look like ice-cream cones. Lovely brow, with stupid little vanilla for a head. And they're good at sex. And at least you know where you are with them. In England, all the sex is is subterranean.'

Kathy Lette's husband is Australian. He is that media-friendly QC, Geoffrey Robertson, a rather charismatic fighter of left causes, truly international. One of the few top-flight lawyers constantly engaged in the global human rights circuit which Lette says causes a dilemma. Every time she wants him to mash avocado he's dealing with the paperwork for three hundred people on death row. He's lived in England for twenty-five years, but he has a TV show in Australia called *Hypothetical*, and that's where they met, when Kathy Lette stood in for Kylie Minogue.

'It's funny having a video tape of your first meeting. It was absolutely love and lust, everything, in the first few seconds.

You can see me on the tape, which we have. Me, getting more and more hormonally flushed. I'm batting my eyes. My eyelash-batting average would rival Alan Border. I'm oozing charisma. I was completely hijacked. I knew he was the person for me, but I was already married. I was married, but it was, well, much more of an intellectual union. There was none of that primal passion, and once I sampled it I knew it was the real McCoy. I gave up my home, my hemisphere, everything, in about two seconds flat. It was wonderful. It does exist. But it was also traumatic and terrible. I had to say goodbye to my husband first, and that was angst city because he loved me. I could only tell my parents I had fallen in love when I was leaving for England the next day. My father looked at me and said, 'Who do you think you are? Zsa Zsa Gabor?'

The Australians joke about poms and she thinks the English see the Australians as the Irish of the Pacific. It was an uncomfortable jolt. To start with, there was the whole class system that she reacted badly to. Appalled by a country where even stamps have a first and second class. 'I would never have come here except for love. It was quite hostile and everyone speaks in euphemisms like when someone says to you, 'Oh, you Australians. You're so refreshing' What that really means is rack off, you loud-mouthed colonial. It took me ages to realize this. And you are also masters of the back-handed compliment. When I first arrived, I was wearing a hot pink suit with flowers on it and one woman said, 'Aren't you brave to wear that in London? But you can't see yourself from the back, so what does it matter?'

Lette says that she's still trying to work out this very difficult tribe. It's not that she isn't used to being an alien. In a way, as a writer, it probably helps. Her first experience as an alien abroad was in L.A., where, after her first couple of novels had been a success in Australia, she was asked to go and work on the writing of a sitcom called *The Facts of Life*. She'd written about girl-bonding and this was about four girls living together, who were 20, 21 but none of them has lost their virginity. The first thing she said when she got there was, 'Can I wrote the episode when one of them does the horizontal tango?' They were shocked, horrified and dipped me in disinfectant.'

It was a visceral experience. 'The thing I like about England is that England likes writers. But in America, on the job-desirability scale, it sort of goes can opener, amoeba, toilet, brush, pond scum, writer. You have no power, muscle, nothing. And in these shows, the actors got up in the morning and took their megalomanic pills and were vile for the rest of the day. They'd been on the show since they were about 9 and now they were 20. We'd write these really funny scripts and all the jokes would be cut out. It was nine Jewish guys and me and we were fabulously funny. But they'd turn it into a kind of joke-zac – a kind of joke version of muzac where the jokes wash over you. It was heartbreaking . . .'

L.A. wasn't for her. 'Tanning salons even though it's sunny all year round, clubs called Densa where you have to sit around and be vacuous, and Vampires Anonymous for people who really thought they were vampires. In L.A. they're all pretty vacuous. They don't read, except their bank balances, their menus and their tarot cards. The first thing you notice there is that everyone's skin sags upwards. The ankle becomes the knee, the knee the navel, the clitoris the chin. You have to look for women doing this too vigorously.'

She's rubbing her chin with unusual dexterity. She was uncomfortable in L.A., but 'I got a novel out of it, so that was fine. Cheaper than an analyst and it's a cure for heartache. Look at *Heartburn* that Nora Ephron wrote when her husband dumped her. She got it all out of her system and made a fortune. Poetic justice is the only justice in the world, and I say that married to a lawyer.'

There is a feeling that with her intensely autobiographically influenced work now necessarily centered around the dilemmas of birthing and rearing, she might want to live her passions vicariously, or maybe she always did. Certainly in *Girl's Night Out*, there's a sadness for a lost wildness before it's even been lost, and behind the cynical sheath there's a sweetness, there's a pungency and a kind of bravery.

She's very much Dame Edna's love-child, with her own parents, Val and Mervyn, coming from Sylvania Waters and having the same names as Edna's daughter and her husband. Her mother is a teacher and her father worked in optics. Optic Merve, Merve the nerve they used to call him. 'It makes me sound like a tadpole. The men in Sylvania Waters disproved the theory of evolution. They were evolving into apes. I think the reason the men are so macho is that hardly any women were transported to the colony early on. They say their version of foreplay is shearing. I used to tell my English girlfriends going to Australia to wear their woollens to bed, put their feet in a pair of gumboots and lie back and go baaaa. Australian women, though, have a sense of cameraderie, rather than rivalry. I miss that.'

Although, once, the cameraderie got a little brutal. I used to keep a passionately detailed diary from the age of 13 till 20. Then I was living with a man in one of those households where everyone was having an affair with everyone else and one of the other women in the house found my diary and we were stick sisters. That's an expression for two women who are sharing the same man. She found my diary. I knew about her but she didn't know about me. You know what it's like at that age, sexual minestrone. But, you know what she did as revenge? She photocopied my diary and circulated it around dinner parties in Sydney. Journalists would ring up and go, 'Kath, your period's due.' But what mortified me was that it was so badly written. You think it's about existential angst when you're writing a diary, but it's not. It's "Am I fat? Am I ugly?" '

No longer able to write a diary but still needing to write things down, to get it all out of her system, writing novels was the only way of 'making sense of the chaos going on all around me.' There were other jobs in the meantime. There was running away to a sheep station, being the only girl for a 100 miles. There was a punk band called the Salami Sisters, and then there was a hippy, tree-hugging phase that corresponded to the extreme feminism and the discovering of Germaine Greer that had caught her reeling from tan-tattoo territory. She is very much an extraordinary wit in a very ordinary world, and the wit *is* extraordinary. The *Mad Cow* book is packed, every paragraph has a lethal one-liner. It's a wit that stands up and shows off. It's a wit that's big ear-rings and barbie dolls, or miniature balconies with champagne. It's hard for women to be funny – funny and sexy anyway. If men want to laugh at you, they don't want you. How did she get to be this funny?

'I feel about as funny as a period cramp, but if you're not really good-looking, you have to try to be funny. All my girl-friends that I grew up with were serious sex goddesses – and then there was me. They never had to try. I noticed this in England. When I met Jerry Hall for instance at a party. All the men, the so-called intellectuals, were so rude to me every time I opened my mouth. Then she walked in and said, "I've never noticed any class system in Britain." All the men went, "Really?" It was as if they had more natural oil than Saudi Arabia. If you're beautiful, it's male meltdown. If you're not beautiful, you have to learn to verbally tap-dance. If you don't have big breasts, it's just a survival mechanism.'

Although she understands that women with big breasts can also feel terrible. 'It's to do with the female condition. We're never happy with what we have. Women I know sit in my kitchen, crying because if they didn't have children, they'd be fulfilled. And women I know who don't have them say if they did they'd be fulfilled.'

She talks about her little boy, Julius, who's 5. She tried to do nurture, but nature kicked in. She gave him dolls, and his truck gene, motor-bike gene and Batman gene all kicked in. And the little girl, Georgie, sadly has an ironing board gene. She wrote *Foetal Attraction* while pregnant with the second one, tantalizingly writing the final paragraphs as she was going into labour. On the trials of childbirth, she is most explosive because 'nobody tells you. It's a silent conspiracy.

They never say how bad it's going to be. It's a case of stiff upper labia. They don't tell you that you'll end up a few nappies short of a full load. They never tell you about the unbelievable pain. There's that female macho thing where it's competitive and women say, 'I did it naturally.' Why? This is like saying 'I'm going to the dentist to have my teeth out. Let's do it naturally,' and they give you gas. Giving gas to a woman in labour is like giving aspirin to someone having their leg amputated. My advice is have the epidural and have the bloke there. If he was there when it went in, he should be there when it comes out. Also, don't have the enema because crapping on the obstetrician is the ultimate revenge. Afer you have the baby, you love everybody for a few days, then you go feral and want to kill. Then you're brain dead and it's so sad, because I realized if someone offered me a night of totally orgasmic sex or a good night's sleep, I'd take the z's.'

She says she doesn't think the children should ever outnumber the adults and two is enough. And on one level she can write about it as analagous of the prison that the character in *Mad Cow* has to endure. But there's another slant to her that's really romantic, even when she talks about the tiredness, the mess, how children are the ultimate contraception. Once 'her hormones had been hijacked and the snooze alarm had gone off in my biological clock, that was it.' And she says it in the same way as that being it when she met Jeff in August 1988, a serious love city that meant her marriage was concluded and her hemisphere transferred by November 1988.

'There's a real dichotomy in western society. People feel sorry for you if you don't have a child, no matter the image of bikini-wax career woman with a couple of portfolios up each sleeve. They still feel sorry for you if you don't have progeny. Once you've had the baby, it's like you get an eviction notice from the human race. When you're pushing a pram, it's as if you've been swallowed up in the invisible man's bandages. I wanted to get a Kafkaesque role going and see it snowball. That's why I used a prison. Of course there are good things about having kids. You can never get pretentious with an epaulet of vomit on one shoulder, even though I'd like my brain back. Sometimes I'm so bored of doing things with playdough I can see my plants engaging in photosynthesis.'

But it's this dichotomy that propels her. What does she think she gets most of her inspiration from?

'Hormones, love, anger. A minestrone of all of these. Whenever someone is rude and horrible, I always think great material. What made me want to write *Mad Cows* was the notion of Stepford mothers, the ones that pretend everything's fine, and everything's coping, coping. After I had my first baby and I wasn't getting any sleep and I was just meals on heels, I rang my friend in Australia and said my baby is crying and I can't cope. She said, 'Just remember, if you shake them too hard, they get brain damage.' I laughed and when I got back to England, I was with some Stepford mothers and said, "Just remember, if you shake them too hard, they get brain damage." And one of them said, "Oh no. You must never shake your baby. Have you thought about therapy?" and I thought I can't be the only career and family juggler who ends up dropping a lot of things. I haven't been wrong about the other things I've written about. Am I wrong this time?' she asks, the very big eyes more knowing than beseeching. 'We'll see when the book comes out.'

The book turned out to be a bestseller. We all love to taste the hormone/love/anger minestrone and she has the recipe.

Erotic Best Friends
18 December 1994

Most people say they want to be loved, ravaged and made love to. But that is not what most people really want at all. Gratification is not the essence of pleasure: it is diminishing because it is finite. Most people flourish when they feel a tacit yearning, they want to want. The most enduring relationships are the ones that have no resolution, that are constantly imbalanced. And the most special of all friendships is one that is more than platonic and is less than sexual.

Such relationships are not always easy to master. Invariably, they will tip one way or the other, as with, for example, the characters portrayed by Meg Ryan and Billy Crystal in the movie *When Harry Met Sally*. Erotic best friends can cause pain for the other permanent sexual partners involved, too. What, for instance, would Hugh Grant make of his girlfriend Elizabeth Hurley and the writer William Cash? There they were, snapped last week in London's West End, hand sweetly cupping hand, shoulders swaying together like a couple of Start-Rite kids.

You will find that people rarely have best friends who they consider ugly, or even plain. I certainly don't. A pleasing physical appearance is a prerequisite in all my male and female friendships. Part of the erotic charge of the friendship depends on just how pleasing the physical package is. When I was in Los Angeles recently I met William Cash, who works there, and he was constantly referring to the 'most beautiful girl in London,' his shorthand for Hurley. He says her name with such pride and apparent romance, yet I'm sure theirs is a friendship, no more and no less.

Erotic best friends can be the most enduring of relationsips. It is often a mentor-pupil dynamic. Sometimes they are relationships that were once full sexual partnerships and that have since transmuted into something else.

The workplace is where they seem to flourish or fester. When Gaby Roslin and Chris Evans used to present the *Big Breakfast* together on Channel Four it was compelling to watch. The teasing, the comforting, the caring. The way he often cocked his head on one side and looked at her. The way they always praised each other in interviews. They are EBF's, erotic best friends. Fiona Foster and Alistair Stewart are exceptionally bouncy together on Carlton TV's *London Tonight* news show. Even Anne and Nick have shown some inklings of an EBF. Torville and Dean were a kind of unrequited, thwarted, erotic best friendship. All their passion was plunged into their skating to the soundtrack of Ravel's 'Bolero'.

Princess Diana has attracted incessant comment through her platonic friendships with police minders. The actor Joe McGann's friendship with his TV-sitcom colleague Diana Weston in *The Upper Hand* seems to have spilled into real life. This was breaking the rules. Kenneth Branagh seems to have a fascination with Helena Bonham Carter. And Emma Thompson and Anthony Hopkins have such a three-dimensional charge onscreen that I suspect that they know each other very well.

This is a very important part of an erotic best friendships – to know the person without having to try to. It shouldn't have to take any effort.

Women often forge erotic best friendship with gay males, because you get the attention, the ego massage, the sexual appreciation, but a clear-cut limit of no sexual action. I would be very disappointed if my best gay male friend was not erotically aware and sexually in tune with me, however. He has another erotic best friend who is a very handsome heterosexual man. They flirt with each other outrageously.

'Flirting without intent is so exciting. Of course I flirt back, I love to be flirted with. It's some kind of evidence that deep down there's a real bond,' the straight man informs me.

Erotic best friends encourage and comfort each other in

areas in which only they know how. You turn to them when you are miserable and sexually rejected. They boost the morale with the assured frisson that exists. Since there is a constant danger that the EBF will turn into a regular boyfriend, however, you must keep the friendship in constant check. Keeping the balance is part of the addiction of an EBF; wondering how far is too far; and the process of learning how to take deep pleasure in the holding of hands can be intriguing.

The point of these special friendships is that, at the same time as never knowing what to expect of an evening, you have devotion and total loyalty. The dynamic means that there will a constant sense of anticipation and sometimes a complete imbalance of intent and attraction. Friendship remains so long as there is a baseline for this.

I have an ex-EBF whom I did not realise was an EBF at the time, but I turned to him for advice and ego-resucitation whenever I had made a bad mistake in another relationship, and he turned to me for the same. We would spend hours discussing our sexual intellects. The friendship ended when he became involved in a relationship that was so happy and peaceful that I felt distanced. The girlfriend, a one-dimensional sort, felt jealous of me – a perennial problem with EBFs. She never quite knew what had gone on. The fact that nothing had happened made her feel that something still could have.

One friend of mine who is in publishing enjoys several EBFs and says, 'I think it is the prerequisite for late twentieth-century man. Wounded, tired or bored, or simply too frightened to have a full-blown affair, he opts for an affair that is not an affair, he finds somebody to amuse, abuse and nurture. It is the perfect antithesis to any marriage. I don't have many friends whom I don't fancy, but I never make a move on them because I don't want to destroy the friendship or my marriage.' That's the thing about EBFs: the relationship meanders, but endures. It never ends because it never really begins. EBFs are perfect for the sexual anorexic who is always hungry but never wants to eat.

You can tell an erotic best friend by two characteristics in particular: they like to talk on the telephone, and they like to talk about the sex they are having with other people, or not having, as the case may be. My EBFs and I always know what buttons to press in each other: the amused button, the reveal button, and the annoyance button. These functions are all semi-erotic: making somebody laugh is erotic, knowing somebody deeply without trying is erotic.

You must not have too many EBFs in your life at the same time because this would be disloyal. I have limited myself to one who is gay, and one other, a new EBF, who is straight.

When I met the EBF I suddenly felt a warm rushing feeling. I was attracted by his eccentricity and immediately felt compassion for him. His instincts about me were also so sharp that I was immensely flattered. This relationship may sound like nascent love-angst, but it is not. Perhaps it is even cowardice, or perhaps it is a hardy endurance test to walk on without ever overstepping the mark. Perhaps we are too mentally attuned to our EBFs to be carnal: perhaps it would be just too much. As he held my hand, my new EBF talked about how anticipation was much more thrilling than gratification, and we knew what we meant. There was never going to be any mess. There would be constant allusion, but never disappointment. Demands would never be uttered and any sex that ever took place would be in the head.

Danny DeVito
17 November 1996

*I had the pleasure of meeting him twice. He'd always rather
ask than answer, but that's not what it's about.*

OK. So he is not tall. A kind of saturnine womble, a squidgy
jelly baby filled with some malevolently sickly substance.
Actually, he probably tastes of very dark chocolate nemesis.
He has been described as a meatball with arms, a hand
grenade with the pin pulled, a cosmic joke, the runt of the
litter, and an accident, a mistake, a little boy born too late to
ageing parents, a boy who never grew. He has allowed himself
to be described as, when he let the lines come out of Billy
Crystal's mouth in *Throw Mama From the Train*, which he
directed, 'a little troll which should be hanging off a rear view
mirror.' He says of himself in *Twins*, 'I am the leftover crap. I
am genetic garbage.' The lines roll pat. Which Shakespearian
character could he play? Richard III's hump. And nobody
offers him the part of Napoleon because he just might get into
it. He got into it enough to have the giant billboard on Sunset
painted with him as Napoleon earlier this year for the
Quentin Tarantino-inspired *Get Shorty*.

He's brash and bold with his shortness. No one in
Hollywood is telling him now, 'Go home. There are no parts
for actors under 5´.' He reinvented the term, little big man,
mini-mogul. Not since Orson Welles or Woody Allen has
there been a more successful, impressive, impenetrable
actor/director than Danny DeVito.

The squidgy bits inside the jelly baby are fairly tight. Sure,
he'll shock you with horribly funny lines, lines that are horribly self-deprecating. But it's him that's doing the deprecating.
And it's rehearsed. All that pocket-sized pain stuff is put in a
compartment, put in a movie, wrapped neatly in a *faux*-spon-
taneous one-liner.

When you meet Danny DeVito you don't ask him how the smallest man in Hollywood has become one of the most successful because, when you're one on one, the twinkling eyes are charm offensive. They roll chocolaty beams that sear your soul and cover it in something dark. You first meet him and you think, 'God. He's even smaller than I thought he was.' After half an hour, you think, 'Oh. Well, he's sort of the same size as me' and after thirty-five minutes you're immersed in his energy and his intrigue and you forget the impossible. In a world where conventional size means perfection and tall means success, attractiveness means proportionate DeVito breaks through these barriers because of his articulate passion and tirelessness. He's not cosy though. Small is shocking and he likes to shock.

He's dangerous because he picks up things, looks at you, sees through you and taunts you in a flirty sort of way. The first time I met him he shocked me by turning therapist and asking penetrating questions about my love life, and then proffering advice that seemed heartfelt, not a couch cliché. But we'll come to that later.

One of his fingernails is dark blue, painted by his daughter, a kind of varnished tattoo which she has placed on him along with several woven bracelets called friendship bracelets, which you are not allowed to take off until they fall apart and you make a wish. It seems like she's marking her territory, as most of the people who work with him have different-coloured fingernails and threads hanging from their wrists.

We are in the offices of Jersey Films in Los Angeles. It's cosy, homey, in a shabby-chic, designery sort of way. Despite his warmth and his twinkling eyes, DeVito is not an easy man to interview, to get to the nub of, because he just keeps throwing the questions back. You know more about him from the questions he asks than what he answers. Except, of course, questions about his work. Everything he does, he does with vigour and he's monumentally proud of it all.

He dismisses the idea that it's difficult to act and direct at the same time. He says that what he's driven by is passion.

He just had to play Harry Wormwood in Roald Dahl's *Matilda* (as well as being the narrator thoughout the story) because he used to act it out when he was reading it as an elaborate bedtime story to his kids. There are three of them, 13-year-old Gracy, Lucy, aged 11 and Jake, 8.

It would be easy to say he loves his kids, he loves being with them, so he thought he'd make a kid's movie. In a way, that's part of it. But there's a much bigger connection between Danny DeVito and the *Matilda* that Dahl created. For a start, there's Dahl himself. He and DeVito are kind of twins of darkness. Dark. Dark is a word he uses a lot. And he always says it very precisely and endearingly.

'I was totally blown away by *Matilda* because the themes are so dark, so funny and extreme. I thought this would be a great movie to make for my kids because it's empowering. There were some great fairy-tale themes to explore.' (Such as Pam Ferris's role as the evil headmistress, the Trunchpole).

This is the story of a small girl, an ignored girl, who is basically a good person and learns to control bad people, or at least people who are doing bad things. If there is a fairy-tale moral, it is one of karma, that you get what you deserve and what goes around comes around, but you can sort of help it along a bit. It beams into the mind of the child where, in child-world, you are told you know nothing and can do nothing. Children all over America got a vicarious thrill. It was number-one children's box-office throughout the summer largely because it does not patronize kids. There is a fearlessness about it which is very attractive. The Harry Wormwood character he plays is a sleazeball dad, a second-hand car dealer addicted to TV game shows who has never read a book in his life and doesn't think his daughter should do either. She is like an alien to this family. But of course it's the alien and the underdog that comes off the thrilling winner.

'I've always felt very strong, empowered. I can't really put my finger on where it comes from and I know that most of my life I have done pretty much anything I set out to do. Maybe it is from something deep-seated,' he shrugs. 'From a lifetime of being told, you can't do this. For the most part though, my childhood was very good in terms of my family.'

The family was Italian-American from New Jersey. Two much older sisters (one is ten years older and one is sixteen years older) who were maternal and protective towards him, a mother who was largely encouraging and a dad who was a bit of a loner, always into this scheme or that. He describes his parents' relationship as typically Italian; volatile, but it was made in the days when Italian marriages ended only in death, never divorce.

Childhood images and imaginings seem very real to him. He's close to it, obviously because of his kids, but also because it was a time in his life when he did not get what he wanted. Those who feel they can do anything and can have everything do so because they once felt they were nothing. It is to do with the survival of the damaged, the baleful humour of horrible human relations he's spitting out of the films he's directed. *War of the Roses* for a start had to come from some place.

'I guess negative things did come from outside my family. Not that there was any teacher like Trunchbull, but there were a couple of nuns who were pretty bad. They were pretty powerful women, but never as extreme as Roald and I are doing in this movie.' He talks a lot about 'Roald and I', as if they are in constant conversation with each other even though Dahl has been dead since 1990. While he was preparing the movie, he listened to Dahl's story *The Fantastic Mr Fox*.

'I had that playing in my car on my way to work and back and I felt that we were communicating on another level.'

He talks about this level being of deep dark secrets and of 'clinging to goodness and positive things' when the negative forces are acting in life. He talks about how hard it was to get this movie made, how Hollywood looked down on a film about a young girl. Even with all his accumulated clout and the soulful eyes of Mara Wilson, who plays Mathilda, it was a passionate struggle. As soon as he decided he wanted the rights to it, he found out from Roald Dahl's widow, Felicity Dahl (known as Liccy) that some screenwriters were already on to it and it was to be auctioned. He kept in constant contact with her and finally the buyers came: 'I went after it full force and it almost slipped out of my hands. Liccy always stuck by me and said, no matter where it went, I was the approved director. It was a delicate thing, this movie. So finally it took another year to get a hold of it and it was one of those things; no matter what, you know you have to make it.'

He makes a point of giving me a *Matilda* book and it is a list of Matilda's tips for survival. Number one: big does not mean smart. Number two: bullies are bullies because they are scared. Number three: don't compete, just know the truth. Number four: be brave and don't let fear stop you. Number five: a punishment never lasts forever. Number six: read, read, read and stick with your friends. Matilda's tips or DeVito's? Just what exactly were those negative forces? The taunting about his height that forced him to fight back with his mouth? Is that what taught him to believe in himself?

'I've always been able to see that energy, that feeling in my work. If a kid grows up fat and everyone's calling him fatso, he learns to develop a thick skin and fight back. I never let the abuse I took as a kid make me bitter.'

It was as if he saw bitterness and savagery and didn't want to taste it. When he was 13 he asked to be moved to a boarding school. 'The great thing about that was that I got away from an incredible demon, and that was drugs. Several of my close friends had come to it. No matter what Danny Boyle says in *Trainspotting*, I chose not to go that road and I think it was a good thing because if I had stayed in town it would have been a bad thing.'

It does seem extraordinary for a teenager to rebel and want to be a good boy. Was this because he was aware even then of a dark side that might want to drag him down?

'I think I was aware that there were minefields that a couple of times came very close to exploding, and I was able to circumvent the dark waters. I saw people being addicted to heroin, and for some reason there was something that got inside of me and said, "you don't want to go there." My family were kind and good and I got along with them, but my father used to tell me about a brother of his who died young of heroin addiction. That story he used to tell me, it broke his heart. His brother was in hospital getting a treatment and his mother went to get him out. His mother was very happy to see him, but when they got him out, there were a lot of people waiting in front of the hospital for him. He disappeared. They would wait outside his hospital, these guys, to sell him more drugs.

'So I could get out. Get out of where people were abusing people, ruining people's lives. I heard that story a lot. I would go home at weekends and hang out with my friends and go to the movies and I loved that. And that's when I knew deep down *I* could do that. Not make them, because I didn't know what the hell that was, but it's a scream and you leave the world behind you, become part of that story, relate to those characters. I could do that, whatever that acting stuff was.'

There is a sense with him that he wants to escape, escape my gaze and the questioning. It is a reaction that must become automatic. It's not that his childhood seems devastatingly bleak and ugly. It's because he is particularly sensitive and there were times, him being so much younger than his sisters, that he was like an only child. Not necessarily lonely, but definitely alone. Part of the urge to escape comes from the urge to merge, to feel part of something.

So, his parents lived together for fifty years 'whether they liked it or not.' His father would escape into an overpowering work ethic and fishing.

'He would get up at 4.00 in the morning and go fishing. We lived in Jersey, and I'm talking about the dead of winter when it was freezing cold. He'd get up with his pail and his poles and bundle himself up with his thermos and out in the snow, sleet, rain. Sometimes I would get up if I wanted to be with him. Sometimes he would take me when I didn't have school. He was always involved in some different business. He had a luncheonette that sold hot dogs and milk shakes and when I was 13 he bought a pool hall. We drove to this place in Philadelphia and picked up five pool tables, and he fixed up this store and called it the Crown Billiard Academy. He didn't want any rough stuff there. It had to be nice, nice and neat. He never made a dime but he had a good time doing it.

'My sisters were so much older than me. I was alone. Yes, I felt alone. I know my kids play with each other. There's always someone in the house. I played with soldiers and records, picture-book records, the "Bugs Bunny Story", "Daffy Duck". They were 78's. They would talk to me and I would listen to the voice of Mel Blanc.

Shopping for clothes was a rather brutal experience. He used it in an episode of *Taxi*, the 1970s show responsible for making him a household name. It had autobiographical twinges, including one where he would go to a clothing-store and have to go to the children's section. He recalls the shopping experience.

'I'd always have to have a wide waist and then the pant legs were always hanging down, so they'd roll them up' (indicated yards of rolling) 'and they'd cut them here. It was kind of embarrassing. I used the story in *Taxi* because it was a poignant moment.

'I was always aware that my parents were older than other kids' parents. My mother was always dying. She was always saying "Danny, you're going to have to take care of yourself. I'm going to be gone soon." That didn't happen until she was 86. "You were right this time, Mom. You're dying." But she was funny about it. She always used to want you to be independent and do things on your own because she was going to die and no one else was going to take care of you. It's a funny concept. For forty years she's dying. She was never ill, not a day in her life, God bless her. She was as strong as an ox. She was my size and she smoked and she'd take a drink. She cooked a lot but she was always telling you that you were going to be on your own. So, in that way, I was all on my own.

'In those days, they did things differently, child-parenting. They'd stick you in the yard in the morning and if you were still there at lunch that was good. They'd bring you a sandwich. I can remember as a toddler crawling around under the table. My mother and my aunts, who weren't really my aunts – they were my mother's girlfriends – all hanging around drinking coffee, and I'd be crawling around with the cat or whatever we had. I remember my Aunt Millie who was my mother's best friend; for my eight-year-old birthday, she made me a lamb cake. It was a beautiful yellow cake covered with frosting in the shape of a lamb. I never forgot it and coconut cake has always been my favourite ever since.'

It's somehow sad hearing about the lamb cake. I don't really know why. Perhaps because it is he who seems curiously touched by it, the eyes twinkly, jewelly. To cheer him or distract him, I tell him the story of when my rabbit had babies and my grandfather cooked chicken and said, 'Did you like that chicken? It was Wopsy.' Everyone round the table thought it was very funny.

Now he's altogether distressed, protective for me, and says, 'I know they thought it was funny, but they didn't understand. They weren't malicious. They didn't set out to hurt you.'

This is an interesting take on humanity. And it's a take which comes from a being who's truly had to survive the kind of taunting that could grab your mind and twist it if you let it. He's kind of set himself apart and never blames other people. He simply thinks what he wants and works for it. He doesn't particularly think that his strength comes from being knocked back.

'If a thing is kept from you, you have to go and get it, don't you? Let it be known, no matter how much encouragement you give your children, and how much positive faith, there are going to be obstacles you have to encounter. If you really want something, you go and do it. Nobody is going to be able to stop you. You have to have courage and conviction to realize victory.'

That's tank-talk, that's talking like you're in the army, like you really do have a Napoleon complex.

'Well, being director is giving commands. It's like you are a general and you are in the fray. You are out there on your trusty steed in the middle of battle and you do it. It's a twenty-four-hour-a-day job and I love it. If you fall madly in love with a project you just have to do it. But it doesn't have to be a movie. It's all part of a journey you're taking.'

He left New Jersey not to be an actor, but to join the Wilfred Academy of hair, to be a hairdresser and work with his sister and maybe get into movies doing make-up. 'I liked working in the beauty parlour. There's nothing wrong with being a hairdresser. There's nothing wrong with being a janitor. I just didn't want to do it for long. But there are no deadlines. There's only one deadline. So you keep going. You deal with things at the time and you stick around until you don't want to stick around. You can't be scared.'

There is nothing much that DeVito fears. You get the feeling that if he has to revisit his fears he does so in a script or a joke, in a way that's somehow separate to him.

'I am really not afraid of anything. Things happen. You can't be frightened.'

Not even of death?

'I don't relish the thought of dying, but I don't live my life as though I'm afraid of death.'

For someone who's so aware of dark forces and bleak things happening, the stance of fearlessness is curious, but there are lots of opposing dynamics going on. He's sitting with his big fat cigar smouldering. He can be blokey, cheeky-chappy, avuncular. And its not just the blue nail polish. It's the way his mind is attuned. He is incredibly in touch and in tune with females. Females surround him in his company. His partner in Jersey Films is Stacey Scherr. He can talk about boyfriends. He can talk girly. He's generally sympathetic, yet he can control like a general. He's ordinary and extraordinary. Warm, but with kind of heat you know could turn ravishingly hot or shudderingly cold within a second.

There's something quite dangerous about him, especially the way he wants to turn the questions around. He wants to know what I am scared of. I tell him rejection and failure because I think that must scare everybody.

'Oh.' He looks askance. 'Do you think about that a lot?'

Doesn't that scare you?

'No. Why would you be afraid of being rejected? For your work? For yourself? You're saying that to be accepted and be embraced or loved or cared for is important. I mean it's important for everybody, but is it really paramount in your mind all of the time?'

Yes, I tell him, feeling pinned down. Isn't it in yours?

'No. When you come in here I'm focused, and you could be focused, thinking, "Danny's talking to you." That's not so frightening, is it? Are you feeling rejected because you fear you're going to write a bad story? I might be afraid of sky-diving, but I'm not going to do that. You just get up in the day, go with the faith that you're going to be victorious. Stop anticipating.'

OK. So he's afraid of sky-diving but he doesn't have to sky dive. He doesn't think about failure because he doesn't want to anticipate it and make it happen. What about falling in love? Isn't that scary?

'Falling in love can't scare you. Something else scares you about falling in love. You're projecting that things might go wrong. I think it's glorious to fall in love. It's the most wonderful thing that can happen. You look at someone in the eyes, at the way they are, the way they treat you and respect you and if they are in love with you, you don't worry about it failing. You're not worried about dying are you? Everybody dies, right?'

Now he's really winding me up. Did you ever have therapy, I ask him.

'Of course. Didn't you? Therapy is a good thing. Don't look at me like it's a negative thing. You thought "How dare you think I need a therapist." That's not the point. It's just good to talk. I like to talk to people who are understanding. I like to talk to people who I respect. If you can talk to a friend, that can be considered therapy.'

However he's come through fear to fearlessness, the journey has served him well. His company, Jersey Films is phenomenally successful. Another partner, Michael Shamberg, has just produced the follow-up to *A Fish Called Wanda* and *The Mirror Has Two Faces*, the Barbra Streisand film. DeVito took on *Reality Bites* and established Ben Stiller who at that time was still completely unknown. He decided to make *Get Shorty* after an instinctive skim-reading of the book and, after he'd laughed himself sick with *Reservoir Dogs*, decided he would love to go into business with Tarantino. Tarantino at that time told him he had an idea for another movie of intertwining tales that was going to be called *Pulp Fiction*, and with that almost psychic insight he has, he said to the then virtually unknown director, 'Let's make a deal and I'll produce your next movie.' A year or so later, 158 pages of *Pulp Fiction* arrived and DeVito said, 'I must be the sickest person in the world because I find this so funny,' and then he went to make the movie and found that other people might be that sick too.

Sick is a word he uses a lot. He overuses sick and dark. Yet the office atmosphere couldn't be brighter, and ask anyone in Hollywood – as I did – and they'll all say how his company is such a credit to him because everyone there is so happy, so energized. There is a kind of contagious passion. Executives at the new Disney Family Channel have been observing him, wanting to mimic his style that can produce entertainment which is family-orientated, which is not patronizing and goody-goody but at the same time not X-ratable.

DeVito is quite censorious about what his children watch. They can see *Grease* a million times, but *Saturday Night Fever* would be too sexy. By all accounts, the picture that he presents of inquisitive children scrambling around animals, games, books, and a need to have their father act rather than direct, seems blissfully accurate. The directing they think takes him too far away, out of the house for too long.

He has been with his wife, Rhea Perlman, most known for the feisty barmaid in *Cheers*, for over twenty-five years. They were together eleven years before they decided she should get pregnant. They got married in order to have a baby, to do the right thing. He just sort of willed the babies to happen.

'The interesting thing is we had been together eleven years and we weren't always careful. She never got pregnant. Then we decided to have a baby. We said let's have it during the season break, and bingo, Gracy was born 25 March. (The spring was the time they gave them a break from the TV show.) Same thing two years later with Lucy. Jake, however, was a different story.'

He recalls one morning when she came in waving a pregnancy test – result positive – and Jake arrived on Hallowe'en. He has hair longer than his sisters, is into roller-hockey and reptiles.

Much has been made that Rhea Perlman could be a female version of DeVito. Did he feel he was meeting a part of himself?

'I think she has a certain energy that's affinitive to mine and vice versa. She's very serious about what she does and likes to have a lot of fun. In the early days, we'd be doing short films together. She was producing, I was directing. Out there on the street, against all odds, going to get it done, roll with the punches, keep it going. We're similar in that way. She's very strong and she takes a lot more care of herself than I do. She works out every day. She's in great shape.'

Then he describes her regime with a kind of expression that is halfway between bewilderment and awe. Her exercise regime seems to be the thing that sets them apart, the thing that stops them from being a couple that are established like overstuffed, overcomfy furniture. He is a consummate flirt, although I'm not quite sure how seriously he takes his flirting. He says he's not often been rejected by a woman and that there are worse things than rejection. He recalls a story from his youth when he was really in love and it was a difficult time because her dad didn't like him and stopped the romance.

'If you're simply attracted to someone and they don't like you back, everyone has to deal with that. The toughest one is when you've not been rejected, but where it's reciprocal and it's dashed by some outside force you can't understand.'

Personally I think it's much worse to be rejected, but we have been informed by different experiences.

'Disappointment is not good. We don't like disappointment. But you just have to use the experience so that you get what you want next time. When I was a kid, I wanted a speedboat. I didn't get it. I wanted a motor cycle. I didn't get it. I wanted to fly a plane. I've never done it. I wanted to catch the brass ring on the carousel every time – when you're going round and round on the carousel, you keep reaching for these rings and if you catch one you get a free ride. I always reach for it and, once in a while, I get it.'

He looks at me like that ought to be enough, but he knows really that it's just a fairy-tale metaphor. He knows that for every time you do get what you want, you need the next thing more acutely. There is a kind of calm about him that perhaps you wouldn't expect. Because perhaps a long time ago he learned to control negative forces with the belief that good things happen to good people and bad things will happen to the bad people. Call it karma, call it come-uppance, whatever.

'I think there's a positive way to live our life. I think there's someone out there. There are angels taking care of Matilda.'

Are there angels taking care of you?

'Absolutely.'

Do you talk to them?

'Absolutely.'

Do they talk back?

'I think so. But it's not something you can articulate. It's a feeling. They're not Botticelli angels, but we're talking about the force of an angel, something that you connect with that you know is there, you are aware of so you can speak to it.'

He seems almost nervous to tell me this because this is something that really matters to him.

'I respect it very much and I don't know what whoever it is feels about me talking about it. So I should stop, only because I cherish it.'

So we do stop talking about his angels, although once you are aware of them, you feel perhaps they have been there watchful for a very long time.

TRUE LOVE

Relationship of the Week
Kate Moss and Johnny Depp
7 July 1996

Never trust a man who has his mother's name tattooed on his forearm – or anywhere else. Johnny Depp has it etched there and, when he dies, he'd like it pickled as a legacy for his children. He is a man defined by his mother, brought up by her alone. He was a regular Hollywood bad boy. He left school at 16, he took drugs and he drank, and his mother said, 'My most precious boy.' From her, he got the idea of intense, unconditional love, that 'a great woman is a great gift.' Schmaltzy stuff.

Next to his mother's name, there is another. I remember actually saying to Kate Moss, can you really trust a man who has Winona Forever as a tattoo? The only comfort she could take from this reference to his former love is that nothing is forever. Now it seems that neither is she. Depp is a serial fiancée. Winona Ryder, Sherilyn Fenn and Jennifer Grey. He promised himself to all of them. He is the man of the big gesture. He once filled Kate Moss's room with thousands and thousands of fresh daisies. He says it was insane but fun. Actually, it was just insane. Never trust a man with a big gesture.

She might be thinking that, now that they have supposedly split up forever. But, just as inevitable as their break-up, is the possibility of the make-up. They have been, these past three years, stapled together in a mutual obsession, fuelled by jealousy, tempestuous fights, hotel rooms wrecked, reunions desperate, addicted to the angst. You can't be torrentially in love unless you feel it. She told me once that relationships have to be angst ridden, the good ones, anyway. What's the point if it isn't passionate?

Moss is 22, a lush lolita full of 'teenage love is a rollercoaster' idealism. She is not as bad-tempered as her boyfriend. She does not explode. She festers. Perhaps she has grown a little weary and this time it really is the end.

Last autumn they were supposed to have broken up for good when Depp allegedly beckoned over the actress Samantha Janus in a nightclub. And then there was the business that Kate Moss was banned from his video of his rock band. He wanted it to be art house and thought her image too commercial. She felt left out. The album, a dismal piece of guitar narcissism, bombed. And this could be the real clue to Depp's moodiness.

For the past decade, he has been the American teen symbol of cool, of sultry machismo. His lank hair, his mean mouth making him handsome in a cold sort of way. Known now for kind of lost-soul characters, outsiders – *Edward Scissorhands*, *Ed Wood*. He was previously exalted to teen idolhood in a cop series, *21 Jump Street*, which got top ratings but eventually drove him mad. He asked that his character, a clean, fresh-faced thing, could be obsessed with peanut butter and be discovered smearing his naked body with it. The producers did not agree with his vision and, soon after, he left. Left for those smouldering weirdo parts with which he seems to have an affinity. He admits to feeling insecure sometimes, having a little voice in his head. It must have been a shock to him that his record failed so completely. Failure was not something he was used to. Men who fail often take it out on women who don't.

Moss, who is not as thin as dental floss, is also not as neurotic, not as much of a flibbertigibbet as she is often portrayed. She was the more grounded one and he needed that. He also needs constant, all-consuming, big love in his life. He needs a woman to be precious for, and a woman to do things for. He is capable of great generosity. Famously, he threw a 21st birthday party for Kate at the Viper Rooms, his Los Angeles club, flew in all her friends from around the world and bought her a rare etching, *Alice in Wonderland* by Salvador Dali. But that was when their love was new and unstoppable and hot.

They met when Moss discovered that the photographer she was working with had recently done Depp. All over the studio were pictures of Johnny. Moss became fixated. She said to the photographer, 'Get me Johnny and I'll get you a model girlfriend.' He did and they went on a date in New York in winter. She went back to his hotel after the dinner and got snowed in. By 6.00 in the morning, there was a snowstorm knee-high. She had arrived the night before in a tiny skirt and high heels. She sent a courier uptown for her clothes and it took seven hours for the clothes to arrive, so she was stuck with him. 'If that hadn't happened, we might never have phoned each other.' She says she believes in fate. She says she's read *Celestine Prophecy*, a book that says divine intervention happens all of the time.

Soon after, there was an engagement ring. And bumper stickers all over Hollywood read, 'Honk if you haven't been engaged to Johnny Depp.' Better to promise nothing than to promise what you can't deliver. The wedding plans were constantly on and off. Moss's capacity for suffering, her sensitivity, is greater than her capacity for articulation. She didn't articulate her needs, her hurt, she festered. He blew up. And then came the familiarity of the traumatic on-off relationship. As volatile as he is, Depp obviously yearns for stability. That's why he can't have a girlfriend. He wants a fiancée, a wife. He said, 'I have a traditional idea of marriage. I go for the idea that people can have a home in the country, a picket fence, a couple of dogs. It's a big dream of mine.' He also says that he doesn't feel like a completely realized human being, which means what he says doesn't have to make sense. He says he doesn't go for fast, easy sex, contrary to what people think. 'I used to ask myself, is it sex? Is it love? Well, one can quickly lead to another if you have heart.'

As he's not a fully realized human being, he thinks he can say that sort of thing. If he really believes the only way to love someone is through sex, I think that's rather limited. However, the sex is all-consuming sex. Each time he's been involved with someone, it's been the greatest, the most, the absolute. That's what he felt for Moss. And she for him.

She was insatiable for him, often saying she'd never felt like this about anyone before. He was ready to kill if he even so much as saw another guy just staring at her. He bought guns to protect her. And now, apparently, she's dancing on the dance floor. With Johnny she never danced. Maybe she didn't have to. Maybe there was enough dancing inside her head.

Since then, I'm always hearing that she's dumped him or he's dumped her and then that they're still crazy for each other and he's recently changed his 'Winona Forever' tattoo to 'Wino Forever' which means what he says really doesn't have to make sense.

Relationship of the Week
Alison Steadman and Mike Leigh
28 April 1996

I was really sad to read the news that the party's over for Alison Steadman and Mike Leigh. Not just because he is such an inspired and driven director, a man who has been able to coax out of his wife meticulous and wincingly observed performances. 'Just a little top-up Tone' from *Abigail's Party* is mimicked in suburbia. It has practically passed into the language. But because after twenty-two years their marriage was a touchstone, it gave you faith that such seemingly difficult people could actually get it right.

They were fantastically individual. Yet, at the same time, it always seemed as if they had a place that was only theirs. Leigh spoke of their private language. Steadman spoke of the jokes that no one else ever got. She'd just be looking at the way a woman was pulling her skirt down and they'd be off into a world of forensically observed suburban minutiae and ironies lost on anyone else except themselves. Time and time again everyone said, 'How can you be with such a moody-broody, dark and difficult man?' And Steadman would say, 'I have the best fun.' Their partnership was not particularly angst ridden and, besides, she herself was not above 'a bit of a mood.'

What crisis could have occurred that has allowed their partnership to fragment, that would have allowed Alison Steadman to leave Mike Leigh allegedly for her co-star in the BBC series *No Bananas*. A man who didn't have it in him to be a proper sex symbol, but almost was once – Michael Elwyn? What could have happened to two people who know each other so fundamentally, who have been used to skirting over a few edges, but finally they've fallen apart?

All the most interesting people are self-absorbed. It just is that way. They have longer to work on themselves, they fester in their own charisma. Film directors are notoriously of this breed. Actresses are self-absorbed, but they have an outlet, a release in the parts they play. Despite the fact that Steadman has always said being with Leigh wasn't some incredibly depressive vortex, I still think that their marriage survived for so long because she learned to deal with moody-broody. She learned not to take it personally. He's bad-tempered, flares up, goes away for months, in his own world.

With over twenty-two years and two children, of course there's a process of learning to not take it personally. It's also something you can very quickly unlearn. Steadman is a brilliant actress. She comes over as sexy, robust, sensitive but not fragile. But who can really know whether she's fragile herself underneath it all? A few years ago, Mike Leigh went off to Australia on a film course and called to say he wasn't coming back, or at least he didn't know when he would be. "He'd gone to find himself," she told me. 'I said, "Oh OK." But, I was annoyed. But what else could I have done?' Instead of screaming and demanding, which probably wouldn't have gotten her anywhere, she bottled up her annoyance.

Maybe the cork came out of the bottle as she ignited with Elwyn, when they were filming last year. I'm not saying that this was revenge exactly, but something that she had to get out of her system. In Leigh's films, her characters are always slightly deranged women, completely without vanity. That doesn't mean to say Alison Steadman is.

She didn't go to Hollywood, not because she isn't ambitious, but because she doesn't want to be a nobody. Here, she's a somebody.

So then, talented, good old sport Steadman is not beyond needing a bit of attention, validation, all the stuff that's usually heaped on to those who look needy. Steadman never looks needy. She is incredibly sexy, everyone says so, and has always said that she didn't mind about getting older. She's 49. Even so, she sounded slightly wistful, when she was making *Pride and Prejudice*, that her character, Mrs Bennett, was simply an onlooker while, all around her, the younger actresses were having onscreen love-affairs (and offscreen in some cases). Sure, she would have enjoyed being swept away, festooned in devotion. The heady unreality of a love-affair.

If you ask me, Elwyn, if indeed he and Steadman are together, is probably a mistake. He may be there with the flowers, the nice lines, but how will she ever have the bond she had with her husband? It will be impossible. I think she just needs a distraction. If she is serious, than she should look seriously at Elwyn's wife, Naomi Butch, a less substantial version of herself. Never trust a man who trades in a wife for the same model.

Leigh must be an incredibly hard act to follow. Most famous for his award-winning *Naked* and *Life is Sweet*, any actor that's ever worked with him never wants to work with any other director. His films begin with a vague but important idea. He teases it out into brilliant dialogue and performances. He is obsessively demanding and thorough. But he is also a man from whom one might need to seek a brief respite. She always said working away from home was not a good idea but she's been doing a lot of this lately, and so has he, making his new film *Secrets and Lies*. It seems to me that this is a hiatus in their relationship. Because I want to believe that true love does exist, I hope that they will get back together. I don't think that Leigh is the high priest of humdrum, the depressive that people like to portray him as. Nor do I think things were as easygoing and jokey as Steadman always used to say. Leigh has a labyrinthine mind. He is anarchic. But that's the price you pay for a creative genius. She is also a genius. There's scarcely a better actress ever existed. Ergo she has her no-fun zone too. They learned to put up with each other because each believed the other was worth it, and I seriously doubt that the alleged affair could fundamentally change this.

We do know, though, that Mike Leigh hates compromising, hates criticism. If someone snipes at a detail or dismisses his method of working, he takes umbrage. He's one of those 'prick him and he haemorrhages' types.

It's usually up to the woman to be big enough to forgive. On the whole, men have a problem with forgiveness and they have more of a problem with jealousy. Leigh, for the past months, has had the outlet in his new film. Perhaps he has been able to compartmentalize his pain to translate it on to the screen. As a result, his best work may be yet to come. I hope that they find some way of being with each other. Otherwise, I'll just have to go on believing that true love can't exist.

OK. So they didn't get back together and true love doesn't exist. And Secrets and Lies *was one of the best films ever made. I suppose you have to suffer for great art.*

Ugly Men
29 October 1995

I have never gone out with a man who is drop-dead gorgeous, apart from when I was 17 and the envy of all my friends because I was dating the most handsome man in North Shields. He was, indeed, achingly handsome, and so was his motor bike. I'm not sure which the more so. He could have had anyone, and he did, which perhaps led me to distrust beauty.

I was into trophies then. It was something that I grew out of and men never do. Men feel defined by the woman on their arm and validated thus. They feel more attractive, potent, sated, by the association. Whereas women do not derive their sense of power and self-worth from the physical appearance of their beau. In fact, just the opposite. They feel threatened, insecure and overshadowed. I would never dream of entering a room and feeling validated because everyone wanted to get off with my boyfriend. I'd prefer that it was me that people wanted, not what was dangling three steps behind. Who needs to be made so insecure? Much better to have someone that nobody else sees the point of immediately.

I have always had trouble finding conventionally beautiful people sexy. I hate perfections of feature and form. I mistrust beauty. It's a terrible prejudice to think the beautiful people are stupid but they so often are because they've never had to try hard, and I like men who try hard, who are desperate charmers. Charm is about sexiness and sexy can be very ugly indeed.

If you think somebody is sexy, you lose perspective. Sexiness is about being a whole being, inside and out, and once you are hooked you forget which is which. If you do go out with somebody who is impeccably good-looking, their looks can become boring after you are used to them. But with the ugly ones, it's vice versa: they become beautiful and you become blind.

Ugly people are the compensators, they have had to become interesting. Interesting men are voracious, cruel, unpredictable, fast, controlling and better at sex. And, I am afraid, that several times in my life I have gone out with men of whom my girlfriends have said, 'How could you?'

I once went out with a painter. He was twenty years older than me, balding and about 5′ 7″. In fact, when I say I went out with him, this is an understatement. I was ready to die for him. I thought we were one person and, because of a deep sense of sexual narcissism, nothing pleased me more than the idea of pictures of myself hanging in the V&A. I felt secure because he wasn't obviously attractive.

It made me feel exceptionally beautiful and powerful.

Once, I surpassed myself and fell in love with a man because of his appalling 1970s haircut. It was his crowning glory – he *was* that haircut. His naffness was sexy because I felt that it was something only I could understand and enjoy. It endeared me totally because it felt publicly uncool.

One day he cut his hair and, although everyone else might have thought it more conventionally aesthetic, I have to say it took a part of me away with it. I was shocked when I saw it and some little scissors twisted in my heart and snip-snip suddenly I didn't fancy him anymore.

An acquaintance of mine used to cut her boyfriend's hair especially badly at the back, so he didn't notice but everyone else did.

She also encouraged him to eat a lot so that he would get fatter and more slob-like and nobody else would want him. He left her anyway, which would seem to indicate the uglier the better.

Men are allowed to be fat. Fleshy bits are grabbable and sexy, warmly protective. Men are also allowed to be thuggish, bits of rough, or existentialist plumbers. Men are more often defined as sexy by a *jolie-laide* quality. Most famously Jimmy Nail or Robert De Niro. Too pretty is too much trouble, too self-absorbed. Vanity is not welcome.

Quite recently, I was approached by an uncommonly

handsome man whose looks are much admired. Initially, I was flattered, then I began to feel awkward, less myself, shrinking. I couldn't fantasize about any potential sexual action because I would have been too afraid to take my clothes off, which leads me to a horrible conclusion. Maybe I felt I was not good enough for him.

A friend of mine who is a model went out for a year with a man who was short and big. She'd had enough of men who felt they'd have to bring her down a peg or two: 'I went out with this guy because I thought he'd celebrate me. It didn't work because he had so many hang-ups about the way he looked. He started to protect himself by projecting those problems on to me, he resented me ultimately,' she says. In other words, ugly men can be just as dangerous as beautiful ones if you go out with them only because you have a self-esteem problem.

The majority of women are sufficiently evolved to look straight through into the soul, anyway. They do not see hair, skin, bone, fat simply in the way it is arranged. They know that it is not the bones in themselves that have the potential to destroy, love, stimulate, obliterate. It is what moves them. A gleaming-haired man can have dandruff of the soul.

One who is in the gym every day can have cellulite of the psyche. The trouble is that a few women are attracted to that inner flakiness. They want to change it, or at least to taste it, because it is more interesting than wholesomeness and goodness.

My husband, Spencer Bright, would like it to be known that he is not ugly and I have never found him so.

DISLOCATED
SOULS

Sindy: Breaking the Mould
7 April 1996

When I was little, and even not so little, I had twelve Sindy dolls and a million accessories. They were my life. I was an only child and I had no friends. I played with them far longer than I should, acquiring Sindy Party Dresses, Sindy Career Girl, Sindy Cordon Bleu Cook.

It was my first taste of retail therapy and I never forgot it.

Yes, I wanted to be Sindy, this child-woman who was my friend, who had it all and through whom I could live vicariously. Who needs the restrictions of childhood when you can have the full thrill of Sindy in her red sports car, or hanging up her clothes in her big white-and-gold wardrobe? And Sindy had Paul. As a result I grew up having a fatal attraction to men called Paul, not to mention far too many accessories to stuff into my white wardrobe.

I also grew up re-enacting the psychological patterns I imposed on Sindy's lifestyle. For instance, I remember one meteoric row with my mother after she had dared to put some of Paul's jumpers in Sindy's wardrobe. His outfits, along with his skis, his Chelsea boots, his Ronson razor, his blue-and-white stripy pyjamas and his Hardy Amies navy suit, lived in batchelor pad, which was a shoebox way out of town. And this is how I like my Pauls, in a separate compartment, to be visited by me, the vicarious Sindy, whenever I choose.

So, last week I had something of an emotionally cataclysmic moment. Instead of me being Sindy, Sindy became me. Hasbro, her makers, had offered to make a prototype Chrissy Iley version of the doll, complete with a tiny version of my dog, Poodle, and thus I finally came face-to face with my mini-*doppelgänger.*

I had taken the process of designing the Chrissy doll very seriously indeed. Unlike the new supermodel Sindys –

Naomi, Claudia and Karen – who merely had their faces sculpted, I sent pictures of my clothes and accessories, as well as photographs of myself and my dog, so that we could be transformed into doll form. I came back as two possible Sindys. Poodle arrived in a copy of his gold coat and curious gold leggings.

These mini-clothes were indeed essential d'Iley. The fabrics had been replicated almost exactly and the shape and stitching had also been adhered to, albeit in simplified form. Sindy's face had been widened, and the eyes painted in a blue-grey-green mix to match mine. Sindy's hair is much more lustrous than my own and her teeth do not stick out, but she wore red lipstick just like mine, breaking the Sindy marketing rules of keeping lips pink and hair babe-blonde. Her skin tone, however, was too outdoor-Malibu to be akin to my own.

Sindy's vital statistics are 36-22-36. That's the body they gave the supermodel Sindys and that's the body they gave me. It is slightly disorientating to be given the same body as Naomi Campbell, but I suppose I have the imagination to deal with it. Sindy's body is, apparently, difficult to change: the clothes wouldn't fit, the adventures wouldn't fit, the image wouldn't fit.

Hasbro are toying with the idea of making Sindy in different sizes, or in a more muscular form, but they know that they have to balance this political correctness with attractiveness, with what little girls will want to buy. But in prototyping me as Sindy, albeit with the doll's existing ludicrous vital statistics, perhaps they realize that there is a need for other role models to encapsulate her spirit. After all, at the moment she seems to have no basis in reality – even supermodels don't have breasts this big.

However, everybody that I showed my new doll to seemed to think it looked like me. So, naturally, I quickly became extremely fond of the Sindy Iley, and was looking forward to being what Hasbro called 'play value' for little girls all over Britain. Just how marketable, I wondered, would I be?

The supermodels and myself, I am told, encapsulate an 'independent spirit and prettiness'. Yes, we have traditional looks, but we have also built our own empires. However, while the supermodels are widely recognized all over Europe, which means there will be no marketing push required to get them up there on the lists of bestselling toys, little girls don't tend to have heard of me. Still, lack of recognition is, it turns out, the least of my worries. The marketing people tell me that not being blonde is my main worry, and that I will only sell in Scandinavia, where black hair is big. In fact, I might have to be made for one target marketplace alone, so they might only make 30,000 of me. And as I will have to sell at £14.95, that doesn't seem hugely economical. The cost, you see, is all in the prototyping and sculpting. Once the Sindy Iley mask has been made, it's as easy to make a million dolls as 30,000.

Sindys are tested all over Europe among different age groups of little girls, all playing together and being intimate. According to Sue Meredith, the marketing manager for Hasbro, a child wants a Sindy so that she can 'cartoon it'. In other words, make up exciting stories for it to enact. And although there is lots about me that is cartoonable, she is not sure if I also have play value. On the other hand a journalist Sindy could have lots of accessories, miniature microphones, laptops and the like and she could use them on an adventurous interview trek. That might work, they tell me; after all, in the early 1970s there was Career Girl Sindy.

Although Sindy's market is for 3-10 year olds, the core market is age 3 to 6. They think pink. They want to feel glittering eyelashes. They want fairy princess Sindy. Meredith, however, said of my look, 'What's more, their mothers certainly do understand it and don't allow it.' But I didn't ask to look like Sex Sindy, I say. Perhaps I could be modified. Perhaps Sindy Iley could have some brightly coloured suits, the kind a journalist might wear. Perhaps if I could look more like a television presenter the smaller girls would like me better, because at the moment I'm too difficult a concept for a 6-year-old to grasp. I'm not amiable enough. This is, of course, the story of my life. I like my Sindy being me. But I also yearn to be accepted and played with.

Forlornly, I tackle Sarah Howard, Hasbro's PR manager, about a possible Press campaign. Little girls shouldn't be patronized into pinkness and blondeness and blandness and the rigid glamour of supermodeldom, I say. There must be something about me that has this thing they keep calling 'play value'.

She sighs. I sense that disappointment is on its way. 'Sindy is wholesome,' she says. 'Sindy cares about animals and her friends, not when her next hot session with Paul will be.' She pauses, and then adds pointedly: 'But we do have an adult collectors' market.'

Paul Verhoeven
Sunday Times Magazine
7 January 1996

Sometimes you meet somebody and you think you've met them before. You think you know them. Perhaps from another life, or maybe another soul. That you were the same soul, even. This is what happened to me, but I tried not to let it bother me.

He likes sex. He likes violence. Most of all he likes to shock. Paul Verhoeven's work has always been distinguished by extremes. A compulsion for the scatological and the grotesque; explicit brutality in *Robocop*, gasp-making actions in *Total Recall*, and the viscerally explosive *Basic Instinct*.

The trouble with crossing the shock barrier is if you're not careful it ventures into the kitsch, the ridiculous, the sated, the boredom of outrage.

This is *Showgirls* territory. The film is to be released here this week. It has already been banned in Ireland and it comes with a reeking resonance. In America it caused havoc because it was promoted as a lascivious, big-time peep-show. Basically, the story is a rather sketchy 'A Star is Porn.' Bad girl makes more bad on a backdrop of iced nipples. Vegas showtime. It comes studded with stiletto thigh-highs, leatherette bikinis and clichéd orgasms.

Verhoeven says it was not about turning people on. It was not meant to be sexy, yet it's full of sex. He says he tells a story of how far women will go to succeed. Violence and viciousness at the bottom gets worse at the top.

Somehow, the story he thinks he told is not the film I watched. Or, at least, I couldn't find it. It didn't so much fail, as fail spectacularly. Nothing could be more dismal than an outrage that fails to excite; baring all, revealing nothing. 'There was a perception problem,' Verhoeven now says rather sadly.

There were many problems, starting with such a big-budget movie being pigeon-holed by an NC-17 rating in the US. (Usually this is box-office death but, in fact, the forbidden quality probably helped get the figures up. It has almost broken even, it cost $25 million, but everyone hates it. They don't just hate it, they deplore it. Is this because it makes them retch, or they're disappointed that it doesn't? I, myself, was rather unmoved by it the first time I saw it.)

Joe Eszterehas wrote the script for several million dollars. It was the same team that agitated gay-rights activists and feminists to verbal carnage over *Basic Instinct*. You can't repeat a thrill. It was hyped as 'the kind of erotic, sexy, pornographic movie that would go through boundaries and would give you the best erection in the world,' says Verhoeven. 'That was wrong. Everybody went and they were all pissed off because they didn't get an erection. Beyond that, there were problems with the script. Perhaps it is a flawed movie. So many people say that it is extremely flawed I have a tendency to believe them.'

He seems hurt but resigned, and certainly not diminished.

So much less frenetic than his films. He's 57, all muted colours, vibrant thoughts. He would have been less interesting had he tried harder to defend the unsexy sex, the pedestrian script that cost a fortune.

Verhoeven has already distanced himself emotionally from it; already had his next project lined up, a science fiction epic, *Starship Trooper*, about baddie big insects and goodie humans – no sex at all, but lots of violence. A precaution he has never taken before. He says that there's something very beautiful about going down spectacularly. 'I've always found that there was at least great drama and glamour, in an artistic way, about making wrong choices. You know the Germans, going to Russia and destroying themselves because of it.' This is a typical boundary-pushing statement of the sort he so loves to embrace.

'Failure you learn from and move on. Without accepting defeat you could never move on and make the next movie. Without learning how this was unerotic sex, you could never learn how to make a movie so sexually erotic that everybody would be masturbating in the theatre.' That's the plan for the next but one. Not for nothing was he chosen to direct the life story of the Marquis de Sade. There'll have to be more of the essence of him in it though, that's why *Basic Instinct* worked. 'It was very personal to me. It was the relationship between me and Sharon, what was not consummated in the bed. To have been involved with her would have been a disaster, but the movie was good because of my feelings.'

The *Omnibus* to be shown tomorrow on BBC1 is an overview of his career which seems to indicate the shock element is most important to him. Certainly the backlash from *Basic Instinct* didn't deter him from more similar stuff. 'Yes, I'm sure I enjoyed it. But you don't enjoy it every day. It's easier to enjoy after a couple of days. When it happens, it's a little bit amazing. It shocks me, so I get what I deserve.' He shocks to be shocked back. He talks often of his feelings of alienation. The shock syndrome is an addiction that perhaps makes him feel real.

Even when he started off, producing a Dutch version of *Ivanhoe* for children's TV, parents got it banned because it was too violent. Then there was a series of art-house, sex-house movies; commercial smashes in Holland. *Spetters*, about maladjusted, disconnected, no-hoper teenage bikers managed to agitate. It was made in 1980. Free love was finished. Violence was no longer considered socially correct. I think his heart is probably still in the 1970s, as much as his hairstyle. The hair, the clothes, say dishevelled academic. After *Spetters*, he was a 'lost son' of Holland. He was 'pushed to the sea', to the Hollywood dream; to the acceptable savagery of *Robocop*. The follow-up, *Total Recall*, was voted the most mindlessly violent picture of all time.

He puts notions of violence down to growing up in the bloodied, wartime suburbs of the Hague where the Germans were picking up pieces of pilots. 'Of course this world was crazy but it was normal because, as a child, you don't know anything different. The natural state of my mind I feel is still more war than peace.'

How is it then that all the other little boys of his generation don't make movies where bits of bloody brains are flung at the screen and rape scenes where women are torn? 'It's a genetic thing. Many people were born into a violent environment, of course, but I always had the need to communicate my feelings about it. I like looking at violence, sure. But in real life I've never used my hands to touch a human being in a violent way.'

Perhaps that's because you have other ways of expressing yourself. Surely in the same way he expects people to be stimulated, they could also be violently inspired by his movies.

'I'm not saying that is not the case. I've studied it a lot because I've been attacked so many times for this. First, I think you have to differentiate between sex and violence. With violence I think there is a correlation between people who like violence in movies and people who are violent themselves. A study they did in a Miami prison showed that when they showed extremely violent movies, the rates of violence diminished. It gets it out. It has a cathartic effect. They are less activated after seeing violent movies.'

Do you enjoy the fact that it has an effect? 'No. I never think about it. I have this old-fashioned feeling about the artist, he does what he wants and fuck the rest.'

Does he feel equally casual about the sexual impact he incites? I wondered if it correlated with on-screen violent/off-screen placid, on-screen sexual omnivore/off-screen anorexic.

So many of his fantasies have shouted their way from his head to the screen. The girl on girl displays, the female sexual predator, the famous Sharon Stone scene in *Basic Instinct* where she uncrosses her legs to reveal no underwear. Of course this was based on a memory of a woman back in university; his observation of the power she had, how men were her victims.

Yet he thinks the most powerful sexual organs are the eyes. 'Because they reflect the soul. You're not going to tell me that an encounter with a woman and a man is about putting your penis into a vagina, that is not the essence of sex. It's about the brains.'

Mm, certainly not reflected in this movie. He sampled the lap dancers in Vegas. Did he find it interesting? 'I didn't get an erection if that's what you mean. Yes, you can fuck just because it's fun for your genitals, but ultimately that's boring. I have never had a relationship in my life for one day. Even when I married I've always had relationships that were for years, never one-night stands. Why bother? I prefer to drink a cup of coffee, that's how much I think the penis means.'

He's been married since 1967. Doesn't his wife mind about the other relationships? 'She minds, it's not that she enjoys it. She has had other relationships. We were living in Holland in the liberated atmosphere of the 1970s where people were supposed to. Life's never easy, even Simone de Beauvoir and Sartre couldn't solve these threesome situations.'

I suggest to him that straightforward monogamy might be less problematic. 'I wouldn't know, I haven't tried, and I know very few people who have.' Perhaps this is why he's sometimes so bemused and alienated that the reality that he's trying to break the boundaries of is only his own and not necessarily other people's. For instance, he introduces his girlfriends to his wife, they have dinner together. Once Martine was in a trio, she's the violinist, and one of his girlfriends played the flute. 'I thought it was cool and very progressive at the time. In retrospect I have a different opinion. Then I thought, this is a new era starting and, of course, I was wrong.'

Ask him what are his sexual fantasies and they're really quite sweet and small-time. 'Making love to people that I think might be interesting that I've met. Floating experiences that come back to me. And breasts.' This seems at odds with the screen in which he so loves to indulge. He talks of pushing the boundaries, but whose? My reality is not his.

One of the problems with *Showgirls* is that its main female character is utterly dislikeable. She's a manipulator, has an attitude. She has no golden heart. 'She does one good thing, which is kicking the shit out of a guy. But it is not a morality tale of redemption. That would be a conventional theme, after all the grizzly stuff you feel very good at the end.

'But Nomi is traumatized, a bit psychotic. I created her character with elements from two or three people, I was even thinking about my mother. She could suddenly explode in an outrageous situation that was based on nothing. I am not a big fan of Freud. I have always rejected him. Maybe he's right, he knew too well about me. Let's reduce it to that. It's all about my mother.' He thinks he's joking.

He thinks women are much stronger than men. That has been his reality. 'Because the person I have most contact with, Martine, my wife, is very strong.'

Probably the most politically incorrect person on the planet, he is at odds with many things about middlebrow America, particularly the belief that sexuality incites, that the effect of doing sexual things in movies leads to decadence, perversity and subversion.

368

'It's a lie, it's just to keep sexuality under cover to keep this so-called Christianity in charge.' But didn't you once want to be a priest?

'A preacher actually. When I was 26 there was a crisis. Martine was pregnant and we didn't want the baby. We had no idea how to get rid of it, it was illegal, even in Holland. I panicked because I felt it would prevent me from pursuing my goal, which was to become a film director, knowing I wouldn't make a penny for the next few years.' The baby was aborted. They went on to have two daughters and an adopted child. 'I always give a lot of money to the Planned Parenthood charity now. But at the time I lost my grip on reality. I was propelled into the ultimate hell, which is God, isn't it?'

You find it a lot with men of power, politicians, leaders. They used to want to be priests because they want to control. 'No, that's not me. I have pleasure giving something over to an editor. I don't want my vision precisely, I want something a little bit beyond or to the side, that is fun. That is artistic freedom.'

He was once very controlled. His parents wanted him to be a maths professor. He did his doctorate in mathematics, he was good at it, but he felt he would never use mathematics to explore the world, he wanted to be a comic-book writer or a painter. After university he went into military service, the filming corps, and told his parents he would study in film school. They were not obstructive but they were disappointed.

He was an only child, which meant that he carried all their hopes. Being an only child also ensured that he was quite alone, not quite part of life. The parents eventually got over it, in that they liked the social aspect of going to premières, but after his mother died he read her diary where she said, 'I still have this simple hope for a simple human being, that ultimately he will become a professor.'

She also left him the genetic legacy of psychotic behaviour. He admits to being 'very explosive. She would do that and she never apologized, but I try to. I am sure I have been an asshole. To a certain degree I enjoy being hated.'

Perhaps hysterical reaction makes him feel loved? 'I don't know if I want to be loved. In the end I think everyone is looking for respect and I have the feeling that respect will come for me ten years later. That things will seem better in retrospect. That guy was crucified and seemed to be a lost cause and then He came back.'

Despite his despising Christianity he's keen on the God metaphor, both visually and verbally. He fears death though. He tells me he thinks about sex regularly, but death every day. His one fear is 'that I will be alone in my soul and unable to communicate with anybody ever. That would be real hell for me.'

Inadvertently, in his attempt to reach out and shock people with *Showgirls*, Verhoeven has misjudged its impact and the kind of sleazy kitsch unreality that pervades it alienates us from it, so we are untouched by it. His soul does not communicate with us: he has created his own version of hell.

Paul Verhoeven: I was never sure if Chrissy was interviewing me or trying to seduce me. Her décolletage was quite distracting but then again shooting Showgirls *had been distracting too.*

Relationship of the Week
Captain Townsend and Princess Margaret
25 June 1995

I do believe there is such a thing as great love, a resonance of souls, a mingling of spirits that can never be untangled. A maelstrom, when certain beings meet, a feeling that they have always known each other and loved each other. When they are separated, even for short times, they feel torn as if something has been ripped out of them. Yet when they are forced to separate for years and then they meet again, they laugh and bond like they last met yesterday.

Sometimes we fear this force, sometimes people imagine they will be safer in denial. Sometimes they feel that the shadow of an immense sacrifice is in itself a love bond. However, I do believe if you deny the course of nature it can only be cataclysmic.

The chronic effort required is like forcing Niagara Falls to flow upwards. Everything in one's life splinters, grows into canker or a cavernous limbo of regret.

This is what happened when Princess Margaret and Group Captain Townsend denied their love. He died this week, the morphine for his stomach pain blotting out agony and loss and the notion of the way things could have been. He'd been married to a beautiful Belgian, Marie-Luce Jamagne, who looked not dissimilar to the Princess – dark hair, creamy skin. But she seemed so smooth, so easy, everything that Margaret was not.

During her marriage to Anthony Armstrong-Jones, which ended in 1978, she'd been clingy, neurotic. She'd annoyed him because she was in constant ill temper and ill health. Then there was the long affair with Roddy Llewellyn. He dumped her for a younger woman – his own age (she was 16 years older than him, in a curious reversal of her relationship with the Group Captain).

One always has the sense of her suffering, smouldering. She's the only one of the Royal Family I've ever found sexy, maybe because she is sad and hungry. A few years ago she had part of her lung taken away and has now stopped chain-smoking. She was also advised to cut down on the booze.

In their years apart, both the Princess and the Captain drank spirits. Their favourite was Grouse Scotch. He always said 5p.m. was his favourite time of the day because that's Scotch time and in latter years he moved it forward because the last half-hour before 5.00 was too tough. Perhaps they had not grasped the way their feelings for each other were to have a stranglehold on their entire lives.

Townsend always used to speak with a tender and archaic language that underlined a wistfulness that things, people, values, duty, were different then. He was public-school stock. His spine stiffened for service to the Empire with a kind of muscular Christianity.

He was a Battle of Britain knight in shining medals and after the war the King's equerry. He was sixteen years older than her. She was only 14 when she first met him – dashing, handsome, vulnerable, sensitive and brave.

It was she who realized the strength of her feelings first. At the beginning he was married, an ill-matched, not planned-out, wartime passion which faded uncomfortably and ended in divorce. The very existence of this divorce defied the code of suitable Christian behaviour. The divorce meant scandal and tumult for the Royal Family.

By the time she was 22 he had declared his feelings to her. She waited a long time to hear them. She listened without uttering a word as the feelings poured, then she said, 'That is exactly how I feel too.' At 22 she was ravishing, with pansy-sized violet eyes and 23˝ waist. And she was funny. He said, 'More than anyone else she made me laugh – and laughter between boy and girl often lands them in each other's arms.'

Their love had a kind of purity and innocence that made them not try to hide it and appear shifty. It was at the Queen's coronation, with an innocent gesture, she brushed a piece of fluff from his otherwise impeccable uniform, and it was as good as a public declaration. The intimacy caused an uproar and he was sent away like a criminal to a post in Brussels.

Those in court circles thought this would be a way to snuff out the affair. After a year they met again on a secret tryst. Townsend later recalled this meeting in his book *Time And Chance*, a tome of sad resonance and freshly hewn hearts-peak. 'We had not met for a year and our joy at being together was indescribable. We were together for a couple of hours and talked as if we had only left off yesterday. We did not discuss the future; all we knew was that for the present our feelings for one another had not changed.'

He returned to Brussels. Under the Royal Marriages Act the princess could not marry before 25 without the Queen's consent. And because of the Queen's constitutional position she could not give it. Margaret must have been desperately alone. Her well-beloved father dead, her sister lost to duty and a suitable prince, and Townsend in exile.

As soon as she turned 25 he returned. The nation was hooked and in constant surveillance. Princess Margaret was free from the Queen's approval, but she still had to obtain the consent of Parliament. It was likely that they would agree if she consented to lose all her Royal rights, including her income under the Civil List. And this wrangling would take a further year at least.

Both of them were 'mute and numbed in the centre of this maelstrom.' A reeking cloud loomed over them. Although Margaret had only been 6 when her uncle Edward VIII renounced the throne for the thin and divorced Mrs Simpson, the abdication had had a shuddering effect.

They both seemed swallowed up with anxiety. In 1955, during a sleepless night, Townsend pencilled an emotional first draft of the statement renouncing him that would be issued later that week by the Princess. 'I would like it to be known that I have decided not to marry Group Captain Townsend. Mindful of the Church's teaching that Christian marriage is indissoluble and mindful of my duty to the

Commonwealth I have resolved to put these considerations before others.'

One wonders why he wrote it. The ultimate sacrifice for duty and honour? Or because he wanted to test her. One is inclined to believe the former because after she read it she said, 'That is exactly how I feel' – showing a sad echo of his first declaration and a singleness of heart. They did not meet again for thirty-seven years – a formal lunch at Kensington Palace where they glowed with a once-shared tenderness.

Human beings are taught to deny the power of feeling and they both must have imagined the pain would end and they would get on with their lives. Instead, in a way, they only buried that pain. Townsend went back to Belgium, eventually settling just outside Paris. Exile was particularly hard for him. It was a tyranny to have been abandoned by the country he had fought for and which had honoured him for his wartime fighter-pilot combat.

He was no straightforward brutal gunner. The German fighter with whom he'd been in combat over Whitby had been gunned down. He went to visit him in hospital and felt like a brutal killer as the man looked at him with sick-animal eyes and forgiveness. He never forgot that either.

It seemed like all the sacrifice and all the fight for a cleaner better world had been in vain. A few years ago he wrote despairingly about the 'shocking Royal Family situation and the behaviour of some of them . . . It reflects so many lapsing values across society. People say anything they like about the Royal Family these days . . . They've become a common old day-by-day family. Such a shame.' Such a shame that the dignity he fought to preserve for England had been so shattered.

Of course he must have asked himself was it not all for nothing. Of course he had to say that the past is the past and he had moved on from it. He was working at a seemingly cosy marriage and bringing up its three offspring.

Did he keep the daily letters from Clarence House recording the Princess's passion? 'Not a line. And I don't know what she did with mine. But I will tell you that I was in the middle of the African veld, miles from anywhere, when I took out a pile of letters – and I tore them up and flung them to the winds and I watched them disappear. And I knew then I was free.' Actually, just the opposite of free. The words that were the bones of that deep love scattered into the universe to exist forever.

Relationship of the Week
Lord Young of Dartington and Dorit Uhlemann
21 January 1996

A radical intellect is always sexy because of the surprising way it fires. Lord Young of Dartington, libertarian socialist peer, is cadaverously handsome. His features even seem finer with age, as if he's grown into them, or them into him.

Now it comes to the point where I have to say how old he is. I always hate putting in the ages of the people I write about. Sometimes I sneakily try to avoid them. It's a means of defining and assessing, but it's not always a correct one. It's completely based on personal prejudice.

Lord Young wrote a book called *The Arrival of the Ageless Society*. He argued that everybody's age of birth should be private property, wiped from Government computers and employers' records because of the widening gap between biological ageing and what he called social ageing – the roles individuals are cast into at different ages by society.

Lord Young has just bridged that gap. He is 80 and to become a father for the sixth time. His new wife Dorit Uhlemann, a 37-year-old milliner, is expecting a baby in the summer.

This was very much planned parenthood. Planned not only because he's always been a very paternalistic sort of chap. For a start he helped give birth to the 1945 Labour manifesto that created what was called the Welfare State. He created the Consumer Association with its *Which* magazine. He helped form Open University, and even wanted Open School for difficult pupils who were truant.

The urge to look after, teach, make better, is in his core. So I expect he'll make a very good father. His mind is still impeccably mannered and fluid. Soon after his marriage last year he said next year he would be celebrating his birthdays backwards so he would become 79, then 78, so that eventually there wouldn't be much age difference between himself and his wife – currently a difference of forty-two years.

And it is almost as if with their brightly coloured sparklers circling their names into the air above the church in Tower Hamlets, where they gave champagne free to a bewildered congregation, they were attempting a childlike stab at innocence, *naïvety*, fun.

The Charlie Chaplin school of parenthood is not unknown. He had babies into his seventies, and Anthony Quinn produced a baby girl, Antonia, when he was 79. I don't want to be rigid and lump them all together, but with Chaplin and Quinn, they definitely saw making their wives pregnant as a kind of penis extension, an ego extension too.

Chaplin was never happier than when his wife Oonagh had bun in tum. Quinn had a voracious appetite for dangerous liaisons. Can it be that this quiet patrician, with his brilliant mind, also needs to prove himself? Prove his own theory, he's not old. And disprove another theory, that he only married Dorit as a substitute after his wife, Sasha Moorsom, died at 62 of cancer in 1993, as a companion, as a substitute.

He and Sasha were indeed a great big love thing. He left his first wife for her and the searing emotions never blunted. Oddly, when she died, he sent a picture of gruesome intimacy, a deathbed picture, to appear with the obituaries. Then he published a volume of romantic poetry that they had written about each other. A hard act to follow.

Although it is not usual, occasionally a sequel is as good as the original. Just look at *Addams Family Values*. And Lord Young would never be such a cliché as one life one love. Or would he?

Dorit and Sasha have got the same intense wet eyes, slinky mouths and short wispy fringes. Dorit is not an intellectual. But for the year before they married, where he was going round introducing her as his friend, they were always holding hands, very touchy-touchy, cosy-coo compatible. If not soul mates at least slipper mates.

I'm not sure if you can ever trust a woman who is a hat-maker; by the very nature of what they do, they know how to change heads. Still, that's what Lord Young and his lifelong educational quest has all been about.

He's had some pretty odd, but some visionary ideas. Recently he wanted school to be compulsory only till 13 and then you get educational vouchers for another eight years which you can take whenever you feel like it. Open School was another innovation that hasn't quite happened yet.

He has spoken of improving the status of children in society. 'Equality between the sexes will prove sterile unless there is a rise in the status of children.' Now that's a nice thing for a dad to say. Most dads go round assuming they're on another planet, believing everything was better in their day.

The new baby will avoid that generational swing that sets children against parents. Oftentimes a child empathizes much more with its grandparents in that there is a two-generation turnaround, one generation always rebels against the one that's preceded it. For instance, he has always been left leaning, and his son Toby, the journalist, sparks to the right.

Much has been made of age differences. Does it really matter? I think there are differences greater than age that matter quite a lot. As long as each component knows who they are and why they are together and they're not trying to be somebody's father or somebody's daughter, age-difference marriages can often work. After a while of being with somebody you don't notice how they look as much as who they are and how you relate to them. It's the extravagance of the connection that matters, its intricacy, not its physicality, the difference between the sex act being a physical act and a love act. It is rather endearing to see that Lord Young and Dorit Uhlemann are not just good friends.

It is hard to imagine the dignified Lord Young boasting about a new baby like the boy with the Porsche keys, the cat with the cream. But, he planned it, it has happened, and he feels very smug and excited even.

The question that some people must ask is, is it fair to the child? Is it better to be part of the gene pool of a visionary and spend an intense but short time with the parent, or is it better for the child to have some stable humdrum thing that goes through the usual suburbia of rebellion and making up with its parents?

As the power is always in the present and not what might be or could have been, I think a short burst with a great person probably wins out. And who knows, he so firmly refuses to believe that rigid biological ageing equals social ageing, perhaps he can really turn the clock back and do the school run with the other dads and no one will notice the difference.

Relationship of the Week
Chelsea Clinton and Hillary Clinton
9 April 1995

When Chelsea Clinton was born, her mother said to her, 'Chelsea, you've never been a baby before and I've never been a mother before. We're just gonna have to help each other get through this.' Most babies would have panicked.

Hillary Rodham Clinton, academically fierce, emotionally taut and religiously staunch, First Lady, so close to rocking the cradle of power, is gushing in her naïvety. She goes on, 'I think our willingness to just learn from Chelsea and respect the person she was meant to be has helped us a lot.'

In the psychodrama of her head, the mother and child roles have reversed. Hairstyle-a-day Hillary feels she can't quite fit into her own skin. But Chelsea, Chelsea must have been born an old soul. Even after all the taunting attention of the American media headlines such as, 'Why are Democrats' daughters so ugly?' and skits of the *David Letterman Show* about the absence of her pulchritude, photographs of her at her most gawky, toothy and lumpen, close-ups of her wobbling chins and the ironmongery in her mouth, Chelsea, 13, when it all began, when most girls are in hormonal hell, was unflappable. Those around her describe Chelsea as level-headed and fun. She likes Pictionary, parlour games and poker.

Even as a pre-teen she was unsettled by her parents' crumbly relationship back in Little Rock. The then governor would slip out in the middle of the night and her mother would flip out, tearing cupboards limb from limb amid all those dreadful allegations about a night-club crooner, Gennifer Flowers.

'Why doesn't Daddy still love you?' she pleaded protectively to her mother. A couple of years later her father's alleged infidelity was to inform her wit. At a school carnival she took on the job of gypsy fortune-teller and gave world-weary readings and promises of 'You will marry young and blissfully but he will be unfaithful.' There has always been a very protective bond between the Pre-Raphaelite-haired, sad-eyed Chelsea, and the power-haired glazed-in-panic-eyed Hillary.

The First Child is an only child, all the more alienated. Only children grow up with an interesting contradiction. They grow old before their time because they yearn to be part of the adult world, as they have no siblings to aspire to or taunt. And the parents, mindful of the fact they have but one childhood to re-live, want to keep the only child a child for as long as possible. Thus, Chelsea is allowed no heels, no mascara, no make-up at all, and skirts must rest at that very unflattering level just on the knee. But rebellion is subtle: it brews.

Hillary says that her idea of bliss is pushing a trolley up and down the grocery aisle, having quality time with Chelsea. She says that her daughter is 'an absolutely wonderful person.' Nobody at 15 is a wonderful person, at least nobody normal is. But of course this is America, where even peanut butter is smeared in sickly jelly, everybody says they love everybody, they still talk about quality time, and all fond emotions are voiced way beyond their integrity.

None the less the outward signs this week are indeed that mother and daughter are aglow. Touring the East together, they are pictured seated in front of the Taj Mahal with matching bright smiles and droopy, sensible clothes.

In *Newsweek*, Chelsea poses on top of a camel, waving majestically. She has lost a lot of weight, her arms are bonier and her face more sculptured. This is the first time that Hillary has allowed her daughter to be a photo opportunity in more than a year, since the hurtful brouhaha about her plainness reached its peak, when 'Leave Chelsea Alone' T-shirts were a momentary fashion item.

Of course, it must have been hell for Chelsea: public humiliation, pubescence raging, personal confusion, and an inevitable estrangement from her friends and distance from her parents as they both propelled themselves into the roles of big-time busy world leaders. Confusing, too, because of Hillary Rodham's own personal transformation from frumpy to foxy. One minute a lank-haired academic with bottle glasses, rearing her in the belief that beauty is a patriarchal tyranny, and the next reconstituted, slimmer and glossy, perky-mouthed, pencilled into Donna Karan's full range of navy and beige.

Often, power-mother syndrome means that the adults dress themselves up, and dress their daughters down: to protect their daughters' innocence, they say. Such a lot of protection going on.

Newsweek reported that Chelsea was a delightful and serene presence on the eastern trip, a sure source of pride for her mother, 'but the First Lady's insistence that her daughter never be used as media fodder, admirable in principle, suddenly seemed inflexible, fiercely dogmatic, a reminder of all that had gone wrong for the Clintons these past few years.'

Is over-protection not always too rigid? Over-protective mothers create masochistic daughters. It is necessary for some symbiosis to exist between mother and child, but if this attachment continues too long it fosters an extreme dependency in the child. A mother who is distant and busy may over-compensate with a rigid protectiveness that binds her child, by refusing to allow the child to move away from her. Unable to recognize the separateness of her daughter, unable to acknowledge the boundaries between them, such a mother refuses to let the child develop her own thoughts and perceptions. This relationship breeds a sense of inadequacy in the child and a passivity that masks as serenity. Perfect manners or nascent masochism? Nobody could get off this ride free.

Chelsea, last year, took her three pals to a party her parents gave for a baseball movie. They waited in turn to get personalized baseball-cards made. Chelsea told her friends, 'You go first, I'll wait until you've gotten yours.'

The last First Child to be victimized was Amy Carter. But

381

that was different then. For a start, the beauty myth hadn't been invented and parents didn't give corrective surgery as a birthday present instead of a pony. Amy Carter was bespectacled, flaxen-plaited, and 9 when she arrived, 13 when she left 1,600 Pennsylvania Avenue. She was scoffed at for yawning at her father's speeches, received nothing like the personalized insults that have been spun around Chelsea, yet she turned weird. She became a peace protester, was arrested several times staging lie-ins in shopping centres in Memphis. Then there was Patti Davis (a.k.a. Reagan), who denounced her parents and took off her clothes for *Playboy* and wrote a spiteful book. One can only wonder what psychological trauma will befall Chelsea.

Last year, there was a hoax known as Chelseagate. A tape of nine rap tracks, allegedly spat out by Chelsea to reflect her teenage angst, were circulating in Washington. One was obscene, and mocked her father's love life. Although it was an elaborate set-up, a joke, I do believe that there is no such thing as a joke. The idea came from somewhere, that old no-smoke-without-fire routine. Somebody has sniffed a singeing of the need-to-please teenage psyche, the first sulphurous whiff of rebellion.

Currently, Chelsea's career ambition is to be a space scientist and head up a team of troubleshooters who will explore the possibility of setting up settlements on other planets. Could this be because there lurks another Chelsea, one who is not as level and serene and parentally bonded, one who would simply like to be an another planet?

Soon, she'll be attending college on the other side of the country.

Relationship of the Week
Margaret Drabble and Michael Holroyd
18 February 1996

Everybody needs love, and space to feel it. The most exciting togetherness is when you know separateness. People never fall out of love violently. They fall out of love slowly, crushed under the weight of domestic trivia and emotional claustrophobia. I know I've had tantrums that shook my building when somebody I was living with moved something. If people are used to a large, inner life, as writers are, and had dislocated childhoods like Michael Holroyd and Margaret Drabble, a detached marriage suits them.

In fact, they agreed, that when she lived in Hampstead and he lived in Ladbroke Grove, which they did for well over a decade, it worked beautifully. It gave them space to pursue their all-consuming literary endeavours. Could he have possibly written his mammoth, three-volume biography of George Bernard Shaw in longhand over several years had he had to share a living space? Could she have banged her manual typewriter like a virtuoso pianist, the house shivering, without disturbing her husband? When she finished her Angus Wilson biography, which was published last year, thirty-six boxes of him, in paper, went off to the archives at the University of Iowa. This made her house seem rather big. This, and the fact that her husband had bought the top floors of the building in which he had been living – a much bigger house now, with separate floors for each of them – seemed to mark the turning point. After thirteen years of marriage, they decided to move in together.

I fear for them. Change is never as interesting or enjoyable as it seems. Better the Devil you know and all that. Because the Devil you don't know could be a complete fresh hell that you've spent your life trying to avoid.

They got together gradually after a kind of erotic friendship. She liked having him for dinner parties. He was good at conversation, manners and flirting. She liked to watch him flirting with other women. After the oblique courtship of driving lessons, the weird eroticism of the shared endeavour, their chemistry really clicked. He made her feel relaxed enough to try something she was not good at. All her life, she'd avoided tests she couldn't pass, and loved exams because she could come top of the class. He made her feel that nothing was at stake when, as it turned out, everything was.

She's 57 and he's 61. The courtship began when they were in their forties and finally knew how to survive themselves. They knew who they were. That's why they didn't make the mistake that they'd seen so many people make. People change when they get married. But it's not the marriage itself. It's the living together. People become more merged and irritated by that. They become more demanding. They take more for granted. They treat each other like pieces of furniture. Sometimes furniture that they don't even like, but they are used to it being there.

In particular, both of them had fairly extreme childhoods that taught them to appreciate their own mental terrain. After his parents split up, Holroyd was brought up by his paternal grandparents. They were in their seventies, generations and a huge expanse of emotional wasteland away from him. His mother was blonde, Swedish and striking. In Stockholm, she'd take him out for dinners when he was a little boy and she would dance on the tables. He shrank from it and has never been able to dance, except on the inside. The dancing inhibited him. And where his mother was an exhibitionist, his aim was to become invisible. 'I didn't speak and I tried to drain myself of interest. I soon gained the power to be overlooked and became very successful at it. In school, I could stand in the middle of the room. Someone could come in and not see me.' Visible meant trouble. Now they're living together, he's going to be very visible indeed.

This is not a man who grew up to thrive on intimacy, sharing, revealing, displaying. He knows about hiding, about finding himself. To make matters worse, his father was some macho thing that showed him about the inner workings of cars, but no emotion. Often, when he came to visit him, he was frightened of him. If he did anything wrong, there would be a beating. He grew up hating all team activities because of his conditioning, he preferred single relationships. Juxtaposed with all of this, he sometimes forgets to sleep at night, while Drabble's hours are more regular.

They were probably able to enjoy each other from afar because Drabble's childhood was also not an intimate, loving one. Her mother used to let her wander off, travel alone on buses in Sheffield when she was only 5. She got used to this negligence and equated it with love. Her mother used to like to clean and tidy things, which she hated. Her mother was an unhappy woman who used to get volcanically angry over trivia. Drabble was married for fifteen years to the actor Clive Swift, but that was the very antithesis of her relationship with Holroyd. It was jealous and claustrophobic. He wanted to write. She wanted to act, almost as if they wanted to be each other.

I think she bravely broke this pattern when she mastered being both with Holroyd and apart from him at the same time. I am very suspicious of the relationship's current turn. Especially as Holroyd says the twist is partly a financial one. After paying for the new floor and the subsidence caused by the great weight of his many books and papers to be repaired, he said they simply couldn't afford two houses in London. Never trust a man who says 'Can't afford.'

Holroyd's parents got married several times themselves, always disastrously. It was his intention never to do so himself. So to be married and not living together seemed the perfect solution. If you never attempt to be all cosy, you never fail. And there is no reason why it should be successful now.

They hint that it's going to be successful because she has a bolt-hole, a cottage in Somerset where she writes her novels. But that's far too decisive, traumatic. It's not seventeen minutes away. You don't go to Somerset for a bit of head-space. You go to Somerset for complete detachment.

When they first got together, they did everything eccentrically. Had the honeymoon before the wedding – and it worked. And although they said it was only a matter of convenience, the separate houses, she still had two children living with her in Hampstead and he had the volumes and volumes of Bernard Shaw and Lytton Strachey and Augustus John, it was really because he was comfortable having only the dead for company. And she was comfortable with him being that way. Most people at least have an office to escape to as a kind of home from home. If you work from home, you have to have another home.

Already he dislikes certain pieces of her furniture and she's already complaining about his kitchen. When she arrived, the oven had no door. For an accomplished cook, his lack of interest in food must be irritating. Holroyd has indulged in creamy new carpets which Drabble hardly dares walk on. She jokes, 'They probably represent his desire not to have me in the house at all.' And we all know what Freud said: there's no such thing as a joke.

No reports of total separation yet – but it's early days.

Valentine's Day
13 February 1994

I do not like foreplay and I do not like romance. Never seen the point in either. Passion doesn't need a middleman. Some people make a big deal about foreplay because they are inadequate in other areas. Same with romance – it's a cowardly business.

Romance is about waiting and pining and self-control. Passion is about wanting something and wanting it now.

Romance comes with presents and flowers. It is the trade of the guilty and the deluded. Passion doesn't have a credit card and doesn't have to Say It With Flowers, better to Say It With A Kalashnikov.

So here it is again. Valentine's Day, the annual romance-fest. It is a benediction of sentimentality, phoney cheeriness and commercial gluttony, like having the worst of Christmas all over again.

Romance is a big fat lie. It is a denial of emotion and a denial of sex. It is anti-nature, it is unnatural, it muffles and mutes the instinct. It is the homeland for the inarticulate and the sexually dyslexic. Passion, on the other hand, is about submission, surrendering to a force that is uncontrollable and overwhelming. Nothing could be more underwhelming than, 'I could die for you, sugar, cutie pie, petal, pet, puds, kitten'.

There it is – the metaphors for romance are about dying, death or displacement. Passion is appetite; romance is being too cowardly to live, too cowardly to draw your own breath, therefore draw someone else's. Romance is about moving all that pain, pleasure and anger that maybe you could feel, or maybe you once felt, into someone else.

Men are much more romantic and sentimental than women because romance is the easy way out, and I don't just mean out of a guilt trip. A romance is a *frisson*, something that never has to be substantiated. It is about the dumb male longing that Frank Sinatra sings about. It is about being able to treat a girl badly because you are bruised. It is about being able to stay out all night and not call when you are supposed to because you are needy.

Romance makes bad behaviour apppealing. Heathcliffe in *Wuthering Heights* was a difficult boy, and he was considered romantic. Romance is user-friendly to men because it objectifies women as love-objects rather than as sexual predators. It denies them lust and voraciousness, which all men fear. And, in the thwarting of this, it provides the male with something to be anxious and guilty about.

Romance is deepened when the relationship is going on *in absentia* – this means sadly or tragically separated or starcrossed, this means having an affair with someone who is married to somebody else. A man once told me that the guilt and angst of this sort of arrangement was the addiction, the maraschino cherry on the cocktail of love and lust. But he was a difficult man.

Looking back, all the difficult men I have known have been intensely romantic. But I don't look back much. In fact, if I ever succumb to romance, it takes the form of looking forward, since a woman's romantic mantra is futuristic. Some day my prince will come. Whereas a man sighs, 'Ah, the one that got away.' Well, she probably didn't get away, she probably got dumped, but romance is all about rewriting history.

'A game for fools'. I think Frank Sinatra said that about love, or romance. Men like it because it is melancholic and self-punishing, and there is the hook, that is the drug. Sentiment is more dangerous than heroin. Romance attracts narcissists because they can project themselves into the vapid sentimentality. It is a substitute for feeling. People feel differently about themselves when they are in love, but they do not love the other person, they love the way it makes them feel.

Romance is pre-sexual. In romance you have pet names: Cuddly Bumps and Huggy Bear are a return to childhood. It's a crush, it's a pash. It has its base in the traditions of medieval courtly love, which was basically an aesthetic love that denied bodily functions, while sexual impulses were diverted into impossible quests. Look at the paradigm of Dante and Beatrice: he projects every emotion he ever felt on to a girl he only meets twice.

Romance doesn't lead to an orgasm, it leads to a pop song. It is middle-brow and middle-class, the stuff of Phil Collins. It is close to religion in that its impulses are about projection and transferral. That is why it is soggy with clichés. It makes dull people feel special and special people feel dull.

Romance happens in the head. It extracts some of the elements from passion and dries them out to rattling bones. Sex is about domination and submission. Romance makes the actual mental, and the active passive. It's a mind-fix, a diluted version of love that makes love handleable, so you don't know, as Cole Porter wrote: 'Is it an earthquake or is it a shock? Is it the good turtle soup or the mock?'

Romance is a candle-lit dinner and love-hearts exchanged over the sticky toffee pudding. Passion is not being able to eat past the starter because your stomach's too liquid and dripping with lust. You don't stay there longing, you go to bed immediately.

Telling someone they are your sun, moon, north, west, south, east, and all the hands on a clock is not an expression of how much you feel for that person, but how little you feel about yourself. It is a denial of the personality.

Romance is inarticulate because it is all wrapped up in symbolism, tantalizingly ambiguous. I once gave a man part of a broken ear-ring. It had three keys on it. He, as a romantic, assumed they were the keys to my mind, body and soul. The relationship ended not in a row or an exclamation, he simply stopped calling. However, he told a friend that in the parallel universe we are still together, me and him.

Romance is big in the parallel universe. Romance is about holding a candle for someone when you could simply turn on the electric light switch. It is about the chase, but not wanting the kill. It is about not saying what you want.

The person who inspired this piece knows who he is. And what I was trying to say at the time was, see there, I don't love you any more. But obviously I did, all that fresh hewn is pain so obvious. I don't love you now though. In fact I've forgotten that burn of excitement and fear. I've forgotten why you were such a particular thrill, why, when it was over, I woke up with bricks on my chest every morning for a month. But I've not forgotten why romance exists. Despite my protestations I went along with it, though I hated myself for it. Romance exists because it provides false hope. I didn't want to know the worst. I was scared to ask. Romance was a stifler. You don't demand because you fear being rejected. You think the proud way is the silent way, but really that is just being a coward. Real power is being told you are not loved and not being devastated by it. Real power is risking telling someone you love them and that not being dependent on them answering that they love you. Real power is knowing what to do about that. Real power is knowing that you can't measure out love in amounts. Just like I get on the scales every day and weigh something different, it can never be a constant. And do you express it by what you do or how it makes you feel? Real power is not caring about any imbalance of emotion, because if you fear that you'll never redress that imbalance. Real power is knowing that imbalance is always redressed. They always come back in the end. Maybe not how and when you want them to, but they do. Real power is knowing that if you want anything badly enough it's yours.